China 1949

China 1890

China 1949

Year of Revolution

Graham Hutchings

BLOOMSBURY ACADEMIC

LONDON · NEW YORK · OXFORD · NEW DELHI · SYDNEY

BLOOMSBURY ACADEMIC
Bloomsbury Publishing Plc
50 Bedford Square, London, WC1B 3DP, UK
1385 Broadway, New York, NY 10018, USA

BLOOMSBURY, BLOOMSBURY ACADEMIC and the Diana logo are trademarks of
Bloomsbury Publishing Plc

First published in Great Britain 2021

Cover design: Terry Woodley
Cover images: Generalissimo Chiang Kai-shek reports to 2,500 National Assembly
delegates on the state of the Chinese nation and Chairman Mao shown reading a
proclamation of the founding of the People's Republic of China. Bettmann/Getty

A catalogue record for this book is available from the British Library.

A catalog record for this book is available from the Library of Congress.

ISBN: HB: 978-0-7556-0733-4
        ePDF: 978-0-7556-0735-8
        ePub: 978-0-7556-0734-1

Typeset by RefineCatch Limited, Bungay, Suffolk
Printed and bound in Great Britain

To find out more about our authors and books visit www.bloomsbury.com
and sign up for our newsletters.

For Maisie Ella (in memoriam), Millicent Grace, Charlotte Anna, Joseph Luke and Jacob Dylan Noah

'Today is the first day of the year [according to the lunar calendar]. I got up at dawn, went to the riverside and gazed up at the surrounding mountains. I reflected on the year that had just passed. As for the year ahead, it is very hard to say what it will bring. It is even more difficult to know how many people are suffering and experiencing anguish during this Spring Festival. The country is drenched in blood and tears. I would really like to be able to say something that is in keeping this festive time of year. But with things like they are, what can I do?'

CHIANG CHING-KUO (CHIANG KAI-SHEK'S SON), DIARY ENTRY FOR
29 JANUARY 1949 (AUTHOR'S TRANSLATION)

CONTENTS

FIGURES

MAPS

ABBREVIATIONS

CCP	Chinese Communist Party
DBPO	Documents on British Policy Overseas
FRUS	Foreign Relations of the United States
GMD	Guomindang (China's Nationalist Party)
GMDRC	Guomindang Revolutionary Committee (formed by prominent 'liberals' and 'leftists' who broke with Chiang Kai-shek and threw in their lot with the CCP)
PLA	People's Liberation Army
PRC	People's Republic of China
ROC	Republic of China
SWB	Summary of World Broadcasts from the BBC Monitoring Service
TNA	The National Archives (United Kingdom)

ACKNOWLEDGEMENTS

Many friends have been generous with their time in reading all or parts of this book. I am extremely grateful to the following for the questions they have raised and the improvements they have suggested: Bob Ash, Cui Cui, Rory Macleod, Rana Mitter, Simon Scott Plummer, Jon Sullivan and Steve Tsang. The finished product is better than it would have been had they not shared their enthusiasm and been committed to the highest standards in the study and interpretation of China. The shortcomings that remain are mine alone.

At I.B. Tauris I had the benefit of working with Jo Godfrey as editor. When Bloomsbury took over I.B. Tauris, Maddie Holder took on the project and was a constant source of good ideas as the book took shape. I am very grateful. Thanks are also due to Jill Hedges, a former colleague at Oxford Analytica, who suggested I approach I.B. Tauris in the first place; and to my agent Christopher Sinclair Stevenson, whose support I have been fortunate to count on again.

I should like to record my gratitude to the staff at the British Library, the archives of the School of Oriental and African Studies at the University of London, King's College London archives, the Church Missionary Society in Oxford, the Salvation Army Heritage Centre and Sheffield University. They were without exception welcoming and helpful in locating relevant materials.

I am especially grateful to Professor Rana Mitter, then Director of the China Centre at Oxford University, and his colleagues, who granted me associate status at the centre. Among other things, this meant that I enjoyed access to the marvellous resources of the China Centre Library. My thanks also go to the library staff, first under Joshua Seufert and then Mamtimyn Sunuodula; Cui Cui, the Readers Service Librarian, was unfailingly well informed, quick in response, patient and supportive.

I should like to acknowledge the authors of four books in Chinese on the topic of 1949 that I have found especially valuable in understanding the events of that year. They are Long Yingtai ('Vast Rivers, Vast Seas, 1949'); Lin Tongfa ('1949: The Great Withdrawal'); Zhang Renyi ('1949: Chinese Society'); and the reference work produced by Beijing's Contemporary China Institute ('Chronicle of the People's Republic of China – 1949'). Full details of all four works can be found in the Bibliography.

My long immersion in this book has taxed the patience of members of my family. I remember with gratitude and affection my mother who, in the last, confused months of her life, suddenly said, 'You are writing a book, aren't you.' I am sorry that she was not able to see the finished product; I very much hope that my father, who will be nearly ninety-nine, will be able to do so. I owe a special debt to Lizzie Hutchings, accumulated over many years. Her support has again made something possible that once seemed beyond reach. Finally, this book is dedicated to my grandchildren in the hope that Millie, Charlie, Joe and Jacob will one day read it and – more importantly – understand why their grandad wrote it.

Graham Hutchings
Charlbury, West Oxfordshire
March 2020

NOTE ON TRANSLITERATION

I have for the most part adhered to the pinyin system of transliterating Chinese words in this book with the exception of some proper names and places that generally are more familiar to most readers in older forms. Thus:

Chiang Kai-shek (rather than Jiang Jieshi)
Chiang Ching-kuo (rather than Jiang Jingguo)
Taipei (rather than Taibei)

However, I have preferred:

Chongqing (rather than Chungking)
Guangzhou (rather than Canton)

In quoting sources that used the older Wade-Gile systems of romanization, I have invariably converted the relevant words into pinyin.

1949 CHRONOLOGY

31 December 1948
Chiang Kai-shek holds New Year's Eve reception and advises senior political and military leaders that he will stand down as president to open the way for peace talks with the CCP.

1 January 1949
Chiang make his decision public in New Year's Day address to the Chinese nation.

Mao Zedong's 'Carry out the Revolution' to the end published.

5 January
Major shipment of cultural treasures and artefacts to Taiwan.

Chen Cheng appointed governor of Taiwan.

14 January
Mao Zedong announces his 'Eight Points' as the basis for peace negotiations with the government.

15 January
PLA occupies Tianjin.

19 January
Fu Zuoyi, Commander of north China, signs agreement handing over Beiping (and thus north China) to CCP.

20–21 January
End of the Huai-Hai Campaign in which PLA troops destroy Chiang's main armies north of the Yangtze.

21 January
Chiang steps down from the presidency, leaves Nanjing for Xikou, his native place; Li Zongren becomes Acting President.

27 January
SS *Taiping*, en route from Shanghai to Taiwan, collides with the SS *Jianyun* and sinks.

Li Zongren cables Mao accepting his 'Eight Points' as the basis for peace talks.

31 January
Formal entry of PLA troops into Beiping.

10 February
Transfer of Central Bank holdings of gold and silver to Taiwan completed.

13 February
Unofficial peace mission to Beiping begins.

March
Military authorities in Hong Kong and London review plans to defend the colony in the case of communist attack or internal unrest.

5–13 March
CCP Central Committee meets in Xibaipo to discuss future work, especially the switch in focus from countryside to the cities.

12 March
He Yingqin succeeds Sun Ke as premier.

25 March
Mao Zedong and other key CCP leaders move from Xibaipo to Beiping.

4 April
Peace negotiations between government and CCP begin in Beiping.

16–17 April
Government refuses to accept CCP peace terms.

20–21 April
PLA troops cross the Yangtze.

Beginning of the 'Amethyst Incident'.

23 April
Government moves to new capital of Guangzhou.

PLA occupies Nanjing.

24 April
PLA occupies Taiyuan, capital of Shanxi province.

1 May
Martial law imposed in Taiwan.

3 May
PLA occupies Hangzhou.

5 May
British government decides to send reinforcements to Hong Kong.

8 May
Li Zongren leaves Guilin and joins rest of government in Guangzhou.

16 May
PLA occupies Wuhan.

27 May
Hong Kong government introduces Societies Ordinance to control CCP and GMD activities in the colony.

PLA occupies Shanghai.

2 June
PLA occupies Qingdao.

3 June
Yan Xishan succeeds He Yingqin as premier.

6 June
British Defence Minister Lord Alexander visits Hong Kong.

15 June
New currency (Taiwan dollar) introduced in Taiwan.

16 June
Start of Liu Shaoqi's secret mission to Moscow.

1 July
Mao Zedong's 'On the People's Democratic Dictatorship' published.

New silver currency introduced in Nationalist-held areas.

10 July
Chiang Kai-shek visits Philippines.

2 August
US Ambassador John Leighton Stuart leaves Nanjing for the US.

4 August
Regional Nationalist leaders Cheng Qian and Chen Mingren turn Hunan province over to the communists.

Hong Kong government announces measures to register the colony's population and to expel those individuals deemed to be 'undesirable'.

5 August
US State Department publishes China White Paper.

13 August
Huang Shaohong and forty-four other members of the GMD announce that they will abandon the government and support the CCP.

17 August
PLA occupies Fuzhou, capital of Fujian province.

26 August
PLA occupies Lanzhou, capital of Gansu province.

1–10 September
In battle of Qingshuping, Bai Chongxi inflicts minor defeat on Lin Biao's forces in Hunan.

13 September–10 October
In Heng-Bao campaign, Lin Biao's forces in Hunan inflict heavy defeat on those of Bai Chongxi, whose main army withdraws into Guangxi.

21–30 September
Meeting of the Chinese People's Consultative Conference in Beiping to prepare for the proclamation of the PRC and the Central People's Government.

25 September
Xinjiang commander Tao Zhiyue agrees to hand over military and political power to the PLA.

1 October
Mao Zedong proclaims foundation of the PRC with Beijing as national capital.

2 October
Soviet Union recognizes the PRC.

12 October
Government shifts capital from Guangzhou to Chongqing.

PLA occupies Guangzhou.

19 October
Chinese communist and British security forces meet at Hong Kong border.

22 October
PLA occupies Xiamen (opposite Jinmen).

24–27 October
Nationalist troops defeat PLA in Battle of Guningtou for control of Jinmen island.

PLA occupies Hengyang, Hunan; Bai Chongxi withdraws all his forces into Guangxi.

PLA troops arrive on border of Hong Kong.

9 November
Pilots of China National Aviation Corporation (CNAC) and Central Aviation Transport Corporation (CATC) fly thirteen aircraft from Hong Kong to Beijing, defecting to the communists.

20 November
Li Zongren leaves China for Hong Kong.

21 November
Nationalists shift capital from Chongqing to Chengdu.

22 November
PLA occupies Guilin.

27 November–7 December
Troops of Lin Biao's Fourth Field Army and the Second Field Army under Liu Bocheng destroy Bai Chongxi's main armies in southern Guangxi.

1 December
PLA occupies Chongqing.

3 December
Bai Chongxi withdraws to Hainan Island.

5 December
Li Zongren leaves Hong Kong for the US.

6 December
Mao Zedong embarks on journey to Moscow, where he will remain until early February.

8 December
Nationalists shift capital from Chengdu to Taipei, Taiwan.

15 December
Wu Guozhen succeeds Chen Cheng as governor of Taiwan.

27 December
PLA occupies Chengdu.

30 December
Hong Kong government introduces emergency powers.

National Security Document 48/2 stipulates that the US will not recognize the PRC and that it will use diplomatic and other means to deny Taiwan to the communists – short of overt military action.

PRINCIPAL CHARACTERS IN 1949

Bai Chongxi (56–57)   Commander of Nationalist troops in Central China who in January forced Chiang to retire in an effort to reach a peace deal with the CCP but who rejected its terms and fought on; his armies – and career – were destroyed by Lin Biao.

Bai Xianyong (11–12)   Son of Bai Chongxi, taken to Hong Kong for refuge and to continue his education.

Chen Cheng (50–51)   Appointed by Chiang Kai-shek as governor of Taiwan to run the island efficiently and ready it as a potential temporary home for the Nationalist government.

Chiang Ching-kuo (38–39)   Chiang's son by his first wife, close confidant and personal companion of his father during the defeats of 1949.

Chiang Kai-shek (61–62)   President of the ROC (until January 1949) and leader of the GMD; gave up his government position but not his power; Mao's armies forced him and his government off the mainland to Taiwan.

Fu Zuoyi (53–54)   Commander of Nationalist troops in north China; turned Beiping over to the communists in January; joined the government of 'New China' in October.

He Yingqin (58–59)   Premier (head of Nationalist government) from March to May; sought to be a 'bridge' between Li Zongren and Chiang Kai-shek; resigned following PLA crossing of the Yangtze.

Hu Shi (56–57)   Chancellor of Beiping ('Beida') University and one of his country's most prominent intellectuals; left Beiping in December 1948 before the PLA arrived and moved to Nanjing but kept his distance from the GMD; moved to the US in April before the Yangtze crossing.

Huang Shaohong (53–54)   Prominent figure on the Nationalist side in the April peace talks with the CCP; close to Li Zongren and Bai Chongxi, whom he sought to persuade to accept Mao's peace terms; broke with the Nationalists moved to Beiping and served in the PRC government.

Li Zhisui (38–39)   Young medical doctor who, inspired by Mao's revolution, returned to Beiping in 1949 to serve the new regime; was assigned to look after the medical needs of the top CCP leadership.

Li Zongren (58–59)   Acting president following the resignation in January 1949 of Chiang Kai-shek, with whom he waged a bitter struggle for control over the government's military and financial assets until he left for the US in December.

Lin Biao (41–42)   The most brilliant of Mao's generals who, as commander of the PLA's Fourth Field Army, defeated Nationalist forces under Bai Chongxi.

Lester Knox Little (56–57)   US citizen and Inspector General of the Chinese Maritime Customs Service; moved from Shanghai to Taiwan (via Guangzhou) with the Nationalist government, of which his service was part, though most customs officers remained to serve 'New China'.

Liu Hongsheng (59–60)   One of Shanghai's leading industrialists who, troubled by the prospect of communist rule, fled to Hong Kong but returned at the end of the year to endorse 'New China'.

Liu Shaoqi (50–51)   Second in the CCP hierarchy to Mao Zedong; responsible for Party work in rural and urban areas; undertook secret diplomacy in Moscow in June–July, paving the way for Mao's meeting with Stalin in December.

Mao Zedong (55–56)   Chairman of the CCP and its principal theorist and strategist; led his party to power over mainland China, overthrowing Chiang's Nationalist regime, founding the PRC and becoming undisputed leader of 'New China'.

Mei Jun (24)   Country girl from rural Zhejiang province who left home to escape the war with her son, placed him with her parents-in-law for safe-keeping, and gave birth to a daughter during a journey that lasted more than a year and ended in Taiwan.

Eva Spicer (50–51)   History teacher at Jinling College, Nanjing, whose letters home shed light on the events of 1949 from the perspective of a missionary-funded educational institution.

Ya Xian (16)   Schoolboy from Nanyang, Henan Province, who fled south with hundreds of his classmates and their teachers to avoid the fighting; left the mainland for Taiwan via Guangzhou.

Yan Xishan (65–66)   Regional militarist who, once evicted from his stronghold of Shanxi province by communist troops, succeeded He Yingqin as premier of the Central Government.

Zhang Zhizhong (53–54)　Leading Nationalist figure in charge of northwest China; close to Chiang personally but abandoned him for the communists after leading the government side in the abortive peace negotiations in Beiping.

Zhou Enlai (50–51)　Number three in the CCP after Mao and Liu Shaoqi; special responsibility for administrative and foreign affairs, and for the CCP's relations with non-political figures.

Prologue

On 1 March 1950, Britain's assistant military attaché based in Beijing submitted a report on military operations during the previous year to his masters in London. '1949 will go down to posterity as a memorable year in Chinese and world history', he wrote.

> This is particularly true of the military sphere. Never before has a civil war been waged with so many troops over so vast an area. Over 5 million Nationalist and Communist soldiers . . . have been engaged, while the victorious armies in many cases have finished up well over a thousand miles from where they started and have crushed all organized resistance by Nationalist forces on the mainland, with the exception of a few armies scattered over West CHINA.[1]

Lt Col R. V. Dewar-Durie knew something of the changes about which he wrote. His despatch was filed on letterhead marked 'British Embassy, Nanking'. But by the time he wrote it the embassy was a shadow of its former self, the Republic of China (ROC) government to which it had been accredited had fled, its authority at an end on the mainland. Britain's diplomatic presence in China was now centred in Beijing, capital of the new People's Republic of China (PRC), which, somewhat controversially, London had recognized on 6 January.[2] Operating from the former Legation Quarter in the centre of the city, the British mission was of modest size and disputed status. Once one of the Great Powers in China, Britain was not even recognized fully as a sovereign state by the new communist regime, and its 'embassy' was seen through Chinese eyes as the office of a 'negotiating agent'.[3]

Historians have often used a single year as a prism through which to view key changes that are said to have shaped an era. This is especially true of the period immediately following the end of the Second World War, with the years 1945, 1946, 1947 and 1948 all claiming advocates.[4] Curiously, while events in China feature in many (though not all) of these accounts, the year 1949 seems to have been singled out less often as decisive, at least in this wider sense.[5]

Contemporaries would have been surprised. Writing at the beginning of that year, under the headline '1949, Decisive Year', prominent American journalist R.H. Shackford contended that 'the New Year might determine whether the Western powers and Russia would "live and let live" in the world without another war'. He set out several factors that would have a bearing on the outcome, including 'developments in China which may virtually wipe out what little Western prestige survives in that unhappy region of turmoil'.[6]

At the end of the year, an author who chose to describe himself merely as a 'student of Europe', offered the following: 'The year 1949 has without doubt been the most important one in world affairs since the end of the war. It has seen a complete shift of scene in the struggle that will decide the fate of our civilisation – a shift to which the West has been slow to react and which leaves it exposed to great dangers.' He continued:

Up to 1949 the chief theatre of the world struggle was Europe. In 1949 the Kremlin, with the suddenness characteristic of totalitarian regimes, switched its offensive to Asia, where it met no prepared political or economic defence of any kind. Within one year China fell; South Korea was isolated; Burma and Indo-China undermined. Before public opinion in Britain and America had even woken up to the new danger, half of Asia was gone; and the remaining half was as immediately endangered as was Western Europe in the spring of 1947, before the Marshall Plan checked Russian ambitions and stabilised the European position.[7]

So far, so convincing. But it may well be asked at the outset: 'What's in a year as far as China, a country of so many years, is concerned?' Even if we take the three years of the Civil War (1946–9) as a turning point in Chinese history, which it certainly was, might we not do better to regard 1947 or 1948 as the critical twelve months that determined whether the communists would conquer China, set their huge country on a new, revolutionary course and extend the Cold War into Asia, making it a truly global conflict? It has been so argued. Two works by Chinese writers – Jin Chongji's *The Turning Point: China in 1947* and Liu Tong's *China's 1948: A Conflict that Decided between Two Destinies* – make the case for their respective years with some conviction.[8]

Jin argues that 1947 was a turning point because of changing patterns of public support for the protagonists in the Civil War. Largely but not solely due to its land reform policies, 1947 was the year in which the Chinese Communist Party (CCP) won the firm support of those under its rule. By contrast, the government failed to rally the public under its own jurisdiction. It was the CCP's success (and the Nationalists' failure) in this regard that made possible the creation of the People's Republic in 1949. For Liu Tong, 1948 was the decisive year because, among other things, a series of stunning communist military victories in the northeast and north brought the Nationalists to their knees.

It is of course true that the events of 1947 and 1948 paved the way for those of the following year. Yet Dewar-Durie's claims about the significance of what happened in China in 1949 and the wider importance he attributes to the year are persuasive. At the start of January 1949, Mao Zedong's communist armies occupied less than half of China. While there was plenty of evidence that it would take little less than a miracle for Chiang Kai-shek's Nationalist government to slow the communist advance let alone reverse it, the speed and completeness with which it collapsed surprised participants and observers alike. By the end of 1949, the Nationalists had been driven from the mainland save for a few isolated pockets, and Chiang's grip on maritime China, chiefly the islands of Taiwan, Hainan and Zhoushan, looked shaky. Within the space of twelve months, the communist military conquest changed the 'meaning of China' and recast the landscape of global politics.

The most important manifestation of this was the creation on 1 October of the PRC – a strong, centralized state that would soon achieve two goals that had defeated the Nationalists during the past two decades: governing all of China (apart from Taiwan) as a unified country and setting radical new terms in its dealings with foreign powers. The new government ruled the world's most populous country of some 500 million[9] people under the ideological banner of a Chinese version of Marxism and in avowed allegiance to the Soviet Union, to whom the CCP leaders looked for security, economic assistance and (for a while) ideological guidance. It at first presented a 'moderate', accommodative face to its own people and the outside world; in Mao's 'People's Democracy', there seemed room for all but 'reactionaries' and 'feudal elements'. But with remarkable energy it inspired, organized and indeed *required* the Chinese people to re-fashion their politics, society and economy along completely new lines in the form of 'mass mobilization' and popular participation. Chinese society became, if not overnight, at least in short order, thoroughly *politicized* in a way that marked another break with the past.

Despite these developments, scholars have in recent years challenged the idea that 1949 (or any other single year such as 1947 or 1948 for that matter) should be regarded as a watershed. They argue that powerful underlying continuities run through China's modern history.[10] It is easy to overlook these wider themes and trends amid the heat of revolution, so the point is well made.

But it ought not to be overdone. Radical changes in China's political behaviour, policy, institutions, national leadership and global alliances make 1949 a pivotal year – as does the fact that the country escaped the orbit of the West and modelled much of its behaviour on Stalin's Soviet Union and the new 'people's democracies' of Eastern Europe. The events of 1949 provided an answer to an extremely important question: Under what political conditions would the next stage in China's quest for wealth and power take place? The answer determined the nature of these goals as well as how they would be pursued. It also had a dramatic effect on much of the rest of Asia – and especially among the Western powers, whose commercial and strategic interests in China and the region were suddenly cast into jeopardy. They responded to the creation of the PRC by seeking (in different ways) to 'contain' the 'New China' and all it stood for.

The case for regarding 1949 as a point of departure is reinforced by the year's legacy and lineage effects in terms of China's 'domestic story'. The communist military victories and the foundation of the PRC constitute key components in the 'creation myth' of today's China. They furnish the current regime with history and purpose, and thus with *legitimacy* – the lifeblood of every government, but especially those that do not depend on a mandate derived from genuine popular elections. During the past seventy years, radical changes in CCP policy, under and after Mao, have caused the Party to downplay and/or sometimes almost ignore various episodes (and, in the case of the Cultural Revolution, a complete era) in its past. No such endeavours have been made with regard to the events of 1949. Nor will they be: Party rule could not survive denunciation of the circumstances that brought it about.

Moreover, many of the factors that accounted for the Party's seizure of power in 1949 form part of the 'furniture' of Chinese politics today. Perhaps chief among them is the belief – not universally shared by all Chinese yet by no means limited to the Party itself – that the leadership of the CCP and its monopoly of political power is inseparable from China's well-being. The Party 'liberated' China in 1949. It has led the country ever since, admittedly disastrously during the Great Leap Forward of the late 1950s and the Cultural Revolution of the 1960s. But in the past thirty years it has pursued policies that have transformed the living standards of hundreds of millions of citizens, made China the second biggest economy in the world and boosted its global standing. Little of this could have happened had it not been for the CCP, runs the official mantra. Its overthrow or its defeat in competitive elections, should they ever be allowed, would surely presage national disaster. Liberation would give way to enslavement of the Chinese people, either at the hands of predatory foreign powers, self-interested domestic forces or possibly both.

From this much else flows in terms of the impact of 1949 on current Chinese life. It includes the fact that the Party, rather than the state, controls the People's Liberation Army (PLA); that the rule of law is subject ultimately to the Party rather than to professional judges; that the media is obliged to adhere to the Party line; and that civil society is allowed to flourish only within Party-set parameters. To this list of legacies might be added the maxim that China's leaders can be praised but not publicly criticized, ridiculed or attacked other than in the context of Party-approved campaigns; the CCP's persistent obsession with secrecy in decision-making; and its extreme sensitivity towards real and perceived slights to China's national sovereignty. All these features were prominent during or immediately after the creation of the PRC. Indeed, many of them made it possible. They remain defining aspects of the way China is governed today.

The year 1949 did something else to 'change the meaning of China': it created two of them. The foundation of the People's Republic of China did not eradicate the existence of the ROC, which it claimed to supersede, but it did dramatically alter the former's status and territorial jurisdiction. With its capital in Beijing, the PRC was by the end of the year in control of virtually the entire mainland. The ROC was driven to 'domestic exile' in offshore, or what for the purposes of this book will be referred to as 'maritime China', so as to include British-held Hong Kong, whose own transformation as a result of the Civil War is part of the '1949 story'.[11] In December 1949, Chiang announced that Taipei, the administrative centre of the island province of Taiwan, would be the temporary seat of his embattled national government. But he insisted that the ROC remained sovereign over *all* of China, despite its sudden, dramatic ejection from the mainland.

The 'two Chinas' were hardly equally matched: Mao had driven Chiang to the very margins of the Chinese world, where his government languished with only half-hearted promises of support from its erstwhile partner, the United States. It looked as though the communist conquest of maritime China (with the exception of Hong Kong, after a period of tension and uncertainty) might soon be complete until the outbreak of the Korean War in June 1950 changed the US calculus and put an end to such prospects. Taiwan was reprieved, Chiang spared political oblivion. Largely because of their international sponsors (the Soviet Union and the communist bloc in the case of the PRC; the United States and some of its allies in the case of the Republic of China or Taiwan), 'both Chinas' were able to play a role in global politics during the 1950s and 1960s. But the price was continued (if intermittent) civil war, decades of tension and enduring national disunity, a matter that grieves many Chinese patriots, irrespective of their political affiliation, to the present day. More than seventy years later it is striking and perhaps something of a puzzle that both communist rule in China and Taiwan's de facto status as an independent state have survived so long.[12]

Historian David Armitage, reflecting on global conflict following the Second World War, observed that civil war became 'the most widespread, the most destructive, and the most characteristic form of organised human violence'.[13] French President Charles de Gaulle expressed the same sentiment but with a twist: 'All wars are bad ... But civil wars, in which there are brothers in both trenches, are unforgiveable, because peace is not born when war concludes.' He was speaking during a visit to Spain, whose full-scale civil war predated that of China, but which scars the country still, nearly a century after the guns fell silent.[14]

China's Civil War is an unfinished conflict, the country's division a scar on the national soul that two decades of close cultural and commercial ties between the protagonists have failed to eliminate. Indeed, at the time of writing, the disposition of political forces in the two states either side of the Taiwan Straits is such that conflict could easily break out again. If it does, it would have huge consequences for China and the wider Asia Pacific region, thanks to the strategic interests of various parties, including the United States and Japan.

So far in this discussion, references to the ways in which 1949 changed the meaning of China have been somewhat abstract. They have been the stuff of revolutions and revolutionaries, politicians, statesmen, diplomats and other professional observers rather than the immediate concerns of 'ordinary people'. This is perhaps inevitable in a book about such an important a country as China in so important a year as 1949. But it is essential to understand the transformation of individual lives as well as changes in national fortunes and global politics during this critical year. Accordingly, I have tried in what follows to explain what it was like to live through it from the perspectives of different individuals, causes and countries.

The triumphs and tribulations experienced by some of the well-known figures on either side of the Civil War come under scrutiny. So do those of a number of lesser-known individuals. They include the Nationalist general Bai Chongxi, whose career ended abruptly in 1949, and Bai's nemesis, the communist general Lin Biao, who cemented his status during the year as the PLA's most outstanding commander. Combatants and partisans further down the chain of command, as it were, also make their voices heard.

And in the spirit of John Milton's 'they also serve who only stand and wait', I also describe the trials of some of the ordinary folk who were caught up in the maelstrom of civil war. Among them are those who were forced to leave home and flee to other parts of the country, often entirely new to them, or even leave China altogether, in some cases never to return, or to do so only after an absence that lasted decades. Then there are the 'victors' – the men and women who were inspired by Mao's doctrines, the prospect of building a 'new China' and of course the sweeping victories of the PLA that made all this possible. I try to tell something of their story, too. In revolutions, as in other matters, nothing succeeds like success.

A final contingent of characters that make up this story might be regarded as 'third parties' as far as China's epic struggle was concerned. They are mainly foreign citizens – the businessmen, missionaries, diplomats and adventurers of various kinds who owed their presence in the country to a previous dispensation. From 1949, if not earlier, they had to contend with a much stronger Chinese government bent on pursuing and capable of achieving a very different set of aims as far as its own and foreign citizens in China were concerned. For many of those in this category, 1949 marked the beginning of the end.

No account of a year in China can be regarded as satisfactory unless it sheds some light on the basic conditions of the people. It is therefore worth saying something about this at the outset. In many respects the condition of the Chinese people was grim in 1949 in both relative and absolute terms. The Civil War and the eight-year struggle against Japan that preceded it brutalized life generally as well as ensuring that for many it was nasty and short.

For example, the average Chinese male born in 1949 could expect to live to the age of forty-one, a woman to forty-four.[15] Atrocious hygienic conditions and inadequate medical treatment meant, in the words of historian Lloyd Eastman, that: 'Approximately one of every three children died within the first year of birth . . . And nearly 50 per cent of all children died before they reached the age of five, often from diarrhoea, malaria and childhood pneumonia.'[16] Gerald F. Winfield, a research biologist who spent many years in China, said of the country in that late 1940s that, 'Seventy-five percent of all deaths in China are due to preventable diseases that are under control in the West.'[17]

High birth rates and high death rates meant that there was an abundance of young Chinese people relative to the elderly. Voluntarily or otherwise, they filled the ranks of China's huge armies, constituted a lively student community in the major cities, and in many cases proved enthusiastic recruits for the cause of revolutionary change.[18]

Literacy rates, though hard to gauge, suggested that only 1.2 per cent of women could read compared with just over 30 per cent of men.[19] Relative lack of access to education for women was just one aspect of a fundamental inequality between the sexes. Among other iniquities, women were usually deprived of the right to inherit property and divorce their husbands.

Despite these grim statistics, social and economic misery was neither universal nor necessarily increasing across the board during the late 1940s. Scholars have in recent years shown that reforms undertaken during the Republican era improved the lives of many people in both quantitative and qualitative terms. The problem was that such progress tended to be patchy, confined to particular parts of the country and, partly because of war, often impermanent.

China's economic performance in historical perspective illustrates the relatively parlous state of affairs in the late 1940s. While Chinese adults in 1949 might have more immediate matters on their minds, many were probably worse off economically than their great-grandparents, as well as their contemporaries in the West. 'Between the 1840s and 1940s, China's economy collapsed', wrote economic historian Angus Maddison. 'Per capita GDP in 1950 was less than three-quarters of the 1820 level . . . [and] . . . [national] GDP was less than a twelfth of that in Western Europe and the Western Offshoots.'[20] Accordingly, China's weighting in the contemporary global economy was modest. In 1952 (after two years of communist reconstruction), it accounted for 5.2 per cent of global gross domestic product (GDP) but 21.8 per cent of the world's population. Its share of global exports was 1.0 per cent.[21]

Such comparisons are telling but in another sense beside the point. Chinese compared themselves with their contemporary counterparts rather than their forebears and foreigners. For millions of them, especially the peasants and the country's much smaller number of factory workers, reality was a daily struggle to survive. For those who were better off – landlords, city dwellers, businessmen, some professionals, higher-level officials and those for whom crime, corruption and connections of one sort another offered advantage and security – it was a question of protecting their livelihoods from the effects of rampant inflation and trying to preserve their place at the upper end of a social, economic and political pyramid that seemed in danger of being swept away.

In many cities, social reforms had made significant headway. But in September 1948, the Ministry of the Interior still felt it necessary to promulgate what it called 'Measures for Suppression of Popular Harmful Practices and Customs'. Such practices included superstitious worshipping of divine powers, including fortune-telling, sorcery, geomancy and healing of illnesses by casting charms; binding women's feet; keeping of slave girls; bringing up of daughters-in-law as 'children of the house'; and abortion or infanticide by drowning.

In a despatch to London about such matters, the British Embassy in Nanjing observed:

> It is a safe assumption that the promulgation of these measures indicates the continued existence, on a considerable scale, of all the practices forbidden by them; many of them indeed can be seen every day even in Nanjing and Shanghai, though others are of necessity covert. The Communists, of course, do their best, probably with more success than the Guomindang, to abolish them.[22]

From many points of view, then, it is plain that China needed to change and that many Chinese yearned that it would do so. Where they differed was on how it should change and who should undertake it. The tragedy for the Chinese people was that it took a civil war to provide an answer to this question.

This book is in some respects a passage through China as well as a journey through a year. The direction of travel is mainly from north to south, with many excursions east and west along the way. Indeed, if there is a single theme that emerges from the 'story' of 1949 in China it is that of 'movement', an issue highlighted in Dewar-Durie's report cited at the beginning of this Prologue. The attaché had in mind the movement on a huge scale of soldiers and military equipment across the country in the cause of conquest. He might also have mentioned the great distances Nationalist soldiers were forced to travel in defeat and the search for sanctuary – where their leaders hoped they could rest, reorganize and resume the campaign against their foes. And of course, it was not just soldiers who were on the move: as mentioned earlier, millions of ordinary people upped sticks and made their often tortuous way from one part of China to another (and sometimes beyond) – both in the revolutionary cause and to escape its consequences.

Lester Knox Little, the last foreign Inspector General of China's Maritime Customs Service, wrote in his diary on 13 June 1949: 'The Chinese all seem to think that, if they only *go* somewhere – anywhere – they will be safe. They have a fleeing complex.'[23] This might seem an odd remark given that the country was convulsed by civil war, that Little himself had just fled from Shanghai to Guangzhou to avoid communist rule and that he, like hundreds of thousands of Chinese, would soon flee to Taiwan in search of sanctuary. Yet his were not merely the jaundiced observations of a foreigner, albeit one who knew China well. The prominent Shanghai literary journal *Lun Yu* in March 1949 devoted an entire issue to the theme of 'running away'. Writer He Fangzhou, introducing the subject, described flight as a 'special characteristic' of the Chinese people. Thanks to circumstances they had become 'adept at it'.[24]

Vital assets were also moved around in this year of dislocation and displacement. Prominent among them was the Nationalist government's holdings of gold, silver and foreign exchange, and as many items as possible among the great collection of artistic and cultural treasures held by China's leading museums that could be packed up and relocated with little risk of loss or damage. Chiang Kai-shek – and, in the case of the cultural objects, a small group of distinguished curators – did all they could to place such resources beyond the reach of the communists. By their own lights this was for good reason. Badly beaten on the battlefield, Nationalist leaders believed that rest, reorganization, new military equipment and fresh financial resources would in time enable them to fight another day. In the meantime, and in any event, their continued custody of a significant proportion of China's national cultural treasures strengthened their belief that the Nationalist regime still enjoyed legitimacy, despite its woeful performance in so many other respects.

There were less tangible but no less important aspects of what might be termed the 'great flow' from the interior to 'external' or 'Offshore China'. This is because it was a movement of ideas as well as of material. In 1949 (and in the years that followed), significant numbers of educated people – businessmen and women, civil servants, professors, teachers, journalists, lawyers, technicians and engineers – left the mainland for Taiwan or Hong Kong. There, despite often dire personal circumstances, the 'exiles' constituted a vital source of talent and ideas that helped transform what had been relative backwaters into prosperous manufacturing and trading centres that enjoyed global connections of the kind largely denied to the mainland, especially once it positioned itself firmly within the socialist camp.

Britain's determination (demonstrated in mid-1949) to hang on to Hong Kong, despite the change of regime across the border, and US resolve (exhibited one year later) to thwart Mao's plans to attack Taiwan provided the security guarantees that enabled these key nodes of maritime China to survive and prosper. The fact that they became new homes for clusters of talent, entrepreneurial skills and wide-ranging international links meant they saw sharp increases in productivity, rising living standards and much else besides. There is thus a sense in which China – defined as a country rather than a state – was reconfigured after 1949: it 'changed shape' economically as well as politically. Agricultural revolution and rapid industrialization, much of it focused on heavy industries, preoccupied the mainland authorities. Land reform was also an important part of Taiwan's post-1949 experience but, along with Hong Kong, it concentrated on trade, finance and light manufacturing, drawing on the influx of mainland talent and capital that had arrived on its shores. Both territories became beacons of relative stability on the periphery of a country convulsed by revolution.

In the seventy-odd years since 1949, much has changed in both of these jurisdictions. The Nationalists have lost, regained and then lost power again in Taiwan. Hong Kong has returned to Chinese rule under an arrangement supposed to guarantee the territory a high level of autonomy. Yet it is reasonable to argue that there has been little, or at least less, change as far as the essential nature and function of these two 'Offshore China centres' are concerned. This is true in terms of their relationship with the mainland and the outside world. In both cases, as will be explained in more detail, the origins of their very different identities lie in the traumatic events of 1949.

It is easy when convinced that a single year, a series of events or the actions of one or more individuals are decisive in defining the era that followed to forget that it need not have been so. 'History is lived forwards but is written in retrospect', observed British historian C. V. Wedgwood. 'We know the end before we consider the beginning and we can never wholly recapture what it was to know the beginning only.'[25] In his reflections on the twentieth century, Tony Judt cautioned that the past acquires meaning 'only by reference to our many and often contrasting present concerns'.[26] Gill Bennett, in her study of crises in British foreign policy, warned that the first thing to do in trying to understand why a decision was taken is 'to forget what we know about its consequences'.[27]

An element of 'unknowing' or 'unlearning' is certainly required when considering what happened in China in 1949. Only with hindsight does history seem inevitable: things could have turned out otherwise. The collapse of the Nationalist government did seem likely to occur in that year, as many contemporaries pointed out. But the manner and speed with which it did so was remarkable and caught many people by surprise. This is true whether they were on the battlefield or in the civilian ranks of either party; whether they were ordinary if deeply concerned Chinese citizens or those following events at a distance from the chanceries and highest councils of the foreign powers. We know the consequences that followed; they did not. The British diplomat Sir Percy Cradock, himself an experienced China Hand, cautioned that if we are truly to understand any situation and make sense of the times, 'we have to put ourselves in the shoes of the contemporary actors, struggling in the dust of current events, to whom there must have seemed not one but a variety of possible futures'.[28] That is the spirit in which I have approached the subject of 1949, the year China changed.

Notes

1   The National Archives (UK) (hereafter TNA) FO371/83274 Microfilm, p. 00009 – PDF, p. 10), 'Annual Report – Military Operations', dated 1 March 1950 (capitals in the original).

2   The cover letter with the report was headed 'British Embassy Peking'; see FO371/83274, p. 0007.

3   Alastair Lamb, *Tibet, China & India 1914–1950: A History of Imperial Diplomacy* (Hertingfordbury: Roxford Books, 1989), p vi.

4   See, for example, Ian Buruma, *Year Zero: A History of 1945* (London: Atlantic Books, 2013); Victor Sebestyen, *1946: The Making of the Modern World* (London: Pan Books, 2015 – Kindle edition); Elisabeth Asbrink, *1947: When Now Begins* (London: Scribe Publications, 2017 – Kindle edition). Asbrink describes 1947 as the year when 'everything is in a vibrating state of flux, without stability and without goals, and all possibilities are still open' (Location 420 of 3164). She does not mention China. See also Jonathan Fenby, *Crucible: Thirteen Months that Forged Our World* (London: Simon & Schuster, 2018). Fenby's '13 months' were from June 1947 to June 1948.

5   This is true of English-language accounts, at least.

6   *The Hong Kong Daily Telegraph*, 3 January 1949, p. 1.

7   *Observer*, 25 December 1949, p. 4.

8   Jin Chongji, *Zhuanzhe niandai: Zhonguode1947* (*The Turning Point: China in 1947*) (Beijing: Sanlianshudian, 2002) and Liu Tong, *Zhongguode 1948 nian: Liangzhong mingyunde juezhan* ('China in 1948: A Battle that Decided between Two Destinies') (Beijing: Sanlian shudian, 2006). In the English language, Richard Bernstein pushes the critical year back to 1945, though his *China 1945: Mao's Revolution and America's Fateful Choice* (New York: Alfred A. Knopf, 2014 – Kindle edition) focuses more on US–China relations than Chinese domestic developments per se.

9   There are conflicting estimates (for that is what they were) of the size of China's population in 1949. The *China Handbook 1950*, p. 17, compiled by the China Handbook Editorial Board for the Nationalist Government (New York: Rockport Press, 1950), put the figure for June 1948 at a surprisingly precise 463,493,418. An official PRC publication, *Zhonghua renmin gongheguo shibiannian: 1949 nianjuan* p838 ('Chronicle of the People's Republic of China – 1949') (Beijing: Dangdai zhongguo chubanshe, 2004), says the 1949 population was 541,670,000.

10 See, for example, Paul A. Cohen, 'The 1949 divide in Chinese history', in Jeffrey N. Wasserstrom (ed.) *Twentieth-Century China: New Approaches*

(Taylor & Francis, 2002. ProQuest Ebook Central, http://ebookcentral. proquest.com/lib/oxford/detail.action?docID=170454).

11 There is no discussion of events in Macau in 1949 in this book, not because they are uninteresting or unimportant, but because they had little bearing on the broader outcome of the Civil War and its wider significance. Readers keen to explore the impact of the communist victory on Macau could start with Moises Silva Fernandes, 'How to Relate with a Colonial Power on its Shore: Macau in the Chinese Foreign Policy, 1949–1965', *Bulletin of Portuguese/Japanese Studies*, December 2008, Volume 17, pp. 225–50.

12 I am grateful to Dr Rory Macleod for this observation.

13 David Armitage, *Civil Wars: A History in Ideas* (New Haven, CT: Yale University Press, 2017), p. 5.

14 Armitage, *Civil Wars*, p. 9.

15 https://ourworldindata.org/life-expectancy (accessed 13 June 2019). Other sources put the figure (possibly for 1946–7) much lower – for example, 34.85 for men and 34.63 for women. See Gerald F. Winfield, *China: The Land and the People* (New York: William Sloane Associates, 1948), p. 106.

16 Lloyd Eastman, *Family Field and Ancestors: Constancy and Change in China's Social and Economic History, 1550–1949* (Oxford: Oxford University Press, 1988). p. 82.

17 Winfield, *China*, p. 111.

18 See Chapter 2, p. 8 and Chapter 8, p. 13.

19 Angus Maddison, *Chinese Economic Performance in the Long Run* (Paris: OECD, 1998), p. 69.

20 Angus Maddison, *The World Economy: A Millennial Perspective* (Paris: OECD, 2001), p. 117.

21 Maddison, *Chinese Economic Performance*, p. 16, p. 56.

22 TNA FO371/F15624, 25 October 1948.

23 Chang Chihyun (ed.) *The Chinese Journals of L. K. Little, 1943–54: An Eyewitness Account of War and Revolution, Vol. 1* (London: Routledge online resource, 2017), p. 691.9/968.

24 He Fangzhou, *Zailun taonan* ('More on Running Away') in *Lun Yu*, 16 March 1949. Introduction.

25 Cited by Condoleezza Rice, *No Higher Honour: A Memoir of My Years in Washington* (New York: Crown Publishers, 2011), p. xiv.

26 Tony Judt, *Reappraisals: Reflections on the Forgotten Twentieth Century* (London: William Heinemann, 2008), p. 5.

27 Gill Bennett, *Six Moments of Crisis inside British Foreign Policy* (Oxford: Oxford University Press, 2014), p. 3.

28 Percy Cradock, *Know Your Enemy: How the Joint Intelligence Committee Saw the World* (London: John Murray, 2002), p. 5.

Introduction

High noon in Nanjing

As darkness fell over Nanjing, China's capital, on the evening of 31 December 1948, fireworks lit up the night sky above the private residence of Chiang Kai-shek, the country's president. Festive lanterns adorned the walls surrounding the red-brick building in Huangpu Road, just a short distance from the imposing Presidential Palace. Inside, attendants scurried between tables laden with delicacies. It was, as one of those present put it, a thoroughly festive scene.[1]

So it appeared on the surface. Most of the forty or so guests at the New Year's Eve reception were senior leaders of Chiang's government and ruling Nationalist Party (or Guomindang) either based in or passing through an anxious capital, a city of 1.1 million people located on the south bank of the Yangtze, some 220 miles upstream from Shanghai. And festivities were far from their minds.

Instead, this largely civilian elite of a fragile, fracturing regime feared that their world was coming to an end. At what speed, under what terms and with what consequences were far from clear, which made matters worse. They probably hoped some clues would emerge this very evening.

Chiang's generals were far from Nanjing and had little time for celebrations. They were desperately trying to stave off (or escape) the latest offensives by Mao Zedong's communist armies. Some were besieged in major cities such as Beiping[2] and Tianjin, the now isolated metropolises of north China; or in Taiyuan, capital of Shanxi province, to the west. Nerves were also jangling in Shanghai, China's mighty commercial centre, where residents, their ranks swollen by refugees, were watching the seemingly unstoppable advance of communism with apprehension. Unless something was done to stop the rot, the fall of all these citadels to the People's Liberation Army (PLA) seemed merely a matter of time.

Large parts of the country had already done so. On 2 November, after a long and bitter siege, the PLA had taken Shenyang, the last major city still

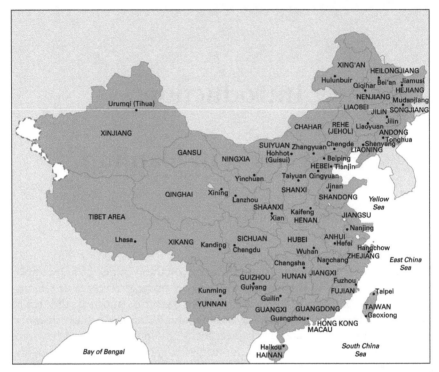

MAP I.1 *A Political map of the Republic of China, 1949.*

under government control in Manchuria, the resource-rich and industrially
developed territory in northeast China, beyond the Great Wall. Manchuria
had been under Japanese occupation for almost fifteen years before Tokyo's
surrender in August 1945 ended the Second World War. Chiang had made a
priority of regaining control over the region: it had been a 'lost' Chinese
territory too long, and its recovery was essential for the security of Beiping
and north China as a whole. Moreover, it had since become a new stronghold
for Chinese communist forces who benefited from the presence in the region
of the Soviet Red Army – a condition arising from the Yalta agreement of
February 1945 between the Allies, from which the Chinese were excluded
and about whose outcome, at least in this respect, they were at first kept in
the dark.

Manchuria adjoined the Soviet Union, which was the Chinese communists'
main source of weapons, money and, when Mao felt like adhering to it,
Joseph Stalin's strategic advice on how to topple Chiang's government and
take over China. Its fall to the PLA had transformed the balance of power
between the two bitter rivals for control of the rest of China; the communists
now controlled the country's largest industrial base, including a string of

former Japanese arsenals from which they could supply their armies. It was a strategic and symbolic asset of huge significance.[3]

During the first days of December, forces under Lin Biao, the communist general who masterminded the conquest of Manchuria, had poured south of the Great Wall. They were now linking up with other units in north and central China whom Mao and his generals had ordered to launch major attacks against Chiang's armies.[4] By the time the guests gathered at Chiang's residence, the largest of these battles, known as the Huaihai Campaign,[5] was well under way and had all but destroyed his best forces north of the Yangtze. Communist guns were now within firing range of the capital and the government had imposed martial law in most of the rapidly diminishing areas under its control.[6]

The government's chances of reversing the tide seemed close to zero. 'Manchuria is a limb that has been amputated', one minister noted soberly. 'The body can live despite amputation. North China is another limb, and even that can be sacrificed. But Central China is the Nationalist heart – and if the heart is pierced, the body dies.'[7] The very survival of Chiang's regime was in question. Drastic action was required.

Among those present at the gloomy soirée in central Nanjing was Li Zongren, one of two key military leaders from Guangxi province, south China. Li had been at odds with Chiang for years over matters of political leadership and military strategy. Chiang had usually come out on top. But eight months earlier, despite vigorous efforts, he had failed to prevent newly empowered National Assembly members from electing Li as vice president, and thus Chiang's deputy. It was a serious setback for the Chinese leader. Indeed, it was said to be the only one in a year of acute troubles that had caused him to suffer insomnia, which he sought to cure by forsaking his Methodist principles and taking a little whisky.[8]

Up to that point a life-long military man, Li, now fifty-eight, was widely admired for his feats on the battlefield during the war against Japan. Exasperated for years, he had decided he could no longer serve under a leader he believed to be incompetent. But Chiang was so self-assured and surrounded by so many acolytes it had proved impossible to weaken his grip on power, even though the government was on the brink of collapse and the country about to succumb to communism.

Ignoring the advice of Bai Chongxi, the other leading Guangxi general and one of his closest associates, Li had decided, as the expression put it, to 'enter politics'. He had swapped his uniform for the tailored Western suits in which he never looked entirely comfortable, precisely to challenge Chiang's leadership and implement urgent reforms before it was too late. He would do what he could to rescue the Nationalist regime – hopefully with the help of friendly foreign powers, chiefly the United States.

Also present was Premier Sun Ke, a veteran politician, less popular with the public than Li, who had served in a string of senior positions under

FIGURE I.1 *Li Zongren, who in January 1949 succeeded Chiang Kai-shek as Acting President, but was at perpetual odds with him over control of the Nationalist government.*

Chiang. The son of Sun Yat-sen, founder of the Republic of China, Sun Ke had also reached the view that change at the top was essential. Still sore over the fact that Li had defeated him in the vice-presidential contest, he had just about managed to put together a new cabinet (or Executive Yuan). It had taken weeks of intense lobbying by the fifty-seven-year old, interrupted by spells of bad health and high blood pressure, to balance factions and bridge personal rivalries in a Nationalist hierarchy demoralized by calamitous setbacks on the battlefield and a bold but ruinous attempt to reform the currency. It was unclear how long the new team would stick together. But it was certain to collapse should it fail to get a grip on the situation.

Other guests included Chiang Ching-kuo, Chiang's son, with whom he was particularly close;[9] Zhang Zhizhong, the left-leaning political strongman of northwest China; and Chen Lifu, a US-trained mining engineer, who with his older brother, Chen Guofu, headed the 'CC clique', a powerful faction within the Guomindang (GMD) that usually – though not always – was fiercely loyal to Chiang.

Chiang's future was on the minds of all those who spent the last few hours of 1948 in his secluded, heavily guarded quarters. Now sixty-one, he was still China's best-known figure at home and abroad, and the symbol of his country's troubled fortunes over the past twenty-two years. Lean, short and wiry, and frequently seen wearing a military cape and brandishing a walking cane, he came across as a dour, abstemious, rather aloof leader. But he was also vigorous, stubborn and proud. And he was completely devoted to his mission of saving China from communism – a plot that he insisted was largely inspired, led and bankrolled by the Soviet Union. Chiang believed that communism was inhuman and that, unless defeated, it would mean oppression for the Chinese people and the destruction of their traditional culture.

Yet military disasters, corruption, inflation and economic chaos in China's major urban centres had caused a collapse of confidence in his government. His insistence on exercising the final say on all major decisions, especially military matters, meant that he was blamed personally when things went wrong. He had proved strategically and tactically inept.[10] War-weariness was acute in a country that had endured eight years of struggle against Japan and now more than two years of civil conflict with the communists. For years, students had demonstrated against what they believed to be rotten in Chiang's state, with the pursuit of civil war foremost among the complaints. Many such protests were small scale. Some were ended violently by the police. But all amounted to a damning indictment of the government, thanks to the traditional regard in which students were held as the country's moral conscience and presumptive elite. The hunger for peace was intense and growing.

So were calls for Chiang to resign as a pre-condition for opening peace talks with the communists. They had come from ordinary members of the public. They appeared in a surprisingly vigorous liberal media, despite heavy-handed government censorship. And they had recently been uttered, if discreetly, by diplomats from the United States – Chiang's sole, increasingly uneasy supporter among the foreign powers.

Washington had for years backed Chiang's government with arms, military training, economic aid and generous diplomatic support. Many Americans had long believed their country was in a strong position to guide and assist China's reform and modernization. The fact that during the Second World War Chiang had been an important if often frustrating ally in the global struggle against Japan and Germany reinforced the sentiment. After the war, Washington helped secure a place for China – which it included in the 'Big Five'[11] countries that had emerged as victors – at the top table of international affairs: Nationalist China was a founder member of the United Nations as well as other important international organizations.

The United States had also tried to broker peace between the Nationalists and the communists after the defeat of Japan. It wanted to prevent a resumption of civil war between the two foes and lay the foundation for a strong, united and democratic China, a broad US aim over the previous fifty years. But General George Marshall's mission of 1946–7 failed in the face of bitter enmity and large-scale hostilities between the government and the communists. Worse, from the US point of view, the communists quickly gained the upper hand thanks to their battlefield skills, disciplined leadership, tight organization, sense of purpose – and support from the Soviet Union.

Chiang's inability to match the communists in the first four of these attributes was the main source of his government's current predicament. He believed that more US aid was needed to rescue the situation. This was essential because much more than China was at stake in this struggle between the Chinese. Historian Steve Tsang has pointed out that Chiang 'was one of the first to see the Chinese civil war as an integral part of the worldwide conflict between communism and capitalism'.[12] It was part of the struggle between the 'free world', led by the United States, and international Bolshevism, championed by the Soviet Union. And the struggle was intensifying, as Soviet moves in Eastern and Southern Europe had recently forced Washington to acknowledge.

President Harry S. Truman had responded in 1947 with the doctrine by now firmly associated with his name of countering Soviet expansion. His administration pledged to resist communism in Greece, Turkey and elsewhere, and with the programme of economic assistance known as Marshall Aid to help lift Western Europe off its knees and render it less vulnerable to Soviet or home-grown forms of communism. Moreover, the Cold War had just produced its first crisis in the form of the Berlin blockade, under way at the very moment when the fate of China, too, was at a critical juncture.

In Chiang's view (and those of many others at the time) the prospect of a third world war loomed between the democratic and communist camps.[13] The United States would have no choice but to wage it – just as it had been forced by Japanese aggression to join the Second World War. Washington should act sooner rather than later, insisted Chiang. It should provide full military support for his government whose survival was now critical to the cause of global freedom. As V. K. Wellington Koo, Chiang's ambassador to the US, put it: 'China and Europe formed two parts of one picture. US policy to contain Communism should not discriminate in favour of Europe and against China.'[14]

Nationalist leaders, in common with many citizens, were angry that the Truman administration was busily building up Japan, the former enemy, as a bastion against communism rather than China, its erstwhile ally. Premier Sun Ke put it plainly in a bad-tempered outburst in front of an American visitor: 'You are fighting a cold war against communism throughout the world, yet in China your policy appears aimed at hastening our government's disintegration. It seems we aren't collapsing fast enough to suit your taste.'[15]

Chiang had been disappointed in November when Republican contender Thomas Dewey, who had promised more aid for the Chinese leader, failed to defeat Truman in the US presidential election. In a thinly disguised sign of desperation, his wife, Song Meiling, who had successfully rallied support for her country in its struggle with Japan during a tour of the United States in 1943, suddenly left Nanjing on 27 November to see if she could win the Americans around again. As a result of the worsening situation in China, 'she was emotionally and psychologically out of control, and both he and his wife were suffering insomnia', Chiang noted in his diary.[16] China's 'first lady' crossed the Pacific on a plane provided by the commander of the US Seventh Fleet.

Song received a courteous reception from US leaders who had already written off her husband's government. A Central Intelligence Agency (CIA) assessment in November concluded: 'The disappearance of the Chinese National Government, as presently constituted, will probably occur within the next few months . . . It is inconceivable that the existing regime can rally to stabilize the situation on a new line in Central China.'[17] Accordingly, Washington had withdrawn its formal military mission, the United States Military Advisory Group (USMAG); a British reporter saw the 'carpets being rolled up at Nanking's Hotel Metropole, where US officers had been quartered, and secretaries busily incinerating confidential documents'.[18]

Nevertheless, while taking tea with the president in Washington on 9 December, Song requested that the US send a new military mission to China and provide a further three billion dollars in aid. Truman demurred. Washington later calculated that between 1945 and March 1949 it had provided no less than 1.6 billion dollars in military and economic support and an additional 400 million in credits to China.[19] This was said to be an amount 'equivalent in value to more than 50 percent of the monetary expenditures of the Chinese Government and of proportionately greater magnitude in relation to the budget of that Government than the United States has provided to any nation of Western Europe since the end of the [Second World] war'.[20] It had also sold to China military and civilian war surplus property worth over US$1 billion for which the US realized US$232 million. Despite such generosity, the Chinese government 'has been nationally and internationally bankrupt for a long time', said *The Far Eastern Economic Review*.[21]

Yet the United States could not look with equanimity on the prospect of a communist victory in China. Neither could the United Kingdom, which had large commercial interests in the country and was concerned about the future of Hong Kong. Significant differences had emerged between London and Washington over China policy and how best to respond to the changing fortunes of the Civil War. But for both, China's fate was important due to its size, strategic location and economic potential, and because its future would have a crucial bearing on the wider global contest between the United States and the Soviet Union and their respective allies.

In this context, Chiang Kai-shek's personal future acquired added importance at the close of 1948. There were few grounds for thinking that his departure alone would revitalize the Nationalist regime: it had a very weak social base, which partly explained its rapid collapse. But perhaps it could at least delay the establishment of communist control over all of China. Perhaps it would result in a condominium of some sort in which the communists governed north China and the Nationalists the south. Perhaps it would pave the way for a national coalition government that the Western powers could deal with more easily than a solely communist or, come to that, a solely Nationalist administration. At least, surely, it would mean an end to the fighting, chaos and disruption that had blighted China for so long.

China's communist leaders had different ambitions. They had long wanted Chiang to go, convinced that his regime would not long outlast him, a view the CIA shared.[22] Since the collapse of US-led mediation efforts in mid-1946, they had vilified China's 'reactionary' leader in the strongest terms. The United States, of which Chiang was said to be the 'puppet', came in for the same treatment. At every turn, the Party tried to persuade Nationalist generals and politicians, and especially the former, to desert their leader, whom they insisted was destined for oblivion, along with the corrupt, reactionary, incompetent elite surrounding him. Just a few days before he entertained guests in his residence, a communist radio broadcast branded Chiang and forty-two of his principal lieutenants 'first-class war criminals', a move said to have driven the Chinese leader into a paroxysm of rage.[23] Nine of those named, (who included Li Zongren) were present at the reception.

Until this point, Chiang had resisted calls that he step aside, even though, as one observer put it, the 'peace-at-any-price tide welled right up to the door of [his] study'.[24] He had broached the topic with a small circle of senior leaders, but had yet to announce a decision. It was an extremely sensitive matter – for him personally, for the wider leadership and for the public.

On the personal front, he was still grieving over the loss of Chen Bulei, his longstanding confidential secretary and close adviser. A man of the shadows, usually well out of the public eye, Chen had committed suicide in Nanjing on 13 November, two days before his fifty-eighth birthday. His loyalty to Chiang was legendary. Corruption and factionalism within the Guomindang, as well as successive military disasters, had driven him to despair; so, it seems, had the knowledge that his daughter, then in Beiping, was a CCP agent. He could not bear the collapse of a cause and a leader he had served so long. The author of many of Chiang's speeches and policy documents, Chen could have been of immense help to his embattled chief in the difficult months that lay ahead.[25]

There was also the impact on the military situation to consider. Though extremely unfavourable for the government, this was still delicate at the end of 1948: communist victory in the Huaihai campaign, the great battle for control of central China, was close but not yet complete. Chiang's sudden departure from the scene, whether forced or otherwise, might weaken what remained of fighting spirit among his besieged commanders and men.

Yet on balance Chiang had come to believe that clinging onto the presidency might prove more dangerous for both him and his government than relinquishing office. The reason for this was what he referred to in his diary as 'betrayal and coercion' by Bai Chongxi, the Guangxi general with whom he had long had a tempestuous relationship, but on whose well-trained troops, battlefield skills and general reputation he now critically depended.[26] In these circumstances, survival required subtlety more than stubbornness. It was a question of knowing when to step down – with a view to stepping up again once circumstances allowed, which Chiang believed they inevitably would.

Broad-shouldered and bony-faced, Bai, fifty-five, was the sword-bearer of the Guangxi Clique, as this powerful military faction was known. A compact man, whose closely shaved head was typical of the Chinese military leader keen to convey a sense of discipline, dedication and duty, he was an ethnic Chinese Muslim from humble origins, close to the traditional Guangxi capital of Guilin. One of China's most admired generals, he acquired the sobriquet 'Little Zhuge' (after Zhuge Liang, one of ancient China's most famous military strategists) thanks to his victories over Chinese opponents and Japanese invaders.

Bai was Commander in Chief of the Central China Bandit Suppression Forces based in the city of Wuhan, the strategic strong point straddling the central reaches of the Yangtze, several hundred miles upstream from Nanjing. Chiang depended on him to prevent PLA forces moving into position to cross the river, seizing the capital and conquering the south. He at first tried to lessen this dependency by splitting the Central Bandit Command into two and entrusting a loyalist with the defence of the central plains north of the capital. But by the close of 1948, this had resulted in catastrophic defeat: Nanjing was dangerously exposed to the communists' next move, which could only be in one direction.

Bai thus found himself in a critical position within a divided camp. He had four armies under his command, in all some 300,000 troops, the best of them his own Guangxi forces. Though ill-equipped and short of funds, they controlled the flow of food (from the rice bowl of Hunan to the south) and such weapons as could be obtained (partly from the arsenals of Sichuan to the west). Perhaps 'Little Zhuge' from Guangxi could prevent the complete collapse of Nationalist power in China and at least delay the communist advance?[27]

Bai thought it possible. As he saw it, the only alternative to total defeat and all that this entailed for China, the national government and for him personally was to sue for peace with the communists. Chiang must step down in favour of vice president Li, who would then try to reach a political accord with the bitter foes whom the Nationalists had been fighting for most of the past twenty years.

At the very least peace negotiations could buy time. Time for the Nationalist armies to reorganize and replenish themselves after their recent

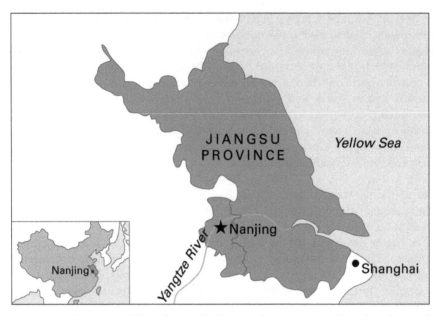

MAP I.2 *Nanjing and Shanghai – The Nationalist government's political capital and economic centre.*

defeats. Time for the foreign powers to wake up at last to what was at stake in China's civil war and either mediate or, in the case of the United States, resume military aid or even intervene in the conflict. Perhaps enough time might be won even for the Nationalists to get their house in order and rebuild confidence in their battered regime.

Such were the calculations at work in Bai's mind, judging from two critical telegrams he sent to Chiang at the end of December.[28] The first, despatched from Wuhan on the 24th, opened with a bleak but realistic assessment of the situation among the public and the military following the destruction of the government's main armies. 'Unless we have a chance to rest, replenish and reorganize, it will be impossible for us to rescue the situation, whatever sacrifices we make', it said. 'We must communicate our sincere desire for peace to the Americans and ask them, the British and the Soviets to use their good offices to mediate to this end.'

Bai spoke of making the most of the pressure that popular organizations across the country were applying to both sides to sue for peace. Government and communist troops should remain in their current positions, pending the outcome of the peace initiative. 'I hope we can speedily unfold this peace plan at home and abroad while Beiping, Tianjin, Nanjing and Shanghai are still under our control, and thus win time.'

Chiang did not reply immediately to Bai's telegram (though he railed against it in his diary), which was one of several from senior generals and provincial governors expressing similar sentiments about the same time. Bai therefore wrote to him again on 30 December, this time with greater urgency:

> In the present situation, it is hard to wage war and the pursuit of peace is also difficult . . . We must promptly declare our sincere desire for peace and seek internal and external support for this cause. If the other side agrees, we will have a chance to overcome our difficulties and gain a fresh start . . . [but] time is not on our side. I humbly request a prompt decision.

Chiang probably received this telegram a few hours before he joined his guests, who did not include Bai, at the New Year's Eve reception. No wonder those marking the arrival of the New Year with the man who had led them for so long wore gloomy expressions. When Chiang entered the room and bade them sit down and eat, they did so in perfunctory manner, seemingly oblivious of the delicious fare in front of them. They were quick to declare that they had eaten their fill, whereupon Chiang addressed them, quietly and solemn in tone:

> The situation is so grim today that some people in our party advocate that we open peace talks with the communists. This is a matter that concerns the very existence of our party and country. Thus, I cannot remain silent but must express my own views on the matter. To that end, I have asked Chen Fang [Chiang's new secretary] to put down my thoughts on paper so that I can deliver them tomorrow in the form of a New Year's Day address to the Chinese people. I am going to ask Zhang Qun (former premier and close friend) to read out this draft and solicit your views.[29]

In common with key speeches by Chinese leaders before and since, Chiang's address contained mixed messages. It combined defensiveness with defiance; statesmanship with shows of sympathy for a public forced to endure the hardships of war. The customary reference to the communists as 'bandits' was dropped, and there was contrite acceptance of Chiang's own responsibility for the setbacks of the past. But he pledged to fight on and rid China of the menace of communism – if necessary, by means of a decisive military victory in the coming battle for control over the Yangtze heartland.

The critical passage occurred in the second half. The government had done all it could to secure peace and dialogue with the communists but to no avail. It was therefore pointless for people to appeal to the government to end the civil war because the matter was no longer in its hands. It was up to the communists. If *they* were sincere about peace, the public would not find the government wanting in terms of a positive response.

But there were certain conditions. They included the preservation of China's independence and national sovereignty; adherence to the constitution and democratic form of government the Nationalists insisted they were practising; the continued integrity of the government's armed forces; and maintenance of the free lifestyle and minimum living standards said to be enjoyed by the people.

And then came the most important section of all: 'As for my own position, I have no concerns at all. As long as peace is secured, I will follow the will of the people.'

These remarks stunned the audience. Chiang asked Li Zongren, seated to his right, what he thought of them. Long an advocate of Chiang's departure, Li must have experienced mixed emotions. For once Chiang stepped down, it would be up to him to salvage a desperate political and military situation. All Li could manage by way of reply was a diplomatic, 'I agree with you, Mr President.'

Several members of the CC faction were less compliant, warning that Chiang's resignation would have a grave effect on public morale. They demanded that the two sentences hinting at his willingness to give up the presidency be removed from the speech. They were lone voices in the discussion that ensued.

Chiang then suddenly exploded in anger, throwing the teacup he was holding to the ground. 'Do you think it is easy for me to do this?' he demanded of his startled guests. 'The fact that I am willing to do so is not because of the Communist Party. It is because of a faction within our own party!' he said in a pointed reference to Li and Bai, leaders of the Guangxi Clique.

He then turned to Zhang Qun, told him that the reference to his willingness to step aside must be included in the next day's speech and stormed out of the room.

Notes

1   The account of the New Year's Eve reception that follows is based largely on the observations of Cheng Siyuan, a junior official, who was present. See Cheng Siyuan, *Li Zongren xiansheng wannian* ('The Later Life of Mr Li Zongren') (Beijing: Wenshi ziliao chubanshe, 1985), pp. 22–4; and, by the same author, *Zhenghai mixin* ('A Political Life Behind the Scenes') (Hong Kong: Nanyue chubanshe, 1988), p. 211. See also *Time*, 10 January 1949, p. 15.

2   Chiang's government on 20 June 1928 declared Nanjing as the capital of China and changed the name of Beijing ('Northern Capital') to Beiping ('Northern Peace'). I have therefore referred to the city by that name when dealing with events before 1 October 1949. With the founding of the PRC, the communists made the city the capital again and I have from that date adopted the form Beijing accordingly.

3   Harold M. Tanner, *The Battle for Manchuria and the Fate of China: Siping 1946* (Bloomington, IN: Indiana University Press, 2013), p. 206.

4 Christopher R. Lew, *The Third Chinese Revolutionary Civil War, 1945–49: An Analysis of Communist Strategy and Leadership* (London: Routledge, 2009), p. 126.

5 In communist historiography, the Huaihai campaign (named after Huai river and Long-hai trunk railway in central China within whose confines it largely was fought) is regarded as the third (and decisive) of the three great military battles in which their forces destroyed Chiang's armies and conquered the entire country. The other two decisive battles were the Liaoshen campaign, in which the communists defeated government forces in Manchuria, and the Beijing–Tianjin campaign, so named for obvious reasons.

6 Liang Shengjun, *Jiang-Li douzheng neimu* ('The Inside Story of the Struggle Between Jiang and Li') (Taibei: Xinxin wencongshu, 1992), pp. 48–9. *Xianggang gongshang ribao* (Hong Kong Commercial Daily), 11 December 1948, p. 1.

7 *Time*, 15 December 1948, p. 17.

8 Dong Xianguang, *Jiang zongtong zhuan* ('A Biography of President Jiang'), Vol. 3 (Taipei: Zhonghua wenhua chuban shiye weiyuanhui, 1954), p. 497. *Time*, 6 December 1948, p. 17.

9 Ching-kuo was Chiang's son by his first wife, Mao Fumei.

10 A short but telling summary (in Chinese) of Chiang's military errors can be found in Wang Chaoguang, *1945–1949: Guogong zhengzheng yu zhongguo mingyun* ('1945–1949: The Political Struggle between the Nationalists and the Communists and China's Destiny') (Beijing: shehui kexue wenxian chubanshe, 2010), especially Chapter 13.

11 That is, the United States, the United Kingdom, the Soviet Union, France and China.

12 Steve Tsang, *The Cold War's Odd Couple: The Unintended Partnership between the Republic of China and the U.K. 1950–1958* (London: I. B. Tauris, 2006), p. 6.

13 Joseph Stalin, the Soviet leader, was among those who believed a third world war was inevitable. Foreign Minister Vyacheslav Molotov quoted him as saying: 'The First World War tore one country [i.e. Russia] away from capitalist slavery. The Second World War created the socialist system, and the Third World War will finish imperialism forever.' Cited by Sergei N. Goncharov, John W. Lewis and Xue Litai in *Uncertain Partners: Stalin, Mao and the Korean War* (Stanford, CA: Stanford University Press, 1993), p. 55.

14 Stephen G. Craft, *V.K. Wellington Koo and the Emergence of Modern China* (Lexington, KY: The University Press of Kentucky, 2004), p. 218.

15 *Time*, 27 December 1948 p. 16.

16 Lin Hsiao-ting, *Accidental State, the United States and the Making of Taiwan* (Cambridge, MA: Harvard University Press, 2016), footnote 66, p. 263.

17 National Intelligence Council (NIC), *Tracking the Dragon: National Intelligence Estimates on China During the Era of Mao, 1948–1976* (Pittsburgh, PA: Government Printing Office, 2004) ORE 27-48 (CD)

18 *Daily Express*, 29 November 1948.

19 Foreign Relations of the United States (hereafter FRUS), *The Far East: China, Vol. VIII*, 13 December 1948. https://history.state.gov/historicaldocuments/frus1948v08/d252 (accessed 13 February 2020). Robert Bickers, *Out of China: How the Chinese Ended the Era of Western Domination* (London: Allen Lane, 2017), p. 272.

20 US Department of State Publication 3573, Far Eastern Series 30, *The China White Paper*, August, 1949, Vol 1 (Stanford, CA: Stanford University Press,1967) (hereafter *CWP*), p. xv.

21 *The Far Eastern Economic Review* (hereafter *FEER*), 19 January 1949, p. 79.

22 National Intelligence Council (NIC) (2004), ORE 27-48 (CD).

23 TNA FO371/75734. 31 December 1948, p. 2.

24 *Time*, 27 December 1948, p. 16.

25 Daphon D. Ho, 'Night Thoughts of a Hungry Ghostwriter: Chen Bulei and the Life of Service in Republican China.' *Modern Chinese Literature and Culture*, Vol. 19, No. 1 (Spring 2007), p. 4; Zhou Hongtao, *Jiang Gong yu Wo* ('The Revered Jiang and I') (Taibei: Tianxia wenhua chubanshe, 2003), pp. 56–9; and John F. Melby, *The Mandate of Heaven: Record of a Civil War, China 1945–59* (London: Chatto & Windus, 1969), p. 292.

26 Lin Tongfa, *Da chetui* ('The Great Withdrawal') (Taipei: Lianjing chuban shiye youxian gongsi, 2009), pp. 72–3.

27 Shengjun, *Jiang-Li douzheng neimu*, p. 47. *Time*, 17 January 1949, p. 15.

28 The extracts from Bai's two telegrams that follow are drawn from Lin Tongfa, *Da chetui*, pp. 72–4; and Bai Xianyong, *Fuqin yu minguo* ('Father and the Republic') (Hong Kong: Tiandi tushu youxian gongsi, 2012), Vol. 1, pp. 318–20 and Vol. 2, pp. 51–2.

29 The quotations from and details of Chiang's remarks in the paragraphs that follow are drawn from Cheng Siyuan, *Li Zongren xiansheng wannian*, pp. 22–4, and Dong Xianguang, *Jiang zongtong zhuan*, Vol. 3, pp. 509–10. An English translation of Chiang's New Year Message for 1949 can be found in *CWP*, Vol, 2, pp. 920–2.

1

Adversaries

'The enemy will not perish of himself'

The tone, content – indeed, the very title – of Mao Zedong's New Year address to the Chinese people issued on 30 December 1948 could hardly have been more different from the solemn yet mild message to be delivered on New Year's Day by the beleaguered Chiang Kai-shek. It was entitled 'Carry the Revolution Through to the End', and whereas Chiang proffered peace talks with his foes, even offering to stand down to facilitate them, Mao pledged to overthrow the Nationalist leadership, eliminate the influence of their imperialist backers and upend the entire social order of which they both were part.[1]

'The Chinese people will win final victory in the great War of Liberation. Even our enemy no longer doubts the outcome', he declared.

> The annihilation of the Guomindang's main forces north of the Yangtze River greatly facilitates the forthcoming crossing of the Yangtze by the People's Liberation Army and its southward drive to liberate all China ... Public opinion the world over, including the entire imperialist press, no longer disputes the certainty of the country-wide victory of the Chinese People's War of Liberation.

Mao castigated the Nationalist leaders as 'gangs of bandits' and 'venomous snakes', demanding that Chinese people show them no mercy. The revolution must not be abandoned half-way for 'the enemy will not perish of himself'.[2]

If Chiang Kai-shek felt that his world was collapsing round him after a year of calamities, Mao, while perhaps not brimming with quite as much confidence as his uncompromising address suggested, felt that he and the communist movement of which he had been the undisputed leader since 1945 was on the brink of what until recently had seemed unimaginable: the conquest of China. Chiang had been chasing Mao around the countryside for years; it now seemed that Mao might be able to drive Chiang out of China altogether. Mao was destined to enter the ranks of the world's greatest leaders; Chiang was about to drop out of them.

Six years and some 450 miles separated the birthdays and birth places of the two men battling for control of their country. Chiang, the elder of the two, came into the world on 31 October 1887 on the second floor of a salt store in Fenghua, Zhejiang province, a traditionally prosperous part of China, south of Shanghai. His father was a salt merchant with whom he was to have a difficult relationship. He had nothing but tender feelings towards his mother.

Mao was born on 26 December 1893 in Shaoshan, a village surrounded by fertile rice paddy in Hunan province, south central China. His father was a rich peasant, a class of person whom his son's revolution would later cast into jeopardy. The young Mao hated his father but, like Chiang, adored his mother.

As they matured, the two men continued to have much in common yet remained a study in contrasts. Intelligent, resourceful, determined, they both immersed themselves in the struggle to change China for the better that dominated much of the political life of their country in the early decades of the twentieth century. Both were shamed by their country's weaknesses; both were determined to do something about it, often at great personal risk. They fought on the same side for a while, rallying to the cause of National Revolution in the early 1920s championed by Sun Yat-sen, leader of the 'reorganized' GMD, and backed by the Soviet Union.

Yet doctrinally and in terms of their visions for the future of their country the two men were miles apart. And while they both possessed extraordinary will power, confidence and sense of mission, it was to very different ends. Ultimately, it was communism that divided them.

Chiang, who had seen something of it first-hand during a study trip to Moscow in 1923–4, was unimpressed, though he admired the discipline of the Red Army, enforced by its political commissars. 'Proletarian revolution was not appropriate for China', he told his startled hosts.[3] Mao was a firm believer in the Marxism to which he had been introduced at an early age and which, so he and his supporters claimed, he had since adapted to Chinese conditions with such extraordinary success. He had never been abroad but was at this precise moment badgering Joseph Stalin for an invitation to visit Moscow in the hope that he could secure an alliance between their two countries.

Chiang was supremely confident in himself and his civilization, thanks to a sense of personal destiny reinforced by his conversion to Christianity. His diary reveals him to have been a devout man, a regular reader of the Bible, reflective and self-critical. Disciplined and restrained in public (except under pressure of the kind that caused him to storm out of the New Year's reception), he was in many ways a traditional figure, Confucian in outlook and convinced that many of the answers to China's problems lay in improving the moral behaviour of its people. 'We must ... endeavour to improve our social customs and habits ... reform our intellectual life and foster a spirit of freedom and government by law', he wrote in the conclusion of his *China's Destiny*, published in 1943.[4]

Mao was made of different stuff. He was a man of more grandiose visions eager to place developments in China in a wider international framework. This was striking given that his knowledge of the outside world seems to have been acquired mainly through Soviet or Marxist sources. Cruder, crueller and even more ruthless than Chiang, Mao's manners and modes of speaking bore the hallmarks of his Hunan peasant origins. The same was true of his dialect, which seems to have been as hard for many of his fellow countrymen to understand as Chiang Kai-shek's thick Ningbo accent.

Yet what ultimately differentiated the two men at the close of 1948 was the simple but critical matter of success – politically and on the battlefield. Mao had led the Communist Party and its armies to the brink of victory. This was striking testimony to his ability to motivate, lead, catalyse and organize a widespread desire for change in a huge, diverse country and in the most difficult of conditions. It was also an indictment of Chiang Kai-shek's failings in this regard.

Heavy-set, stocky, by now thrice married and the father of at least six children, Mao had just turned fifty-five at the close of 1948.[5] He was in indifferent health thanks to what would later be diagnosed as a low-grade malarial infection, bronchitis and what probably was both cause and effect of his condition: insomnia.[6] Usually clad in matching baggy jacket and trousers, his hair long and floppy rather than the coiffured look of later years, he had since late May been living in Xibaipo, a small village on the eastern edge of the inaccessible Taihang Mountain range in Hebei province, some 200 miles southwest of Beiping. The Taihang marks the eastern boundary of China's loess plateau, separating Shanxi province to the west from Hebei in the east and pushing south into Henan province. Xibaipo was a hamlet of 100 households or so, on the north bank of the Hu river. The yellow baked-mud walls of its simple dwellings were surrounded by mountains and set among cypress trees. The nearest city, Shijiazhuang, was 60 miles away to the southeast. The PLA had taken it from the government the previous December, the first urban centre in north China to fall into communist hands.

Mao had settled in this small, picturesque location after more than a year wandering through remote parts of northern Shaanxi with his personal bodyguards and small detachments of troops. He spent much of this time avoiding (often without much apparent difficulty) government forces under General Hu Zongnan, which in March 1947 had forced the Party out of its wartime base of Yanan. Chiang made much of his capture of the CCP's headquarters; at the time, he seemed to have the upper hand in the struggle against his rival. But it was an illusion. His troops, desperately needed elsewhere, soon evacuated Yanan, which the communists reoccupied in April 1948.

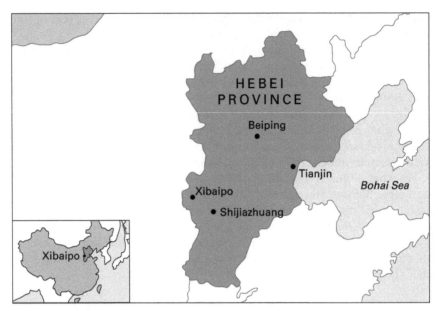

MAP 1.1 *Xibaipo, location of Mao Zedong's headquarters in early 1949.*

At home in the courtyard house in Xibaipo that he shared with his wife, Jiang Qing, Mao concentrated on the conduct of military operations and plans for China's political future. Key Party leaders moved into houses nearby. They included Zhou Enlai, fifty, perhaps best described as Mao's 'fixer' both within the Party but especially in terms of relations with those outside of it, including foreigners; Liu Shaoqi, second-ranking figure after Mao, just a few months younger than Zhou, a labour leader, specialist in Party organization, and most recently architect of a tempestuous but transformative land-reform movement; and Zhu De, some dozen years older, who was commander in chief of the PLA. Secure in their rural enclave, and far removed, in every respect, from the modern offices and grand government buildings of Nanjing, from which Chiang and his coterie watched their regime crumble, these disciplined, committed, battle-hardened men put the finishing touches to their plans to conquer and transform China.

Following a Politburo meeting held in the village in September 1948, Mao delivered a progress report. The communists were by now in control of about one-quarter of China and one-third of its population. In areas of North China with a population of 44 million a 'unified people's government' had been set up in which the Communist Party was cooperating with 'non-Party democrats'.[7] Two months later, he declared that communist troops (whose number he put at three million) had achieved numerical superiority over government forces (which, after the 'loss' of Manchuria, he said totalled 2.9 million). The war would therefore end quicker than had been expected.

'The original estimate was that the reactionary Guomindang government could be completely overthrown in about five years, beginning from July 1946. As we now see it, only another year or so may be needed to overthrow it completely.'[8]

Accordingly, his New Year address was full of plans for the future. In 1949, a Political Consultative Conference would be convened, 'with no reactionaries participating and having as its aim the fulfilment of the tasks of the people's revolution'. The People's Republic of China would be proclaimed, and a central government established. It would be 'a democratic coalition government under the leadership of the Communist Party of China, with the participation of appropriate persons representing the democratic parties and people's organizations'. Mao set these measures in an almost cosmic context: 'In our struggle, we shall overthrow once and for all the feudal oppression of thousands of years and the imperialist oppression of a hundred years. The year 1949 will be a year of tremendous importance. We should redouble our efforts.'[9]

Making China 'modern'

When Mao uttered these words, barely twenty-seven years had passed since the founding congress of the Chinese Communist Party in Shanghai's French Concession in July 1921. To all but the participants, it was fledgling movement that seemed destined to fail. That events proved otherwise was due in large part to deep forces at work in the country since at least the collapse of the imperial system of government in 1911, and the series of crises that followed. Contingency and character, those fickle forces of history, also played their part.

The year 1911, when the last imperial dynasty was overthrown, in many ways marked the end of the 'old world' as far as China was concerned. For centuries, power had been exercised by a highly trained, supposedly morally superior Confucian bureaucratic elite with the emperor at the apex. In 1911 this system collapsed, largely under its own weight. It had proved incapable of responding to acute internal challenges and external threats posed by a hostile, rapidly changing world. The rot had set in to such an extent that when a small group of republican revolutionaries associated with Sun Yat-sen joined disaffected gentry and young, modern-minded military men to stage a revolt in Wuhan in October of that year, it spread quickly across the country. Two thousand years of imperial rule came to an end in little more than a few weeks.

On 1 January 1912 a Chinese Republic was proclaimed. But how should it be organized politically, socially and economically? What path should the country take? What was its place in the family of nations? Such questions were at the heart of Chinese political discourse in the first half of the twentieth century, especially following the May Fourth Movement of 1919, which sought to come up with the answers.[10]

4 May was the day on which students in Beijing protested against their government's failure at the Versailles Peace Conference to stop the victors in the First World War from rewarding Japan's participation by granting Tokyo parts of Chinese territory. But May Fourth, often more accurately described as the 'New Culture Movement', was more important than the day after which it was named. For it lasted years and constituted a profound often painful exercise in national self-examination. Its adherents critically evaluated China's intellectual, political, social, economic and international situation and found it wanting. They insisted radical change was required if their country was to survive and flourish in the modern world.

Youth, or rather 'New Youth', to use the title of one of the most prominent of the new periodicals of the May Fourth era, was at the heart of the movement. Its champions (there were no leaders as such) were men such as Cai Yuanpei, president of Beijing University, Chen Duxiu, dean of the university and founder of 'New Youth', and Hu Shi, a noted philosopher. Other prominent figures tended to be writers, such as Lu Xun, often regarded as the father of modern Chinese literature, journalists, academics, students and political activists, most of them in their late teens, twenties or early thirties. What united them was a sense of national crisis, patriotic ardour, spirit of self-sacrifice – and determination to fashion China's future.

Their indictment of 'old' (but in fact largely still current) China was as damning as it was profound. 'All our traditional ethics, law, scholarship, rites, and customs are survivals of feudalism ... When compared with the achievement of the white race, there is a difference of a thousand years in thought, although we live in the same period', declared Chen Duxiu, soon to become the first leader of the Chinese Communist Party.[11] China was weak militarily. It was backward in terms of ideas and institutions. It was socially regressive thanks to manners and morals based around respect for age, the family and a deeply embedded patriarchy. It was poor due to the size and stagnation of the rural sector, and weak industrial base. And its people were blighted by the absence of adequate health care, modern schools and efficient communications. Even its written language was archaic and unfit for communication in the modern age.

The appropriate cures for these ailments was a matter of contention. 'Science' and 'democracy' were bandied about as potential saviours. But that left open the *kind* of democracy China should practise. There was no lack of models. Some May Fourth activists were impressed with Japan's modernization drive: it had transformed another East Asian country where tradition once prevailed. Others favoured emulating Germany's political institutions, those of the United Kingdom or the United States. All such 'modernisms' had their advocates; so did more conservative creeds.

What mattered was what would *work*. China needed doctrines and forms of political authority capable of satisfying the demands of its people for

wealth, power and ensuring greater political participation; of putting an end
to national division, backwardness, poverty and weakness; and of securing
a place for China among the world's most advanced countries. This was all
very well, but China was far from starting from scratch. National renewal
had to make headway in a land of lingering tradition and deep attachment
to the past, even though the emperor had abdicated, his palaces deserted.
New ideas had to take root in a vast, hugely populated, economically
undeveloped country that, especially since 1911, had fallen prey to political
violence and civil wars.

This meant the pursuit of change was likely to be brutal. Arms as well as
arguments would be needed to win the day; ideals quickly abandoned in
favour of coercion. 'Political power grows out of the barrel of a gun', Mao
had written in his report on the1927 peasant uprisings in Hunan.[12] The
phrase was new but not the sentiment. It was not *impossible* to change
China without recourse to force; attempts would be made to do so, some of
them quite successful. But many activists believed the future was bound to
be contested, probably violently. Opponents would have to be swept aside,
popular consent imposed.

Raising the Red Flag

Marxism, with its notions of contest, struggle and revolutionary upheaval
had obvious appeal to many of those active in the New Culture Movement.
Among them was Li Dazhao, China's first major Marxist theorist, who
influenced the young Mao and was much inspired by the Bolshevik
Revolution of 1917. 'The bell is rung for humanitarianism!', he wrote in the
November 1919 edition of *New Youth*. 'The dawn of freedom has arrived!
See the world of tomorrow; it assuredly belongs to the Red Flag!'[13] Marxism
was compelling because it could explain why, as seen from the point of view
of many patriotic Chinese, the world was in such a sorry state. Capitalism
and industrialization had made Western countries (plus Japan) strong,
enabling them (even *obliging* them) to prey on China and other less
developed countries. It was a grim but 'necessary' truth.

Yet it was also a contingent one. History's dialectic could not be denied.
Crisis eventually would engulf capitalism. The proletariat would triumph
over the bourgeoisie, giving birth to the era of socialism, a prelude to the
highest stage of history: communism. Such a scheme offered comfort of a
kind to the weak and dispossessed, especially in China.

The Russian Revolution offered more. Lenin and the small group of
Bolsheviks around him, rather than waiting for the tide of history to move
in their favour, had seized power and created the world's first socialist state.
This had happened in a huge, largely agrarian, relatively backward country
whose parallels with China, though easily overdrawn, could hardly be
ignored. A small, tight-knit, committed, well-led political organization with

a global vision had upended Russia's *ancien regime*. Among other things, its leaders were quick to renounce Tsarist privileges in China.

Spreading revolution beyond the borders of the new socialist state was the task of the Comintern (the Communist International), whose agents were soon active in China. They spread the word, provided funds and presided over the creation of the Chinese Communist Party. For the theorists among them, China looked like a weak point in the network of global imperialism and thus of capitalism generally. Advances in the distant frontiers of the capitalist world, would take the fight to the 'enemy', mainly the British and later the Japanese. They would also ensure greater security on Russia's eastern flank, an important consideration for the Kremlin, custodian of international Bolshevism.

But such advances would not come easily. China's proletariat was small and widely scattered. In the countryside and elsewhere, the forces of conservatism, political as well as social, were well entrenched, those with power in no mood to relinquish it. Marxism did not enjoy a monopoly among intellectuals; there were rival '-isms'. Communist revolution would have to be *made*, the revolutionary tide *created* rather than merely ridden to power.

Moscow's tactics sought to acknowledge this reality. On Soviet orders, members of the CCP in 1924 joined what was soon called the 'reorganized' Nationalist Party led by Sun Yat-sen, whom the Russians backed with funds, military expertise and modern weapons. Sun (and Moscow) hoped that troops loyal to his National Revolutionary Government, based in Guangzhou (Canton), would march north and unify the country, then in the grip of regional warlords, some of whom pretended to constitute a 'national' Government in Beijing. In the process, they would put an end to imperialism and the 'unequal treaties' that privileged foreigners and insulted every Chinese citizen.

The CCP's role was to mobilize peasants and workers in the path of the armies with the aim of speeding up the revolutionary process. It did just that. Chiang Kai-shek, Sun's successor, launched the Northern Expedition in July 1926. By March the following year Nationalist troops had defeated many of their regional foes and were in command of much of the Yangtze Valley. But the CCP had an additional agenda: it was under Soviet instructions to seize power from the 'bourgeois democratic' leaders of the GMD (such as Chiang) at a suitable point in the proceedings. He was having none of that. 'I treat the Soviets with sincerity', he complained in his diary in 1926, 'but they reciprocate with deceit.'[14]

As keen on overthrowing the warlords as he was on ending foreign privileges, Chiang nonetheless loathed the idea of rural revolution, as he did social upheaval in general. In April 1927, to forestall both, he purged the Guomindang of Communist Party members and Soviet influence. The Guangxi leaders were right behind him, Bai Chongxi, in particular. It was a sanguinary episode: the death toll, unclear to this day, probably ran into the thousands, and the killings took place across the country, wherever communists and leftists were to be found.

The 1927 coup, purge, 'massacre' or 'cleansing' of the Guomindang ranks, depending on whether one was victim or proponent, provoked a profound split among the young men and women, the soldiers, activists, peasant leaders, students, writers and intellectuals who constituted China's revolutionary camp. Twenty-two years after the event, an apparently still shocked Liu Shaoqi told Stalin whom he met in Moscow: 'we were not at all prepared, we suffered a terrible defeat and were terribly "taken in" [by Chiang]'.[15] It marked a parting of the ways for the Nationalists and the communists and their respective leaders, most obviously Chiang Kai-shek and Mao Zedong, though he had yet to achieve prominence in the communist movement. The same was true for the many talented, dedicated people in their ranks, who now pursued different, indeed conflicting visions for the future of their country.

Among those who ended up on different sides, and who were to play an important part in the events of 1949, were two of modern China's most gifted military leaders – the communist Lin Biao, whom an early biographer said his comrades ranked 'with the half dozen military geniuses of recent Chinese history', and the Guangxi leader Bai Chongxi, whose battlefield renown and role in Nationalist politics have already been touched upon.[16] Both men were of lowly origins. Both dedicated themselves to the revolutionary cause when they were little more than children.

Bai, born in Guilin, and the oldest of the two by some fourteen years, joined a Youth Army in 1911 and marched north to Wuhan (close to where Lin was born) to support the Republican Revolution. Lin, affable and self-assured on the surface but in fact nervous and highly strung, was more interested in revolutionary student politics than the curriculum at the various schools he attended; he was a committed communist by the age of eighteen and would play an important role at almost every stage in the Party's march to power.

Pursuit of their respective revolutionary causes took Bai and Lin from one end of the country to another and eventually into bitter personal conflict as they pitted their military skills against each other. They clashed first in the spring of 1946 during the struggle to control Manchuria that marked the start of the Civil War. The battle for Sipingjie, a strategic railway junction on the borders of what is now Liaoning and Jilin provinces, was hard fought because its occupation by Lin's troops prevented government forces marching north and conquering the rest of the region. Bai, as Minister of Defence, was in overall charge of the campaign and claimed credit for forcing Lin's forces to abandon Sipingjie in a state of panic and disorder.

He urged hot pursuit, the speedy occupation of Changchun to the north, and a Nationalist advance as far Harbin, close to the Soviet border, whose capture he claimed would eliminate the communist menace from Manchuria

FIGURE 1.1 *Bai Chongxi, one of the Nationalist's most accomplished generals, whose career ended in ruins at the end of 1949 at the hands of rival Lin Biao, the most brilliant of Mao's military commanders.*

completely. Chiang, under pressure from US mediator George Marshall to impose a ceasefire, rejected the idea. For Bai, this was a cardinal error that granted Lin the breathing space he needed to recover, reorganize and two years later conquer the entire region. 'To the very end of his life Father bitterly regretted this matter', noted his son.[17] Bai would not fare so well in the 1949 encounter with Lin's by then vastly superior armies.

Despite the 1927 purge, the Nationalists and the communists would cooperate again, at least notionally, in the form of a United Front in the war of resistance against Japan. But the solidarity was barely skin deep. In this respect, the events of April 1927 marked the start of what might be called a local, Chinese 'hot war' between the forces of capitalism and communism that, after 1945, when championed respectively by the United States and the Soviet Union, took on wider significance in the form of the Cold War that dominated the international landscape.

FIGURE 1.2 *Lin Biao, architect of the communist victory in Manchuria, Northeast China, went on to lead his Fourth Field Army to the southern extremities of the country, destroying Bai Chongxi's armies in the process.*

For Mao and the communists, the events of 1927 were a disaster. The Party's ranks were decimated; its organizations in the cities rolled up. Yet it marked the beginning of what turned out to be a journey of exploration, experiment and self-discovery for Chinese communism that, though at times it veered close to disaster, resulted in extraordinary success. For Chiang, the crackdown stripped the GMD of much its revolutionary purpose and *élan* but did not make it easier for him to control either the party or the national government it formed. Rather, he had to wage a constant battle to assert his personal ascendancy – on and off the battlefield.

Chiang's republic

The 'new China' of the Guomindang (the communists were not the first to use the phrase) came into being in 1928 with the formation of the central government in Nanjing. It was quick to rebuild the capital along grandiose lines as a 'source of energy for the whole nation', and a 'role model for the whole world'.[18] A huge mausoleum for Sun Yat-sen was constructed in the outskirts, where party leaders and dutiful citizens could pay homage. The major powers, including the Soviet Union, established diplomatic relations with Chiang's new government which, like its leader, they hoped would impose order and undertake reform.

According to the schema laid down by Sun Yat-sen, the national government would embark on an unspecified period of 'political tutelage' of the Chinese people until they were deemed ready to elect their leaders and inaugurate the longed-for era of constitutional rule. It would in the meantime pursue Sun's 'three principles of the people' – nationalism, democracy and people's livelihood (a poorly defined form of socialism). Chiang's aims, in practical terms, were to end territorial disunity, recover some of the rights lost over the decades to foreigners (notably tariff autonomy), promote social change and, ideally at faster pace, engage in economic modernization. This was envisaged as a state-driven project, directed from the 'top'. Success therefore required the creation of strong government, an end to civil wars and the absence of foreign invasion. Neither of the first two conditions was fulfilled during what came to be known as the 'Nanjing Decade' (1927–37) and the outbreak of full-scale war between China and Japan in July 1937 brought this era to an abrupt end.

Recent scholarship has provided a more balanced assessment of the strengths and weaknesses of Chiang's republic than once prevailed. The same is true of the Republican period generally. It is now understood, for example, that modern education and medical care, delivered by public and private agencies, some of them foreign (usually of missionary origin), made significant inroads in the 1930s and 1940s. Road building, railway construction, urban planning, the establishment of telephone and telegraph links, and the development of an aviation network, to mention other aspects of national reconstruction, all took place on a larger scale than thought. The Republic was more than a story of national weakness and war, a kind of grim interlude justifiably ended by the triumph of communism.[19] 'Reading back' in this fashion proved politically convenient after 1949 but made for poor history.

So does an inadequate understanding of the difficulties Chiang faced, even if many of them were of his own making, including his leadership style. A would-be rather than an actual dictator, his relied largely on manipulating the numerous factions that bedevilled his party to get his way. Some of these factions, though powerful, were little more than informal political groupings based on common associations and personal loyalties: the 'CC Clique', encountered earlier, was one example.[20] The 'Political Science Clique', which took as its purpose 'the study of political affairs and the practice of reform/ progress', was another.[21] There were factions in the Nationalist army, too, such as the Huangpu (or Whampoa) Clique, named after the military academy of the same name near Guangzhou. During the 1920s this was the main training ground of the Nationalist military. Since Chiang was then its principal it often (though not always) gave him special leverage over this clique in later years.

Then there were the regionally based cliques. While the central government controlled most major cities and many important provinces, vast territories beyond the Yangtze valley in effect went their own way. Their leaders were often old-fashioned warlords who wrapped themselves in the Nationalist flag in the hope it would keep Nanjing at bay. It often did so.

But other regionalists posed a more direct challenge to Chiang. The Guangxi leaders Li Zongren and Bai Chongxi sided for and against him during the tortuous struggles for control of Nationalist politics in the 1920s and 1930s, playing a leading role in the events that forced him to stand down as Nationalist leader twice during this period.[22] They confronted him again in the 1930s by transforming their province from one of the most backward, bandit-infested parts of the country into a model of reform and modernisation. Brandishing the slogan 'Reconstruct Guangxi and Revive China', they hoped to inspire other regional leaders to follow suit and expose what they insisted were Chiang's failures as a reformer. In 1936 they even fought (and lost) a war against central government troops that, briefly, forced them to flee their province and seek refuge overseas. Chiang's bad-tempered outburst on New Year's Eve 1948, when he criticized the Guangxi leaders for forcing him to give up the presidency, thus had deep roots.

In essence, Chiang's regime was too weak to impose its will yet too strong to be overthrown. It had but shallow social roots outside of the major towns and cities of the Yangtze Valley. It came to power by military means and was to a large extent captured by the military. As a party, the GMD was weak organizationally, and lacked discipline. Once in government, its members easily exchanged the virtues of reform for the vices of bureaucracy. The entire edifice was much less solid than it looked, as events in the 1940s would soon demonstrate.

The Party and the peasants

The Nationalist government's inability to root out insurgency was apparent from its foundation. The CCP, caught unaware by Chiang's purge and much reduced in numbers, retreated into the south China countryside after 1927. There, in remote areas, often close to provincial borders where governance tended to be weak, they set up local governments or 'Soviets', mobilized the peasantry, redistributed land and attempted to reorder rural society. Violence and killings were staples of these and later attempts to impose communism in the countryside. As Mao put it in his 'Report on an Investigation of the Peasant Movement in Hunan', written a few weeks before the April 1927 purge, a revolution cannot be so refined as embroidery, literary composition or (most famously) a dinner party. Rather, it is the 'violent action of one class overthrowing the power of another'.[23]

Mao did not 'discover' the peasantry as a revolutionary force. Neither did the CCP rebuild its power around the issue of rural land ownership simply because China's working class was numerically small and concentrated in the cities. Rather, Chiang's superior armies drove what remained of the communist movement deep into the countryside. Party leaders then had to 'weaponize' China's farmers politically.

Peasant rebellions, of course, were the stuff of Chinese history; folk tales and popular fiction told of righteous rebels and armed uprisings that swept corrupt emperors away and ended social injustice. Soldiery provided an avenue whereby poverty-stricken peasants might survive *and* serve a just cause: they formed and filled the ranks China's armies. Yet in the Republican period, though peasants in many parts of the country were subject to appalling poverty, they were not bent as a class on upending established rural society or bringing down Chiang's government, chafe at both though they certainly did. Deep-seated rural resentments had to be turned to political account. 'Communism in China', contended Gerald Winfield in his portrait of the rural scene in the 1940s, 'has been essentially a political movement designed to gain power through stressing and manipulating the poverty and conflicts that exist in the rural community.'[24]

China in the first half of the twentieth century was what it had always been and would remain for decades thereafter: a country of cultivators, principally of wheat (in the north) and rice (in the south). Agriculture, including fisheries and forestry, accounted for about 60 per cent of economic output, compared with roughly 10 per cent for industry, with the remainder attributable to government spending and services. Perhaps 80 per cent of all jobs were on China's farms, fields, forests, rivers and coastal waters.

Peasants went about their often back-breaking business within the confines of tiny plots that resembled what in the West would be regarded as gardens rather than farms. The landscape was crafted accordingly, whether it be the 'shattered mirror of paddy fields catching every mood of the sky' in the south, the open country of timber, beans and millet in the northeast or the 'central plains where canals carry junks with brown tattered sails between low-lying rice fields', as writer Peter Townsend put it.[25]

Where possible, mountainsides were terraced so yet more crops could be grown. Animal power was put to work wherever farmers were rich enough to feed their beasts. Water, or more importantly the means of getting it to the right place, was essential. Night soil and animal manure were the primary fertilizers but also the source of dangerous parasites. Families tended to be large, sons a highly valued source of security, daughters generally less treasured. Rural homes, save those of landlords, often were crude and hardly designed to outlive those who built them. Temples and clan halls, both of which usually had lands of their own, might last longer, but there was often little that was permanent about the look of Chinese villages – beyond their location and the family names of those who lived in them. Illiteracy was common in the countryside; among rural women it was rife.

The social and economic circumstances of China's farmers varied according to the crop, and the nature and location of the countryside they cultivated. This meant that investigations into rural life undertaken by those, such as US agronomist John Lossing Buck in the 1930s, who wanted (at least at first) to *understand* the plight of China's peasantry, and the young Mao, who was keen to *change* it, were necessarily partial, in every respect of the term.[26] Yet they provided a useful picture. According to Buck, some 44 per cent of China's farmers were working proprietors; 23 per cent were part-owners, part-tenants; and 33 per cent were tenants. The average farm size in the early 1930s was about 4 acres for an average family farm of 6.2 persons.[27] Buck found that rents averaged about 43 per cent of the crop on tenanted land while other sources put them at the much higher figure of 50–70 per cent of the main harvest.[28] Land values (and therefore rents) were high because competition for land use was so heavy.

Such data do not capture the harshness or of much of rural life. Winfield described the farmer's lot as follows:

> On his tiny farm, the Chinese farmer must produce three-quarters of the food he consumes and enough of some cash crop to pay his taxes and purchase the things he does not produce. He normally buys about one quarter of his food . . . Then, too, he buys most of the cloth from which his clothes are made . . . And in addition to food and cash crop, the Chinese farmer must produce fodder for animals . . . and its own fuel.[29]

This description is of 'typical' or perhaps 'ideal' circumstances. It leaves aside the impact of crippling rents and taxes, especially when harvests were poor; peasant indebtedness and immiseration; the scourges of floods, famines and disease; the impact of rural disorder and war; and the often harsh treatment landlords and other rural big-wigs meted out to tenants and 'lesser' rural folk in general.

There was no lack of plans to alleviate such suffering. Chiang's government passed a Land Law but devoted most of its efforts to building a modern urban economy in the hope that this would eventually benefit the countryside. It would repent of its failure to redistribute land in the late 1940s by when it was far too late.[30] Several provincial governments launched rural reforms in the 1930s despite lack of resources and a reluctance to challenge vested interests. A more ambitious effort was undertaken by the Rural Reconstruction Movement, described by its historian, Kate Merkel Hess, as the work of 'a loose coalition of reform-minded elites who sought to create a rural alternative to urban modernity that would mobilize rural people and strengthen the nation'.[31] 'Rural Reconstructionists' wanted to change the 'quality' of the Chinese peasants and thus Chinese society. Education and technology figured prominently among the remedies championed by what, thanks largely to the disruption caused by the Japanese invasion, turned out to be 'the last non-Communist effort to remake rural China'.[32]

Mao and the communists, virtually isolated in a rural world from which they would not escape for years, reached a different view. For them, the entire structure of rural life, presided over by the economic power of the landlords and the political influence of the gentry and local officials, was predatory and unjust. It had to be overturned. The beneficiaries, the 'liberated' peasants, would have a stake in the new order and fight to the end to preserve it. Once given land, they would, in Winfield's words, 'fight to keep the Communists in power or risk punishment by any local or central government group that may regain power. Once across the divide there is no way back.'[33]

The most important, though not the first, rural Soviet was the one Mao and his gifted military commander Zhu De created in Jiangxi province.[34] It was based in Ruijin, an otherwise unremarkable county town briefly dignified with the status of capital of the 'China's Central Soviet Republic'. It was there that Chinese people in any number were first organized, led, coerced or simply forced into compliance with the Communist Party's prevailing vision of revolution.

Little of this would have been possible without the creation of the Red Army. The Party had to have a military of its own, otherwise the Revolution would be crushed by Chiang's vastly superior forces, which had by now employed German military advisers to help defeat its foes. The Red Army proved up to the task until October 1934, when the fifth of Chiang's 'bandit suppression' campaigns forced the communists out of Ruijin, on to their Long March, the heroic trek that took the revolutionaries deeper into south China before they turned north in search of sanctuary. They found it in the loess country, around the borders of Shaanxi, Gansu and Ningxia provinces, where perhaps one tenth of the 100,000 or so Party members, soldiers and supporters who had left Jiangxi managed to regroup and awaited Chiang's next move.

It was not long in coming. Chiang ordered the Manchurian generals Zhang Xueliang and Yang Hucheng, whose homeland the Japanese had incorporated into their puppet state of 'Manchukuo', to wipe out the communists before they could rebuild their forces. The generals declined. They had already secretly agreed with the communists not to turn on them and believed, in common with much public opinion, that Japan, not Yanan, where Mao had made his headquarters, was the real menace to China's well-being. They forced the point home in December 1936 by kidnapping Chiang while he was visiting Xian in north-central China to urge them on.

On pain of execution, and in the face of patriotic exhortations from his rebellious subordinates as well as Zhou Enlai, the CCP's emissary, Chiang agreed to halt 'bandit suppression' in favour of resisting Japan. The Soviet leaders let him know they would support his government if he agreed to form a United Front that included the Communist Party, a cause Moscow was now championing in the wider struggle against fascism. Released from captivity on Christmas Day, Chiang returned to Nanjing amid widespread popular acclaim and a new sense of national purpose.

Yanan years

If the Xian Incident spared the Chinese communist movement from probable extinction, the Japanese invasion and occupation of China that began the following year enabled it to expand its influence and power on a previously unimaginable scale. It allowed the Party to consolidate control over its 'core area' and move into 'occupied' territory evacuated by the central government but only nominally occupied by Japanese forces. It provided Mao and his fellow leaders with space and time to develop the techniques of governance, organization, mass mobilization, land reform, economic production and army-building inseparably associated with the critical 'Yanan phase' in the Party's history. No less important, it subjected Chiang's government (and the people under its control) to eight years of brutality, driving it out of its capital, cutting it off from the outside world, decimating some of its best armies, and destroying much of the infrastructure and modernization efforts undertaken during a decade of nation-building. Chinese communism flourished amid China's national crisis.

Then a dusty isolated township in northern Shaanxi, surrounded by hills of eroded yellow earth, Yanan became a kind of Mecca of Mao's version of Chinese communism. Its core diagnosis was that China was suffering from centuries of feudalism and a century of semi-colonialism. This was why it was so weak, backward and most of its people so poor. Feudalism had made serfs of the Chinese in economic terms and blighted their mental outlook thanks to the grip of the past. China was enfeebled, Japanese aggression being the latest example in what by now amounted to a century of national humiliation.

For some, this way of looking at things seemed to explain the ills of landlordism, the prevalence of usury, peasant land hunger and growing rural misery in many parts of the countryside. Rural gentry, large-scale urban capitalists, government officials and foreign powers all preyed on the Chinese people. They constituted an unholy alliance. They must be overthrown, destroyed, 'reformed' or expelled, as appropriate. Land must be given to the peasants, the landlords destroyed as a class. Chinese society must be remade from the ground up – and in the countryside first.

China's workers, the proletariat, would play a role in making the new order, as orthodox Marxism insisted. But they were few and confined to the cities, which the communists had yet to occupy. That would change eventually. And when it did there would be important roles in the Revolution for the patriotic bourgeoisie, intellectuals, business leaders and other 'progressive' urban citizens.

The magic of this message, which did not emerge whole or complete but which Mao and the Party refined over the years, was that it was both mundane and millenarian, if only in a secular sense. It was what today would be called a 'master narrative', promising the end of backward, downtrodden, humiliated 'old' China and its replacement by a 'New China' in the vanguard of global history, alongside the world's other socialist states. Chiang and the Nationalists could not compete with this in terms of what they were offering China and its people. All too often, their most visible contribution was the incompetence, corruption and disunity that for many became bywords for their administration.

Yanan, by contrast, seemed to stand for a new type of society. Visitors, foreign and Chinese, found it brimming with purpose, equality and hope. Many students and intellectuals chose to leave areas under the control of a central government they felt lacked a sense of justice, as well as the will to confront the national enemy, for life in the border regions and the communist or 'progressive' camp. It was not always an easy pilgrimage: Chiang's troops tried to blockade the communist areas, pending the anticipated resumption of hostilities once Japan had been defeated.

Patriotism and plain living were on display in Yanan. Less evident but no less important to life there was the Party's mastery of the mass purge – the techniques of social and psychological command over the rapidly expanding ranks of Party members to ensure their loyalty and weed out waverers or foes. Much of this was the work of Kang Sheng, Mao's Moscow-trained security chief, who was granted licence to display his grim arts, said to include personally supervising the torture of his victims. Kang's biographers described him as 'the ideological entrepreneur who imported the Stalinist armoury of repression and control into the Chinese Communist movement'.[35] He helped ensure that beneath the innocuous terms 'rectification movement', 'self-criticism' and 'ideological re-moulding' – practices that in future would be intricately associated with the Chinese version of communism – lay a darker reality: one in which confessions were encouraged but often extracted, criticism suppressed, critics persecuted, and sometimes killed, and absolute conformity required. There was little free-thinking in Mao's republic. In 1942, he told artists and writers that they 'must gradually move their feet over to the side of the workers, peasants, and soldiers, to the side of the proletariat'.[36]

Mao was not yet the tyrant he later became: not every criticism of the Party was traitorous; and he was not (yet) so sure of himself that he forbade discussion of major issues in its highest councils. But by the time of the Party's Seventh Congress in April–June 1945 he was the undisputed leader and theoretician of the Chinese Communist Party. Both his 'Thought', described as a creative adaptation of Marxism to Chinese conditions, and his personal authority prevailed. As Chairman of the Party's Central

Committee, he came to exercise the kind of hold over his movement that Chiang Kai-shek could only dream of in respect of his own. Chiang rejoiced in the title 'director' of the GMD; in reality, he was often *primus inter pares*.

The control and manipulation of information was another feature of Yanan life, especially when it came presenting a favourable image of the communist movement to the outside world. Targets ranged from the extremely hostile, in the case of the central government, to the intensely curious, as was true of foreign, mainly US, journalists based in China. The 1936 visit to Mao's headquarters of journalist Edgar Snow, a communist sympathiser, set the broadly complimentary tone. Snow spent four months in communist territory, including many hours with Mao, Zhou and other leaders. They spoke about their lives more intimately than they were ever to do so again in a front of a foreigner. Snow's *Red Star over China*, published in January 1938, broke the news blockade Chiang had imposed on Chinese communism.[37] Eleven years later, when *Time* magazine put Mao on its front cover and sought to explain to the world the extraordinary rise of his movement, it drew heavily on *Red Star*, claiming it had still not been surpassed as a source of information about the man of the moment.[38]

Other journalists followed in Snow's footsteps, reporting positively about life in the communist areas in contrast with the grim conditions of those under Nationalist control. There certainly were contrasts to be drawn between the two. But they were often overdrawn, notably when it came to the subject of the two sides' secret police. 'The world hears little about the communist secret police in China for the same reason that it hears little about it in Yugoslavia or Russia', wrote Winfield in 1948. 'More is heard about the GMD secret police because, in spite of all that is said and written to the contrary, the central government of China still permits more foreign correspondents to see and write more about it than do the communists.'[39]

US foreign service and military officers were not far behind the journalists. What drew them to Yanan was China's desperate military situation following Japan's spring offensive of 1944, which soon saw Japanese troops penetrate deep into previously unoccupied areas, briefly threatening Chiang's temporary capital, Chongqing. Washington feared China would be knocked out of the war. In such circumstances, Chiang had at least to pay lip service to the US desire for closer military collaboration with the communists. He reluctantly permitted the US Army Observation Group to visit Yanan (the 'Dixie Mission') in July 1944.

Members of this mission, many of them well versed in Chinese affairs, had little to say about purges, the absence of critical voices and the presence (admittedly small and well hidden) of Soviet agents in the communist areas. They said much more about the nature and goals of the Chinese communists, whom they described as 'agrarian reformers', and whose methods were said to resemble the practices of US democratic politics rather than those of the Soviet version of socialism.[40] 'All of our party have had the same feeling— that we have come into a different country and are meeting a different people', enthused John Service, a State Department officer based in the US embassy in Chongqing.[41] Such characterizations would prove a rich source of trouble for the US government, and many of its China analysts, once the communists seized power and proved themselves to be more dedicated Marxists – as well as closer followers of Joseph Stalin – than had been believed at the time.[42]

Chiang: emboldened, embattled, eclipsed

With the dropping of atomic bombs on Hiroshima and Nagasaki in August 1945, the war in the Far East ended even more dramatically than it had begun. Dominant in East Asia for the past thirty years, Japan was prostrate. Britain, chief among the Western colonial powers, was much weakened in East Asia as elsewhere. The Soviet Union, although the main casualty of Nazi aggression, was emerging as a global power. And the other beneficiary of the war, the United States, would soon deploy its immense resources to defend a liberal, capitalist order apparently threatened by the advance of Soviet communism.

China's Nationalists and communists had both relied, in some respects critically, on their respective US and Soviet backers as they struggled to survive at home. But after the war, as both Moscow and Washington soon realized, sometimes to their alarm, the Chinese were for the first time in more than a century beginning to shape their own destiny.

The key question in 1945, amid widespread relief in China that the war of resistance against Japan was at last over, was whether the GMD and the CCP would halt their attacks on each other and share power. It seemed unlikely, but in August Mao and Chiang met in Chongqing, still the country's capital, for talks to that end. In this rather strained and as it turned out final encounter between two men who were determined to rule China alone, it was agreed that negotiations would start to form a coalition government, draft a democratic constitution and unify command over their respective armies.

This was a welcome fillip for a public yearning for a fresh start. Between 20 and 30 million soldiers and civilians are thought to have died during the war against Japan, while the number of refugees is put at 80–100 million.[43] China's large population must be borne in mind when considering these figures; but so must the disproportionate impact in certain parts of the country. In Guangxi, for example, one in every fourteen people died, even though the province was either unoccupied or only partially occupied for long periods during the conflict.[44]

Though less quantifiable, the physical damage was no less appalling. Manchuria, or northeast China, the country's industrial base, was partly an exception because it had been occupied and developed by the Japanese since 1932. But the great seaboard cities of Tianjin, Shanghai and Guangzhou, inland hubs such as Wuhan, many provincial capitals and other important centres across the country had all been occupied, bombed (by both Japanese and the Allies) and/or partly reduced to rubble. Again, Guangxi provides an example: the United Nations Relief and Rehabilitation Administration reported in 1945 that 5,000 of the province's 24,000 villages had been 'completely destroyed', agricultural production had fallen by 50 per cent, 'over 1,000kms of main highway were practically impassable' and 'transportation by river was extremely limited, difficult, uncertain and slow' due to lack of dredging and maintenance.[45] In her study of Guangxi at war, historian Diana Lary noted that 'much of Guangxi's stock of public buildings, bridges and roads was destroyed, some by bombing and some by pre-emptive destruction'.[46]

Yet hopes that peace would at last come to China proved illusory. With Japanese troops about to withdraw from China, Chiang and Mao were more interested in seizing control over as much of the country as possible than they were about ceasefires and power-sharing. The chief targets were the Manchurian provinces, north of the Great Wall. The Soviet Red Army was in control of most major centres in the region, having declared war against Japan on 9 August, after the atomic bomb was dropped on Hiroshima (6 August) and just before Nagasaki suffered the same fate (9 August). As noted, the Russians aided the Chinese communist armies by supplying them with the stocks of Japanese weapons and ammunition that had been left behind and by turning a blind eye to their own infiltration of the Manchurian countryside. Lin Biao, already ensconced as Mao's military commander in the region, suddenly found he had more arms than he did men to put them to use. He promptly stepped up recruitment, drawing heavily on former soldiers of Japan's puppet Manchukuo state.[47]

The US, concerned that the Soviet Union alone or in partnership with the Chinese communists, would gain control over northeast China, transported by air and sea hundreds of thousands of Chiang's troops into Manchuria's major cities and key centres in north China. It was at the time the largest airlift of its kind in the world.[48] US marines were also deployed to maintain order in some of China's key ports and along major lines of communication, pending the restoration of Chinese government rule.

The military stand-off in the northeast and parts of north China quickly sparked clashes and casualties that first jeopardized and then destroyed talks about a political solution to China's internal divisions. Efforts by former US Army Chief of Staff George Marshall, whom President Harry Truman tasked with bringing the two sides together, provided a tantalizing glimpse of progress before grim reality set in. Exasperated and unaccustomed to failure, the general returned to the United States in January 1947 complaining of the 'complete, almost overwhelming suspicion with which the Chinese Communist Party and the Kuomintang regard each other'.[49]

He had been thrust into a world of irreconcilables. Chiang had to
countenance some political reforms if his faction-ridden government was to
secure the US military aid and advice needed to defeat the communists on
the battlefield. But he could not agree to demands from the US and some
quarters at home for measures that would make it possible for a combination
of liberals and communists to 'capture' the central government.

More disciplined, tightly led and highly secretive, the CCP was less
troubled by such internal divisions. And though it often chafed, Mao
responded as best he could to Stalin's orders that he temper his radical
inclinations on everything from the pace of land reform to his refusal to
cooperate with the GMD for fear it would draw Chiang and Washington
closer together. But there could be no question of ceding territory voluntarily
or subordinating communist military forces to a coalition government
unless the communists, as part of it, could be sure of overruling any decisions
that might be taken on the military front.

However, another factor was at work: the belief, especially on Chiang's
part, in the possibility of a battlefield victory. Although this would mean
more misery for the Chinese people, it promised to deliver more to whoever
emerged as victor than any gains that might result from political compromise.
The personalities and predilections of the leaders on both sides were crucial
here: save for fleeting purposes of political convenience, neither Chiang nor
Mao could contemplate sharing power. Conquest and control were always
more attractive than compromise.

Communist forces had expanded significantly by 1945, as had the territory
under their control. But Chiang still enjoyed overwhelming superiority
across the board. Notionally at least, the government had 4.3 million people
in uniform compared with 1.37 million for the communists. Its troops were
also much better equipped, thanks in part to a large quantity of modern
weapons supplied by the United States. The government controlled most of
the country's munition plants, ensuring adequate supplies of at least basic
weapons and ammunition.[50]

By mid-1946, Chiang decided that he could wipe out the 'communist
bandit menace' on the battlefield in short order. Bai Chongxi, newly
appointed defence minister, concurred. Chiang had already moved to
neutralize the threat posed by Moscow's aid to the communists by signing a
treaty with the Soviet Union under which Stalin agreed that Chiang was
leader of the sole legitimate government of China. He felt sure he could
count on unconditional if not uncritical backing from the United States,
particularly as relations between Washington and the Kremlin were headed
for trouble over the struggle for influence in the post-war world.

Yet if this at first looked as though it was a sound calculation it soon
proved otherwise. Several factors were responsible for this turn of events,
many of them noted by observers at the time and examined by scholars
since.[51] But the primary reason lay with Chiang, in his role as military

commander in chief, and the ineptness of his armies when faced with a smaller but better-led, more adroit, agile, committed and determined foe. After a few months in which government forces enjoyed the initiative, he squandered his military advantage with remarkable speed and on a staggering scale. With it went his control over much of China, his prestige at home and what remained of his international reputation.

To the extent that Chiang had a military strategy to defeat the communist menace it was often hard to fathom. 'It's impossible to know what Mr Chiang's strategy is', complained Cheng Qian, whom the Chinese leader had tasked with imposing government control in Manchuria. 'Is the focus to be north or south of the Great Wall? Is it to move from south to north or from north to south? It's anybody's guess. No wonder we keep suffering setbacks.'[52]

In Manchuria and elsewhere, Chiang insisted on holding as many cities and lines of communications as possible. He believed that 'government forces' should above all occupy territory, and that the communists could not present much of a military threat as long as they were confined to the countryside and kept on the run. He failed to understand that Mao the tactician thrived on mobility, including guerrilla warfare, and that his peasant revolution was 'transferrable', despite the different conditions prevailing in the various parts of rural China where the Party operated. Neither did he foresee that government forces occupying major cities would soon prove reluctant to stray far from them – either because they were afraid to fight a formidable enemy or because they had grown used to such creature comforts as the cities provided. Before long they were forced on to the defensive. In many cases, they fell prey to bitter siege from which often heroic relief efforts failed to spare them from utter destruction.

Other weaknesses contributed to stinging Nationalist defeats in 1947 and 1948, among them passivity, fear of fighting at night and at close quarters, and poor coordination between different units, notably when one army was required to come to the aid of another. Weak intelligence added to such woes. 'Our own signals are not secret, but when we do manage to break those of the enemy, we cannot decipher them', complained Xu Yongchang, Bai's successor as defence minister. 'The enemy has a good grasp of our own military situation while we have only a perfunctory sense of his.'[53] There is some dispute over the extent to which alleged communist spies in the upper ranks of the Nationalist armies contributed to Chiang's downfall: Mao biographer Jung Chang believes it was critical; Chinese academic Yang Kuisong is sceptical.[54] But dissension and subterfuge made life much easier for the communists than might otherwise have proved the case, aided, no doubt, by espionage of the conventional kind.

Factionalism among military commanders and personal antagonism towards Chiang intensified as the setbacks mounted and potential rewards diminished along with the amount of territory under the government's control. Chiang could not safely delegate, even had his domineering temperament allowed. Neither could he motivate his senior commanders in the field or the often brutally conscripted, poorly paid, ill-fed and inadequately clothed troops serving under them. Many of the peasants in the communist armies were incentivised by the promise of land reform once the war was over – the 'weaponizing' of peasant land hunger. Those in the Nationalist ranks had little if anything to look forward to in the increasingly unlikely event of their victory. Peace, however attractive, was a diminished reward for the average farm boy if it simply meant a return to the social and economic status quo.

By mid-1948, some 800,000 government troops had changed sides and joined the communist armies. Thus, former Nationalist soldiers constituted no less than 28 per cent of the then total of 2.8 million communist forces. This was several months before Lin Biao sealed his victory in Manchuria, and at a time when Liu Bocheng, Chen Yi and Su Yu, generals whom Mao would entrust to launch the Huaihai campaign in central China, were still planning the moves that were finally to destroy Chiang's armies north of the Yangtze and force him to step down as president.

The flow of equipment to the communists was similarly extraordinary. Chiang's Deputy Chief of Staff Guo Gan described both developments as a new form of 'Nationalist–Communist Cooperation', following that undertaken in the mid-1920s and later during the war against Japan.[55] This was grim humour indeed. So, in a different but equally telling vein, was an observation by Brigadier L. F. Field, Military Attaché at the British Embassy in Nanjing: 'Supposing one were given the task of raising and training a worthwhile Chinese Army, one would have to start by getting rid of all the officers and virtually all the men.'[56]

Plainly, the conduct of the Civil War to this stage, and indeed its final outcome, cannot be explained solely in terms of Nationalist military weakness, failings and errors. Christopher R. Lew, who studied the PLA high command during the war, reminds us that the communists, at various times and in different respects, suffered from precisely these defects. Yet Mao and his military leaders overcame them, learning from their mistakes – often the difference between successful and unsuccessful leadership.

Nor will it do to focus on military matters alone in weighing up the performance of each side at almost any stage in the conflict. Social, economic and political factors were among the wider dimensions of the Chinese Civil War that should not be lost sight of, as did Chiang and many of those around him at the time. But it is hard to argue with Lew's judgement that these 'pale in comparison with critical military decisions that took place at the levels of high command . . . [which] did more to crown the CCP and exile from the continent the GMD than any reform programme or political movement.'[57]

What is indisputable is that, in thinking that he could crush his foes by military means, Chiang overlooked the political, social, economic and foreign policy dimensions of failing to do so quickly or effectively. This struggle was *civil* war, a fight to the finish of Chinese against Chinese, not a mere battle against a foreign invader or a 'bandit extermination' campaign. Thus, as the military losses mounted so did the economic chaos, corruption, political unrest and general misery of the population – along with a popular demand for peace at almost any price. Chiang's government lacked both the capacity and, it often seemed, the willingness to deal with such problems. This is why, during that gloomy *soirée* at his residence on New Year's Eve in 1948, he decided that he had no alternative but to step down and open peace talks with the old enemy, whose huge forces were bearing down on the banks of the Yangtze, just a few miles north of Nanjing. The very survival of the Nationalist government seemed to depend on it.

Notes

1   Mao Zedong, *Selected Works Vol. IV* (hereafter MZD *SW*) (Beijing: Foreign Language Press, 1961), pp. 299–307. http://www.marx2mao.com/Mao/CRE48.html (accessed 16 February 2020).

2   MZD *SW*, Vol. IV, p. 301. http://www.marx2mao.com/Mao/CRE48.html (accessed 16 February 2020).

3   Jay Taylor, *The Generalissimo: Chiang Kai-shek and the Struggle for Modern China* (Cambridge, MA: Harvard University Press, 2009), p. 44.

4   Chiang Kai-shek, *China's Destiny* (New York: Da Capo Press, 1976 edition), pp. 236–7.

5   The best recent biographies of Mao are: Philp Short, *Mao: The Man Who Made China* (London: I. B. Tauris, revised edition 2017) and Alexander Pantsov (with Steven I. Levine), *Mao: The Real Story* (New York: Simon & Schuster, Kindle edition, 2013). The best introduction to Mao's thought is Stuart Schram, *The Political Thought of Mao Tse-tung* (Cambridge: Cambridge University Press, 1989).

6   Li Zhisui (with the editorial assistance of Anne Thurston), *The Private Life of Chairman Mao* (New York: Random House, 1994), pp. 72–3.

7   Tony Saich (ed.), *The Rise to Power of the Chinese Communist Party: Documents and Analysis* (New York: M. E. Sharpe, 1996), p. 1201 and pp. 1317–22.

8   MZD *SW*, Vol. IV, pp. 287–8. http://www.marx2mao.com/Mao/MC48.html (accessed 16 February 2020).

9   MZD *SW*, Vol. IV, p. 306. http://www.marx2mao.com/Mao/CRE48.html (accessed 16 February 2020).

10 See Rana Mitter, *A Bitter Revolution: China's Struggle with the Modern World* (Oxford: Oxford University Press, 2004); Vera Schwarcz, *The Chinese Enlightenment: Intellectuals and the Legacy of the May Fourth Movement of 1919* (Berkeley, CA: University of California Press, 1986).

11 Orville Schell and John Delury, *Wealth and Power: China's Long March to the Twenty-first Century* (London: Little, Brown Book Group, Kindle edition), pp. 153–4.

12 Saich, *The Rise to Power of the Chinese Communist Party*, p. 317.

13 Wm Theodore deBary, *Sources of Chinese Tradition Volume* II (New York: Columbia University Press, 1960), p. 201.

14 Odd Arne Westad. *Restless Empire: China and the World since 1750* (New York: Basic Books, 2012), p. 164.

15 Wilson Center Digital Archive (hereafter WCDA). https://digitalarchive. wilsoncenter.org/document/113440.pdf?v=ab9ae0aa6cd3c36a5b6e4991a019 db10 (accessed 16 February 2020).

16 Nym Wales, *Red Dust: Autobiographies of Chinese Communists* (Stanford, CA: Stanford University Press, 1952), p. 163.

17 Bai Xianyong, *Fuqin yu minguo* ('Father and the Republic') (Hong Kong: Tiandi tushu youxian gongsi, 2012), Vol. 1, p. 228. China scholar Arthur Waldron took a similar view to Bai on the significance of Sipingjie – see his 'If Chiang Kai-shek Hadn't Gambled in 1946' in Robert Cowley (ed.), *What If? Military Historians Imagine What Might Have Been* (London: Macmillan, 2001 edition), pp. 377–92. However, the author of the most detailed study of the battle for Sipingjie disagrees. See Harold M. Tanner, *The Battle for Manchuria and the Fate of China: Siping 1946* (Bloomington, IN: Indiana University Press, 2013).

18 C. D. Musgrove, 'Building a Dream: Constructing a National Capital in Nanjing, 1927–37' in Joseph W. Esherick (ed.), *Remaking the Chinese City: Modernity and National Identity, 1900–1950* (Honolulu: University of Hawaii Press, 2000), pp. 139–57. Schell and Delury, *Wealth and Power*, p. 178.

19 See, for example, Frank Dikotter, *Things Modern: Material Culture and Everyday Life in China* (London: Hurst & Co., 2007) and the same author's *The Age of Openness: China Before Mao* (Hong Kong: Hong Kong University Press, 2008).

20 See Introduction, p. 16.

21 Lin Tongfa, *Zhanhou Zhongguode bianju: yi Guomindang wei zhongxinde tantao* ('Post-war Changes in China: An Exploration Focusing on the Guomindang') (Taipei: Taiwan shangwu yinshuguan youxian gongsi, 2003), p. 230.

22 See Lin Tongfa, *1949 Da chetui* ('1949: The Great Withdrawal') (Taipei: Lianjing chuban shiye youxian gongsi, 2009), pp. 88–90.

23 Saich, *The Rise to Power of the Chinese Communist Party*, p. 201.

24 Gerald F. Winfield, *China: The Land and the People* (New York: William Sloane Associates, 1948), p. 394 and p. 396 et seq.

25 Peter Townsend, *China Phoenix: The Revolution in China* (London: Jonathan Cape, 1955), p. 89.

26 See John Lossing Buck, *Land Utilisation in China: a Study of 16,786 Farms in 168 Localities, and 38,256 Farms in Twenty-Two Provinces in China, 1929– 1933*, 3 vols (Nanjing: Nanjing University Press, 1937); and, for Mao, see Saich, *The Rise to Power of the Chinese Communist Party*, pp. 198–210.

27 Angus Maddison, *Chinese Economic Performance in the Long Run* (Paris: OECD, 1998), p. 69, citing Buck.

28 Felix Wemheuer, *A Social History of Maoist China* (Cambridge: Cambridge University Press, 2019), pp. 55–7.

29 Winfield, *China*, pp. 58–9.

30 See Chapter 7 p. 191.

31 Kate Merkel-Hess, *The Rural Modern: Reconstructing the Self and State in Republican China* (Chicago: University of Chicago Press, 2016), pp. 2–3.

32 Ibid., p. 3.

33 Winfield, *China*, p. 400.

34 The first rural Soviet was created by Peng Pai (1896–1929) in the Shantou region of Guangdong, south China.

35 John Byron and Robert Pack, *The Claws of the Dragon. Kang Sheng – the Evil Genius behind Mao – and His Legacy of Terror in People's China.* (London: Simon & Schuster, 1992), pp. 18–19.

36 Schell and Delury, *Wealth and Power*, p. 119.

37 Edgar Snow, *Red Star Over China* (Harmondsworth: Penguin, 1972).

38 *Time*, 7 February 1949, p. 16.

39 Winfield, *China*, p. 417.

40 British diplomats were later scathing about what they called these 'stage-managed visits of war-time correspondents' and the fallacious reporting to the effect that 'the Chinese Communists are not Communists at all'. See S. R. Ashton, G. Bennett and K. A. Hamilton (eds), *Documents on British Policy Overseas, Series I, Volume VIII: Britain and China 1945–1950* (hereafter *DBPO*) (London: Routledge, 2002), p. 104.

41 Richard Bernstein, *China 1945: Mao's Revolution and America's Fateful Choice* (New York: Alfred A. Knopf, 2014 – Kindle edition), p. 92.

42 See Chapter 7, p. 197 and Afterwards, p. 267.

43 Rana Mitter, *China's War with Japan, 1937–1945: The Struggle for Survival* (London: Penguin, 2013), p. 387; Stephen R. MacKinnon, Diana Lary and Ezra Vogel (eds), *China at War: Regions of China, 1937–45* (Stanford, CA: Stanford University Press, 2007), p. 1.

44 Diana Lary, *The Chinese People at War: Human Suffering and Social Transformation, 1937–1945* (Cambridge: Cambridge University Press, 2010), p. 173.

45 Hans van de Ven, *China at War: Triumph and Tragedy in the Emergence of the New China, 1937–1952* (London: Profile Books, 2017), p. 228.

46 Lary, *The Chinese People at War*, p. 174. See also Graham Hutchings, 'A Province at War: Guangxi during the Sino-Japanese Conflict, 1937–45', *The China Quarterly*, no. 108 (December 1986), p. 677.

47 F. F. Liu, *A Military History of Modern China, 1924–1949* (Princeton, NJ: Princeton University Press, 1956), p. 228.

48 Wu Yuexing (ed.), *Zhongguo xiandaishi dituji, 1919–1949* ('Atlas of Modern Chinese History, 1919–1949') (Beijing: Zhongguo ditu chubanshe, 1997), p. 210.

49 *CWP*, Vol. 2, p. 686.

50 Wang Chaoguang, *1945–1949: Guogong zhengzheng yu zhongguo mingyun*
    ('1945–1949: The Political Struggle between the Nationalists and the
    Communists and China's Destiny') (Beijing: shehui kexue wenxian chubanshe,
    2010), p. 260.

51 See, for example, Suzanne Pepper, *Civil War in China: The Political Struggle,
    1945–1949* (Berkeley, CA: University of California Press, 1978); Pichon P. Y.
    Loh (ed.), *The Kuomintang Debacle of 1949: Conquest or Collapse* (Boston:
    D. C. Heath and Company, 1965); Odd Arne Westad, *Decisive Encounters: The
    Chinese Civil War, 1946–1950* (Stanford, CA: Stanford University Press, 2003);
    and Diana Lary, *China's Civil War: A Social History, 1945–1949* (Cambridge:
    Cambridge University Press, 2015).

52 Wang Chaoguang, *1945–1949*, p. 267.

53 Ibid., p. 274.

54 Jung Chang, *Mao: The Unknown Story* (London: Jonathan Cape, 2005),
    Chapter 29; and Yang Kuisong, *Guomindangde liangong yu fangong* ('The
    Guomindang's "Unity with the Communists" and "Anti-Communism"')
    (Beijing: Social Sciences Academic Press, 2008), p. 674, footnote 2.

55 Wang Chaoguang, *1945–1949*, p. 277.

56 TNA FO371/75734, 3 January 1949, p. 1.

57 Christopher R. Lew, *The Third Chinese Revolutionary Civil War, 1945–49: An
    Analysis of Communist Strategy and Leadership* (London: Routledge, 2009),
    p. 140.

2

'The event on the horizon'

Watching, waiting, plotting, fleeing

At the end of November 1948, Shen Congwen, one of China's best-loved writers, wrote to a friend: 'Two million people are waiting silently for the event on the horizon. It is truly the most uncanny and profound chapter of history.'[1] Shen was writing from Beijing, whose formidable Nationalist garrison and large population were encircled by the People's Liberation Army. The 'event on the horizon' was the terms under which the siege would end, communist troops march into the city and the residents of China's weary, somewhat shabby but still imposing former imperial capital join the growing ranks of the 'liberated'. Only then would the waiting be over; only then would this 'most uncanny and profound chapter of history' come to an end.

A sense that change, profound change, was in the air was widespread in China as 1948 gave way to 1949. It may have been too much for Shen Congwen, forty-six, who suddenly fell prey to mental illness. Weeks later he came under attack because his novels and stories, many of which celebrated traditional customs and depicted human nature as he observed it in his native Hunan, were deemed to be at odds with the spirit of the new age. Against the advice of friends, he decided to remain in Beiping rather than move south into Nationalist-held territory. But he would keep a low profile, abandoning contemporary fiction for antiquarianism and research. If he thought this would spare him from a sea of troubles under the country's new masters, he was proved wrong; silence on the part of such a renowned and productive literary figure was hardly more acceptable than political errors.

Shen's was a singular voice, a product of his refined sensibility. But it was part of a much wider chorus – heard over the past year or so in the country's academies, the media, around the family dining table, in correspondence and anxious conversation among friends – that rang out with hopes, fears and more often deep-seated uncertainties as the Civil War moved towards some sort of conclusion. China was about to change. Much of the country had already done so. Communism, still for many an unknown quantity, was coming. Its leader Mao Zedong, something of a mystery to many, was set on

conquering the entire country and creating a 'new' China. An enfeebled
Chiang Kai-shek seemed incapable of stopping him. Many Chinese feared
what was coming and tried to escape. Others welcomed the prospect of
change. The majority decided there was nothing for it but to wait and see,
protecting their families and belongings as best they could. Judging from the
diplomatic traffic and media coverage, the same was true of the major
powers; they watched and waited, taking such steps as they could to preserve
their national interests as the battles raged, the killing continued and China
suffered.

The scale of the fighting in China during the second half of 1948 was
staggering, even in the light of the huge battles of the Second World War of
recent memory. Millions of troops were engaged across thousands of miles
of territory. Communist forces had abandoned guerrilla tactics in favour of
pitched battles and positional warfare between 'standing' armies – though
for the most part, government forces did more 'running' than standing. Both
sides deployed artillery and, in some cases, tanks. The Nationalists bombed
and strafed their enemies from the air, usually to little effect other than to
harm non-combatants and damage property. Communist Field Armies,
hitherto operating largely independently, mounted coordinated engagements,
often with stunning success, outsmarting and outfighting the slow-moving,
poorly led Nationalist formations at almost every turn.

Conflict on this scale was a disaster for millions of ordinary Chinese.
Everywhere in the war-torn areas they were on the move, fleeing their homes,
clogging the roads, crowding into trains and buses to escape the fighting,
avoid communist rule and settle in a quieter part of the country until
hostilities were over. The course of the war meant that the direction of flight
was from north to the south and east; from 'liberated' to government-
controlled areas; from inland to coastal cities; and, if necessary, out of
mainland China altogether to Hong Kong, Taiwan and, should circumstances
permit, further afield.

Such journeys tended to be made in stages, as was the case of the family
into which Li Ao, later a famous Taiwanese activist and writer, was born in
1935. Li's father, a professor of Chinese who later worked in the government's
opium suppression bureau, believed the Nationalists, despite their defeats in
the north, still had some fight left in them and would retain control of China
south of the Yangtze. Rather than leave Beiping for Taiwan in 1948, he
decided to move his large family (plus maid) in four separate groups to
Shanghai. 'This turned out to be a mistake', the younger Li wrote. By trying
to settle in Shanghai, 'the family squandered an opportunity as well as its
financial assets.'[2] They would have been better off heading straight to
Taiwan.

At least Li's family were spared some of the panic, tragedy and sorrow
visited upon others desperate to get away. The attempted withdrawal of
government forces, officials and ordinary citizens from the port of Yantai,

Shandong province, in mid-October 1948 was an example. Shandong, whose eastern half forms a huge promontory that juts into the Yellow Sea, was a province of immense importance in the battle to control north and central China. Its main ports, Qingdao and Yantai, and the former British but by now Chinese naval base at Weihaiwei, provided vital supply lines for troops as well as, in happier times, for goods and services destined for the heavily populated cities in the north China interior.

But by the autumn of 1948 the communists had expelled government forces from almost every part of Shandong. Jinan, the provincial capital, a city of nearly 600,000 people, had fallen on 24 September after a siege of several months in which it was completely isolated save by air. Despite US advice to the contrary, Chiang had refused to abandon it, with predictable results. 'Red forces battered and blackmailed their way into Jinan', reported *Time*. They were aided by the defection of General Wu Huawen, one of its key defenders, whose relatives had fallen into communist hands.[3] The loss of Jinan put Mao's forces astride a key north–south–east–west rail network, solidifying their hold over the area of the newly proclaimed 'North China People's Government', one of the communist's embryonic administrative organs that in just over a year's time would be incorporated into a new national government.

Despite the fall of Jinan, Chiang was not yet ready to evacuate Qingdao, the former German concession on the south of the Shandong promontory, subsequently occupied by the Japanese but since 1945 back in Chinese hands. Qingdao was home for part of the US Seventh Fleet, and Nationalist troops would hold on there for a few more months. But in Yantai, to the north, pitiful scenes unfolded as soldiers and citizens sought to escape the advancing communists by sea. 'People rushed towards the wharves like a tsunami, the adults crying, the young shouting, the able-bodied leaping into the small fishing boats tied up alongside, several of which sank under the weight, drowning many would-be passengers', *Da Gong Bao* newspaper reported. 'The larger boats were controlled by the military and nobody tried to jump on board those . . . Instead, people plunged straight into the water, and some even threw their children into the sea. Nobody cared about anybody but themselves.'[4]

Amid the chaos, rumours abounded that the Nationalist air force was about to flatten Yantai, intensifying the panic. But there were not enough boats, and many people were left stranded on the dockside to await an uncertain future. Tragically, the last-minute exodus from Yantai could have been avoided. The port served no useful military purpose as long as the government held on to Weihaiwei and its evacuation 'might well have been made many months previously', noted the British Embassy drily in its monthly round-up of key events.[5]

In Henan province, several hundred miles inland, a large party of school children endured a no less tragic ordeal as they tried to escape the carnage unfolding in the Central Plains. The arrival of the war in this province, celebrated as the historic homeland of Chinese civilization but plagued in more recent times by famine, drought and flooding, was as brutal as it was sudden. In May, the communist Central Plains Field Army, led by Liu Bocheng and Deng Xiaoping, launched the Wandong (Eastern Expeditionary) campaign, one of the first great coordinated offensives against government forces south of the Great Wall. A fierce battle ensued. Nanjing launched air attacks to blunt the assault. Nanyang city, in southwest Henan, and its environs suffered appallingly. When the fighting died down and the city's middle school students turned up for class, they found their school had become a 'scene from hell'. Classrooms and corridors were littered with body parts. 'Outside the city, the fields were covered with corpses rotting under the scorching summer sun. It was impossible to gather in the harvest.'[6]

So precarious was the government's hold on the region that, in November, teachers of some sixteen Nanyang schools decided, with the reluctant blessing of parents, that it would be best for the education, and very possibly the survival, of the students to leave the city and head for the still relatively peaceful south of the country.[7] On 4 November, the day the communists claim to have 'liberated' Nanyang, some 5,000 children assembled inside the city ready to tramp south. Among them was Ya Xian, then sixteen. Winter had arrived and snow covered the ground. Crowds gathered around. Parents and family members bade farewell to loved ones about to embark on a journey to an unknown destination from which there was no guarantee they would return.

'We students didn't really understand what was going on. It seemed like fun', Ya Xian recalled.[8] His mother baked some cakes (*bing*) for him to take on the journey and then accompanied him until the group reached Nanyang's city walls. She stuffed the cakes and a pair of cotton-soled shoes into his back pack. Ya Xian did not look back at his mother but simply kept walking. The students were quickly swallowed up in the much greater exodus of wounded and retreated troops tramping south. 'At that time, I had no idea of what goodbye or farewell meant; it was an alien concept to me', Ya remembered.

> My grandfather came to see me set off, but I did not even acknowledge him. We just marched on following our teachers ... I was alone, independent. When we reached Xiangfan [in northern Hubei, just across the border from Henan] my father must have arranged for someone to provide me with some cotton socks. They seemed strange to me; further north, we never wore such things ... That was the last contact I ever had with my family.[9]

To stop panic spreading, the Nationalists tried to suppress news of the huge military setbacks they suffered during December. A Nanjing-based correspondent from the pro-GMD *Hong Kong Commercial Daily* complained that that he could find nothing at all in the local Chinese-language press about government losses in the Huai Hai campaign, then in its closing stages. As a result, people feared the worst, and many junior- and mid-level civil servants decided to flee. There were pitiful scenes at the city's bus and train stations where the weak, the old and the young were left behind having failed to win the fight for a seat or standing room on whatever means of transport were available.[10] Senior officials tended to be better informed about the way the war was going and were often one step ahead in the race to get away. Among them were high-ranking military officers, some of whom had been entrusted with direct military commands but had decided to desert, taking their dependants with them. 'In such circumstances, how can one expect soldiers in the front line to fight with courage, and ordinary citizens in the rear areas to feel at ease?' the paper asked.[11]

Beiping besieged

In Beiping, as Shen Congwen pointed out to his friend, anxiety about the prospects of life under communist rule was more common than panic, though the issue of whether to stay or try and flee to the south was no less pressing – at least for those who still had a choice. Residents had watched as the PLA tightened the noose around the still formidable, relatively well-equipped troops of General Fu Zuoyi, the government's military and political strongman in north China. As recently as late October, Chiang had flown in to discuss with Fu the launch of a surprise attack on Shijiazhuang, the city to the southwest. If they could take this back from the communists, they might even be able to force Mao to abandon his temporary HQ in nearby Xibaipo. However, the planned attack seems to have been a poorly guarded secret and was shelved.

In the weeks that followed, there was a large influx of defeated soldiers, officials and students from Manchuria and elsewhere, many of whom now lived in squalor, camping near the Temple of Heaven and other national landmarks. Electricity and water were rationed and frequently unavailable. The corridor to the port city of Tianjin in the southeast had been cut. The garrison's days were clearly numbered.

China's cultural capital and seat of learning, Beiping was home to a high proportion of the country's leading scholars and students, many of them attached to its most prestigious universities: Beiping, Yanjing (Yenching) and Qinghua. The arrival of the communist armies posed a dilemma for members of this community, guardians of Chinese culture and intellectual life generally, on whom both tradition and a sense of patriotic duty placed a heavy responsibility to respond to the national crisis. It posed a challenge for the CCP and the Nationalists, too. Both were keen to win the country's leading scholars over to their cause – the former by encouraging them to remain in place and at least acquiesce in communist rule; the latter by trying to persuade them, and their entire institutions, to leave the city for Nationalist-controlled territory before it was too late. This was a battle for China's most prestigious human assets, for the talent and influence that each of the rivals coveted, knowing it would enhance their reputation and legitimacy.

The Nationalists concentrated their efforts on the presidents and principals of Beiping's leading universities, members of Academia Sinica, the national institute of learning, literary figures based in the city with connections to the government and as many other prominent figures as possible. Chiang appointed Professor Fu Sunian, a founder of Academica Sinica, as president of National Taiwan University, where he was charged with making life as agreeable as possible for those among China's leading intellectuals tempted to move to the island. Relatively few would do so in terms of the total number of scholars and academies of various kinds based in Beiping. There were several reasons for this, including enthusiasm for or willingness to tolerate CCP rule, relief to see the back of the Nationalists, unease at the prospect of life in Taiwan and doubtless other personal considerations.

But their dilemma was real enough. And it was especially true for China's 'liberals' – those public figures in Beiping and beyond – who were members of minor political parties or of none, who were generally highly critical of the GMD, in some cases willing to look favourably on the CCP, and yet also concerned about what they regarded as the Party's dictatorial tendencies.

The last gasp of Chinese liberalism

By the late 1940s liberalism had enjoyed a long life in China but had failed to come of age. There were several reasons for this though they can easily be oversimplified. The prevailing political narrative during the first half of the century emphasized the threats to China's national existence posed by external and internal foes. With its attachment to individual rights and the need to hold state power to account, liberalism seemed more of an opposition creed than a means of achieving national salvation, which according to majority opinion, required the creation of a strong state. It is also true that the bias of traditional Chinese thought and social custom favoured the welfare of the community over the sanctity of the individual. Yet if liberalism was a minority voice, and one all but drowned out by the roar of guns as two dictatorial parties slogged it out on the battlefield, it was to have a long echo that would linger and eventually haunt both victors and vanquished in China's Civil War.

As might be expected, China's liberals were city types, professors and teachers, journalists and artists, lawyers, civil servants, a few bankers, traders and other professionals. Their commitment to their country was as deep as that of the communists and the Nationalists, it was just not so dogmatic, ideological and therefore so partisan. For many of a liberal cast of mind, serving their country meant retaining their status as independent voices, and serving as arbiters and guardians of the people's interest.

The liberals lacked their own legions, the only safe way of making their voice heard in China's militarized politics; but they enjoyed prestige and influence, both of them powerful weapons of a kind. Some were members of the Democratic League, a small party formed in 1941 but outlawed by Chiang in November 1947 because of its alleged communist sympathies. Its leaders, notably Luo Longji, fifty, a US-educated political scientist and theorist of human rights, became even more critical of Chiang and were soon co-opted by the CCP as evidence of its willingness to rule in partnership with what it called 'democratic personages'.

Some liberals travelled in another direction. Zhang Junmai (Carsun Chang), a prominent philosopher and public intellectual, was one of the architects of the 1946 constitution that Chiang hoped would dignify his rule but which critics intended to use to curb his power. An important figure in the Democratic League, he had founded another small party, the Democratic Socialist Party, which was prepared, within limits, to work with the government. Yet Zhang, sixty-three, scion of a scholarly family in Jiangsu, and a man whom visitors to his Nanjing home often had trouble locating among his book-filled rooms, was exasperated by Chiang's personal failings and those of the Nationalist party. The government needed a complete overhaul, he insisted. In November 1948 he wrote to Chiang: 'My advice is that it will be better for you, as the President of the Republic to go abroad. You should delegate your power to someone else who should have the full power to do the housecleaning for you.'[12] Zhang's name was among the 'war criminals' Mao publicly singled out for punishment once the communists came to power. Three months later he left the mainland for Macau.

Chu Anping, who as editor of *Guancha* ('The Observer') was perhaps the most prominent and widely admired liberal journalist in China, responded to the dilemma of his times in a different manner. Barely forty, tall, and often nattily dressed in a Western-style three-piece suit, Chu had accumulated an education and wealth of experience that belied his years. Much of the former had been acquired during the 1930s at the London School of Economics where he became an Anglophile, praising, among other things, British policemen 'as the most admirable in the world'.[13] On returning to China he worked for the GMD's *Central Daily News*, chafing under strict censorship and refusing to toe the party line. Once the war with Japan was over, he and his wide circle of liberal friends formed *Guancha*, an independent political weekly. Chen described himself as a 'freedomist' determined to serve his country with his pen.

Witty, cynical, its articles penned by some of the country's leading writers and its pages enlivened by pointed cartoons, *Guancha* was easily the most influential weekly magazine of its kind. In reporting the horrors of the Civil War, the Shanghai-based publication generally lived up to its claims to be independent even though many of its writers were favourably disposed towards the communists and most highly critical of the government. The regime responded by using every available means to harass the publication and those who wrote for it.

Chu himself had no illusions that the communists, while highly likely to run the country better than the Nationalists, would tolerate much criticism – either from the media or from other quarters. As far as liberty was concerned, while it was a question of how much there would be under the Nationalists, under the communists, the issue was whether there would be any at all, he wrote.[14] And in November 1948, in what turned out to be its final few issues, at least in the form in which it was founded, Professor Yang Renbian of Peking University warned that: 'Since we never expected the GMD militarists to be so high-handed, what makes us sure that the CCP militarists will not be imperious?' The following month, another academic, Professor Yan Rengeng, stated that Chinese liberals were waiting for the dawn of a new era 'with mixed feelings of fear and joy'.[15]

On 24 December, the government finally lost patience and closed *Guancha* down. Chen had left Shanghai by then, flying to Beiping just as the communist forces were tightening their siege of the city. Chiang's police tried to hunt him down but failed to do so before the city changed hands a few weeks later. Chu then resurfaced in public life where, at first feted by senior CCP leaders, he was soon to find out that there was less scope for independent journalism in 'New China' than there had been under the Nationalists.

Chen's 'journey' provides a contrast to that undertaken at the same time by a fellow liberal, if one of very different stamp: Hu Shi. President of Beiping University and perhaps the pole star of China's intellectual life as far as the humanities were concerned, Hu was a key figure in the May Fourth Movement and a philosopher and linguist of international renown. He trusted neither the Nationalists nor the communists though he had served as China's ambassador to the US during the Second World War. He insisted that political partisanship was the enemy of scholarship, even in a country as divided as China. And in 1948 he at first rejected appeals from Nanjing to move south and take as many staff of Beiping University as possible with him. China was fighting a civil war, he responded. It was not as if a foreign invader was about to take over the country's premier university. There was no need to flee.

However, Hu, by now fifty-eight, had long been critical of the rigid dogma of Marxism and the CCP's recourse to violence. Perhaps this explains why, when a colleague rushed into his office in mid-December to tell him that he had just heard a communist radio broadcast urging the learned man to stay in post, he responded calmly: 'The communists want *me*?', and decided immediately that it was time to leave.[16] By now it was not so easy to do so: PLA troops had cut the city off from the rest of China, and the only route in and out was by air, thanks to frantic efforts to build makeshift landing strips inside the city walls, one of which was on the site of the former polo field of the British Legation. Hu left Beiping on 16 December, not long after Chu Anping had arrived, on a flight organized by the Ministry of Education. He was to spend the next few weeks in Nanjing carefully keeping his distance from the government. Hu Shi left China on 6 April 1949 for the United States, where he was to spend the next ten years before moving to Taiwan.

Beijing's large student community was generally less inclined to leave campus, though with PLA soldiers bivouacking on university grounds, most of which were in the northwest suburbs, and a fierce battle for Beiping still a possibility, some parents urged their offspring to return home or move south. Others, short of money because of the government's failure to pay their stipends, simply gave up attending classes.[17] But many more, their liberal principles offended by the oppression, corruption and incompetence of the Guomindang, had taken part in months of protests against the war, police brutality and the heavy-handed arrests of suspected communists among their ranks. They were not about to leave, even if they had the means to do so. In what seemed to be the dying days of GMD rule, as at other key moments in their country's recent history, China's educated young felt impelled to speak out, fulfil their role as the conscience of the nation, and condemn those, in this case the Nationalists, whom they blamed for the current catastrophe.

Doak Barnett, who provided posterity with the best account in English of the last few months of Nationalist rule, described students as 'the most vocal opposition group' in the entire country.[18] 'Almost all students are anti-government', a professor told him.[19] A prominent student said there were few 'actual communists' on campus (though some students did leave the classroom to work for the Party in the countryside around Beiping), but that 'at least 50 per cent are sympathetic to communism'.[20] Many certainly made no bones about their enthusiasm for a change of regime. Maria Yen, a Beiping University student, recalled that she and her classmates felt that 'Mao Zedong's victorious fighters would bring us not just the promise of food and peace, but the bright hope of a new China, young and strong with the power of the liberated masses, standing up to take our rightful place in the world'.[21]

A New Year's Day editorial in the 'liberal' newspaper *Da Gongbao* (it carried the word *L'impartial* on its masthead) captured the moment for such people. Unlike Shen Congwen, the paper looked forward with enthusiasm to the end of Nationalist rule and the creation of a revolutionary new order (under which, incidentally, *Da Gongbao* would soon be required to abandon its 'impartiality' for adherence to the Communist Party line):

The year 1949 ought to be a watershed that marks the end of old China and the creation of a new China . . . This deep-seated and longstanding civil war should conclude with a victory for the people . . . The Republic of China should become a state in which the people are genuine masters

... It should never again become a state in which one person or a few people rule over hundreds of millions of Chinese as if they were slaves. If [the people become masters], the bitter three-year civil war will have proved worthwhile ... [and] if a country of 450 million people gains a new life, it will naturally make a huge impact on the wider world ...'[22]

By New Year's Day, General Fu Zuoyi had entered secret talks with the CCP. He hoped to start a 'new life' of his own with a political role in the new order yet leave him in command of his troops and spare ancient Beiping from physical destruction. In fact, he did not have much choice. 'The future of Beiping depends more on Red intentions than on General Fu's plans', noted a Reuters despatch from the city. 'There are several ways it could become a red blot on the map. By conquest, by compromise; by revolt; by starvation.'[23] The writer wondered whether a deal on the handover of Beiping might be reached as part of a bigger agreement with the central government that would put an end to the conflict. In any event, it was only a matter of time before the curtain came down on Nationalist rule in the city for, as the *Hong Kong Telegraph* reported, 'not a single mile of railway in the entire area under General Fu's command is now operated by the Nationalists'.[24]

Shanghai sunset

Though the sound of battle remained distant during much of 1948, anxiety also stalked the Chinese residents, officials and military personnel, to say nothing of the large, diverse foreign community of Shanghai, China's by now somewhat battered 'global' city.

Shanghai was the largest city in China (the population was around six million) as well as its richest, hosting the greatest concentration of wealth in the entire country. It was China's biggest trading port and its financial centre. It was the location of the lion's share of China's light industry, holding 'in its terrible embrace almost half of the country's industry south of the Great Wall, nearly half of its spindles and looms, a third of its machine industry', as writer Peter Townsend put it.[25] It formed the hub of complex transport networks that transferred goods and services deep into the interior and swapped materials and products for imports of food, energy and the other vital supplies that kept the city going and linked it to the global capitalist economy. Finally, there were more foreigners in Shanghai than anywhere else in the country, meaning among other things, that a great cloud of witnesses would be on hand to tell the outside world what happened if and when the communists arrived.

A 'place apart' in a host of respects, Shanghai was nevertheless critically dependent on the rest of China for its economic survival and well-being. The Civil War had already taken a heavy toll. Shanghai people were war weary, the vitality of their city at low ebb, its former physical splendour tending towards the shabby. The prospect of a communist takeover seemed to cast its rationale, indeed its very future into doubt. Many Chinese residents, their ranks swollen by growing numbers of refugees, and the foreign community, then put at some 40,000, made plans accordingly. *Life* magazine photographer Jack Birns in 1948–9 depicted the dilemma they faced in a stunning visual study of a city on the brink of change.[26]

The activities of Shanghai's British community to some extent carried on regardless. When the local branch of the British Community Interests committee met on 11 August 1948 the first item on the agenda concerned an attempt by the Very Revd ACS Trivett, Dean of the city's Anglican Holy Trinity Cathedral, to enquire whether funds might be raised to restore the Cenotaph. This was the imposing monument to those from Shanghai (and elsewhere in China) who had lost their lives in the First World War, which Japanese troops had destroyed during their occupation of the city. Committee members were not hopeful. The cost of restoring the edifice, erected in 1924 towards the southern end of the Bund, the city's famous waterfront, opposite what at the time was called Avenue Edward VII,[27] was an estimated £5,000 at current prices. There was little comfort to be had from the fact that the angel of victory, which had topped the Cenotaph, had since been found (presumably intact), and that the bill might therefore be a bit smaller.[28]

Here was irony of a kind. Communist troops were closing in to 'liberate' the great commercial centres along the Yangtze, of which Shanghai was the greatest of all. The curtain was surely coming down on more than a century of foreign involvement in China. Yet a least a section of the British community calmly went about the business of protecting cemeteries, monuments, schools and other symbols of the domination that its forebears once exercised over the most unique city in China.

Of course, this was just once slice of local life – the 'stiff upper lip' slice, perhaps. In fact, the entire foreign community, along of course with large sections of the Chinese population, had grounds for anxiety about the advance of the PLA. Shanghai was an archetype of the contest at the heart of modern Chinese history between tradition and modernity, reform and revolution, and the vexed question of China's relationship with the outside world. It was the icon – an impressive one in the eyes of some; an underlying source of shame to others – of the foreign presence in China, what it stood for, and what patriotic Chinese ought to do about it. The verdict on Shanghai of Jiang Menglin, former President of Beijing University, though harsh and hardly the whole story, contained an element of truth:

In Shanghai both Western and Chinese civilisations were at their worst. The Chinese misinterpreted the West and foreigners misunderstood the Chinese; the Chinese hated the foreigners, who in turn despised the Chinese, both with reason. But they had one thing in common – their equally deculturated state; and one mutual understanding – hoarding. These two elements welded Chinese and foreigners together in a common brotherhood of money. 'You exploit me, I squeeze you.'[29]

By the late 1940s Shanghai had changed enough to challenge this rather bleak stereotype. The Allies' renunciation of their extra-territorial privileges in 1943 meant that, since the defeat of Japan, Chinese rather than foreigners were in charge. The foreign concessions were no more; foreigners even needed a passport and visa to live and work in the city. The municipal government, under the redoubtable mayor, Wu Guozhen ('K. C. Wu') had been keen to advance *Chinese* interests, commercial and otherwise. 'The symbol and pride of white superiority [had begun to look] rather dilapidated', wrote Indian Ambassador to China K. M. Panikkar with thinly disguised approval.[30]

The British felt these changes most keenly. The rules of the road in Shanghai, as in most other parts of China, had in 1946 changed from left-hand to right-hand drive. The dollar had become dominant. American firms were keen to benefit from their government's longstanding support for Chiang's rule. One of them, Westinghouse, had even announced plans to standardize China's frequency and voltage, 'because the Americans felt inconvenienced by the old British system of 220 volts and sixty cycles'.[31] Tsai Chin, later to achieve fame as an actor and singer in Britain and the United States, but then a sharp-eyed teenager, recalled: 'All of a sudden, Shanghai was transformed. Americans were everywhere ... Coca-Cola culture was upon us.'[32]

Yet some things had not changed. 'The boundaries of the old foreign settlement still seem to contain Shanghai and its milling hordes', noted a correspondent in the summer of 1948.[33] The city's modern, commercial heart, compressed between the west bank of the Huangpu river, the route to the mouth of the Yangtze and the Pacific Ocean, and the south bank of the Suzhou Creek, a narrow Huangpu tributary, was still headquarters of the great foreign (largely British) trading houses, shipping companies, banks and other industries, along with the clubs, cultural associations and places of worship that had grown up to support the diverse foreign population. The broad thoroughfares, modern vehicles, European-style buildings, godowns, clubs, tennis courts – those most striking physical attributes of China's greatest treaty port – were still intact if far from thriving. Shanghai was 'enjoying its sunset glow', said Ambassador Panikkar on his second visit, later in 1948.[34]

Something similar could be said of the role that foreigners and foreign interests played in China's national economy. Overseas capital still dominated the relatively small modern sector, including iron ore production, coal mining, the supply of water, gas and electricity, manufacturing (notably of textiles), and the financing and transport of foreign trade. Britain was responsible for the largest share of foreign direct investment. Roughly 80 per cent of this was invested in Shanghai, where names such as Jardine Mathieson, Butterfield & Swire, Sassoon & Company, the Hong Kong and Shanghai Bank and Chartered Bank were still bywords for British commercial power. The United States, though a long way behind Britain in terms of direct investment, was by far China's largest trade partner, thanks to the close political relationship between the two governments and a controversial treaty the two sides had just signed to strengthen ties still further.

Furthermore, foreign influence extended well beyond the economic sphere. The terms of engagement might have changed with the end of the treaty port era, but foreigners were still active in many walks of Chinese life, thanks to the power and privileges their governments had exerted when China was weak and easily bullied into submission. This was why, for example, Britain still operated a string of some dozen or so consulates in major ports and cities across China. It was why, on another note, there were still some 100 foreigners (an estimated three-quarters of them Britons) serving in the Maritime Customs Service, a branch of the Chinese government in which non-Chinese nationals held the most senior positions. More generally, it was why thousands of foreigners, many of them with the best of intentions, were still working across the country to educate, heal, aid, reform and generally try to change China and its people.

Missionaries were prominent among this group. On the Protestant side, there were still an estimated 4,000 scattered across China in 1947–8 from just over 100 different organizations scattered across the country.[35] Catholic missionaries, of whom there were about 5,500, were more numerous and served a much larger flock. Their links to the spiritual *imperium* of the Vatican would soon create special problems for their adherents, along with the fact that they tended to prove less ready than their Protestant counterparts to bend to the winds of change, from whichever quarter they blew.

In short, China's diverse and still relatively influential foreign community was a legacy issue, one that harked back to an earlier and, for many Chinese, unhappy era in their country's history. This was true of the presence of White Russians and Jews, many of them stateless, who had made their homes in Shanghai and other cities; the medical missions, foreign-funded universities and colleges in major cities; the great trading firms, finance houses and shipping concerns with deep roots in the coastal ports; the adventurers and chancers who generally found it easier to flourish in China than at home; the evangelists, often deep in the interior; and, of course, the diplomats. Ultimately, they and their enterprises could be said to be operating on *their* terms rather than China's. The coming of communism strongly suggested these 'terms' were going to change.

This was because Mao had pledged that the armies advancing rapidly towards Shanghai would liberate China from its *semi-colonial* as well as its semi-feudal condition. It was not just a question of finally ending the era of real or supposed foreign supremacy, welcome though that was to every self-respecting Chinese. In the CCP's scheme of things, the post-war rendition of Shanghai and the other treaty ports (though not, notably, of the British and Portuguese colonies of Hong Kong and Macau) was of no great consequence. Rather, given the intensifying struggle between the world's capitalist and socialist camps, liberation meant eliminating every aspect of the hold that global capitalism exercised everywhere in China through the presence of the United States and its Chinese 'puppet', Chiang's regime, along with the 'bureaucratic capitalists' who fed off it and preyed upon the Chinese people. In other words, the issue was as much 'cultural' as it was commercial. After the overthrow of the GMD, the 'economic and cultural establishments run directly by the imperialists [will] still be there, and so [will] the diplomatic personnel and journalists recognised by the Guomindang', Mao warned, apparently with Shanghai in mind. It would be necessary to 'deal with these people properly'. Only then will the Chinese people 'have stood up in the face of imperialism'.[36]

No wonder Shanghai was anxious. The mood at the close of 1948 was still something short of panic, though that would change in the next few weeks as hundreds of thousands of Chinese left the city by train, ship or plane carrying as many of their belongings as could be crammed into a suitcase. By and large, Britons, who had by far the largest commercial stake in Shanghai, hoped life would continue as normal. Much of the talk in the clubs and in the diplomatic correspondence to London pointed to the belief that, while Mao and his fellow leaders might profess doctrinal and ideological fealty to Moscow, even they would need to trade. There was surely no better place to do that than Shanghai. Funded by local interests, a group called British Emergency Planners was set up with a budget of £11,000, more than twice that deemed necessary to restore the Cenotaph. It began laying in stores of rice, foodstuffs, petrol and camp beds in Holt's Wharf, across the Pudong River opposite the Bund, to sustain the British community should Shanghai be cut off completely from the outside world.

Other foreigners were less confident. Many US nationals, perturbed by the hostility the Communist Party reserved for their government in its broadsides, and alarmed by reports of the mistreatment of their diplomats in parts of the country already under communist control, decided to leave. 'The North China Daily News [the city's largest English-language newspaper] was filled with advertisements for houses, cars, refrigerators and other household goods', noted historian Beverley Hooper. In early December 1948, shortly after the US government had recommended that its citizens leave the city, second-hand cars were selling for between US$400 and US$500. 'A few months earlier, they would have brought from US$1500 to $2000.'[37] Already under way, the Shanghai exodus would soon resemble a stampede.

Power plays

Each of the three powers with a major role or interest in China – the United States, the Soviet Union and Britain – viewed the communists' rapid advance in 1948 with some degree of alarm: they were as surprised by the speed of events as everybody else, including Mao and Chiang. Each of their leaders, Harry S. Truman, Joseph Stalin and Clement Attlee, understood that more was at stake than preserving their country's commercial interests and political influence in China itself. The Cold War was rapidly dividing Europe into two opposing camps, a contest that might be expected to spread to the Far East, a region of strategic flux. Japan, dominant in East Asia for the past thirty years, was still prostrate. The Western colonial empires, lingering shadows of their former selves, were frail, their populations at home more interested in welfare provision than imperial prestige. India had already achieved statehood. The Philippines had done the same. Indonesia was on the point of doing so, despite Dutch attempts to slow or even stymie the process. The French, for the moment, were determined to hold on in Indo-China, but would soon find themselves humiliated on the battlefield. Such considerations lent an unwelcome wider salience to the struggle for supremacy inside China.

As far as Washington was concerned, strategic disaster loomed in China. Chiang's government had been an ally since the start of the Second World War. While admiration for the Chinese leader's pluck in resisting the Japanese had disappeared long ago, America's overall commitment to China, or perhaps to the 'idea' of China in the American mind, was deeply rooted. This powerful strain of thinking, evident in the missionary, medical, social and cultural impulse to 'change China for the better', reinforced the more pressing strategic goals of building a united, democratic, modern China that Washington deemed advantageous to US, as well as China's, interests. It involved extensive support – military, economic and political – for Chiang's government in exchange for reform, political unity and economic modernisation, from which US firms were expected to benefit.

The trouble was, so the administration thought, that the US delivered its part of the bargain (though critics demurred) while Chiang proved incapable of delivering his. Millions of dollars of assistance and mediation in the form of the Marshall mission had all failed. Chiang had decided to destroy rather than deal with his communist foes. And in the past few months, the US had watched with alarm as his armies were torn to pieces on the battlefield, the urban economy teetered on the brink of collapse and public confidence in his regime evaporated in the face of waste, corruption and sheer incompetence.

In this context, it was easy to overlook the CCP's past refusal to disarm, adhere to various ceasefires and share political power – factors which were also responsible for the breakdown of mediation and outbreak of full-scale civil war. This was reinforced by the secrecy that surrounded most of the communists' activities, and the lack of clarity as to their exact nature and aims. By comparison, the cause and nature of government's ills were highly visible and easier to personalize. They had their origin in Chiang's resistance to reform and his refusal to share power, the fruit of his domineering, highly personalized system of rule.

The dispatches of US Ambassador to China John Leighton Stuart recorded with relentless anguish the disintegration of Chiang's regime, and the US position in China along with it. Born into a China missionary family, and a former president of Beiping's prestigious Yenching University, Stuart counted many key Chinese figures among his friends. 'Dealing with present realities one must begin as always with President Chiang', he wrote to Marshall, by now Secretary of State, at the end of 1948. 'It is distressing to observe how completely he has lost public confidence in recent months and how widespread is [the] desire he retire. This sentiment is shared by most officials of all ranks in Government and is almost universal among politically conscious citizens.'[38]

Yet Washington faced enormous pressure from the 'China Lobby' – a powerful combination of senators, congressmen, philanthropists, media owners and other parties interested in China – to provide more support to Chiang. 'The Republicans, having lost the '48 election, decided to win the Chinese revolution instead', recalled Jerome Holloway, who served in the US Consulate in Shanghai at the time.[39] The Truman administration resisted, as noted, spurning desperate personal attempts by Chiang's wife, Song Mei-ling, during her December visit to Washington to extract fresh promises of US military support for her husband's stand against global communism.

But the US was in an unenviable situation. Leighton Stuart sought to explain his country's dilemma to the premier, Sun Ke.

> We are opposed to the spread of communism all over the world and anxious to assist in preventing this in China, but, on the other hand, we cannot do this through a Government that has lost the support of its own peoples; to do so would be contrary to those democratic principles, the violation of which is a principal reason for our objection to communism.[40]

Washington had set its face against rescuing Chiang's regime yet could not disassociate itself from it. It was thus closely aligned with and still providing substantial aid to the losing side in a struggle, not just over the future of the world's most populous country, but one that acquired dangerous wider dimensions due to the Cold War.

In November, despite strong objections from Chiang, who feared the effects on public morale, the US government told its citizens in north China that they should leave before the communists took control of the area. It had a different view about its diplomats, who were at first instructed to stay at their posts. That changed shortly after communist forces occupied Shenyang, the Nationalist's last major redoubt in Manchuria. Largely on

Soviet advice, Chinese communist troops surrounded the US Consulate General, confined most of its staff *incommunicado* to quarters, ordered the removal of wireless equipment from the premises and, later, carried off Angus Ward, Consul General, to prison.[41]

Tentative attempts would be made to establish contacts between US diplomats and the communists as they extended their control over the rest of the country, but Washington soon set its face against any moves that might lend the CCP communists international respectability. Instead, it prepared a range of economic sanctions designed to make life as difficult as possible for the new communist regime.

London had by this time parted company with Washington on its China policy, causing a rift between allies grown used to moving in step on most major issues. Ultimately, the differences were grounded in the unequal strength of the two nations as they emerged from victory in the Second World War. The Labour government resented having to turn to the United States to remain financially afloat, while Washington bridled, at least until the Cold War cast things in a different light, at London's persistent imperial pretensions. Events in China brought some of these tensions to the surface; and by the end of 1948 the two countries had adopted different approaches to the prospect of communist control of China, in line with their different national interests in the country.

Like Washington, London regarded the prospect of communist victory in the civil war with concern. Unlike the United States, it had remained aloof from the conflict and declined to side with or provide support for Chiang: Britain had neither strategic nor sentimental affiliation to the Nationalist regime. Chiang reciprocated, having no love for the British. 'How can we emancipate mankind if we cannot annihilate the English', he had recorded in his diary at an earlier stage in his revolutionary career. He peppered this record of his innermost thoughts with anti-British sentiment.[42]

British policy was set out in a December 1948 memorandum by Foreign Secretary Ernest Bevin and the conclusions of the cabinet meeting that discussed it. London's assessment of Chiang's prospects was as pessimistic as Washington's: 'The present position in China is that the Communists already virtually control north China and it is merely a matter of time before this control is extended', it stated.

> The result may either be the disappearance of Chiang Kai-shek and the creation of a coalition dominated by the Communists, or an attempt by Chiang Kai-shek to keep his government in being in some part of China, which would result in a continuance of civil war. It is assumed that in either event Communist domination of China will only be a matter of time.[43]

The paper's second assumption, on the nature of Chinese communism, was at the time more controversial. London had never been convinced by the notion, cultivated by various US journalists and diplomats following their visits to Yanan during the Second World War, that the Chinese communists were not Marxists but a party of 'agrarian reformers' willing to share political power for China's common good.[44] Neither were they greatly taken with the idea, much discussed in the wider world during 1948 when Yugoslavian communist leader Josip Broz Tito fell out with Stalin, that Mao's brand of communism was sufficiently different from that of the Soviet Union to make him less a disciple of Stalin than a dissident whose growing stature would weaken the communist bloc. Bevin's memorandum said: 'It is ... assumed that the Chinese Communists, if ever they succeed in surmounting their economic difficulties, will adopt the policies of orthodox Communism.'[45] Support for this view was not long in coming: when police in Hong Kong discovered a trove of communist documents in a raid on a house in the colony, London said they showed 'that the Chinese Communist Party is just as orthodox in its ideology and just as highly organized as any of its European counterparts'.[46]

Britain had a much larger commercial stake *inside* China than America and was reluctant to relinquish it. British firms, independently and through the influential London-based lobby group the China Association, did all they could to ensure that the UK government could not easily abandon them. Many felt the end of Nationalist rule and its replacement by an efficient communist administration would improve business conditions in the major commercial centres and enable them to prosper again. The Foreign Office held that the country's new rulers 'would be under stronger pressure than the Nationalist Government to take active steps to increase the volume of exports', which was bound to benefit the British.[47]

There was also Hong Kong to consider. British investment in the colony was smaller than in Shanghai. But thanks to its status as a free port, Hong Kong's commercial importance had increased with the end of extraterritoriality in China proper. Now the future was uncertain again. If the communists managed to take over all of China, 'the colony could continue its life, but would be living on the edge of a volcano', the Bevin memorandum warned.[48]

Communist control of China was likewise seen as a grave threat to the British position in Malaya where, under the 'Emergency', the army was trying to suppress attempts by the predominantly Chinese Malayan Communist Party to overthrow colonial rule. And London also worried (though not as much as Paris) about the situation in Indochina, where it was held that, in the event of a communist-controlled China, 'the situation might well become untenable for the French, at any rate in the north'.[49]

For all these reasons, the British government decided it would try and keep a 'foot in the door' in China, as the memorandum memorably put it: 'provided there is no actual danger to life we should endeavour to stay where we are, to have *de facto* relations with the Chinese Communists in so far as these are unavoidable, and to investigate the possibilities of continued trade in China'.[50] The beauty of the 'foot in the door policy' was that it might also benefit Britain should the communists *fail* to take over all of China. For then it 'may be possible to take advantage of internal strains as they manifest themselves to maintain and even improve our position. In order to do this it is essential that we should not abandon our position in China'.[51] It was a stance that allowed London, with some subtlety, to open the door to formal recognition of a new communist government, should it prove expedient.

There was a further important consideration in the UK's approach: Mao's relationship with Stalin. Close ties might well develop between Moscow and a communist government in China, the cabinet said. But in a thinly disguised dig at the US position of declining to deal with the communists, it said that the Western powers should avoid a policy 'which might have the effect of gratuitously driving a Chinese Communist Government into the arms of the Soviet Union'.[52]

Though less apparent at the time, it is now known that Moscow was as taken aback by the swift advances of the communists and the dramatic Nationalist collapse as its rival powers. Broadly speaking, things were going Stalin's way in China, but he was perturbed by what he understood to be the personality and policies of Mao. Both men, along with their respective parties, approached the issues facing them at the close of 1948 – as they would well beyond – through the prism of their past and often troubled relations.

While Moscow had played a leading role in the creation of the Chinese Communist Party, it was also to blame for some of the setbacks that followed. It was seldom out of touch with the Chinese communist leaders, even when they were forced to take their revolutionary message into the remote countryside. But it was less often in tune with them: during the late 1920s and 1930s, arguments over the progress (or otherwise) of Chinese communism became entangled in wider, often personal, struggles in the Kremlin over how and who should lead the international socialist movement. It was not until after the Long March, and the CCP's creation of base areas in north central China with their headquarters in Yanan, that relations with Moscow stabilized to some extent.

With the defeat of Nazi Germany and Japan, Stalin prioritized the national security of the Soviet Union over supporting revolutions in other countries – unless such upheavals were under his tight control. China was no exception. Stalin believed the United States would provide all the support needed to keep its ally Chiang Kai-shek in power, and that the CCP, though much stronger than before the war, was still too weak to topple the Nationalists. A long struggle was envisaged and, from Moscow's point of view, deemed desirable given the circumstances.

Events soon proved him wrong. As Mao's armies swept all before them in 1948, the Soviet leader was suddenly presented with a different prospect:

communist conquest of much, perhaps *all*, of China. Though welcome in many respects this, too, was problematic. China's revolution was made at home, even though, over many years, Moscow had supplied instructions, advice and more practical forms of aid to the CCP. Stalin was still troubled by the independent line Tito's revolution had taken in Yugoslavia, the country he had expelled from the Soviet camp just a few months earlier. Yet perhaps he was even more anxious that, as a US diplomat advised Washington in May 1949, 'Mao has no idea of emulating Tito, but aspires to be an Asian Lenin.'[53]

China's communist leaders had backed Moscow's handling of its dispute with Belgrade. But as the authors of a study of the Soviet leader's attitude towards Mao put it: 'Stalin's mania for subservience defined the "ideological dimension" of his perception of the Chinese revolution.'[54] Mao was too much of his own man on ideological matters for Stalin's liking.[55] 'What kind of man is Mao Zedong?' he is said to have asked his confidants around this time. 'He has some sort of special views. A kind of peasant's outlook.'[56] Even if Mao failed to conquer the whole of China, it was plain that the large part of the country already under communist control was not going to be a Soviet satellite along the lines of the new 'people's democracies' taking shape in Eastern and Central Europe.

There was also the more immediate question of what Mao might do next. His armies, busily mopping up Chiang's forces that were still trying to salvage something from the disastrous Huai-Hai campaign, would soon be gathering strength along the north bank of the Yangtze. As Stalin saw it, communist control of northeast and north China, where US influence and assets were relatively modest, was a relatively low-risk affair. Things might be very different should the communists push too quickly into the south, the bastion of Anglo-American influence in the country. Even after Dewey's defeat in the US presidential election, the Soviet leader could not quite bring himself to believe that Washington would not intervene and rescue Chiang's regime. Impetuosity on Mao's part might lead to a clash with US troops over which Stalin would then have to take sides, an outcome he was keen to avoid.

By the end of 1948, many people – combatants or civilians, political or military leaders in either camp, diplomats and reporters on the ground, leaders of foreign powers trying to keep track of events from distant capitals – believed the communists were going to win China's civil war. The 'event on the horizon' was drawing closer. Chiang Kai-shek's Nationalist government seemed destined for defeat, with uncertain consequences for China and its relations with the wider world. The Soviet Union was set to gain an advantage in its struggle for supremacy with the US-led West, despite Stalin's reservations about Mao and the movement he led.

Yet major questions also remained at the turn of the year. Chief among them, as far as ordinary Chinese citizens were concerned, was when the fighting would stop, and the risk of death and injury, the agony of flight, loss, hunger and homelessness come to an end. That would depend on the end game – on whether the adversaries might yet reach a peace accord, on when and whether the communists would crush their foes completely, and on the capacity of the Nationalists to continue the fight in the south, the southwest, Hainan Island or, as looked increasingly likely, Taiwan. In a despatch on 18 December, British Ambassador Sir Ralph Stevenson captured the mood, advising London that the 'general atmosphere remains one of eternal doom but nobody any longer ventures to predict date of final defeat and disappearance of existing discredited regime'.[57] A week later he wrote: 'The year 1948 therefore ends in apprehensive suspense.'[58]

Notes

1 Xiaojue Wang, *Modernity with a Cold War Face: Reimagining the Nation in Chinese Literature across the 1949 Divide* (Cambridge, MA: Harvard University Press, 2013), p. 59.

2 Li Ao, *Li Ao Huiyilu* ('The Reminiscences of Li Ao') (Taibei: Li Ao chubanshe, 1999), p. 38.

3 *Time*, 4 October 1948, p. 20.

4 Zhang Renyi, *1949 Zhongguo Shehui* ('1949: Chinese Society') (Beijing: Shehui kexue wenxian chubanshe, 2005), pp. 47–8.

5 Robert L. Jarman (ed.) *China: Political Reports 1911–1960, Volume 8: 1946–1948* (Cambridge: Archive Editions Limited, 2001) p. 244.

6 Long Yingtai, *Da Jiang Da Hai 1949* ('Vast Rivers, Vast Seas 1949') (Hong Kong: Cosmos Books, 2015 edition), p. 122 et seq.

7 Communist accounts differ on both the causes and numbers of the student exodus, claiming, for example, that Nationalist forces evacuated the city – but not before organizing its plunder. See Zhengxia Nanyangshi (ed.), *Nanyang jiaoyu qunqiu* ('The Spring and Autumn of Nanyang Education') (Nanyang wenshi ziliao No. 9, 1993).

8 Long Yingtai, *Da Jiang Da Hai* 1949, p. 127.

9 Ibid., pp. 128–9. For the continuation of Ya Xian's story see Chapter 7, p. 204.

10 *Xianggang Gongshang Bao* ('Hong Kong Commercial Daily'), 13 December 1948, p. 2.

11 *Xianggang Gongshang Bao* ('Hong Kong Commercial Daily'), 13 December 1948, p. 2.

12 Carsun Chang, *The Third Force in China* (New York: Bookman Associates, 1952), pp. 241–2.

13 Young-Tsu Wong, 'The Fate of Liberalism in Revolutionary China: Chu Anping and His Circle, 1946–1950', *Modern China*, Vol. 19, No. 4 (October 1993), p. 463.

14 Ibid., p. 468.

15 Ibid., p. 484.

16 Zhang Renyi, *1949 Zhongguo Shehui*, p. 190.

17 Ibid., p. 3.

18 A. Doak Barnett, *China on the Eve of Communist Takeover* (New York: Frederick A. Praeger, 1963), p. 43.

19 Ibid.,p. 46.

20 Ibid.

21 Maria Yen, *The Umbrella Garden: A Picture of Life in Red China* (New York: Macmillan, 1954), p. 2.

22 *Da Gongbao*, 1 January 1949, p. 1

23 *The Hong Kong Telegraph*, 27 December 1948, p. 1.

24 Ibid.

25 Peter Townsend, *China Phoenix: The Revolution in China* (London: Jonathan Cape, 1955), p. 54.

26 Carolyn Wakeman and Ken Light (eds), *Assignment Shanghai: Photographs on the Eve of Revolution* (Berkeley, CA: University of California Press, 2003).

27 Now Yanan Road East.

28 Archives of the School of Oriental and African Studies, London University (hereafter SOAS archives). 'Minutes of the General Committee meeting of the British Community Interests, 11 August 1948.' CHAS/S1/13, p. 68.

29 Chiang Monlin, *Tides from the West* (Taibei: China Culture Publishing Foundation, 1957) pp. 184–5.

30 K. M. Panikkar, *In Two Chinas: Memoirs of a Diplomat* (London: George Allen & Unwin, 1955), p. 19.

31 Lanxin Xiang, *Recasting the Imperial Far East: Britain and America in China, 1945–1950* (New York: M. E. Sharpe, 1995), p. 94.

32 Tsai Chin, *Daughter of Shanghai* (London: Chatto & Windus, 1988), pp. 66, 67.

33 Justin Littlejohn, 'Chinese Shanghai', *The Spectator*, 23 July 1948.

34 Panikkar, *In Two Chinas*, p. 31.

35 Figures, respectively, from Beverley Hooper, *China Stands Up: Ending the Western Presence* (London: Allen & Unwin, 1986). p. 13 et seq.; and George Hood, *Neither Bang Nor Whimper: The End of a Missionary Era in China* (Singapore: The Presbyterian Church in Singapore, 1991), p. 57.

36 MZD *SW*, Vol. IV, p. 370. http://www.marx2mao.com/Mao/RCP49.html (accessed 17 February 2020).

37 Hooper, *China Stands Up*, p. 50.

38 Kenneth W. Rea and John C. Brewer (eds), *The Forgotten Ambassador: The Reports of John Leighton Stuart, 1946–1949* (Boulder, CO: Westview Replica Editions, 1981), p. 290.

39 Nancy Bernkopf Tucker (ed.), *China Confidential: American Diplomats and Sino-American Relations, 1945–1996* (New York: Colombia University Press, 2001), p. 40.

40 Rea and Brewer, *The Forgotten Ambassador*, p. 287.

41 N. Goncharov, John W. Lewis and Xue Litai, *Uncertain Partners: Stalin, Mao and the Korean War* (Stanford, CA: Stanford University Press, 1993), pp. 33–4; see The Association for Diplomatic Studies and Training Foreign Affairs Oral History Project, 'Elden B Erickson', Interviewed by: Charles Stuart Kennedy Initial interview date: 25 June 1992. See also Chapter 8, p. 227.

42 Jay Taylor, *The Generalissimo: Chiang Kai-shek and the Struggle for Modern China* (Cambridge, MA: Harvard University Press, 2009), pp. 49–50 for the quotation; p. 700 for further references.

43 *DBPO*, p. 170.

44 Ibid., p. 71.

45 Ibid., p. 170.

46 Ibid., pp. 213–14, 217–30.

47 Ibid., p. 182.

48 Ibid., p. 175.

49 Ibid., p. 177.

50 Ibid., p. 185.

51 Ibid.

52 Ibid., p. 188.

53 FRUS, *The Far East: China*, Vol. VIII, 26 May 1949. https://history.state.gov/historicaldocuments/frus1949v08/d409 (accessed 17 February 2020).

54 Goncharov, Lewis and Litai, *Uncertain Partners*, p. 28.

55 Ibid.

56 Alexander Pantsov with Steven I. Levine, *Mao: The Real Story* (New York: Simon & Schuster, Kindle edition, 2013), p. 354.

57 Jarman, *China*, p. 569.

58 Ibid., p. 571.

3

Peace postures

Chiang's short goodbye

'Dear History Majors', wrote Eva Spicer on 5 January 1949 in a letter to her Chinese students at Jinling College, the US missionary-funded college of higher education for women in Nanjing. 'There are a great many uncertainties about the present situation, but it is at any rate a challenging and interesting time in which to be alive, and as History majors I hope you are all glad to be here when History is so very much in the making.'[1]

Jinling College, founded in 1913, was a remarkable institution. Its largely secular and liberal curriculum was designed to produce 'intellectual and spiritual leaders who would transform their people and nation not so much through evangelisation as through their work and lives of "Christian consecration"'.[2] Its President, Dr Wu Yifang, fifty-six, a University of Michigan-trained entomologist, was in 1928 the first Chinese woman appointed head of a college, and in 1945 one of only four women to sign the UN Charter after attending the San Francisco Conference.

Spicer, fifty-one, an Oxford graduate and one of eleven children of a British Liberal MP, was a perceptive and longstanding observer of the Chinese scene. She had joined Jinling in 1923 and been involved in many of its vicissitudes, including the evacuation of the college deep inland in 1937 to escape Japanese occupation of Nanjing. With communist armies now bearing down on the capital, the Jinling leadership had debated moving the college again but decided that, given the way things were going for the government, no place of safety was to be found anywhere in the country.

A sense that history was in the making was widespread at the start of the year. Chiang Kai-shek's New Year's message, which set out his government's willingness to open peace talks with the communists and implied that he was ready to step down if that would end the war, sent hopes surging among the more than 200 million people still under Nationalist rule. US Ambassador Leighton Stuart was among them. Though discouraged by what he said were its 'fatal flaws' of condescension, stubbornness and failure to go far enough, he conceded that Chiang's message, which had so astonished his fellow leaders when read out in draft during that fateful New Year's Eve reception, had changed the situation. 'A movement was started on New Year's Day which would seem to be the beginning of the end of military conflict on a national scale', he told Washington.[3]

Yet the protagonists did not think in these terms. Chiang tended to be more susceptible to public opinion than Mao, largely because he could not so easily control it, but the rivals for mastery of China viewed 'peace' in different ways. Mao responded to Chiang's address by ridiculing the idea of a 'war criminal suing for peace', and on 14 January substituted Chiang's conditions for holding talks with 'eight points' of his own.[4] They called, in effect, for the dissolution of the GMD state, its armed forces and the punishment of many of its leaders.[5] A propaganda campaign mocked the Nationalists, insisting that 'if Chiang doesn't quit, the CCP won't talk peace'; and 'if Chiang doesn't quit, the US won't come [to the government's aid]'.[6]

Desperation had forced Chiang's hand: the recent string of setbacks – military, political, economic and the associated collapse of public morale – made some sort of retreat unavoidable. But he believed the government's predicament was the result of deeper problems that it was still possible to put right. 'I have been speaking to Ching-kuo [his son] about the current situation', he wrote in his diary on November 1948.

> The selfishness, incapacity and corruption on the part of those in the party, government and army is staggering. It is also irreversible. The only way in which we will be able to revive the national spirit and our revolutionary cause is to discard the current set-up and start afresh. We must do so in a 'clean' environment and on a smaller scale if we are to undertake the fundamental reform . . . that is required for our survival.[7]

The GMD had lost its revolutionary will, purpose and discipline, Chiang believed. He shared with Mao a conviction that tight discipline within the ruling party was essential to China's well-being. The Chinese people needed a strong party to lead and guide them. Otherwise, they would fall prey to factionalism and foreign intervention, and the country would have little prospect of reform and modernization. But whereas Mao and his fellow leaders, buoyed by battlefield victories, were united and strong thanks to their control over a tightly organized, highly motivated revolutionary movement, Chiang's power was evaporating fast, within the party, government and military.

He was immensely frustrated by such developments. The party had let him down. His failure to prevent the election of Li Zongren as vice president the previous year was a notable example. China's lawmakers were taking their role of holding the government to account far too seriously. Chiang wanted them, and the party factions that made his life so difficult, brought to heel. Yet this was incompatible with the commitment to practise 'constitutional government', the third and final phase of the Nationalist's long-term plan to rejuvenate China, which had started with military unification in 1926–7 and entered the stage of 'political tutelage' in 1928.

In late 1947 and early 1948 elections had been held for the National Assembly and other bodies in those parts of the country under government control. It was a remarkable exercise in the circumstances, even if voting was often marred by corrupt practices as Nationalist factions fought to gain the upper hand. It was hardly representative: the CCP and the much smaller left-leaning Democratic League were prohibited from taking part, and in any event would have refused to do so. But whereas Chiang hoped constitutional rule would entrench his power as president, it curbed the ability of the ruling party, and of Chiang himself, to 'get things done', a situation only partially improved by the passage of the so-called 'temporary provisions', which suspended key aspects of the constitution during the present emergency, including term limits on the presidency.[8]

Bai Chongxi would later regard the decision, taken under both US and domestic pressure, to introduce constitutional government at a time when the Nationalists faced a major armed rebellion as a critical error. 'The Americans frequently make a big mistake, which is to try and impose their democratic system on other countries,' he complained in his memoirs. 'Marshall [the US general who had led the mediation effort] wanted us to practise democracy and form a coalition government. He held that we were the "big" party and that we should not dominate the "small" parties. But he did not appreciate the malevolent nature of communism.'[9]

Yet if Chiang was correct in believing that the government's dire situation was due mainly to the failure of the Nationalist Party to live up to the ideals of its founder, Sun Yat-sen, what might be done about it? Where, given the precarious military situation, might the work of rebuilding the party, army and government take place? And since Chiang had now signalled his willingness to stand down, who would lead this enterprise?

There was never any doubt about the answer to the last question: it would be Chiang himself, in his capacity as party leader now that he was being forced to relinquish the presidency. Stepping down was a personal humiliation but one from which he would recover. He had done so on the two previous occasions he had been forced from office – in 1927 (also thanks to pressure from the Guangxi Clique) and 1931 (due to public anger over his perceived weakness towards Japanese designs on China). The critical requirement on this third occasion was to get the timing right, and then do whatever was necessary to secure the survival, renewal and recovery of the Nationalist regime.

Chiang had to bear several factors in mind. On the military side, the great battles for control of the central plains, north of the Yangtze, though shaping up to be a disaster, were not quite over. Nationalist commander Du Yuming, his battered troops running out of ammunition and so hungry that they were 'eating tree bark and grasses, and burning houses, clothes and furniture to keep warm', had yet to be defeated.[10] Chiang did not want to discourage them by stepping down. Neither did he want his departure from the scene encourage Fu Zuoyi in Beiping to throw in the towel sooner than necessary in his semi-secret negotiations over the surrender of the city. He warned Bai in Wuhan that it would be disastrous to hold peace talks with the communists from a position of military weakness, and that unity was essential at this critical moment. If he was to step down, it must be clear that he had done so of his own volition, for the sake of party and country.

With Nanjing threatened, it was also important to transfer critical military assets, the government's gold and foreign exchange reserves, and as many of the nation's arts and cultural treasures as possible to places of safety. Chiang wanted to put them beyond the reach of the communists, but also those of his own generals, notably the Guangxi leaders, whom he feared might make them part of a 'peace deal' with Mao.

Chiang chose Taiwan as the destination for these assets. Even before announcing that he was ready to stand down, he had ensured that the island was under his political control by appointing Chen Cheng, a favourite, as governor of the province, and Chiang Ching-kuo, his son, as local Nationalist party chief. In the three weeks that followed, he transferred key bureaucracies of the three service arms there, along with most of the air force, many ships and as much of the weapons and ammunitions, including that provided by the US, as could be shipped safely.

Chiang and Chen Cheng, then fifty-one and a fellow native of Zhejiang province in the southeast, met first in the early 1920s when Chiang carried out a nocturnal inspection of the Huangpu Military Academy, of which he was commandant and Chen a cadet. 'All was quiet in the dormitory with the officers fast asleep after heavy training,' according to one account. But not Chen Cheng. 'A light gleamed from a window, and when Chiang, unbeknown to the occupant, pushed open the door, he found Chen deeply engaged in the study of Sun Yat-sen's works. Chiang quietly left the scene with a very high impression of the young man.'[11] A fierce critic of the corruption that stained public life under the Nationalists, Chen Cheng turned out to be one of the most capable – and loyal – of Chiang's military commanders. He was at first reluctant to take on the job of running Taiwan but Chiang prevailed, advising him that he should not regard himself as subordinate to the government in Nanjing, soon to be headed by Li Zongren.[12]

It was no secret that Chiang was rapidly moving resources to Taiwan; it was hardly the sort of thing that could be concealed. The harbour at Keelung (Jilong) is 'so filled with Chinese vessels, employed in conveying officials and other evacuees, that they have had to lie four abreast at the wharves', noted *The Far Eastern Economic Review*. Taiwan 'seems to be turning into an armed camp awaiting his [Chiang's] arrival'.[13] Yet it was premature to assume he had already decided to make the island his base because he thought the mainland lost. He was still exploring the options. And he needed to: bad news kept pouring in.

The PLA's eventual destruction of Du Yuming's remaining two armies in the Huaihai campaign was a bitter blow. Canadian diplomat Chester Ronning wrote in his diary: 'The way to Nanjing is now open.'[14] On 10 January, Du himself was captured; he would spend ten years in a prison camp before being granted an amnesty at the age of fifty-four. Total GMD losses in this, the longest and largest in scale of the three 'great campaigns' that destroyed the government's military and political power north of the Yangtze, came to some 320,000 captured, 171,000 killed or wounded and 64,000 defections.[15] Almost at a stroke, Chiang was deprived of an organized, centrally controlled military machine.

A few days later, the communists captured Tianjin, the port southeast of Beiping, and major commercial and trade hub for whole of north, northwest and northeast China.[16] For the previous two years a shadow of its former self due to disruption caused by the Civil War, Tianjin's economy had come to a virtual halt once Lin Biao's forces laid siege to the city in late November. Garrison commander Chen Changjie ordered fortifications erected in preparation for street-by-street fighting. An emergency landing strip was created on the racecourse and (as in Beiping) the polo ground. Lin Biao opened talks with Chen, who refused to surrender and pledged to defend Tianjin using the same methods that Marshall Georgi Zhukov had employed in Stalingrad. The British Consul General condemned the analogy as 'utterly wrong'. The mood of the local British community was one of 'the sooner the communists come, the better', and 'almost the entire population' wants peace, he told London.[17] Mayor Du Jianshe rejected Chiang's attempts to persuade him to escape on a plane that he provided for the purpose, preferring to remain in post, as requested by local business and financial leaders who hoped he could maintain local order.

On 14 January 1949, the PLA launched a fierce assault on the city centre, which fell in just over twenty-four hours. 'We have all passed through a very hectic time', wrote Mary Layton, a young missionary with the Salvation Army, after a month of what she described as 'day and night bombardments'. 'All day on January 14th from early morning the din was terrific and continued non-stop for 24 hours. The southwest corner of the city was razed to the ground . . . Next morning at 6.30 . . . [our] compound was overrun with soldiers.'[18]

Chen was taken prisoner along with many of the 90,000 troops under his direct command and the roughly 20,000 who had sought sanctuary in Tianjin after defeat in Manchuria. An estimated 36,000 Nationalist troops managed to escape to Shanghai.[19] Mayor Du was captured, too: he was arrested outside the door of his 'secret lodging' in the city, thanks to information supplied by his wife, a secret CCP member.[20] Both Chen and Du Jianshe would spend most of the following ten years in prison undergoing 'study and reform'.[21]

With the main port serving Beiping now in communist hands, there was little prospect that the besieged former capital could hold out much longer.

The situation was even bleaker for the cities further inland still in government hands, such as Taiyuan and Xian: both relied on Tianjin for supply by rail or air. The communists were quick to turn their victory to propaganda advantage, warning their Nationalist foes that the PLA could either conquer cities by deploying overwhelming force in fierce battles – the 'Tianjin method' – or take them over as a result of 'peaceful liberation' – negotiated agreement or surrender of the kind that seemed to be on the cards in Beiping.

Chiang was unmoved, telling his generals they must be prepared to fight irrespective of whether peace talks got under way. A military conference in Nanjing on 14 January focused on plans to defend the line of the Yangtze and particularly the Nanjing–Shanghai area, which Chiang had described in his New Year's message as 'the political nerve centre of the country' and pledged to hold 'at all costs'.[22] Bai Chongxi pointedly decided not to attend, an act observers referred to as 'polite insubordination'.[23] In any event, Chiang had already earmarked General Tang Enbo, another of his favourites, to defend the critical sector of the Yangtze, appointing him Nanjing–Shanghai Garrison Commander.

A few days later, Chiang strengthened his personal hold over other parts of the country. He promoted senior figures whom he trusted to key political and military positions in Guangzhou, the major port of south China; Fuzhou, capital of Fujian province, opposite Taiwan; and Chongqing, capital of Sichuan, the huge landlocked province in the southwest, that had been the temporary seat of the central government for much of the war against Japan. In his mind, Taiwan was an investment for the future; he had not given up on the mainland. But he was now ready to step down and – nominally at least – hand over the reins of government to Vice President Li Zongren.

He did so in a subdued fashion. Early on the morning of 18 January, Chiang Ching-kuo summoned Zhou Hongtao, his father's aide-de-camp, to tell him that the president was going to resign and retreat to his native place, Xikou, a tiny village near the port of Ningbo in Zhejiang, due south of Shanghai. Zhou should get ready to accompany him.[24] 'The president was silent during these days', Zhou said of Chiang's last few days in office. 'He seemed worn down by events and setbacks. He was isolated, nobody could share his worries. He alone bore all the responsibility.'[25]

On the afternoon of Friday 21 January, wearing a plain khaki uniform without insignia, Chiang addressed senior party and military figures who had packed into a small room in the National Defence compound. 'With the hope that hostilities may be brought to an end and the people's sufferings relieved, I have decided to retire', he told them. 'As from January 21st, Vice-President Li Zongren will exercise the duties and powers of the President in accordance with Article 49 of the constitution . . .'[26]

He then changed into the long blue gown and black jacket traditional of the Chinese gentleman and got into the black Cadillac bearing the licence plate 'No 1' for the journey to the military airport. Once there, he climbed aboard his special plane, the *Meiling*, named after his wife, China's (absent) first lady. It took off at 4.15 p.m. He would never again see the capital that he had established in 1928, and that had become a byword for his regime.

Ninety minutes later, he landed in Hangzhou, where he was greeted by Chen Cheng, and Chen Yi, Governor of Zhejiang, whom, just days later, Chiang would have arrested for showing undue interest in reaching a private peace deal with the communists.[27] 'Now I have laid down that heavy burden, my heart feels at ease', Chiang confided to his son before retiring for the night.[28] Early next morning, he flew to Ningbo, from where he completed the final stage of his journey by car. The first thing he did on arrival at Xikou was meditate alone at his mother's tomb. Chiang's retirement 'symbolised one of the great shifts in the 20th century's turbulent history', said *Time*. 'Some 460 million Chinese, a quarter of the human race, were passing under the domination of Communism.'[29]

'Plucked like ripe fruit': Beiping surrenders

The day after Chiang, the 'ordinary citizen', left Nanjing for his native place came another sign that time was running out for the Nationalists: announcement of the surrender of Beiping. Skilful tactics by Mao's generals, notably Lin Biao, aided by lack of resolve on the part of Fu Zuoyi, head of the government's North China Bandit Suppression Headquarters, and the incompetence of the Nationalist high command, secured the prize of the former imperial capital.[30]

For several crucial weeks at the end of 1948, the communists had managed to bottle up Fu's roughly half a million men in the Beiping–Tianjin region. They prevented them from moving into Manchuria, where they might, if only briefly, have shored up the government's hold over a few centres. They stopped them from fleeing northwest, where in time they might have presented a threat in the communists' rear. And they made it hard for Fu, assuming he was so inclined, to move his forces south to aid the huge central government armies locked in a life or death struggle with the PLA in the Huaihai campaign. Finally, they prevented his potential flight east, along the Beiping–Tianjin corridor, where the bulk of his forces might have embarked for Shanghai and reinforced the government's position along the Yangtze.

Fu himself, convinced that neither Chiang nor his government could survive, had spent his time under siege fitfully exploring options for his own future and that of his men in semi-secret negotiations with the communists. The fact that he was on the communists' list of forty-three Nationalist 'war criminals' probably concentrated his mind. So did the public's desire to see an end to the siege and spare the architectural and other treasures of central Beijing from harm. Remarkably, the historic centre of Beiping had so far managed to survive virtually all of the political upheavals that had engulfed China during the past century. Both Nationalist and communist leaders were keen to keep it that way; apart from anything else, their reputations were at stake.

It was a question, then, of coming to terms on the handover of the city to the communists. Fu's position was compromised by the fact that his daughter, Fu Dongju, and her fiancé were Communist Party members, and his own command had been infiltrated: the communists were listening in to his military communications with both Tianjin and Nanjing while insisting that Fu keep the peace talks secret for fear that Chiang's forces (or his agents) might try and remove him.[31] On 1 January they had announced the formation of a 'shadow government' – the Beijing Military Control Commission and the Beijing People's Government – headed by Ye Jianying, a Cantonese from the south, a longstanding communist and senior military figure. Set up in the southwestern suburbs, these new bodies readied themselves to take over responsibility for running the city when the moment came, a pattern repeated in the takeover of other cities later in the year.

Among the wider public, weariness over the siege exceeded popular enthusiasm for a communist government. The CCP underground had been active for some time, but with only some 3,300 members at the close of 1948 it had its work cut out given Beiping's population of 1.72 million people.[32] In the Party's favour, of course, was widespread disillusionment with Chiang's regime – fertile ground for spreading a message that things could only get better once the city changed hands. Underground party members played a part in persuading workers in the municipal administration, the telecoms, railway and broadcasting bureaux to remain in post and resist attempts by the Nationalist authorities to disrupt services and damage equipment before a handover could take place.

But despite the importance of the urban working class in the communist scheme of things, and the fact that communist armies were at the city gates, the Party had neither the intention nor the capacity to foster an uprising among Beiping's relatively small, poorly organized proletariat. Neither did it promise that property would be transferred to them once the city was 'liberated'. It was thinking along different lines. Mao wanted to gain control over Beiping intact rather than in a state of insurrection. He had already decided that it would be the capital of the new socialist state. In a pointed reversal of roles, Nanjing would be reduced to municipal status.

Chiang's agents undertook a belated to attempt to thwart or at least delay the inevitable. On the night of 17–18 January, two bomb explosions in the home of former Beiping mayor He Siyuan, head of a citizen's peace committee, killed his twelve-year-old daughter, injured other members of his family and reduced his house to rubble. This was a family tragedy for He but otherwise had little effect: on 20 January, Fu's representatives and their communist counterparts signed an eighteen-point agreement, handing over Beiping to Ye Jianying's shadow administration, some of whose members entered the city centre two days later to organize the takeover. The agreement was signed in the house of a former Chinese foreign minister who, in 1921, had given in to Japan's infamous and humiliating 'Twenty-One Demands'. 'When news of *that* deal broke, there was a wave of public anger', observed one of Fu's representatives, having put his name to the Beiping accord. 'When news of this agreement on the peaceful handover of Beiping gets out, the public will be ecstatic.'[33] Fu had the grace to keep the deal a semi-secret until the day after Chiang had flown out of Nanking.

Shortly afterwards, 'Peiping's massive gates swung open and through them General Fu ("I will defend the city to the last") marched 100,000 troops for reorganization', noted *Time*.[34] A liaison office was set up to manage military and political affairs during the transition. Normal life was to resume as rapidly as possible. Communications were opened with the rest of China. Residents prepared for Chinese New Year (on 29 January) in a brighter frame of mind than many had known for some time.

It was A. Doak Barnett, the young US scholar observing the scene, who found the imagery that best captured events. Beiping had been 'plucked like a piece of ripe fruit', he wrote. The old regime had been 'placed in receivership. The Military Control Commission acted as receiver and was the supreme local authority during bankruptcy proceedings.' Its job was to 'take possession of the Nationalist's assets and then pass them on to the Beijing People's Government . . .'[35]

On 31 January, PLA troops marched into the city. 'Anti-Communist signs had been hastily removed from walls; Communist proclamations appeared mysteriously instead', *Time* reported.

A few days later, 20,000 smartly uniformed communist troops marched in, with two brass bands. They had left their Russian trucks outside the city, displaying only the US ones, which they had captured from Chiang's armies. Picked Nationalist soldiers grimly guarded the Reds' line of march. Beneath pictures of Communist boss Mao Tse-tung (none of Joseph Stalin), sound trucks blared: 'Long live the liberation'. Crowds watched the Reds in silence.

Reports on the reception of the new arrivals tended to be partisan. Dr Jakob Rosenfield, who entered the city with the troops, said the 'joy of the masses was boundless'.[36] Derk Bodde, another US scholar among the crowds, wrote that there was genuine enthusiasm among those taking part in the victory parade but that the reaction of spectators was 'like that of most Chinese crowds, less outspoken'.[37] Some of the foreign press coverage of what the communists were keen to see depicted as a major triumph for their cause merely infuriated them. Despatches by the Associated Press and United Press were found particularly objectionable. The former said the city crowds adopted a 'wait and see attitude' towards the arrival of the PLA, while the latter opined that inhabitants welcomed the communists in the same way that they did the Japanese in 1937 and other conquerors in earlier times. The communist authorities soon halted the activities of all foreign correspondents in the city.[38]

As for Fu Zuoyi, any anxieties that he might have had about his future were soon eased. He was ceremoniously forgiven, his status as 'war criminal' quietly forgotten. 'I'm guilty', were the first words he uttered on meeting Mao in Xibaipo village three weeks after he had handed over the city. The communist leader was all amiability, describing what Fu had done as 'a great deed'. 'The people will not forget you', he told his doubtless relieved visitor.[39] Fu's forces were given the choice of incorporation into the PLA 'without loss of rank or seniority' or leaving the army with three months' pay and all of their personal belongings; officers were allowed to 'depart with one or two orderlies, the number depending on the officer's rank'.[40]

Li 'takes charge'

Acting President Li Zongren had few illusions about the tasks facing him when he assumed the powers relinquished by Chiang Kai-shek on 21 January. He had abandoned the military life for politics with a view to reforming the regime before it was too late. He had instead witnessed its collapse on all fronts, military, political and economic. The government of which he was nominal head was barely functional and deeply unpopular. Yet Chiang had stood down 'to pave the way for peace' and it was up to those who remained, chiefly Li Zongren, to deliver it.

Li also feared that Chiang's 'retirement' would prove illusory. He had led the country for the past twenty-one years and still regarded himself as indispensable to the Nationalist cause. He had vacated the presidency and left the capital, but he was still 'director' (zongcai) of the GMD and retained a tight grip on such levers of power as remained. Even Li's personal safety in Nanjing was not guaranteed. 'Those who were constantly in touch with me were mostly loyal to Chiang', he recalled. 'Even my bodyguards ... were Chiang's men. I had to be careful in my words and actions.'[41]

Neither were Mao and the other communist leaders going to make things easy for the 'acting president'. PLA advance units were even now probing the north bank of the river opposite Nanjing. There were signs they were in the early stages of preparing an armada of small boats for the anticipated river crossing. 'The goal is in front of them and the goalkeeper is crippled; so why not kick the ball through?' wondered Britain's military attaché in Nanjing.[42]

Nevertheless, Li set about his work with a will, issuing a flurry of announcements within a few hours of assuming office designed to impose his authority and show that policies had changed with Chiang's departure. He promptly accepted Mao's 'Eight Points' as a basis for conducting peace talks with the communists. He appealed to leading independent figures and GMD dissidents such as fellow Guangxi politician Li Jishen, who had broken with Chiang but whom he hoped to recruit to the peace cause now that the latter had stepped down. And he announced measures easing censorship, curtailing the activities of the security services, lifting restrictions on public protests and providing for the release of political prisoners.

He soon learnt that his writ barely extended beyond the grounds of the large grey-brick house where he lived and worked, close to the Ming dynasty Drum Tower in the centre of Nanking. Chiang was already calling the shots from Xikou, his native home, where special communications networks had been installed so that he could issue direct commands to various branches of the government and the military just as he had as president. Within hours of stepping down, Chiang cabled Liu Anqi, in charge of forces in Qingdao, the sole port north of the Yangtze still in government hands and a base for US marines. 'Although I stepped down yesterday, there is to be absolutely no change in all matters of military and political appointments and affairs generally. Everything should carry on as normal – especially in these times of turbulence.'[43]

Neither were Li's troubles confined to Chiang's 'meddling'. Premier Sun Ke, with whom Li had long been at odds, slipped out of Nanjing just before Chiang, taking most of the cabinet with him. Its members, like many legislators, were soon scattered between Shanghai, Guangzhou and Taiwan. In Nanjing, Li found himself, in the words of a close aide, presiding over an 'empty city' – a personal humiliation.[44]

Plans to move the government to Guangzhou had been drawn up weeks earlier, to the displeasure of some local authorities. Guangzhou Mayor Qu Yangju is said to have 'assaulted, mauled, threatened with death and forcibly evicted from his official residence' the special delegate from the Ministry of Foreign Affairs managing the transfer.[45]

The exodus of civil servants, their dependants, and the files, archives and effects needed for their work virtually monopolized all means of transport out of Nanjing throughout January and February. The Foreign Ministry had encouraged ambassadors of the leading powers to follow suit. With the sole and singular exception of the Soviet Union, they declined to do so – though some embassies sent senior representatives south to stay in touch with such government departments that were moving there. Moscow's decision was based on the desire to keep the lines of communication open to the Nationalist government and because, as *The Times* reported, it 'wished to give the impression that the Chinese Communists' success owes nothing to the Soviet Union'.[46] The influx of politicians, civil servants and refugees quickly turned Guangzhou, already home for some 1.1 million people, into a boom town. Inflation rivalled that in Shanghai with hotel prices sometimes increasing twice a day. The move went down badly with the newly reassigned diplomats, most of whom found accommodation in a hotel 'whose Chinese name means universal love but whose unreliable amenities cause universal irritation'.[47]

*

Yet in an interlude easily overlooked amid the wider drama, Li managed to slow if not exactly reverse some of the disintegrative forces unleashed by Chiang's departure and the wider sense of despair that had gripped the Nationalist regime. Much of this was due to his energy, reputation as a patriot and 'homespun' personality, reflected in an apparently straightforward approach to political and military problems. He was, of course, under fire on several fronts. 'Li's friends called him a Liberal and his enemies a Communist', said *The Times*.[48] But compared with Chiang, he seemed almost guileless, an attribute he craftily put to good purpose. Deft bargaining among key power-brokers, and a widely praised visit to Guangzhou towards the end of February, resulted in the return of most of the government to Nanjing and Sun Ke's resignation.

By early March, with Nanjing basking in unseasonably warm sunshine, things were looking slightly better for the government. Li managed to secure the appointment of He Yingqin as premier or head of the executive branch of government. A leading figure in the Huangpu military clique of which Chiang was nominal head, He Yingqin had spent much of the past three years in the United States as head of the Chinese military mission to the UN. Since his return to China in 1948, he had twice refused Chiang's invitation to become premier because he felt he would not be permitted to undertake essential social and economic reforms. He told Li he was willing to take on the job now on one condition: that Chiang did not object. He did not. Li hoped the new premier would be able to curb Chiang's influence over government operations – a matter of critical importance now that peace talks with the communists seemed about to begin. I have 'jumped into a pit of fire', He Yingqin told his colleagues.'[49]

Li and Bai Chongxi had been putting out peace feelers from at least the start of the year. It is not clear how much Chiang knew of these supposedly secret activities, which were potentially far more dangerous than those for which he had just ordered the arrest of Zhejiang Governor Chen Yi. But he would not have been surprised, given his deep distrust of the Clique. Before he stepped down, he ordered the Telephone Bureau to share with him details of conversations between Li, Bai and their 'middleman' and former close associate Huang Shaohong.[50]

Two days after Chiang resigned, Li sent two envoys to Beiping. Both Huang Qihan and Liu Ronghua were close to the Clique but by this time were already committed to the communist side. Huang, whom Li had entrusted with a secret telegraphic code so that the two men could stay in touch, shared this with the communists on his arrival in Beiping. Their presence paved the way for a public, if 'unofficial', peace mission to the north. It arrived in Beiping on 13 February and consisted of five elderly figures revered for their long records of government service led by Yan Huiqing, seventy-two, a former diplomat whose medical doctor gave the all-clear for his patient's first experience of plane travel, but who decided to accompany him just in case. Mao gave instructions that the visitors were to be treated courteously, which meant subjecting them to the mixture of flattery, warning and, finally, the 'reward' of an encounter with the most senior leader that was to become a characteristic of Chinese communist diplomacy.

Flattery came in the form of a banquet attended by many of the communist political and military elite. Fu Zuoyi was present – a reminder of the favourable treatment that awaited senior GMD figures who broke with Chiang and 'sided with the people'. New mayor Ye Jianying delivered the warning: there were two ways of achieving a new China, he told a large reception at the Beijing Hotel to which the peace delegates were invited: the 'Tianjin method', in which the military might of the PLA was used to smash diehard revolutionary forces who resisted the revolution; and the 'Beiping method' of 'peaceful liberation' via negotiations.

Finally came the meeting with Mao. The delegates, together with Fu, flew to Shijiazhuang, southwest of Beijing, and travelled on to Xibaipo, the Party's temporary headquarters. The Chairman and Zhou Enlai received them cordially. It was agreed that postal and telephone communications could resume between the north and south of the country, an important matter for many people in both the communist-controlled north and Nationalist-held south. But Mao said communist troops would cross the Yangtze whatever the outcome of any peace talks; that the Communist Party would form a new national government that would include independent figures and certain members of the GMD; and that land reform would be carried out throughout the country. Despite these uncompromising statements, Zhang Shijian, one of the delegates, left the meeting 'feeling that the obstacles to peace lay in the south rather than the north'.[51]

City life: Mao moves in

In the final week of March, Mao, Zhu De, Liu Shaoqi, Zhou Enlai and the other senior communist leaders left the hamlet of Xibaipo for the grandeur, status and relative comfort of Beiping. A much shorter journey than the Long March, it was hardly less significant in the wider story of the triumph of Chinese communism. Neither was it without danger: Nationalist forces had been defeated or reorganized throughout the region, but bandits and government spies were active. A special plain-clothes force was formed to secure the route taken by the leaders, which involved travel by train as well as motor vehicles. First stop was the Xiyuan airfield in the northwest of the city, just over a mile from the Summer Palace, where Mao reviewed his troops.

For security reasons, Party leaders were not ready to take up residence inside the city proper. Mao and his senior comrades instead occupied

FIGURE 3.1 *Mao Zedong 'tours' Beijing, soon to be the capital of the People's Republic of China.*

sprawling pleasure gardens in the Fragrant Hills, to the northwest, which had been favoured by Manchu emperors in search of solitude and mountain air. Here the chairman occupied Shuangqing ('double purity') Villa, part of a complex renamed the 'Labour University' to ensure secrecy. Grander in appearance than the two-storey residence to which Chiang had 'retired' in Xikou, Shuangqing villa would be Mao's home for the next six months. His number two in the Party, Liu Shaoqi, and military chief Zhu De, along with the leading CCP organizations, took up residence in this closely guarded quarter, well away from the city centre and prying eyes generally.

As he exchanged the privations of a remote Hebei village for the pleasures of an imperial recreation park, Mao's personal and political standing had never been higher. 'Very soon we shall be victorious throughout the country', he had told the Central Committee a few days earlier. 'This victory will breach the eastern front of imperialism and will have great international significance.'[52] Though part of a collective leadership, Mao was by now the uncontested theoretician, strategist, organizer and articulator of a compelling 'story' about China's ills and how they might be cured. Many of the ideas,

FIGURE 3.2 *Farmer Yu Jinyu is allocated land by the People's Government. Land for the peasants was one of the foundations of Mao's victory.*

policies and new institutions that would be set up to run the country were either his in origin or at least issued in his name.

This was certainly true of the change in the Party's attitude towards the cities, which it had now begun to conquer with unexpected speed. Chinese communism was grounded in rural revolution: the 'countryside had surrounded the cities', as the formula had it. China's cities were citadels of imperialism and bureaucratic capitalism, home of the country's 'reactionary' elite. In none of them was the urban working class large or well organized enough to overthrow the old political and economic order. They had to be conquered from the 'outside' by peasant armies if their proletarian (and bourgeois) inhabitants were to assume the leading role in the revolution assigned to them by communist theory. Otherwise, China would remain poor and backward.

Zhang Wentian, Party leader in charge of urban work in the northeast, put it this way: 'The city represents a higher productive force, industry, technology, science and culture ... If society abandons urban industry and the urban working class, society cannot progress, and socialism cannot be fulfilled.'[53] The CCP had to secure the cities politically, administer them efficiently and manage them economically. Urban construction and economic production – relative novelties for the revolutionaries to date – had to take first place among Party members with little experience of either and, in some cases, a distrust of the beguiling, politically dubious comforts associated with urban Chinese life.

This in turn touched on the question of *how* and *with whom* the CCP would govern the territories, including the cities, it now controlled. Mao had previously indicated that all other political parties would be banned once the Chinese communists seized power. This was not at all to Stalin's liking. The Soviet leader had during the past few months taken a growing interest in the development of the Chinese revolution. He held that China's 'bourgeois' political parties would play a role for sometime given that the Chinese revolution was essentially anti-imperialist rather than communist in nature [54]

Mao duly trimmed his sails, championing what he called the 'People's Democratic Dictatorship', a concept he would elaborate in greater detail in an essay of the same title later in the year.[55] The 'dictatorship' would be exercised by four classes: the proletariat, the peasantry, the petty bourgeoisie and the national bourgeoisie (deemed to be those not in hock economically or otherwise to 'imperialist forces'). This meant there was room in the new order for 'patriotic capitalists' and for those the Party deemed 'democratic personages' – meaning intellectuals and others who in Western parlance might pass as liberals, or those with no political affiliation but who were glad to see the back of the GMD. But the 'dictatorship' would be led by the working class, of which the CCP had long fancied itself the vanguard, as Marxist doctrine required yet Chinese experience had to date denied.

Such relatively arcane matters created tensions in Mao's relationship with Stalin. The chairman had long been angling for an invitation to visit Moscow and meet the man whom he respected as leader of the global socialist camp. He wanted to confer with him on matters of policy and, above all, secure Soviet diplomatic, military, economic and other forms of support for the government he would soon form. But Stalin was in no hurry to meet Mao. On at least one occasion during the course of 1948 he told him not to travel to Moscow, presumably on the grounds that communist victory in China was far from assured. When in the summer of that year Stalin again told him to stay at home, Mao was displeased. A Soviet radio operator assigned to the CCP leadership advised Moscow that Mao's suitcases had already been packed and 'even leather shoes were bought (like everybody here, he is wearing fabric slippers) and a thick wool coat tailored'.[56]

By the start of 1949, the military situation favoured the CCP. Yet Stalin, rather than receive Mao in Moscow, still preferred to assign a member of his Politburo, Anastas Mikoyan, to spend a week with the Chinese leaders at Xibaipo. Stalin welcomed the prospect of the collapse of the US-backed

Nationalist government in China. But he was not yet convinced that this was imminent, and still feared that Washington might intervene to rescue it. On the other hand, complete victory for Mao and his party could present problems of its own, both in ideological terms and with regard to relations between the Soviet Union and a communist China.

Mao's confidence in victory was justified as events on and off the battlefield over the past few months had shown. But this did not mean that taking over the south would be easy. 'Our organisations there are not strong; the masses have not been mobilised', the Party acknowledged. 'Supplies to our army will meet many difficulties in the initial period.'[57] Much might depend on the speed and the manner of the conquest of the south; that is, whether it would be the 'Tianjin method', the 'Beijing method' or a third that Mao now evoked: the 'Suiyuan method', which referred to that adopted in the province of the same name that is now part of China's Inner Mongolia Autonomous Region. GMD armies in Suiyuan were left unmolested in order to neutralize them and allow communist forces to concentrate on the main task at hand – securing control of southern China.[58]

But there was also the option of bringing China's civil war to an end through a comprehensive (as opposed to partial or local) peace deal. The CCP had spent much of the past few weeks ridiculing Li Zongren's efforts to get talks started. But at the end of March, much to Li's relief, Mao relented.[59] He, too, had cause to play for time.

The 'peace general' flies north

Amid noisy scenes at Nanjing airport at 10 a.m. on 1 April, six men, some smiling, some more solemn, clambered up the steps to board the aircraft that would take them and their small support team to Beiping to start peace negotiations with the communists. Cries of 'good luck with your mission!' rang out among the cautiously optimistic well-wishers on the ground. 'The plane was bearing so many people's fervent expectations', said *Da Gong Bao* newspaper.[60] It also contained, more prosaically, the sum of 10,000 silver dollars to cover the delegation's expenses and several bags of mail from Shanghai, which the postal service had been waiting for an opportunity to send to Beiping.[61] Jinling history teacher Eva Spicer wrote to a friend: 'Peace negotiations are due to begin on Friday April 1st, [and] one hopes the day is not a bad omen. I am afraid that this side [i.e. the government] has almost no assets to bargain with.'[62]

Li Zongren and his allies had worked out a negotiating position that, while based on acceptance of Mao's Eight Points, differed from them substantially. It called for an immediate ceasefire; military de-escalation across a wide front; and the temporary acceptance of the political status quo either side of the Yangtze – in effect a north–south division of the country. Such measures were designed to give the government some breathing space, strengthen its military defences in the south and be in a position to benefit from a 'change in the international situation' of the kind Nationalist officials believed would rescue the anti-communist cause in China. As for Mao's conditions, Nanjing held that there was no reason for the peace talks to address the war criminal issue at this stage. Any re-organization of government troops should take place at a time and place of Nanjing's choosing. And an equal number of delegates from the communist and Nationalist side should be represented in any new government organizations.

Such was the mandate that Zhang Zhizhong, leader of the government peace delegation, took to Beiping. A graduate of the Huangpu Military Academy and close to Chiang personally, he was also a known quantity as far as the communist leaders were concerned. He had on many occasions over the years sat opposite Zhou Enlai during previous attempts to bring to the two parties together. He was about to do so again: Zhou was head of the CCP delegation in the talks. Lin Biao was in the line-up but seems to have played a minor part in the proceedings, perhaps because inflicting military defeat on the enemy was more to his liking than negotiating a surrender.

Zhang was one of the few senior GMD figures whose name was not included in Mao's infamous list of war criminals. Yet he was under no illusions about the difficulties he faced; he knew too much about Chinese communism and the personalities of its leaders for that. There was also his own side to think about. Just prior to his departure for Beiping, Zhang had flown to Xikou to brief Chiang on the peace mission. The latter apparently expressed no views on the matter but took strong exception to Zhang's suggestion that he leave the country 'for a rest', implying that his absence from the scene would help bring the Civil War to an end. 'You can forget that idea!' Chiang exploded. 'I'm willing to step down as president, but I'm not willing to become an exile.'[63]

Nevertheless, as the plane's engines roared into life for the flight to Beiping, Zhang clung to the hope that he might be able to pull off a miracle. If the government's military setback in the Huaihai campaign and Chiang's 'resignation' meant that Bai Chongxi and his central China forces were the main military pillars of the Nanjing regime, Zhang was now its leading statesman whose mission was to make the guns fall silent on terms acceptable to both sides. This was why he had acquired the sobriquet 'peace general'.

Second to Zhang in importance in the delegation was Huang Shaohong, a politically gifted and still ambitious former member of the Guangxi Clique who had left the province in 1930 to serve the central government. He was still close to Li and Bai. Shao Lizi and Zhang Shijian, frail but respected luminaries of the past rather than figures of the future, were members of the unofficial Shanghai People's Peace Delegation that in February had met Mao and Zhou in Xibaipo. Li Zheng, the only delegate who was not a

FIGURE 3.3 *Students in Nanjing, the Nationalist capital, demonstrate in favour of a peace deal with the CCP.*

member of the Nationalist Party, had been head of Beiping Normal University. Liu Fei was a former official in the Ministry of Defence and military adviser to Bai.

In his diary, Chiang Kai-shek wrote that these men were on a 'surrender mission' and that 'the only question was whether the CCP would accept the government's surrender'. The purpose of Li Zongren's peace plan was 'to cooperate with the communist bandits in the destruction of the government's military power'.[64] Chiang had a point: the delegates would soon prove more sympathetic to Mao's cause than Li Zongren's. Shao Lizi's wife, a Russian speaker educated in Moscow (where her husband had briefly served as ambassador), had already moved to Beiping. The spouse of Li's personal envoy Huang Qihan had done the same. As for Liu Fei, he admitted later that, before he agreed to Li's request to serve as a peace delegate, he had moved his family out of Nationalist-controlled areas to Hong Kong 'so he wouldn't have to worry'.[65] His opponents later accused of him of being a CCP spy.

'This is your last chance. Don't lose it'

The Nanjing delegation's first encounter with communist negotiating style and strategy, and the realities of power on which it was based, occurred when their plane landed in Beiping. Expecting to be greeted with public fanfare of the kind they had left behind in Nanjing, they found a 'welcoming committee' consisting of a few junior officials who arranged for the delegates to be driven to the city centre.

The second was the discovery, in their rooms at the Wagons-Lit or Six Nations Hotel in the city's old legation quarter, of newspapers branding the Guomindang as criminals, Chiang Kai-shek as a traitor and Zhang himself as Chiang's 'running dog'. In the CCP's view, Zhang was not so much the representative of a government or a potential peace partner as a man who had come to Beiping to sign a surrender document.[66] The communists quickly imposed a news blackout on the activities of the delegation and threw such a tight military cordon around the Wagon Lits that 'not even the hostelry's barber Martelliti was allowed to pass the barricade'.[67]

To some extent Mao had agreed to the negotiations on sufferance: he was under some pressure from Stalin to parley; communist armies were not (quite) ready to launch the Yangtze crossing; and he probably felt there was nothing to lose from responding positively to the public yearning for peace in the south. Yet the real purpose of the peace talks was to clarify the terms under which the Nanjing government and its military forces would be 'wound up'. He drove the point home in an article published on 4 April, the day after he met the government delegation at his residence in the Fragrant Hills. 'This is your last chance. Don't lose it. The People's Liberation Army will soon advance south of the Yangtze River. We are not bluffing. The People's Liberation Army will advance whether or not you sign [an] agreement accepting the eight terms.'[68]

The communists kept the Nanjing delegates on tenterhooks in Beiping with an unpredictable schedule of informal discussions, individual meetings with Mao and the sudden announcement, a few hours beforehand, that formal talks would take place on the evening of 13 April. They would do so in the Hall of Diligent Governance, where the Qing Dynasty Kangxi Emperor had conducted his official business inside the Forbidden City. Government delegates were also kept off-balance by interventions from their own side, particularly Chiang and the GMD party chiefs in Guangzhou, who kept issuing hard-line terms and insisted that the two parties be treated equally in any accord.

Nonetheless, a late-night meeting in the Fragrant Hills with Mao and Zhou on 8 April boosted Zhang Zhizhong's hopes that agreement might yet be reached. The Chairman was courteous and correct when referring to the Nationalists and their leaders. He said there was no need to include the names of war criminals in the peace accord. The terms under which the Nationalist armies would be reorganized were open for discussion. And the government in Nanjing would not have to disband immediately: it could continue to exercise power until the formation of the new coalition government. Encouraged, Zhang cabled Li Zongren accordingly.

The optimism proved fleeting. On 13 April, Zhou, leader of the CCP negotiating team, placed in Zhang's hands a draft agreement for discussion at formal talks scheduled for later the same day. It consisted of Mao's Eight Points and twenty-four additional associated clauses. His heart sank when he read it. He remained crestfallen when, during the formal talks, Zhou denounced the GMD and most of its works.[69] Zhang responded with a polite but weak rebuttal, admitting the many failings of his own party and government, views from which his fellow delegates did not demur. On the contrary, they now realized the game was up. It was just a question of accepting the best terms they could get and pressing for the most dignified language possible to wrap them up in.

Zhou presented Zhang with a revised version of the accord the next day. It included minor alterations in the precise timing with which the Nanjing regime might wind itself up. Zhou said it was a 'final' version of the accord, the government must sign it by 20 April and that if it did not the PLA would immediately cross the Yangtze. Zhang sought to rationalize political defeat in homely language. 'The GMD and the CCP were two brothers who had been fighting too long', he told Zhou. 'The older brother [the GMD] had made mistakes and it was time for the younger brother [the CCP] to take over. The two parties shared many goals, and it was still possible for a reformed GMD to work with the CCP.'[70] Zhou rejected such folksy language. 'It had not been a case of brother fighting brother during the past 2–3 years but a struggle between the Revolution and Counterrevolution.'[71]

Liu Fei cast the issue in more immediate, practical terms:

We started off as government delegates tasked with negotiating with the Communists. We've ended up as representatives of the Communists tasked with persuading the government to accept the peace deal. My one fear is that Nanjing will look upon it as a surrender document and decide that, since it will lose if it fights on *and* if it gives in, it will have no alternative but to fight to the bitter end.[72]

The delegates decided that Huang Shaohong, closest among them to Li and Bai, should immediately fly south and try to persuade the two Guangxi leaders to swallow the bitter medicine. Huang landed in Nanjing on the afternoon of 16 April, alighting from the plane with 'a five-inch thick sheaf of papers (presumably) containing the Communists' terms'. Besieged by waiting reporters, he responded to their questions with a short remark about the weather and went straight to Li's house. 'There the Nationalist leaders conferred until 2am. Li Zongren's dream of decent peace and a non-communist China south of the Yangtze was fading fast.'[73]

Nanjing says 'no'

If Li hoped a last-minute deal might be snatched from the jaws of defeat in Beiping, he was not banking on it. The trouble was there was little else to bank on. Attempts to strengthen the Yangtze defences, under way for several weeks, were not going well. Frontline troops grumbled about being paid in the gold yuan, demanding silver dollars instead. They were also insufficient in number and poorly equipped. Li appealed to US ambassador John Leighton Stuart to redirect to US aid already earmarked for China to Guangzhou. He replied that there were plenty of US-supplied weapons and equipment sitting in warehouses in Taiwan; it was up to the Chinese government to transfer them where they were most needed.

The ambassador was no more helpful when on 15 April, the day the peace talks ended, Li asked if Washington might issue a statement to the effect that the United States would regard a communist crossing of the Yangtze as a threat to its own national security and take measures accordingly. 'I have every sympathy with the Acting President in his efforts to contain the Communists north of the Yangtze ... Any statement of sympathy from the U.S. at this time would encourage him enormously', Leighton Stuart advised Washington. 'I am not, however, able to support Li's request unless the U.S Government is prepared to back up such a statement by some kind of effective assistance.'[74] The administration was not prepared to do so.

Upriver, Bai was anxious about the reliability of the Hunan military faction (after the strategically critical province of the same name), a key part of his Central China forces holding the middle Yangtze. Its leader, Hunan Governor Cheng Qian, had long been at odds with Chiang. There were signs, soon vindicated, that he had decided that the ascendancy in the communist leadership of fellow Hunanese Mao and Liu Shaoqi meant it might be prudent to explore the possibility of shifting his allegiance to the likely winners in what looked like a pointless battle to prop up Chiang's regime in the south.[75]

On the night of 17–18 April, all the senior military and civilian leaders of the Guangxi Clique assembled at Li's residence. It was one of the last occasions on which the key players in this formidable faction in Republican politics would get together. The stakes could hardly have been higher, given what they had achieved together over the years, in Guangxi and elsewhere, and their present position as power brokers in a regime on the brink of collapse. It was another 'high noon' moment in Nanjing.

Huang opened by saying the communist terms were very tough but better than abject surrender. He had met Mao who promised that the communists would treat the Guangxi Clique favourably should their leaders sign the peace accord. Li could become a vice chair in the new government. Bai could remain in command of his central China forces if he agreed to withdraw them to Guangxi and Guangdong, where the PLA would not molest them.

There would be no change in the political and economic status quo in these two provinces, which in time would be treated fairly by the new central government. And there would be a place for other leading Guangxi figures in the new administration. Huang concluded by saying that, should there be a military disaster in the south, at least the people of Guangxi might be spared some of its effects.

If those listening found this offer tempting they kept it to themselves. Li did not say a word once Huang had finished speaking. Bai, however, exploded: 'How could you bring back a document of this nature and expect the government to sign it?' he demanded of Huang, his face contorted with rage. 'The Communist plan to leave Guangxi and Guangdong alone is merely a matter of timing; they want to cut the fat off the chicken first and [enjoy] the head and feet later', he said and stormed out of the meeting.[76]

This was a critical intervention. Rather as Liu Fei had feared, on listening to Huang in that critical late-night conclave, Bai – possibly along with some of the other Guangxi leaders – was made forcefully aware of the kind of future that awaited him and his associates. If it came to a choice between siding with the communists or with Chiang, they would opt for the latter. It was a matter of survival: the power and influence of the Guangxi Clique could not outlast the life of the Nationalist government. The dismantlement of their personal network of power and its attendant interests, and their absorption into a new communist-dominated regime, would mean political oblivion, even if the communists granted them a short grace period. It was not to be countenanced, even this late in the day. Like Chiang, who could expect no such 'special treatment' at the hands of the communists, the Guangxi leaders would fight to the bitter end.

The government peace delegates in Beiping waited anxiously for Nanjing's formal response to the CCP's terms. It came on the evening of 20 April. There could no question of the government signing such a 'humiliating surrender document', they were told. 'Its entire spirit is that of imposing victor's justice on the defeated. The communists must put the interests of the people above everything and change the tone and the contents of the document.'[77] Zhang Zhizhong was instructed to request more time for negotiations and demand that the communists agree to a ceasefire. Nanjing hoped, even now, that the rising waters of the Yangtze would make defence of the river a little easier. But it was too late for that. Within a few hours of Zhang receiving this message, he picked up some gossip from the Beiping streets: 'Mao and Zhu have ordered the People's Liberation Army to advance into southern China!'[78]

Notes

1   SOAS archives, 'Papers of Eva Dykes Spicer', PP. MS92, Letter of 5 January 1949.

2 Jin Feng, *The Making of a Family Saga: Ginling College* (Albany, NY: State University of New York Press, 2009), p. 9.

3 *CWP*, Vol. 1, pp. 288–9.

4 MZD *SW*, Vol. IV, pp. 309–13. http://www.marx2mao.com/Mao/WC49.html (accessed 18 February 2020).

5 On Mao's 'Eight Points' see MZD *SW*, Vol. IV, pp. 315–19. http://www.marx2mao.com/Mao/SM49.html (accessed 18 February 2020). The first of the Eight Points called for the punishment of 'war criminals', of whom Chiang had already been identified as chief. The other points included the abolition of the 1946 constitution, the reorganization of the government's forces into the People's Liberation Army, land reform, confiscation of 'bureaucratic capital' and the formation of a new government without the 'participation of reactionary elements'.

6 Lin Tongfa, *1949 Da chetui* ('1949: The Great Withdrawal') (Taipei: Lianjing chuban shiye youxian gongsi, 2009), pp. 75–6; Dong Xianguang, *Jiang zongtong zhuan*, Vol. 3 ('A Biography of President Jiang') (Taipei: Zhonghua wenhua chuban shiye weiyuanhui,1954), pp. 511–12.

7 Lin Tongfa, *1949 Da chetui*, p. 71.

8 The full title, in English, of the 'temporary provisions' was 'Temporary Provisions Effective during the Period of National Mobilization for Suppression of the Communist Rebellion', The National Assembly approved them in May 1948. They were not abolished until April 1991, by which time the Nationalist government had been based in Taiwan for forty-two years. See Afterwards, p. 276.

9 Zhongyang yanjiuyuan jindaishi yanjiusuo, *Bai Chongxi xiansheng fangwen jilu* ('A Record of Interviews with Mr Bai Chongxi') (Taipei: Zhongyang yanjiuyuan jindaishi yanjiusuo, 1984), Vol. 2, p. 874.

10 Jay Taylor, *The Generalissimo: Chiang Kai-shek and the Struggle for Modern China* (Cambridge, MA: Harvard University Press, 2009), p. 396.

11 Wang Weili (ed.), *Jiangjieshide wenchen wujiang* ('Jiang Jieshi's Civilian and Military Officials') (Taibei: Balilulun chubanshe, 1992), p. 165.

12 Lin Tongfa *1949 Da chetui*, p. 47.

13 'China – A Survey', *The Far Eastern Economic Review*, 19 January 1949.

14 Chester Ronning, *A Memoir of China in Revolution* (New York: Pantheon Books, 1974), p. 133.

15 Christopher R. Lew, *The Third Chinese Revolutionary Civil War, 1945–49: An Analysis of Communist Strategy and Leadership* (London: Routledge, 2009), p.123. I have rounded the numbers to the nearest thousand for convenience.

16 The account of events in Tianjin that follows draws upon Lew, *The Third Chinese Revolutionary Civil War, 1945–49*, p. 127; Kenneth G. Lieberthal, *Revolution and Tradition in Tientsin,1949–1952* (Stanford, CA: Stanford University Press, 1980), p. 22, pp. 28–9; *Daily Express*, 6 December 1948; *The Crusader*, March–April 1949 (Salvation Army Heritage Centre: File No. CH1/4/3); and *The Times*,11, 12, 13 January 1949.

17 TNA FO371/75734, 1 January 1949 and 2 January 1949.

18 *The Crusader*, March–April 1949, p. 2. (Salvation Army Heritage Centre: File No. CH1/4/3).

19 Zhonggong zhongyang dangshi yanjiushi (ed.), *Zhonggongdang shi dashi nianbiao* ('A Chronology of Major Events in the CCP's History') (Beijing: Renmin chubanshe, 1987), pp. 216–17.

20 Joseph K. S. Yick, *Making Revolution in Urban China: The CCP–GMD Struggle for Beiping–Tianjin 1945–1949* (New York: M. E. Sharpe, 1995), p. 174.

21 'Du Jianshi' in *Baidu Baike*. https://baike.baidu.com/item/杜建时 (accessed 18 February 2020).

22 *CWP*, Vol. 2, p. 921.

23 *Time*, 17 January 1949, p. 15; K. M. Panikkar, *In Two Chinas: Memoirs of a Diplomat* (London: George Allen & Unwin, 1955), p. 39.

24 Zhou Hongtao, *Jianggong yu Wo* ('The Revered Jiang and I') (Taibei: Tianxia wenhua chubanshe, 2003), p. 83.

25 Ibid., p. 84.

26 *CWP*, Vol 1, p. 292.

27 Chen Yi (1883–1950) was dismissed as Zhejiang Governor on 16 February 1949 and detained in Shanghai. He was executed in Taipei on 18 June 1950.

28 Zhang Liangren (ed.), *Chiang ching-kuo xiansheng quanji* ('The Complete Works of Mr Chiang Ching-kuo'), Vol. 1. Chiang Ching-kuo, diary entry for 29 January 1949, p. 386.

29 *Time*, 31 January 1949, p. 16.

30 The observations in this and the subsequent paragraph draw upon Lew, *The Third Chinese Revolutionary Civil War, 1945–49*, pp. 124–5. On Fu's lack of resolve and failure to break out to the northwest see TNA UK FO371/75734, 13 December 1948, p. 2.

31 Dangdai zhongguo yanjiusuo bian, *Zhonghua renmin gongheguo shibiannian: 1949 nianjuan* ('Chronicle of the People's Republic of China – 1949') (Beijing: Dangdai zhongguo chubanshe, 2004) (hereafter: 1949 nianjuan), p. 336; Yick, *Making Revolution in Urban China*, p. 172.

32 Yick, *Making Revolution in Urban China*, p. 68 for estimate of number of people in CCP underground.

33 Dong Shigui and Zhang Yanzhi, *Beiping hetan jishi* ('A True Record of the Beiping Peace Talks') (Beijing: Wenhua yishu chubanshe, 1991), p. 257 (my emphasis).

34 *Time*, 31 January 1949, p. 17.

35 A. Doak Barnett, *China on the Eve of Communist Takeover* (New York: Frederick A. Praeger, 1963), pp. 339–40.

36 Diana Lary, *China's Civil War: A Social History, 1945–1949* (Cambridge: Cambridge University Press, 2015), p. 149.

37 Derk Bodde, *Peking Diary: A Year of Revolution* (London: Jonathan Cape, 1951), p. 104.

38 Robert L. Jarman (ed.), *China: Political Reports 1911–1960* (Cambridge: Cambridge: Archive Editions Limited, 2001), Vol. 9, p. 5; *The Times*, 4 February 1949, p. 4.

39 Dong Shigui and Zhang Yanzhi, *Beiping hetan jishi*, p. 344.

40 Lionel Max Chassin, *The Communist Conquest of China: A History of the Civil War, 1945–1949* (London: Weidenfeld & Nicolson, 1966), p. 216.

41 T'ong Te-kang and Li Tsung-jen, *The Memoirs of Li Tsung-jen* (Boulder, CO: Westview, 1979), p. 510.

42 TNA FO FO371/75734, 3 January 1949, p. 2.

43 Lin Tongfa, *1949 Da chetui*, pp. 60–1.

44 Liang Shengjun, *Jiang-Li douzheng neimu* ('The Inside Story of the Struggle between Jiang and Li') (Taibei: Xinxin wencongshu, 1992), p. 58.

45 FRUS, *The Far East: China*, Vol. 8, 19 January 1949. https://history.state.gov/historicaldocuments/frus1949v08/d746 (accessed 18 February 2020).

46 *The Times*, 29 January 1949, p. 4.

47 *Time*, 21 February 1949, p. 18 and *The Times*, 19 February 1949, p. 4.

48 *The Times*, 22 January, 1949, p. 4.

49 Peter Worthing, *General He Yingqin: The Rise and Fall of Nationalist China* (Cambridge: Cambridge University Press, 2016), p. 266.

50 Yang Kuisong, *Guomindange de 'liangong' yu 'fangong'* ('The Guomindang's "Unity with the Communists" and "Anti-Communism"') (Beijing: shehuikexuewenxian chubanshe, 2008), p. 694.

51 Zhongguo renmin zhengxie shanghuiyi guangxi zhuangzu zizhiqu weiyuanhui (ed.), *Guangxi wenshi ziliao xuanji* ('Selected materials on Guangxi history'), Vol. 9 (Nanning: 1981), p. 17.

52 MZD *SW*, Vol. IV, p. 373. http://www.marx2mao.com/Mao/RCP49.html (accessed 18 February 2020) The Central Committee had met in Xibaipo on 5–13 March 1949.

53 Yick, *Making Revolution in Urban China*, p. 186.

54 Sergey Radchenko and David Wolff, 'To the Summit via Proxy-Summits: New Evidence from Soviet and Chinese Archives on Mao's Long March to Moscow, 1949', *Cold War International History Project Bulletin*, Issue 16 (Fall 2007/ Winter 2008), p. 106.

55 See Chapter 7 p. 197.

56 Radchenko and Wolff, 'To the Summit via Proxy-Summits', p. 107.

57 Tony Saich (ed.), *The Rise to Power of the Chinese Communist Party: Documents and Analysis* (New York: M. E. Sharpe, 1996), p. 1335.

58 MZD *SW*, Vol. IV, pp. 361–2. http://www.marx2mao.com/Mao/RCP49.html (accessed 18 February 2020).

59 The announcement, and the terms, came on 26 March: MZD *SW*, Vol. IV, p. 375 n. 3. http://www.marx2mao.com/Mao/RCP49.html (accessed 18 February 2020).

60 *Da Gong Bao*, 2 April 1949.

61 Cai Dengshan (ed.), *Huang Xuchu huiyilu – Li Zongren, Bai Chongxi yu Jiang Jieshi lihe* ('Reminiscences of Huang Xuchu – The Separation and Reunion of Li Zongren and Bai Chongxi with Chiang Kai-shek') (Taipei: Duli Zuojia, 2016), p. 332.

62 SOAS archives, 'Papers of Eva Dykes Spicer', PP. MS92 Letter dated 29 March 1949.

63 Wang Meizhi and Zhang Huoshi, *Jinling tanmeng: Li Zongren in 1949* ('Nanjing Illusions: Li Zongren in 1949') (Beijing: Tuanjie chubanshe, 2007), p. 79.

64 Zhang Liangren (ed.), *Chiang ching-kuo xiansheng quanji*, p. 412.

65 Liu Chengang and Wang Yuping, *Liu Fei jiangjun, zhuanlue* ('A Short Biography of General Liu Fei') (Beijing: Tuanjie chubanshe, 1998), p. 64.

66 Liang Shengjun, *Jiang-Li douzheng neimu*, p. 108; Yang Kuisong, *Guomindangde 'liangong' yu 'fangong'*, p. 715.

67 *Da Gong Bao*, 2 April 1949; *Time*, 18 April 1949, p. 20.

68 MZD *SW*, Vol. IV, p. 384. http://www.marx2mao.com/Mao/WNG49.html (accessed 18 February 1949).

69 Zhang Zhizhong, *Zhang Zhizhong huiyilu* ('The Reminiscences of Zhang Zhizhong') (Beijing: Wenshiziliao chubanshe, 1985), p. 805.

70 Ibid., p. 838.

71 Ibid.

72 Yang Kuisong, *Guomindange de 'liangong' yu 'fangong'*, pp. 726–7.

73 *Time*, 25 April 1949, p. 18.

74 *CWP*, Vol. 1, pp. 303–4.

75 See Chapter 7, p. 199.

76 Cai Dengshan (ed.), *Huang Xuchu huiyilu – Li Zongren, Bai Chongxi yu Jiang Jieshi lihe*, p. 336.

77 Yang Kuisong, *Guomindange de 'liangong' yu 'fangong'*, p. 729.

78 Zhang Zhizhong, *Zhang Zhizhong huiyilu*, p. 847. Mao and PLA chief Zhu De issued the Order to the Army for the Country-wide Advance on 21 April 1949. MZD *SW*, Vol. IV, p. 387. http://www.marx2mao.com/Mao/CWA49.html (accessed 18 February 2020).

4

'Offshore China'

Taiwan: island refuge?

The dramatic shift during the first few months of 1949 in the struggle to control 'China proper' – the country's economic and political heartland from Manchuria to the Yangtze Valley and beyond – had a profound effect on China's periphery, or what might be called 'offshore China'. The territories most affected were Taiwan and Hong Kong. Their role in the wider Chinese world would be recast as a result of the Civil War, their political, social, economic arrangements, along with their international connections, re-fashioned accordingly. In both cases, this was an extraordinary turn of events. It occurred rapidly and to a large extent against the odds as Mao's communist armies continued their apparently unstoppable march into every part of the country. Taiwan and Hong Kong managed not only to survive the traumas of 1949 but thereafter to prosper, despite their troubled relations and, in the case of Taiwan, state of war, with the 'new' China.

Since March, Mao Zedong and his closest leaders had been busy establishing their headquarters in Beiping, which they had decided some time ago would be the capital of the new People's Republic of China. Yet when it came to forging a new centre of power, Chiang Kai-shek was for once ahead of his foes: as pointed out in the previous chapter, he spent the first months of the year few transferring as many critical resources as he could get his hands on to the island of Taiwan, where he planned to revive his party, government and armed forces, and from where he intended to stage a comeback.

The contrast between the two settings in which these arch-rivals concentrated their nation-building (or in Chiang's case 'rebuilding') was striking. Beiping, thanks to its history, location, size, economic weighting, communications links, educational and cultural prowess, and longstanding foreign presence was at the 'centre' of Chinese life. Taiwan, by comparison, sat at the margins. A largely tropical island of some 13,900 square miles, roughly 110 miles off the coast of Fujian province in the southeast, it would almost certainly have languished in relative obscurity during the late 1940s were it not for China's Civil War. It was home for just over 7 million of

MAP 4.1 *Taiwan, China's offshore province.*

China's roughly 460 million people. About 430,000 lived in the provincial capital of Taipei.

In terms of 'high' Chinese culture, Taiwan was a backwater. Indeed, you did not have to be a particularly well-educated Chinese from the mainland to wonder whether it was 'Chinese' at all. It had only become a formal province of the Qing dynasty in 1885. Ten years later, Japan occupied the island under the terms of the Treaty of Shimonoseki, following Tokyo's victory over the Qing in the Sino-Japanese War. It was not returned to China until Japan's defeat in the Second World War, in line with the undertakings the Allies made to Chiang at the Cairo Conference of November 1943. On 25 October 1945, his government formally declared that Taiwan was China's thirty-fifth province.

Traditionally, the Taiwanese economy was tied closely to that of Japan. Its major products were rice, sugar (in the late 1930s it produced more sugar than anywhere else in the world after Java and Cuba), fruit and tea. Industry was largely confined to food processing. Before 1945, there was relatively little in the way of trade or indeed of many other connections, between the mainland and Taiwan.

Yet in relative terms, the average standard of living on the island was higher than that on the mainland. And though they had chafed at certain aspects of Japan's rule, particularly during the war, many Taiwanese appreciated Japanese culture, spoke Japanese and, in many cases, chose to adopt Japanese rather than Chinese names. Even Japanese wartime mobilization 'spawned no literature of resentment or resistance expressing outrage at Japanese abuses', the leading historians of 1940s Taiwan point out.[1] Indeed, it 'was the one place in East Asia that seemed to have prospered throughout the entire war', notes Stephen R. Mackinnon. 'Its export economy was relatively unaffected until the very end.'[2]

Nevertheless, Japan's surrender and the prospect of Chinese rule generated a degree of patriotic spirit across the island. US ships and planes helped transport Chiang's troops across the Taiwan Straits to disarm the occupiers. Society was stable. Communism had made few inroads, either among intellectuals or the rural community at large. It was indeed a different part of China. These attributes impressed Chiang when he and his wife made their first visit to Taiwan in October 1946, prompting one of his biographers to wonder whether the Chinese leader may even then have considered the island as a refuge in need.[3]

The unruly behaviour of newly arrived Chinese troops and the grasping, monopolistic attitude of the mainland officials who took over the provincial administration soon disturbed the peace in Taiwan. So much so that the *Far Eastern Economic Review* said that once they came under Chinese control, the Formosans (the term widely used for Taiwanese at the time) found themselves 'the most progressive colony of the most backward country'.[4] A Taiwanese reproached a US military officer: 'You only dropped the atom bomb on the Japanese; you have dropped a Chinese army on us.'[5]

In February 1947, a local fracas in Taipei over the sale of untaxed cigarettes prompted protests and a bloody crackdown by the military in which perhaps as many as 30,000 people were killed, including many members of the Taiwanese elite. Poor governance and weak police capacity contributed to the disaster; the central government, absorbed with events in the mainland, failed to ensure that its newly reacquired island province had the resources to deal with large-scale local unrest. The '28th February Incident' formed an unhappy backdrop to the arrival of vast numbers of exiles from the mainland keen to escape the Civil War. It also poisoned political life for much of the following four decades, reinforcing the polarization of Taiwanese society between 'mainlanders' (those who arrived in or fled to the island during the 1940s) and 'locals' (most of whom originated in Fujian province and who had arrived in earlier waves of immigration).[6]

In ordinary circumstances, then, Taiwan was hardly an attractive destination for many mainland Chinese. But these were not ordinary times. Military conflict, revolutionary upheaval and social and economic collapse on the mainland made Taiwan's remoteness, and relative social order (bloodily imposed in February 1947), attractive to Nationalist leaders. The offshore province had the Pacific Ocean at its back. If necessary, it would be easy for a third country (i.e. the United States) to supply a government based on Taiwan. It could also serve as a valuable if occasional outpost for the US Pacific Fleet – perhaps to replace the port of Qingdao on the mainland, which currently, though not for much longer, served that function.

Washington appeared to concur, at least in part. In February 1949, Admiral William D. Leahy, advisor to the Joint Chief of Staffs, responded to an enquiry from the National Security Council about the strategic significance of Taiwan and the Penghu islands (Pescadores), off the west coast of the main island. He said that while there was no case for basing US forces there, naval ships could patrol the region and dock in Taiwan ports to demonstrate US military capacity.[7] US strategic interest in Taiwan was widely discussed in foreign media; *The Economist* described it as the 'Isle of Refuge' while Britain's *Daily Express* wrote about Taiwan under the headline 'Adopted by US – Chiang's Island'.[8]

Transferring the treasure

Chiang worked hard to make Taiwan his own. The build-up of military personnel and supplies on the island in late 1948 was just part of the story. Hardly less important was the transfer of China's gold reserves and foreign currency, and a large proportion of the artistic and cultural treasures held by the country's leading national museums and libraries. They would provide his embattled Nationalist government with the means of economic survival and enable it to pose as custodian of the nation's cultural treasures, perhaps helping it regain something of the legitimacy it had lost on the battlefield. Both were necessary for Taiwan's survival and, later, its reinvention as the 'temporary' seat of the Republic of China.

This great shift of financial and cultural treasures occurred around the same time. The first shipment of financial assets, which included some two million taels (1 tael = 50 grams or 1.76 ounces) of gold from the 4.6 million then said to be held by the Treasury in Shanghai, took place on 2 December on the *Star of the Sea*, a coastal protection vessel operated by the Maritime

Customs Service. Secrecy surrounding the move was broken by a British reporter, George Vine, who happened to look out of his office window on Shanghai's Bund to see 'workers walking in and out of the central bank, in single file, carrying two parcels on a bamboo pole; each was a parcel of gold bullion'.[9] The crew had no idea where they were going until they left Shanghai, whereupon the captain told them they were headed for Taiwan.

A few days later, Bai Chongxi in Wuhan thwarted Chiang's plans to ship 3 million silver coins stored in the city from being transferred to Guangzhou, and used them to stabilize economic conditions in central China.[10] However, the exodus of financial resources from the mainland continued: a second shipment – in mid-January – followed the same procedure as the first, though this time the military sealed off the loading area along the Shanghai Bund and gold (estimated at 900,000 taels), silver and foreign currency were placed on board two naval vessels. They sailed, not to Taiwan, but to the south-eastern port of Xiamen (Amoy) as part of Chiang's 'plan to confuse Mao as to where he intended to make a stand', says his biographer.[11] The treasure was stored on the nearby island of Gulangyu until July, when the communist advance into south China forced the government to move it to Taiwan. Chiang also wanted to transfer jewels and precious stones in the possession of the Central Bank that had been confiscated during the war against Japan and were valued at some 20 million dollars. However, Acting President Li Zongren got word of this and blocked the move, with the result that they fell into communist hands when the PLA occupied Shanghai.[12]

Further shipments of gold and silver were made by civilian plane (on 7 February), a military aircraft (on 9 February), and by two naval and one civilian vessel just days before the PLA completed its conquest of the city.[13] A detailed account of the transfer of these valuable assets appeared in 2010 based on a diary of General Wu Song-ching, whom Chiang entrusted with the secret operation. The total value of the treasuries – gold, silver, foreign exchange – moved from Shanghai to Taiwan was said to be $300 million.[14] Some of these assets were remitted back to the mainland during the course of 1949 to finance military operations and meet government expenditure in the rapidly diminishing areas under Nationalist control.[15] A larger proportion was earmarked as a reserve for Taiwan's new currency – the New Taiwan Dollar – launched in June.

The removal of many of China's priceless cultural treasures from the mainland to Taiwan, including paintings, porcelain, and other artefacts, rare books and government archives, was more controversial. This was partly because more people were 'in the know' as far as the operation was concerned, and because some of them were not well disposed to Chiang and his government. Indeed, several were amenable to appeals from the communists and others to leave China's national heritage where it lay – in the custody of the Palace Museum (in Beiping), the (new) Central Museum (in Nanjing) and the Beiping Library among other national institutions. Moreover, professional curators, many of whom had given their lives to the study and preservation of China's past, were concerned about loss and damage that might arise during the shipment of precious objects at a time of war.

It is true that many of China's treasures had been moved before: the government shipped the cream of them out of Beiping in the late 1930s to prevent them from falling into the hands of the Japanese invaders. But in 1948–9, the 'enemy' were fellow Chinese, and the case for depriving them of their nation's inheritance, at least in the minds of some, was less persuasive. This was especially true of Ma Heng, Director of the Palace Museum, who declined to cooperate in the transfer, earning him instant condemnation in Nanjing but praise once the communists took power.[16]

Nevertheless, due in large part to the efforts of Jiang Fucong, President of the Central Library, and Han Liwu, Deputy Minister of Education, the heads of the key state museums and libraries agreed in December 1948 to select significant parts of their respective collections and prepared them for shipment to Taiwan. The Archive Department of the Foreign Ministry, custodian of the international treaties China had signed with other countries (including the Treaty of Nanjing of 1842 that ended the Opium War with Britain), did the same. Chiang Kai-shek personally ordered that the necessary transport and military protection be made available.

In all, some 6,256 cases of precious objects, many of them today in the custody of the National Palace Museum in Taipei, were transferred to Taiwan in three shipments between 21 December 1948 and 30 January 1949. The first was undertaken by a naval vessel, the *Zhong Dian Lun*, a landing craft converted to a transport. Its mission was nearly aborted when members of the sailors' families, learning that it was bound for Taiwan, stormed on board leaving little space for anything else and ignoring appeals to disembark. Admiral Gui Yongqing, head of the navy, had to be summoned to the dockside in Nanjing to deal with the situation. He told those on board that, on this occasion, 'national treasures had to take priority over passengers'.[17] Many of the dependants reluctantly went ashore, and the flat-bottomed *Zhong Dian Lun* set out for Taiwan on an uneasy passage during which many of the cases containing China's national treasures shifted alarmingly and repeatedly from one side of the ship to the other.

The second shipment, which left Nanjing on 6 January aboard a merchant vessel, the *Haihulun*, enjoyed a smoother voyage. It contained by far the largest of the three consignments, including the Complete Library in Four Sections, a huge collection of books commissioned by Emperor Qian Long of the Qing dynasty. On arrival in Jilong, the contents were disbursed to various warehouses across Taiwan for safe keeping.

The final shipment was more problematic. By the end of January, the military situation in Nanjing was tense and the public anxious about the future. No naval vessels were available for the operation but Admiral Gui secured the services of a 3,000 ton freighter, the *Kun Lun*. Military exigencies were such that the captain, Chu Lianfang, was keen to berth, load and set sail in as short a time as possible. This meant that museum staff had to leave the crates containing their prize possessions on the dockside, ready for loading but concealed by tarpaulins for the purposes of secrecy and protection against incessant Nanjing drizzle. Chu's heart sank when he saw what awaited him: 'My ship was old and could not accommodate such a large load', he observed. 'Yet these were extraordinary times and national treasures like these just had to be moved to a place of safety.'[18]

This was easier said than done. First, it was Chinese Year and dock workers refused to load the *Kun Lun* unless a suitable holiday bonus was paid. Word then again got around that the ship was bound for Taiwan and sailor's dependants, now more concerned to get out of harm's way than ever, flocked aboard. Admiral Gui's entreaties were of no effect on this occasion, so he ordered that the cabins be broken up to make extra space, and the crates be crammed into every available space, including the canteen and the ship's hospital, and spread over every spare inch of deck. *Kun Lun* set sail on 30 January for Shanghai where it berthed for three days and then docked at a nearby shipyard for repairs. It did not arrive in Jilong until 22 February, in all a twenty-four-day journey.

The communists as well as those otherwise dissatisfied with the government worked hard to persuade officials and curators to resist Chiang's relocation of the nation's cultural assets. CCP leaders branded Han Liwu and Jiang Fucong 'cultural war criminals', and Fu claimed that Li Zongren, infuriated by Chiang's 'meddling' despite standing down as president, thwarted his plans for a fourth shipment of artefacts to Taiwan. But by then it was too late. Enough of China's treasures had left the mainland to make a difference in both substantial and symbolic terms. Rival claimants to rule the present, the Nationalists and communists were also rival custodians of a glorious past.

Lurking in the background of these developments was the question of the precise legal status of Taiwan, a matter that would cast a shadow over China and East Asia for decades – and which to some extent remains at issue today. In the late 1940s, as far as the Allies and especially the United States were concerned, Taiwan's status could only be settled as part of a peace treaty with defeated Japan. Until then, whatever the 'facts on the ground', the matter was ambiguous at best.

In fact, Washington had plans, largely unknown to Chiang as he stepped down and devoted himself to rescuing his embattled regime, to deprive both him and Mao of control over Taiwan by fostering independent sentiment on the island. Taiwanese nationalists, alarmed that Chiang was about to move his government to their homeland, had demanded a plebiscite to determine its future. 'Formosa's future status should be decided by Formosans (excluding those Chinese entering Formosa and the Pescadores after August 15, 1945)', they said in a statement issued to the Allies and the UN.[19] 'If Formosa unfortunately falls into the turmoil of China's civil war, this beautiful island will certainly be overrun by the international communist conspiracy.'[20]

Washington's dalliance with the notion of an independent Taiwan soon came to nothing and it changed tack. Once it was clear that Chiang would indeed seek to relocate the Nationalist government to Taiwan, US officials floated what they regarded as the more agreeable idea of turning Taiwan into a 'free province' run by a 'liberal' Chinese leader. Again, largely unknown to Chiang, they cultivated Sun Liren, an outstanding US-trained general whom Chiang had tasked with training a new Nationalist army in Taiwan, to this end. This move, too, would yield to realities as the balance of political power changed within Taiwan, in China and the wider region.

Getting there

Such concerns mattered little to the hundreds of thousands of defeated soldiers, business owners, prominent citizens, civil servants and ordinary civilians desperate to escape war and revolution at home. Taiwan might not be up to much from many points of view, but it did seem to offer sanctuary.

Among those who thought so, at least at first, was Liu Hongsheng, patriarch of a Shanghai-based business empire that encompassed textiles, cement and much else besides. A graduate of the missionary-founded St John's University in Shanghai, Liu was aged sixty in 1948. His sobriquet 'King of Matches' and 'King of Textiles' reflected his company's prowess in these areas. Under his direction, the family business had prospered by not putting all its eggs in one basket, as a history of the family puts it.[21] He maintained cordial relations with the Nationalists but was more interested in ensuring a future for his business empire than the political welfare of Chiang Kai-shek. With communism creeping closer, he decided in mid-1948 to send two of his sons to Taiwan to place certain family assets in what he hoped would be a place of safety. They were instructed to open businesses on the island.

Liu soon changed tack – not because of developments in Taiwan so much as the behaviour of the Nationalist government in Shanghai. Under its radical currency reforms in the autumn of 1948, Liu like other Shanghai business owners and well-off citizens, was required to turn over the family's gold, silver and foreign currency in exchange for the new 'gold yuan', the GMD's last throw in the battle against hyperinflation. In a matter of weeks, the value of the new currency was as worthless as the silver one it replaced. Liu, in common with almost everyone else who had assets worth the name, was angered by what he regarded as thinly disguised expropriation of private wealth by a corrupt and incompetent government. 'Taiwan would not be a safe place', he told his children at a family meeting towards the close to the year.[22]

He did not withdraw his investment from the island but decided against moving any more assets there: the Liu family business would not be following Chiang lock, stock and barrel, as it were. But neither would Liu sit tight in Shanghai and simply wait to see what happened. Concern about the freedom to do business under communist rule and questions of personal safety meant other options had to be explored if the family firm was to survive and prosper.

The several hundred passengers who on 27 January, the night before Chinese New Year's Eve, crowded on board the SS *Taiping* in Shanghai bound for Taiwan's main port of Jilong had already decided what they were going to do.[23] Passenger traffic across the Taiwan Straits had increased in recent weeks as communist forces advanced south towards Nanjing and Shanghai. On the busiest days in January as many as fifty-five vessels crossed between Shanghai and Jilong. Ticket prices soared in accordance with demand. People used their personal or government connections, privileges or plain bribery to get hold of tickets, some of which were exchanged for gold bullion.

Desperate scenes unfolded at the dockside as passengers, their children and other dependants, struggled to board ships that were quickly overloaded with people and their possessions, along with the government files, artefacts and many other valuable items being shipped out to safety. This was despite the fact that a tragedy had occurred just a few weeks earlier, when the SS *Jiangya*, packed full of evacuees, had exploded and sank shortly after leaving Shanghai, probably as a result of hitting a mine. Between two and three thousand passengers may have lost their lives in one of the world's most serious shipping disasters.[24]

The *Taiping*, built as a cargo ship but converted for passenger use, left Shanghai's Huangpu Dock late in the afternoon. She was carrying an estimated 1,000 passengers, hundreds of boxes of government and GMD files and a consignment of steel girders among other cargoes. An estimated one-third of those on board had not purchased tickets, having secured passage by other means. She was undoubtedly overloaded. She also sailed without lights, as required under the terms of the curfew imposed by the military authorities. And she did not have adequate lifeboats and safety equipment on board, as soon became tragically apparent.

About 11.30 p.m., the *Taiping* was struck by the *Jianyun*, a cargo ship, near the Zhoushan group of islands. The *Jianyun* sank immediately, and the *Taiping* picked up some of its crew. But before long the *Taiping* took on water, listed heavily and, about 2.30 on the morning of 28 January, sank. Only about forty people survived, most of whom were rescued by a passing Australian warship, HMAS *Warramcunga*, which, unlike other vessels in the vicinity, responded to the *Taiping's* distress signal.

It was a grim end for those not rescued. 'Conditions in the water were pitiful, with people struggling with armfuls of valuables, attempting to barter for pieces of floating driftwood', said survivor Yeh Lun-ming.[25] Relatives waited in vain at Jilong on 30 January; news of the sinking did not appear in the media until the next day. Many families lost their sole sources of support as well as all their possessions in the catastrophe. It was a life-changing event for them, too. Huang Shilan, whose mother had been on board, now found herself suddenly orphaned. She had to return alone to Guangzhou 'where her "capitalist" origins made her a target for communist hatred in the newly-founded People's Republic of China'.[26]

The *Taiping* tragedy did not stem the flow of people to Taiwan; fear and the desire to flee grew in the weeks that followed as the Nationalist government crumbled and the communists advanced. Two years after the event, a monument was erected in Jilong in memory of those who lost their lives, but no details or names of the victims were included. The story of the SS *Taiping* was only 'rediscovered' in the early twenty-first century, when it also became the subject of a two-part feature film, John Woo's *The Crossing*.[27]

Those on board the *Taiping* had consciously set out for Taiwan. For hundreds of thousands of others, the island province would become, so to speak, an accidental place of refuge. When they were forced from their homes or decided to leave family and friends behind to find a place of safety, Taiwan was perhaps the last place on their minds, let alone the idea that it might be a final destination. Many refugees had little idea what life was like on the island. In his study *China's Homeless Generation*, Joshua Fan says that those fleeing there 'were going to a place where the customs, language and level of modernisation were so different that their experience was . . . perhaps closer to migration to a foreign country than an internal migration'.[28]

Even much later during the exodus, many senior Nationalist figures, including the captains of troop ships packed with defeated soldiers desperate to flee mainland ports, did not know where Taiwan was. It is said of one group of them, trying to escape from Hainan Island off the southern coast, that though 'they were under bombardment in the port, they had to open up their maps and charts to find Taiwan's location [before setting sail]'. Officers on board, asked by their men when they might expect to reach Taiwan, responded: 'I've never been there and neither have you. You will know when we arrive. In any event, I have heard it's a fine place!'[29]

It is not clear when Mei Jun, a twenty-four-year old woman from Chunan, some 60 miles southeast of the city of Hangzhou, in Chiang Kai-shek's home province of Zhejiang, heard about Taiwan. But it can be assumed that it was some time, perhaps rather a long time, after she decided to leave home, which she did around the time of the sinking of the *Taiping*. She carried her baby boy, Yingyang, in a sling and was accompanied by two young soldiers.[30] She set out first for Changzhou, in neighbouring Jiangsu province, where her husband, Long Huaisheng, was then serving as a military policeman.

Her departure was hurried and involved little planning. Mei Jun told her elderly, ailing mother that she would 'be back soon', but steadfastly refused to look back as she set out on her journey, leaving her mother gazing at her from the doorway of the family home. It would be the last she saw of the place.

In the story related by her daughter, Mei Jun boarded a train in Hangzhou bound for the imagined security of the south. It was crammed with passengers, who had crowded in through doors and windows to occupy every bit of available space. Those who failed to find room inside squatted on the carriage roofs. The train did not travel far before the engine ran out of coal. Those in charge solicited donations from the passengers so that they could purchase coal in the neighbourhood and get moving again. Even then it proved to be a stop-start journey: sections of the track ahead had been torn up, presumably by communist guerrillas or bandits.

The train's destination was Guangzhou, the major metropolis in south China, a comforting distance from communist armies and some 80 miles north of Hong Kong. But Mei Jun and her party alighted at Hengyang, a city in the centre of Hunan province, which was the closest stop to the village where her mother-in-law lived. She decided to leave Yingyang in her care. Conditions on the train were too dangerous and unhygienic for so young a child; there had already been several fatalities. Mei Jun and her escort then boarded another train bound for Guangzhou, where she again hoped to join her husband, by now based in the city. She was barely half-way through an epic journey that would take this country girl across war-torn China in search of safety.[31]

Chen Cheng, Taiwan's new governor, soon had his hands full managing the chaotic influx into his domain of people, organizations and materials, including those provided under the terms of US aid. He told Chiang that up to the end of 1948 an estimated 200,000 people had arrived from the mainland and that the number was bound to increase. He was right: a further 400,000 did so during the first half of 1949.

Many were not welcome. *Da Gong Bao* newspaper reported what it said was a widely held view among the local public: 'Top-flight refugees fled to the United States, second order people went to Hong Kong, and the third class people ended up in Taiwan. Since even third class people were richer than ordinary Taiwanese, their presence contributed to inequalities in society.'[32] In May 1949, the editor of the GMD's official *Zhongyang Ribao* (The Central Daily), was blunter. He complained about the 'influx of political rubbish from the mainland' and said refugees ought not to rely on the local government for support 'since it was known that many of them had arrived loaded with gold bars and US banknotes'.[33]

The island's two main harbours – Jilong and Gaoxiong – could not handle the influx of goods and people; in Jilong, vessels sometimes had to wait for as long as a month or more to unload. Both harbours needed dredging and the construction of warehouses. Iron and steel were urgently required. The local economy could not bear the strain. Inflation was as rampant on the island as on the mainland.

In May, Chen Cheng imposed martial law in an attempt to cope with the crisis. The British consul in Taipei reported that the move was a wake-up call for the local population:

> . . . the imposition of martial law in this hitherto peaceful island has come as rude shock to the native population. The feeling that Formosa, being separated from the mainland would somehow be preserved from actual involvement in the Chinese Civil War is gradually giving way to despondency and it is generally feared that as reverse follows reverse on the mainland military control will be tightened and the discipline of the ever increasing numbers of troops will deteriorate until little is left of social order and this island too is reduced to a battlefield in China's Civil War.[34]

Chiang urged Chen to use Taiwan people of talent as much as possible when rebuilding the local government and the economy, and to employ as many young people as he could. And, aware that the governor could be harsh towards subordinates, Chiang urged him to be as accommodating as possible in handling what had become a potentially explosive situation: Taiwan could hardly prove a sanctuary for the Nationalists if it was not politically stable.

Hong Kong: an imperial dilemma

On first appearances, Britain's crown colony of Hong Kong looked much less troubled by events across the border. *Time* magazine in February 1949 described it as 'the only place in China last week that seemed unaffected by the tragedy of China's fall'. While chaos, uncertainty and fear gripped many mainland Chinese cities, forcing those who could to flee, Hong Kong's streets during the Chinese New Year holiday were 'crowded with shiny Cadillacs and Rolls-Royces. The city's overflowing stores were guarded by armed Sikh policemen with greying beards, the last scattered sentinels of the West's past day in Asia. In Hong Kong hotels, Britons still dressed for dinner.'[35]

It is true that Hong Kong, the speck of territory that the British had carved out of the Cantonese-speaking world of southern China more than a century earlier, seemed a place apart given the calamities unfolding elsewhere in the country. British rule over the enclave partly explained this. So did the fact that, perched on the maritime periphery, Hong Kong was far removed from the main arenas of conflict in the Civil War, which had yet to spread south of the Yangtze.

Yet the calm, if not exactly the colonial formality so conspicuous to American reporters, was only skin deep in the early weeks of 1949. Little more than three years after they had reoccupied the territory following the surrender of Japan, its British rulers were eyeing the growing strength of the Chinese communists with concern and fretting about its implications for the longer-term future of their colony. Even sections of the business community, usually more impervious to pessimism, were growing anxious. The threat of communism had been around in China so long that people had placed it in the same category as 'floods famines and other ills to which China is prone', said the *Far Eastern Economic Review*, voice of the colony's traders.[36] But things were different now. The defeat of Chiang's armies had brought the movement's 'dangerous tendencies to the very doorstep of foreign trade and, as a result, it must be considered from an entirely new point of view – ie how far is the foreign merchant likely to be affected and how much can the situation be helped or hindered?' Uncertainty had 'filled Hong Kong with refugees, driven stout-hearted missionaries from their work and shut the door, temporarily or otherwise, to shipping and trade generally'.[37]

Looked at from London's point of view, communist advances in China in the late 1940s coincided with, and for a while deepened, Britain's imperial dilemma. The Second World War had re-cast the rationale and to some

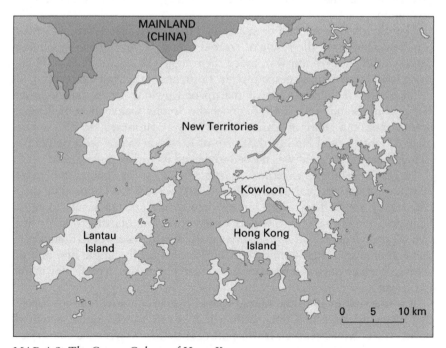

MAP 4.2 *The Crown Colony of Hong Kong.*

extent the legitimacy of the entire European imperial enterprise. It had also made empire ruinously expensive. Britain, a victor but a financially vanquished one, felt this dearly once peace arrived. It had been forced to re-pay its wartime loans to the United States; was committed by its Labour government to introduce expensive welfare schemes at home; and was determined to fund an independent nuclear weapons programme. In peaceful times, Hong Kong might not prove much of a financial burden for London. In less happy ones, it was an added responsibility that might prove expensive – in several respects.

Yet Clement Attlee's Labour government was no more willing than Winston Churchill's Tory predecessor to abandon imperial prestige: Britain's socialists might not like imperialism, but they were quite fond of the empire. It was an attachment that survived US pressure on its wartime ally to curb the imperial impulse, the creation of the United Nations, whose Charter contained troubling (for the British) if vague hints about the rights of dependent territories to full independence, and even the 'loss' of India in 1947. Moreover, the way the Cold War was shaping up suggested, even to Washington, that there was strategic merit in the British retaining some their key overseas possessions.

But in present circumstances how practical was it to hang on to Hong Kong, a densely populated trading city, superb harbour, scattered mountain ranges, scores of islands and modest rural hinterland located precariously on the southern edge of a country convulsed by communist revolution?

The way these assets had been acquired in the first place was part of the problem. They were the result of treaties that in 1842, following China's defeat in the First Opium War, ceded the roughly 32 square miles of Hong Kong Island to Britain in perpetuity; in 1860, under the First Convention of Peking, added 3 square miles at the tip of Kowloon Peninsula, opposite Hong Kong Island; and in 1898, under the Second Convention of Peking, granted Britain a 100-year lease over the New Territories, some 359 square miles of largely rural land to the north of Kowloon (along with numerous islands) that Britain said was needed to defend its earlier possessions.

Successive Chinese governments regarded these as among the more egregious of the 'unequal treaties' that foreign powers had imposed on their country by force. They were morally repugnant and an insult to most Chinese. China's loss of sovereignty over territory and tariffs, to name just two areas of acute sensitivity, spawned the powerful forces of nationalism – and communism – that dominated Chinese political life in the first half of the twentieth century and which were on such visceral, violent display in the Civil War.

It is true that in 1943 the Allies brought the curtain down on one aspect of foreign privilege in China, ceding the extraterritorial rights acquired during the previous century. It was part of the effort to treat the country as an equal, in line with its status as one of the post-war 'Big Five', but Britain specifically excluded Hong Kong from the 1943 treaty and Portugal retained sovereignty over Macao, its tiny colony on the west side of the Pearl River.

Chiang Kai-shek was put out by this latest example of British perfidy. He complained that the move had left 'something to be desired in the cordial relations between China and Great Britain', and advised London that China reserved the right to re-visit the issue in future.[38] This sparked soul-searching in the Foreign Office over whether Britain should relinquish its rights over the territory in whole or in part rather than let Chiang drive it from the China coast on unfavourable terms. The arguments were said to be finely balanced. But Britain decided in November 1946 that 'it would be wiser on the whole to refrain from taking the initiative', largely because of the 'uncertain political situation in China'.[39]

Thus, as the Civil War reached its decisive phase, British possession of Hong Kong was still predicated on China's internal divisions and national weakness: Chiang's government had too much on its mind – notably, *survival* – to focus on the recovery of Hong Kong. London had always hoped that the presence of a well-managed city port on China's southern extremity would compensate for the loss of national pride over the fact that it was run by a foreign power. Hong Kong 'never pretended to be anything more than a trading port offering entrepôt services on a commercial basis', wrote a British champion of the territory around this time, half-apologetically. It was an assertion much weakened by his admission, almost in the same breath, that 'China of today suffers nothing, except the remembrance of an old wrong, from the present status of Hong Kong'.[40]

Yet this had never been an acceptable bargain for Chinese patriots. And it could hardly be expected to count for much on the part of a future communist government for whom fierce opposition to imperialism was at the centre of its revolutionary creed. The question, then, was whether Britain was willing, if necessary, to defend its occupation of Hong Kong by force in the face of opposition from what looked certain to prove a much stronger government in China than it had ever encountered before.

Uncertainty of another kind stalked Hong Kong during the late 1940s: how the colony should be governed. After the war, some among both British and Chinese elites felt that change was necessary if the territory was to keep up with moves towards self-government in Britain's other colonies – to say nothing of the nationalism sweeping through Asia generally and so powerfully at work in the struggle for control of China. Thus, resuming his governorship of the territory in 1946 after more than four years in a series of Japanese prison camps, Mark Young had announced a modest reform plan. It was designed to give Hong Kong residents a greater say in running their affairs – a controversial cause that Britain would address again at the very end of its rule under the last governor, Chris Patten.[41]

The Young Plan was not exactly still born: six years would pass before it and its various derivations finally were buried without fanfare and little explanation. But a combination of bureaucratic foot-dragging, claims that there was little evidence of popular demand for change in Hong Kong itself and, above all, the ominous events across the border in China meant constitutional reform soon slipped down the agenda. It certainly was not a priority for Alexander Grantham, who succeeded Young as governor in July 1947, and who would remark, with some justice based on his own experience, that: 'In a crown colony the Governor is next to the Almighty.'[42]

A man of wiry build, admired for his practical intelligence rather than gift for 'schemes',[43] Grantham would remain in post for the next, critical, ten years. He had begun his career as a colonial administrator as he would end it: with a long spell of service in Hong Kong. In between, he served the empire in the Caribbean, West Africa and the Pacific. If this experience had not already taught him that Hong Kong was different from other British colonies (and therefore would at some point face a different future than independence), it would quickly be borne in upon him once he became the territory's twenty-second governor. 'Hong Kong is "China irredenta"', Grantham recorded in his memoir of colonial service. 'And this applies whatever the complexion of the [Chinese] government, communist or non-communist.'[44] It would fall to this reserved, generally unexcitable colonial administrator to preside over the transformation of Hong Kong from a sleepy, foreign-run commercial port on China's periphery to a potentially volatile 'front line' in the Cold War.

'A bit of a riddle'

By the time Grantham took office, Hong Kong was recovering rapidly from its wartime depredations. Much of the place still had an air of dilapidation: post-war Hong Kong had few high-rise buildings of the kind that then graced the waterfront in Shanghai, and whose construction would later turn the colony into an unrivalled spectacle and symbol of enterprise and ingenuity. One exception was a new telephone exchange, a twelve-storey construction described in 1948 as Kowloon's 'first skyscraper'.[45] Another was the new headquarters of the Bank of China under construction in Hong King's Central District, then as now, the prime site for real estate whose owners/occupiers wanted above all to make a statement. It was carefully designed to exceed in height the Hong Kong and Shanghai Bank headquarters next door. Begun on instructions from Chiang's government, by the time it was finally completed in 1951, the tallest, arguably most prestigious, building in British-ruled Hong Kong was under the control of communist Beijing, whose influence it sought to radiate in the colony.

If there was little change in the way in Hong Kong was governed after the war, the same was true broadly of social relations between colonial masters and subjects. Some of the worst pre-war excesses were abandoned, such as rules forbidding Chinese to purchase property in areas of the Peak, the most elevated, expensive and desirable place to live on Hong Kong Island. But even enthusiasts of British rule conceded that snobbery persisted, and that segregation between Chinese foreigners (meaning mostly Britons) was the rule in leisure and off-duty hours.[46] Racial discrimination discomforted Governor Grantham when it was brought home to him, as was the case during casual conversation over dinner at the private residence of the manager of the Bank of China, that his host was not a member of the territory's yacht club because Chinese were not admitted. 'I was much embarrassed, but am glad to say that a few years later the Club opened its doors to admit non-Europeans', he recalled, still apparently squirming.[47]

Yet blatant discrimination had other effects. The young Barry Lam (Lin Baili), who would go on to found Quanta computers, one of the world's largest suppliers of laptops, was a few months old when his parents fled Shanghai for the safety of Hong Kong. His father managed to secure a job as an accountant in the exclusive Hong Kong Club, where both father and son lived but where entry by the front door was reserved for Europeans. 'This discrimination between whites and Chinese sharpened my sense of shame and national feeling', he recalled. The family's poverty, emphasized by the price of goods in the shops surrounding the Hong Kong Club, had a different effect. 'It encouraged me to work hard so that I could buy everything on display should I wish to do so.'[48]

Despite their anxieties about the coming of communism, Hong Kong's business community responded to the chaos in China by opening trade routes elsewhere in Asia. Much of the region was hungry for prosperity after years of war and disruption. Hong Kong thus became an entrepôt for East and Southeast Asian trade rather than merely a link, albeit an important one, in China's domestic and foreign trading network. Remarkably, it conducted more trade in 1948 than at any time in its history, prompting an outburst of lyricism on the part of Eric Himsworth, the territory's Director of Commerce and Industry:

> To the average layman, Hongkong must appear a bit of a riddle. There are no large industries within its borders; in size it is one of the smallest British Colonies: there are no large mines. It doesn't seem to make anything, it doesn't seem to produce anything. . . . and yet its harbour is teeming with ships from all the four corners of the earth; a thousand airplanes use its airport monthly: it has a population of nearly 2 million people and the total value of its import and export trade is greater than that of the whole of China. It is the largest city in the British Colonial Empire. It is one of the great cities of the world.[49]

Yet if this prosperity was something of a riddle it also looked precarious given the unsettled situation in China. True, the communists had yet to cross the Yangtze and peace talks were under way. But it seemed to many that the Civil War was in 'its final act', and a communist-dominated government would be in power within the next year.[50] However, nobody could be certain about this. And even if this proved to be the case, what might happen in the meantime, and how it would affect Hong Kong, were causes of conjecture and anxiety.

Typhoon shelter

Some of the consequences of the tumult over the border were already plain: thousands of Chinese people were arriving in Hong Kong each week to escape war, dislocation, poverty and the risk of ending up on the 'wrong side' of the revolution across the border. When Japan surrendered in 1945, the territory's population had sunk to some 600,000 compared with 1.6 million in December 1941. Civil war in China reversed the flow. By the end of 1948, Hong Kong was home to some 1.8 million people, all but 15,000 of them (excluding British servicemen and women) ethnic Chinese.[51]

At first, the authorities believed the influx would differ little from that seen in the past: Hong Kong had always been the home of itinerants, so to speak, who tended to seek safety, visit family and/or pursue commercial advantage in that part of China or Hong Kong best placed to offer such advantages. The colony functioned as a safety valve. There were no immigration controls and no 'hard' border as such. Ebbs and flows were determined by conditions either side of the border, especially the Chinese side. Things would surely settle down, despite the upheaval in China.

Yet the numbers were growing fast. Some 50,000 people from central China were estimated to have reached the territory via Guangzhou between mid-November and the first week in December 1948 alone. They gave up 'houses and businesses and converted everything into foreign exchange, gold or were lucky to find buyers abroad for their "gold" yuan holdings in China'.[52] Those who brought a small fortune with them could expect a welcome. But those 'who may, sooner or later, become destitute will present the Colony with a "social problem" of no mean magnitude in view of the large number of refugees now *en route* for the typhoon shelter of Hong Kong'.[53]

Overcrowding was a problem even before the arrival of those desperate to reach the 'typhoon shelter'. The colonial government's Annual Report for 1949 noted that population density in the most crowded tenement areas was as high as 2,000 persons per acre while up to 30,000 people, including public servants and employees of large public utilities, were forced to live as squatters in crude primitive shacks in bombed areas or on the hillsides.[54]

The 'squatter colonies' were worlds of their own. A survey revealed that:

> some consist almost solely of brothels or opium dens; some are flourishing trading centres dealing in reputable wares; some are inhabited only by Chiuchow-speaking immigrants from Swatow [a port some 200 miles

northeast of Hong Kong]; some have a very high proportion of bread-winners in regular, legal and well-paid employment; some consist of nothing but matting roofs two or three feet off the ground which cannot even be called shacks.[55]

All of them were growing rapidly as refugees flocked into the territory. The new arrivals added to the diversity of the squatter communities, many of which became linguistic and cultural microcosms of China as a whole, set within the local Cantonese-speaking majority. Hong Kong was becoming the repository of Chinese humanity at large, much of it broken, fearful, poor and distressed. It was home for the 'refracted shards of culture, history and ethnicity swept into Hong Kong by war and revolution from the vastness of China', as Paddy Ashdown, the British politician, would recall of his (much later) days in the colony as a language student.[56]

But the new arrivals also included those who were determined to rebuild their businesses in this unfamiliar, unusual part of China that was mercifully free, at least so far, of tumult. Prominent among the latter were Shanghai textile magnates, many of whom managed to bring large parts of their workforces with them, hastening the industrialization (and the labour unionization) of Hong Kong.

Senior Nationalist government officials, army officers who had made their names resisting the Japanese, county magistrates and leaders of academic institutions also sought shelter in Hong Kong. So did legislators and politicians who preferred, at least for the time being, not to move to Taiwan. Similarly, the safety of exile, despite its obvious discomforts, was attractive to journalists, intellectuals and religious leaders who feared there might be little role for them in the new order taking shape across the border.

Yet the largest group of those who sought shelter in Hong Kong were ordinary soldiers, most of whom had been defeated in battle or who had chosen to escape the horrors of combat and privations of military life. In the words of Long Yingtai, a custodian of the memories of many of the 1948–9 exiles: 'The sight of these soldiers limping around, crutches to hand, many of them mere children, dressed in filthy clothes, bewildered by unfamiliar streets, and desperately looking for somewhere to live, became an all too familiar, pathetic Hong Kong scene.'[57]

Tightening control

It is easy to overlook the fact that, even by 1949, the authorities in Hong Kong and London knew far less about the intentions and nature of Chinese communism than they wished. Neither was there much clarity about more immediate matters, such as when, how far and how fast Mao's forces would advance into south China and, critically, whether they would stop at the Hong Kong frontier. There was less doubt about the prospect of further significant Nationalist resistance: outside of certain sections of the GMD government and military, few observers set much store by it.

In the absence of such critical information, some form of insurance seemed the best option. This is why, with its investments in Shanghai much in mind, Britain decided at the close of 1948 to 'keep a foot in the door' and retain its commercial and diplomatic presence in China proper. The assumption was that London would recognize a new communist government of China once it was established and Chiang's regime defeated beyond repair, despite Washington's objections.[58]

Only time would tell whether this approach would do any more to protect the future of British assets in Shanghai than it would preserve British rule in Hong Kong. In any case, the two places were quite different. In Shanghai it was a case of 'staying on'. In Hong Kong, where British *rule* rather than merely British *money* was at stake, it might be a question, literally, of 'digging in' – that is to say, mounting a military defence of the colony, which was another prospect entirely.

In the meantime, the Hong Kong government kept a close watch on Communist and Nationalist Party activities in the territory to contain the spill-over effects of the bitter struggle across the border. Until recently, the GMD had enjoyed the upper hand in terms of visibility, influence and status. London was keen not to offend Nanjing. Despite misgivings, it had allowed the Nationalist government to maintain a de jure, official presence in Hong Kong in the form of the office of the 'Special Commissioner for Guangdong and Guangxi', the two provinces closest to the colony.

For much of 1948, the Hong Kong government had tried to curb the activities of anti-Chiang dissidents such as Li Jishen, a leader of the Guomindang Revolutionary Committee (GMDRC), who with several other prominent figures had thrown in their lot with the communists and were taking advantage of Hong Kong's safety and freedoms to pursue their cause. At the end of the year, after several warnings that they were taking advantage of their hosts, many of them, Li included, left quietly for north China to join communist leaders in drawing up plans for a national coalition government. On Li's departure, Grantham received 'a courteous letter of thanks for the kindly manner in which he had been treated whilst in the Colony'.[59] Mao would later claim that winning Li over 'probably saved the lives of twenty or thirty thousand comrades and won the military victory one or two years ahead of time'.[60]

But as the communists gained the upper hand in the Civil War, the activities of the Party in Hong Kong attracted more attention – and caused greater anxiety. The Central Committee had set up its Hong Kong Bureau in 1947 and appointed Fang Fang, a Cantonese, as its leader. The Party's aim at this stage was not to challenge Britain's control of Hong Kong but rather to gather intelligence about the GMD; win support in Hong Kong for the communist cause across the border; coordinate guerrilla activities in Guangdong and Guangxi provinces; and liaise with communist movements elsewhere in Asia.

Yet much of this was more apparent later than it was at the time. Even assurances, given as early as November 1948 by Qiao Mu, head of the Hong Kong branch of the communist New China News Agency, that the CCP had no intention of changing the status of the colony provided only limited comfort to officials in London and Hong Kong. More revealing, though not especially encouraging, was information about the Party disclosed in documents captured in police raids on premises used by communists. These suggested, among other things, that the Chinese Communist Party was ideologically orthodox rather than moderated by 'Chinese' factors; that 'there was no trace of Titoism', as a Foreign Office analyst noted; and that the Party's 'United Front policy' of trying to win over political groups and leaders from widely different backgrounds was a temporary measure, and one whose targets were described by the communists themselves in the most contemptuous terms.[61]

Given the changing situation in China, Governor Grantham decided that the government had to exert stricter control over both GMD- and CCP-affiliated organizations. Otherwise, the colony risked being caught up directly in the Civil War, undermining its impartiality in the conflict, and jeopardizing local law and order. Explaining his case to London in early April 1949, he said it was important to act before communist organizations became too powerful. Under his proposed legislation, all local societies would be required to register with the government and 'foreign' ones would be banned. Such a measure would 'also facilitate control over subversive influences in education and labour'. It would 'provide a means of control over the Communists singing groups and dramatic societies which act as vehicles for Communist propaganda and penetration'.[62]

A few days earlier, the British chief of staff had prepared a revised assessment of the threats to Hong Kong and the measures required to meet them. A large-scale communist attack aimed at rendition of the territory was deemed a remote possibility. More likely was internal unrest inspired by communist-dominated trade unions, the large-scale influx of refugees and external aggression by communist-dominated guerrilla bands. The first of these threats might occur with little advanced notice, while the second and third, both of which were less likely, might do so 'at any time after March 1949, with probably a month's warning'.[63]

These challenges could be met in several ways. Among the more drastic was a proposed attempt to seal off Hong Kong by imposing control over the entire frontier with China, which 'could be completely wired in 14 days, the essential minimum being completed in 4 days'.[64] It would be much harder to close the sea frontier. And it would be impossible, should it even be deemed desirable, to evacuate all Europeans from the territory. On the other hand, rationing could be expanded, since supplies of essential foodstuffs were being built up. The size of the police force could also be increased. And the governor had a plan in hand to register the entire population.

Separately, the Hong Kong government had accelerated plans to create a volunteer Defence Force. A total strength of some 6,000 was envisaged with by far the largest portion (2,750) denoted as the Auxiliary Force, and committed, not to any of the service arms, but deployed for internal security duties.[65]

In the light of the above, London decided there was no need to reinforce the Hong Kong garrison, though a brigade could be held ready in Britain for that purpose. The colony faced serious challenges, of that there was no doubt. But its rulers appeared to believe that plans and preparations were in hand to meet most contingencies. Events on the middle Yangtze would soon force them to change their minds.

Notes

1   Lai Tse-han, Ramon H. Myers and Wei Wou, *A Tragic Beginning: The Taiwan Uprising of February 28, 1947* (Stanford, CA: Stanford University Press, 1991), p. 45.

2   Stephen R. Mackinnon, Diana Lary and Ezra Vogel (eds), *China at War: Regions of China, 1937–45* (Stanford, CA: Stanford University Press, 2007), p. 342.

3   Jay Taylor, *The Generalissimo: Chiang Kai-shek and the Struggle for Modern China* (Cambridge, MA: Harvard University Press, 2009), pp. 362–3.

4   *Far Eastern Economic Review*, 4 May 1949 (title page).

5   *The Economist*, 23 July 1949, p. 195.

6   The distinction is also expressed linguistically in terms of the predominantly Mandarin-speaking mainlanders and the earlier, Fujianese (*minnan hua)* speaking inhabitants who formed the majority of the population.

7   Lin Tongfa, *1949 Da chetui* ('1949: The Great Withdrawal') (Taipei: Lianjing chuban shiye youxian gongsi, 2009), pp. 49–50.

8   *The Economist*, 25 December 1948, p. 21; *Daily Express*, 3 January 1949, p. 2.

9   Mark O'Neill, *The Miraculous History of China's Two Palace Museums* (Hong Kong: Joint Publishing (HK) Ltd, 2015), p. 221.

10 Zhongyang yanjiuyuan jindaishi yanjiusuo, *Bai Chongxi xiansheng fangwen jilu* ('A Record of Interviews with Mr Bai Chongxi') (Taipei: Zhongyang yanjiuyuan jindaishi yanjiusuo, 1984), Vol. 2, pp. 864–5.

11 Taylor, *The Generalissimo*, p. 399.

12 Dong Xianguang, *Jiang zongtong zhuan*, Vol. 3 ('A Biography of President Jiang') (Taipei: zhonghua wenhua chuban shiye weiyuanhui, 1954), pp. 519–20.

13 Mark O'Neill, *The Miraculous History of China's Two Palace Museums* p. 222.

14 Lin Hsiao-ting, *Accidental State: Chiang Kai-shek, the United States and the Making of Taiwan* (Cambridge, MA: Harvard University Press, 2016), p. 83.

15 Wu Xingyong, *Huangjin midang: yijiusijiunian dalu huangjin yuntai shimo* ('The Chinese Secret Archives of Gold: How the Mainland's Gold Was Moved to Taiwan') (Nanjing: Jiangsu renmin chubanshe, 2009), p. 7, note 4.

16 O'Neill, *The Miraculous History of China's Two Palace Museums*, pp. 203–9; Lin Tongfa (2009) p. 254.

17 Lin Tongfa (2009) p. 240.

18 Lin Tongfa (2009) p. 244.

19 TNA FO371/75734, 4 January, 1949, p. 81

20 TNA FO371/75734, 4 January, 1949, p. 84

21 Sherman Cochran and Andrew Hsieh, *The Lius of Shanghai* (Cambridge, MA: Harvard University Press, 2013), p. 357 et seq.

22 Cochran and Hsieh, p. 282

23 This account of the fate of the SS *Taiping* draws on Lin Tongfa, *1949 Da chetui*, pp. 291–4; 'The Forgotten Wreck', *China Report*, January 2015, pp. 42–6, 68; and 'Taiping Sinking Recalled', *Taipei Times*, 28 January 2008, pp. 2–3.

24 Helen Zia, *Last Boat out of Shanghai: The Epic Story of the Chinese Who Fled Mao's Revolution* (New York: Ballantine Books, 2019), p. xxiv.

25 'The Forgotten Wreck', p. 45.

26 Ibid., p. 46.

27 Ibid., p. 68 et seq.

28 Joshua Fan, *China's Homeless Generation: Voices from the Veterans of the Chinese Civil War, 1940s–1990s* (London: Routledge, 2009), p. 7.

29 Long Yingtai, *Da Jiang Da Hai 1949* ('Vast Rivers, Vast Seas 1949') (Hong Kong: Cosmos Books, 2015 edition), pp. 38–9.

30 This account of Mei Jun's wandering is based on that told by her daughter, Long Yingtai, ibid., pp. 35, 56–7 and passim.

31 See Chapter 7, p. 203.

32 Zhang Renyi, *1949 Zhongguo Shehui* ('1949: Chinese Society') (Beijing: Shehui kexue wenxian chubanshe, 2005), p. 54.

33 Monitoring Service of the British Broadcasting Corporation, *Summary of World Broadcasts, Part V: The Far East* (hereafter *SWB*) No. 3, 10 May 1949, p. 29.

34 TNA FO371/8246, 23 May 1949, pp. 9–11.

35 *Time*, 7 February 1949, p. 15.

36 *Far Eastern Economic Review*, 19 January 1949, p. 66.

37 Ibid.

38 Chiang Kai-shek, *China's Destiny* (New York: Da Capo Press, 1976 edition), p. 143. (*China's Destiny* was first published in 1947.)

39 DBPO, pp. 80, 84.

40 Harold Ingrams, *Hong Kong* (London: Her Majesty's Stationery Office, 1952), p. 272. Ingrams conducted his research for this book during a visit to Hong Kong from March to May 1950.

41 Graham Hutchings, *Modern China: A Companion to a Rising Power* (London: Penguin Books, 2000), pp. 327–9.

42 Alexander Grantham, *Via Ports: From Hong Kong to Hong Kong* (Hong Kong: Hong Kong University Press, 2012 edition), p. 107.

43 Kwasi Kwarteng, *Ghosts of Empire: Britain's Legacies in the Modern World* (London: Bloomsbury, 2011), p. 353.

44 Grantham, *Via Ports*, p. 138.

45 David Bellis, *Old Hong Kong Photos and the Stories They Tell*, Vol. 1 (Hong Kong: Gwulo, 2017), p. 101.

46 Ingrams, *Hong Kong*, p. 114.

47 Grantham, *Via Ports*, p. 129.

48 Long Yingtai, *Da Jiang Da Hai 1949*, pp. 152–3.

49 *Far Eastern Economic* Review, 13 April 1949 (title page).

50 *Far Eastern Economic Review*, 9 February 1949 (title page).

51 *Colonial Reports, Hong Kong 1948* (London: His Majesty's Stationery Office), p. 9 and *Colonial Reports, Hong Kong 1949*, p. 12.

52 *Far Eastern Economic Review*, 8 December 1948, p. 601

53 Ibid.

54 *Colonial Reports, Hong Kong 1949*, p. 88.

55 Ibid., p. 82.

56 Paddy Ashdown, *A Fortunate Life: The Autobiography of Paddy Ashdown* (London: Aurum Press, 2009), p. 128.

57 Long Yingtai, *Da Jiang Da Hai 1949*, p. 146.

58 See Chapter 2, p. 71.

59 Grantham, *Via Ports*, pp. 132–3.

60 Michael Y. M. Kau and John K. Leung (eds), *The Writings of Mao Zedong, 1949–1956 Vol 1, September 1949–December 1955* (New York: M. E. Sharpe, 1986), p. 53. Mao was responding to complaints by some Communist Party members that Li Jishen received preferential financial treatment once he had joined the government in Beijing.

61 DBPO, p. 217.

62 Steve Tsang (ed.), *A Documentary History of Hong Kong: Government and Politics* (Hong Kong: Hong Kong University Press, 1995), p. 283.

63 DBPO, p. 226.

64 Ibid., p. 227.

65 *Colonial Reports: Hong Kong 1948*, p. 3.

5

Crossing the river

'Oh, the South is great!'

In early March, a member of the communist Third Field Army arrived on the northern shore of the mighty river to conduct reconnaissance. Along with the Second Field Army, the Third had been ordered, when the moment came, to force its way across the Yangtze and take Nanjing, Shanghai and the other cities that lie on the southern banks. But the officer did not like what he saw. 'We took Weixian [a small town in Shandong, his home province] despite the height of the city walls', he declared. 'We have no fears about fighting on the plains. But fighting on the water is another matter entirely. We can't cope with that.'[1]

He was not alone. During the past year, communist soldiers had proved themselves superb fighters, and their commanders gifted strategists. They had been remarkably successful at making the transition from guerrilla to positional warfare involving large standing armies. They had inflicted huge defeats on Chiang's at first far superior forces.

But for the most part the big battles that destroyed Nationalist power had been fought in the hills and plains of Manchuria and North and Central China. What confronted them now was a type of amphibious war, followed by fighting in the hills, valleys and rivers of tropical south China, a 'huge waterland'.[2] In almost everything from culture to climate, this was a part of the country and the home of people unfamiliar to the northerners, who formed the majority of the Field Armies' rank and file. It is no wonder that artillerymen, surveying the scene in front of them, feared that their weapons would fall overboard during the crossing, that communications teams fretted over the lack of telephone and other links between north and south banks of the river, that military runners worried that, once over the other side, they would soon lose their way, and that members of the observer corps doubted they would be able to conceal themselves in the unfamiliar territory that beckoned in the distance. Some soldiers even complained about the 'numerous poisonous snakes in the Yangtze delta'.[3]

On 10 February, the Central Military Committee had alerted the Field Army commanders responsible for leading the charge south how important it was to acquire some basic understanding of the terrain. They were asked to produce 'basic maps' of the south (and other parts of the country yet to be conquered), 'showing the main rivers, mountain ranges, provincial borders, the names of large and medium-sized cities . . . complete with figures on their respective populations' for distribution to officers at various levels.[4] No doubt such requests were designed to quell anxieties of the kind that gave rise to comic verse often heard among the ranks that went as follows:

Oh, the South is great, the South is great!
You can't understand the language
The food leaves you hungry
The roads are narrow
And you sleep in the rice fields
The muddy roads are so slippery you can't move
It's cloudy all day
And the weather is really atrocious[5]

Such sentiments reflect the fact that the communists not only had to overcome a formidable physical barrier before they could conquer the rest of the country. They also had to cross a cultural, political and economic divide. For the Yangtze divided, as it still does, the predominantly wheat-eating, Mandarin-speaking, rather more conservative people of north China, with their generally closer association with the country's 'grand tradition' of imperial power, from the rice-eating, dialect-speaking, more freewheeling, commercially minded southern Chinese, whose prosperous towns and cities enjoyed close links with the Chinese diaspora and the wider world in general. It was the boundary, if not exactly between two worlds, at least between the main two 'sub-regions' that make up China.

It is true that, in keeping with China's modern revolutionary tradition, Chinese communism had been born in the south. Many of its leaders, Mao, Liu Shaoqi and Lin Biao among them, hailed from the southern provinces and knew conditions there well. But largely because Chiang's military campaigns had driven the communists out of south China, the movement had grown to maturity in the different social and economic settings of the north. It was there, and in Manchuria, that they had won their most significant victories to date. And it was there that they had recruited most of their soldiers, cadres and supporters. Thus, as expert on the communist military William W. Whitson put it, conducting 'people's war' in the south was, 'dependent on the organising energies of northern outsiders'.[6]

Of course, communist organizations had remained active on a small scale south of the Yangtze since the Long March, both in the larger cities and parts of the countryside. And they had by now stepped up their activities, drawing strength (as well as government reprisals) from the stunning victories their comrades had chalked up in the north. Guerrilla units operated in the more remote parts of several southern provinces; and were a force to be reckoned with in the special conditions that obtained on Hainan Island, China's second largest island after Taiwan, which was then part of Guangdong province.

Pan Zongwu, thirty-eight, a county magistrate in the relatively prosperous eastern part of Guangxi around Wuzhou, the major trading port on the West River, was among those officials who found themselves dealing with insurrection at the grassroots level. Guangxi was still a long way from the front line. But in the spring of 1949, local communists raised a small force just over the border in Guangdong province. They began to move towards the richer towns and villages within Pan's jurisdiction. 'I mobilised the county militia to block their approach and patrol the region so as to gather intelligence about what was going on', he wrote. Such measures 'comforted the local people'.[7] In Wuzhou itself 'hidden communists' were said to be at work. They included a female official who was arrested but later released because of lack of evidence, and a man who had worked in the city government for years before suddenly leaving Wuzhou to join the guerrillas in Guangdong. 'He had been very skilled in the art of concealment', Pan grudgingly conceded.[8]

The CCP had an underground network in many southern provinces but it was small in scale and obviously dangerous for its members to 'break cover' too soon. Until communist armies crossed the river, the middle and lower Yangtze provinces were by and large 'Nationalist country': the government faced little significant threat to its control of the major cities, towns and main lines of communication in south China, despite its unpopularity, economic mismanagement and the public yearning for peace.

This meant that the communists had to tread carefully once they had accomplished the crossing. Su Yu, second in command of the Third Field Army, warned his troops: 'Nanjing, Shanghai and Hangzhou form the economic, political and cultural core of the Guomindang reactionary clique and exercise an important influence in the wider international world . . . If we do not carry out Party policy well, we shall be politically isolated.'[9] Soldiers should expect to encounter prosperity of a kind they had not seen before. But they should not jump to conclusions and risk losing public support by adopting harsh, confiscatory measures. 'It is important to understand the conditions of the Southerners', Su Yu insisted. 'In Nanjing and Shanghai people eat "large pancakes"', meaning living standards were relatively high – or at least they were so as seen from the perspective of Shandong (where many of the East China Field Army troops came from). 'But it would be a great mistake to imagine that everyone who eats "large pancakes" is a landlord. And the same is true for those middle peasants who might have several dishes at each meal; they too are not to be thought of as landlords.'[10]

Thus, to cross the Yangtze was for the communists a momentous matter in many respects. Mao and his commanders had to surmount a major physical obstacle and then wage revolutionary war in what to some extent amounted to another world – one marked by political, social and economic complexities, and one still in the (admittedly weakening) grip of an apparently formidable Nationalist military machine that might yet be capable of putting up something of a fight.

The Yangtze is 'worth 300,000 soldiers'

The Yangtze 'front' extended for some 1,100 miles, from close to Shanghai in the east to Wuhan, the 'city in the centre of China'. Along it flowed one of the mightiest rivers in the world, rising in the Tibetan plateau and coursing eastwards, often in the form of great arcs and loops, watering the fertile lowlands, China's food basket, sustaining the vast population of some 180 million in the towns and great cities along its banks, and finally debouching into the East China Sea. There was not a single bridge along its entire length; instead, ferry boats linked north and south at hundreds of points along the riverbanks.

FIGURE 5.1 *The Great Retreat – 1: Nationalist troops head south for the Yangtze.*

FIGURE 5.2 *The Great Retreat - 2: Nationalist armies board ship for the imagined safety south of the 'Long River'.*

The span, depth and flow of the river varied dramatically, depending on its course and the season. At Jiangyin city, at the eastern end of the front, a major government fortress presided over a relatively narrow point, down river of which the span opened up to some 10,000 yards, a few miles above Shanghai. At the capital Nanjing, 2,000–2,500 yards of water separated the north and south banks, depending on tide and season. Along the stretch between the southern riverine cities of Hukou and Wuhu, in the critical western section of the front, some 1,000 and 1,500 yards of water lay between 'north' and 'south' China.

Further west still, the appearance of the Yangtze in Wuhan was little changed from that described half a century earlier by Isabella Bird, the great Victorian explorer: 'The glory of Hankow [part of Wuhan], as well as its terror, is the magnificent Yangtze, nearly a mile wide even in winter, rolling majestically past the bund, lashed into a dangerous fury by storms, or careering buoyantly before breezes; in summer an inland sea fifty feet deep.'[11]

In some stretches, the tidal effects were significant, the current fast flowing. At low water in some parts, various islands were exposed, potentially making a military crossing easier. Yet water levels could rise quickly, especially during the spring floods. Low-lying rice fields on both banks were then flooded, making large-scale movement of troops difficult. In other respects, conditions on the northern and southern banks differed: with the partial exception of Wuhan, the centres of population were on the southern side of the river, along with the road, rail and other means of communications that linked them together.

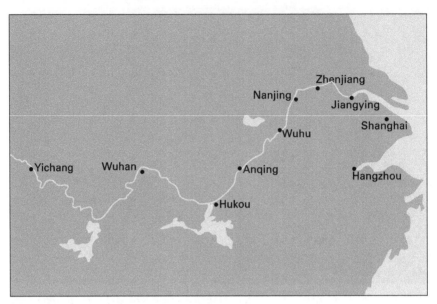

MAP 5.1 *The 'Yangtze front' in the spring of 1949.*

On paper, Nationalist plans to defend the Yangtze were impressive. In practice, they were impaired by disagreements between Chiang and Li, each of whom wanted to preserve the military forces loyal to them to fight another day – in Chiang's case, eventually from a new base in Taiwan; in Li's, by keeping a grip on the south and southwest provinces, where his support was strongest. This discord would cost the government dear.

Chiang's man, Tang Enbo, Commander of the Nanjing–Shanghai Garrison, had 450,00 men under him spread along some 500 miles of the Yangtze 'front' from Hukou to Shanghai, with some troops occupying fortified strong points on the north bank. He was responsible for the defence of South Jiangsu, South Anhui, Zhejiang and Jiangxi provinces. His aim, with air and naval support, was to halt the communists in mid-crossing or decimate them in the shallows on the southern side. Should this fail, Li hoped Tang's forces would fall back on the Zhejiang–Jiangxi railway, about 120 miles to the south where they would form a new defence line. Instead, Chiang ordered Tang to concentrate his forces in and around Shanghai, from where, if necessary, he could evacuate them to Taiwan, via Zhoushan Island, which he had ordered be turned into a fortress. Chiang Ching-kuo said that the very first thing his father did when he stepped down from the presidency was to order the construction of a large airfield at Dinghai, on Zhoushan, and that he constantly asked for updates on how the work was progressing.[12]

Bai Chongxi, Commander, Central China Headquarters, had at least 250,000 men at his disposal, the best of them his own Guangxi forces. He was responsible for the defence of the Yangtze from Hukou, west, through

Wuhan (location of his HQ), to Ichang, beyond which navigation was difficult and a military crossing implausible. Bai also had strong garrisons to the south in Nanchang and Changsha, capitals of Jiangxi and Hunan provinces respectively.

Alongside these land forces, the government could call, at least notionally, on two naval flotillas consisting of roughly 100 vessels of various sizes deployed around major towns and cities along the Yangtze front. That all was not well in the Nationalist navy was apparent at the end of February, when the crew of the cruiser *Chongqing*, unhappy about not being paid and disillusioned with the way the war was going, mutinied. They forced the captain to sail north to communist-controlled territory where, just as the PLA launched the Yangtze crossing, Nationalist planes bombed and sank her. Further naval defections were in store, as would soon become apparent. Yet the fact remained that the Nationalists had a navy (of sorts), while the communists did not.

The same was true of an air force: the government could deploy about 300 aircraft to patrol the skies above the Yangtze Valley from bases in Nanjing, Shanghai and Wuhan. The communists had no air cover at all – another potential hazard to their enterprise, should the Nationalists prove capable of mounting a coordinated defence from land, water and air.

There was a further consideration on the minds of Mao and his military chiefs: the presence of British and US warships in Shanghai, which, according to an official PLA history, they feared 'could mount an armed intervention as our troops crossed the river'.[13] Such anxieties would to some extent be realized – though in the form of the clash between communist troops and the British warship HMS *Amethyst* and the ships that tried to rescue her, rather than a determined or organized effort on the part of the powers to stop or slow the communist advance.

In principle, then, government forces ought at least to have been able to give military planners on the communist side pause. Indeed, US Ambassador Leighton Stuart, hardly one to overestimate the military capabilities of the Nationalists, noted that 'one of the highly competent younger men in the Ministry of National Defense' had told him that the Yangtze, in defence terms, was 'worth 300,000 soldiers'. And the ambassador's own military aides were of the view that 'with the coordination of the ground, naval and air forces and unified command in their Ministry, together with payment of the troops in silver and decent care of them, they could have at least held the river for several months and quite possibly have led the Communists to change their overall policy'.[14] Such an assessment was based on big assumptions.

A question of timing

If the embattled leadership in Nanjing was playing for time in demanding peace talks with the communists and sending delegates to conduct them in

Beiping, so were Mao and his lieutenants. Whatever might happen at the negotiating table, they were set on the conquest of south China. But the communist armies had to be rested and reorganized after their recent stunning victories. They were also re-designated, exchanging their regional affiliations for a simple numerical classification that reflected the fact that they would soon be operating in parts of the country far from where they had made their name and raised most of their recruits. The reshuffle reinforced an affiliation between commanders and men, and a relationship between both and the Central Military Committee, that would have a lasting impact on political and military affairs long after the civil war.

The reorganization took place between February and March. It resulted in the formation of four Field Armies with a total strength of some four million. This compared with 1.4 million on the government side, perhaps half of whom were effective fighting troops.

The Northwest Field Army became the First Field Army under Peng Dehuai, fifty, an outstanding military leader from Hunan. It operated mainly in the northwest and was tasked with bringing this vast region under communist control. The Second Field Army, formed from the Central Plains Field Army, was commanded by Liu Bocheng, fifty-six, known as the 'one-eyed general' thanks to a wound sustained in an earlier battle, and who had recently (and erroneously) been reported to have been killed. Deng Xiaoping, forty-four, the short and stocky fellow Sichuanese who as an octogenarian would transform his country in the 1980s and 1990s, was the Second Field Army's Political Commissar. His role was to ensure that the men in uniform were indoctrinated in the Party's political goals.

Chen Yi, forty-seven, led the Third Field Army, formerly the East China Field Army. A rakish figure who often wore a beret, a habit acquired as a student in France, Chen was said to have 'grim features, cruel eyes, tightly clamped lips and a rugged jaw'.[15] He had spent much of his career in the south and commanded communist troops in the Huaihai campaign. He would later direct the conquest of Shanghai and serve as its first communist mayor. Rao Shushi, forty-five, later to fall victim to Mao's first post-1949 purge of senior Party leaders, was appointed Political Commissar. Lin Biao, the gifted architect of victory in Manchuria, was commander of the Fourth Field Army, formed from the Northeast Field Army. Luo Ronghuan, forty-six, a Sichuanese, was Political Commissar.

As early as 12 January 1949 Mao had instructed the commanders of what would become the Second and Third Field Armies to prepare for the Yangtze crossing and be ready to move by the end of March. A month later a General Front Committee was set up to plan and direct the operation. It concurred that a March crossing was desirable: to leave it much later would grant the enemy too much time to strengthen his defences, while the river's notorious spring tides might make things difficult.

Reconnaissance teams soon established themselves on the north bank and crossed the river on a regular basis to gather intelligence. One mission captured three Nationalist soldiers and took them back to the north bank for interrogation. The most senior among them told his captors that 'defences were weak and that there was no military strength in depth on the southern bank'. He helpfully went on to 'point out suitable landing points'.[16] Here was a comforting indication, alongside several others, that though crossing the Yangtze carried risks, enemy resistance might not amount to much. During March and April, troops of the Second, Third and Fourth Field Armies moved close to the northern banks, ready for the signal to take to the water and surge across into south China.

On the issue of timing, Mao may not have had the free hand he would have wished for. Stalin was still wary of what he regarded as Mao's 'adventurism' and troubled by his questionable adherence to the Soviet leader's definition of ideological orthodoxy. He had pressured Mao into holding peace talks with the Nationalists. And if remarks at the time, unearthed in recent years, are to be believed, he was still concerned that the United States would intervene militarily if it looked as though the Nationalist government was about to collapse. 'In January 1949, although a tremendous shift in power had occurred between the GMD and CCP forces, Stalin's position would still not change', wrote scholar Kim Donggil.[17] The Soviet leader hoped that the peace talks might deliver a less risky outcome than war as far as Moscow's interests were concerned.

Complaints by Chinese leaders that the Soviet leader had tried to halt the crossing of the Yangtze would later surface on several occasions. What is now clear is that Mao voiced them at the time, noting, shortly before the peace talks started on 1 April, that: 'Some of our international friends hold a doubtful attitude towards the victory of China's War of Liberation, advising us to stop and together with Chiang Kai-shek establish "Northern and Southern" dynasties with the Yangtze River as the demarcation line.'[18] The assault across the Yangtze was certainly delayed on several occasions to see if peace talks could result in an accord.[19]

There was discord, too, over exactly when the communists should set up their new state and national government. At first, Moscow wanted this to take place as soon as communist forces had captured Nanjing and Shanghai. This was too soon as far as Mao was concerned, for it suggested, as Kim notes, that he would have to compromise with the remnant Nationalist forces who were bound to try and regroup and resist from a new base in Guangzhou or elsewhere. 'We don't need to hurry, we still need one or two years to take complete control of China both politically and economically', Mao insisted.[20]

Mao could not afford to wait much longer in moving his armies across the Yangtze and deal what he hoped would be the death blow to Chiang's regime. Certainly, there could be no question of a north–south split along the river that runs through the heart of China. China's long history furnished at least one example – the Southern Song (1127–1279) – of a dynasty that used its control of the rich resources of the Middle Yangtze to perpetuate a division of the country between north and south. This was exactly what the Nationalists hoped to do in order to survive. They controlled much of south China by retaining their grip on the provinces and cities of the delta. Any 'northern regime', including that of the communists, would find it hard to prosper, perhaps even to survive for long, if it did not exercise control over the huge population and commercial wealth of the Yangtze Valley.

Mao was therefore determined to dislodge Chiang's regime from its base and destroy it, not simply drive it deep into the southwest as the Japanese had done in the late 1930s, where it might survive and secure renewed US support. And the only way to do this was to cross the river and unify the country from the north. Historian Wang Gungwu, reflecting on patterns of unity and disunity in Chinese history, noted: 'Conquest from the north . . . seemed always to lead to the unification of China. Control of this region [the Yangtze Valley] was therefore a critical factor in the balance between unification and division.'[21]

Agents of change: the 'south-bound cadres'

So much for strategic logic, grounded in China's long historical experience. Yet the military dimension was only part of the story: the communists intended to rule *and* reorder society in the cities, towns and countryside of the south just as they had in the north. That meant mobilizing large numbers of politically reliable, competent administrators. Their role would be to take over the functions of government, support the front-line troops, restore production and normal commercial life, set up new 'people's organs of power', suppress what would often prove to be severe, widespread and protracted outbreaks of banditry, organize the peasantry to carry out land reform, and generally build the new revolutionary society from the ground up. Such people would be expected to work alongside members of the local CCP underground, which varied from place to place in both number and quality, and those mid- and lower-ranking GMD officials who either chose not to flee or lacked the means to do so, and whose experience and expertise would be needed to help stabilize the new regime.

Recruiting the right sort of people on the required scale was an enormous task. As Deng Xiaoping pointed out as early as August 1948: 'Based on the experience of administering the Central China region, for every area with a population of 100 million, we will need 30–40,000 cadres [officials]. I hope the Central Committee will make plans accordingly.'[22] It did, calculating that during the next one to two years the Party could end up administering an additional population of 160 million spread across 500 counties and several medium-sized and large cities. To do so, it would need an estimated 53,000 administrators at various levels.[23]

This new force, though not part of the regular army, would perform both military and civilian duties, and would be recruited in the 'old liberated areas', namely northeast, north and central China. Large contingents were to be raised in Shanxi, Shandong and Henan provinces, especially in those areas where the communists had established 'base areas' and acquired experience in running things.

'Rawer' recruits would be sought among students and staff of leading universities and middle schools in Beiping and Tianjin, injecting a welcome supply of educated people into the Party's ranks: there were at this time only about 40,000 college graduates among its 4.4 million members, less than 1 per cent.[24] Lin Biao's Fourth Field Army thus appealed for 10,000 'young intellectuals' to accompany or follow its planned drive south, where its main task was to destroy Bai Chongxi's military power and impose communist rule in Hubei, Hunan, Guangdong and Guangxi provinces. CCP leaders feared that many people in this vast region of China would respond without much enthusiasm to the idea of 'liberation'.

Yet there was no lack of eagerness among the academic communities of Beiping to the idea of going south, if a communist account is to be believed. 'Once the appeal had been launched, numerous people signed up, in an atmosphere of great excitement', said one of the organizers. 'Several professors were among those who registered ... and before long the recruitment [quota] was complete.'[25]

The raising, training and assignment, often to distant places in dangerous circumstances, of the 'south-bound cadres' (nanxia ganbu), as they were known, would continue throughout 1949 and in some areas remain an important feature of life in the early years of the People's Republic. During the Civil War, recruitment took place in 'waves', as new groups of would-be administrators were sent south in the wake of the rapidly advancing communist forces. 'The Party has entrusted to us the glorious task of liberating the great southwest', First Field Army General He Long told cadets at a cadre training school in Shanxi in May 1949. 'In the past, Southern comrades came to the North to fight the Japanese imperialists and liberate Northern people ... It is now the job of comrades from the North to wage revolution in the South and liberate the people there, thoroughly eradicating the reactionary rule of the GMD.'[26]

Shanxi's role in the recruitment of south-band cadres bears closer examination because it helps explain the outcome of the Civil War as well as some of its consequences. On the one hand, it illustrates the resourcefulness of the communists as they went about their capture of the country. On the other, it was part of the large-scale movement of Chinese people that took place during the conflict – in this case of those who travelled great distances in the cause of building of a 'new' China, as distinct from the even larger numbers of refugees who were desperate to escape from it.

In short, like the Sino-Japanese War before it, the Civil War uprooted many millions of Chinese people, willingly or unwillingly. Most of them ended up in unexpected, unfamiliar even alien places where they were subjected to widely different experiences. For many, it boiled down to bitter loss and painful separation. For others, notably the south-bound cadres, the personal and collective odysseys were a source of personal as well as national pride and the cause of genuine revolutionary enthusiasm. In many cases, the fact they worked and settled in 'distant' parts of the country – often for years, even decades – challenged and changed longstanding provincial identities, certainly at the elite level. Traditional bonds of native place and ties to local leadership networks were weakened by freshly minted 'revolutionary' affiliations forged during the construction of 'new' China.

It was not all smooth sailing: many locals in the southern provinces at first regarded the outsiders or 'northerners' almost as invaders, their doctrines as unwelcome and unintelligible (at least to many) as their language. Yet it is not only for propaganda purposes (though it certainly aids that function) that both a popular and scholarly literature has emerged in China in recent years, celebrating the contribution of the *nanxia ganbu*.[27] They made a mark on their country that will not easily be forgotten.

In the case of Shanxi, between Japan's surrender in August 1945 and the establishment of the People's Republic in October 1949, the province mobilized more than 20,000 cadres to work in communist administrations at various levels, along with several hundred thousand labourers and militia who supported front-line troops engaged in major battles.[28] As the need for capable people intensified in 1948–9, recruiters turned to the Taihang and Taiyue districts of the province, respectively northeast, close to the border with Hubei, and southwest of Taiyuan, the provincial capital, where regional Nationalist chief Yan Xishan managed to survive a bitter and bloody communist siege until late April. Both regions had been in communist hands for some time.

Recruits, some of whom had taken part in the Long March, conducted land-reform campaigns, or administered communist-held-territory during the war against Japan, were moved south in stages and given special training in the Party's latest policies. Much attention was devoted to the new focus on the cities, how they were to be run, and how residents and Nationalist officials who had stayed behind were to be treated. They also spent time studying conditions, insofar as this was possible, in the various places to which they were assigned. Some were to form the kernel of new Party and government organizations set up to run the south or perform support functions for the regular troops as they brought the new territories to heel.

Detailed regulations were drawn up setting out, among other things, that each cadre was to be 'issued with one suit of clothes and one pair of shoes . . .' for the journey south; that those above a certain rank 'could take with them an ox and one horse and rider'; while those at another level could, when travelling in a group of forty, hire a truck to carry their belongings. Anyone who owned a bicycle was welcome to take it with them, but there was no question of the Party paying for repairs.[29] The length of journey and types of transport varied enormously, as one might expect. It was usually undertaken by train, jeep or ferry at some stage, but it always meant much walking, often in difficult terrain physically or because of the presence of marginal groups opposed to the presence of 'outsiders' of any kind.

Some of the south-bound cadres were not at all keen on the idea of life in the south, as was the case with many regular soldiers. Some deserted en route.[30] Many more were reluctant to leave family or dependants behind for an indefinite period. The Party tried to meet these anxieties by promising to treat such family members on the same basis as military dependants, supplying them with basic necessities until families could be reunited again, in some cases a matter of many years.

For all the planning and organization that went into this enterprise, things often had to be changed at the last minute. In the case of the so-called 'Yangtze Detachment', a 3,500-strong unit raised in Shanxi during the first few weeks of 1949, it was at first decided that it would administer much of newly 'liberated' southern Jiangsu – that part of the province where the Nationalist capital was located. Its members would cross the Yangtze a few days after the PLA and hopefully set to work. But by the time they arrived in Nanjing, which they did on 12 May, another contingent of cadres had beaten them to it and taken up the reins. The Yangtze Detachment was thus told to move southeast to the suburbs of Suzhou and await further instructions.

When these eventually came, nearly two months later, another journey was in store: the detachment was told to follow units of the Third Field Army into Fujian province, much further to the south. The mission now was to help administer large parts of a province in which Nationalist troops were still active, and whose people were not only famously suspicious of outsiders but, unhelpfully, spoke a dialect that was impenetrable as far as northerners and most other people in the country were concerned. The peregrinations of the Yangtze Detachment, which ended up hundreds of miles from the river after which it had been named, reflected the unexpected speed with which the PLA would conquer the south, and the communists' ability to deploy personnel critical to their cause so effectively.

Other south-bound cadres from Shanxi were assigned to the southern province of Hunan, and to Sichuan and Xikang, respectively the largest and smallest provincial units in the southwest. When the Hunan contingent was raised, Bai Chongxi's Central Army controlled this province from his HQ in Wuhan. It was far from clear that he could easily be ejected from the area. But the communists were determined to do so and planned accordingly.

In March, they proclaimed a 'Hunan Provincial People's Government' headed by Huang Kecheng, a Hunanese communist who had worked with Mao for years. It was at first based in Tianjin, hundreds of miles away. Governments and party organizations for other provinces were set up in convenient, secure centres from which they might be moved rapidly south to takeover responsibilities in their designated areas once the PLA had cleared or crushed organised military opposition. For example, in August, some 3,000 south-bound cadres from Shanxi would move swiftly into the towns and cities of Hunan when the provincial Nationalist leaders threw in their lot with the communists and Bai's armies were forced to retreat further south. Like the regular troops, many of them would they end up hundreds, sometime thousands, of miles from their home.

Ships and sailors

Of course, the south-bound Cadres could accomplish little if the PLA failed to cross the Yangtze and inflict a heavy blow on the Nationalist armies. The General Front Committee in charge of planning the operation thus bore a heavy responsibility. Its Guiding Document declared: 'Provided we are successful in carrying out the river crossing, no matter what the enemy does, the military situation is going to change in our favour; and it could cause complete chaos in the enemy camp.'[31]

Third Field Army units had begun training for the crossing in early March. On lakes and rivers in the two-thirds of Anhui province that was north of the Yangtze and thus in communist hands, troops had practised embarking and disembarking on small boats, loading and unloading weapons, acquiring navigational skills, plugging leaks, swimming and conducting life-saving exercises. Third Field Army commander Chen Yi said: 'These rigorous preparations had the effect of turning northerners into southerners, a land army into a water army, and the vast and mighty Yangtze into a main road.'[32]

To cross the river the communists needed boats – sampans, junks, narrow fishing vessels, rafts, anything they could get their hands on. That is why, when the Nationalists withdrew from the north to the south bank, they took with them as many craft as they could and destroyed those they left behind. The communists thus had to look further afield for means of crossing the river, which in turn meant conscripting both boatmen and their vessels over a wide area, well away from the Yangtze. Many locals, seeing what was coming, hid their craft before they could be commandeered.

Nevertheless, communist accounts state that by the beginning of April, the Third Field Army alone had obtained some 20,900 craft of various kinds, of which around 8,300 could be used for fighting their way across the River. Deng Xiaoping reported that of these, the small boats could carry eight to ten people, the larger ones fifty and the largest of all a hundred.[33]

So much for the armada, which essentially was a vast fleet of civilian, unarmed and unprotected craft. Sailors were also needed to get the communist armies across the Yangtze. Again, this was not easy. Boatmen were in those days organized into feudal guilds, to which most were fiercely loyal. The PLA used blandishments and doubtless less agreeable methods to persuade these independently minded craftsmen to ferry them to the opposite bank, which they would very possibly have to do under fire and for an uncertain reward. Promises of compensation and efforts to induce class consciousness among members of this specialist profession and win them over to the revolutionary cause can have gone only so far.

To preserve the advantage of surprise, thousands of commandeered vessels were kept some way from the riverbanks until the actual crossing. Otherwise, they would have been an easy target for the Nationalist air force, which having failed to distinguish itself in the war to date, might this late in the day make some amends. The flotillas were thus secreted in creeks, inlets, behind dikes and on small lakes. This proved an advantage when the order to advance came because the Nationalists did not know where the boats were coming from. It was not so much from the waterways but overland: many were dragged to the banks of the Yangtze along gullies specially cut for the purpose.

Arms, ammunition and equipment had to be transported across the Yangtze, too – though not military rations. The Central Committee made it clear that it was up to the southern provinces to feed their liberators, not the northern 'rear' areas from which they had sprung. The PLA would impose grain levies, much as the Nationalists had, with the difference that the biggest obligations would be placed on large landlords and rich peasants. Poor peasants would be exempt. Provisioning the PLA turned out to be problematic. This was especially true of the Fourth Field Army, whose thrust south from Wuhan placed a heavy burden on farmers.[34]

By early April, with preparations close to complete, communist forces were concentrated in four key theatres along a vast stretch of the north bank. The Central Assault Group, made up of some 300,000 troops drawn from the Third Field Army, was tasked with crossing southwest of Nanjing, between Wuhu, a former treaty port on the south bank, and Anqing, on the north bank, about 100 miles to the southwest. Since the Yangtze flows in a northeasterly direction along this stretch, the communist thrust would be towards the southeast. Its aim was to trap those Nationalist troops that were expected to flee south to escape communist armies that crossed the river lower down. It was therefore decided that Central Assault Group would begin its offensive a day earlier than the other formations.

The Eastern Assault Group, some 350,000 men also drawn from the Third Field Army, was responsible for forcing its way across the generally much wider reaches east of Nanjing. It massed along the stretch from Jiangyin to Zhenjiang, another former treaty port, close to the capital. The immediate aim, once across the water, was to cut road and rail connections to Shanghai and Hangzhou, the city that formed the southern tip of an inverted triangle constituting the bastion of Nationalist power. Thus isolated, it was hoped that Nanjing would soon fall to the invaders.

The Western Assault Group, also comprising 350,000 troops but drawn mainly from the Second Field Army, constituted the PLA's right attacking flank. Its mission was to take the key centres from Anqing in the north to

Hukou in the south – in effect, the western end of the 'front'. Further west still, on the extreme right flank, was a mixed force of 200,000 troops, mostly composed of soldiers from Lin Biao's Fourth Field Army. Its function was to put pressure on Bai Chongxi, tie his troops down in Wuhan, and prevent them from attacking the flank of the Western Assault Group, whose aim was to advance as rapidly as possible and drive a wedge between the main Nationalist forces under Bai and Tang Enbo.

Crossings, crises, collapse

Events along a vast stretch of the Yangtze during the four days that began on 20 April surprised even those who had set little store on the Nationalists' ability to stem the communist tide. *Time* magazine told its world-wide readers of a 'stunning, swift disaster in China'. It went on: 'Nearly a million Communist troops along a 400-mile front poured across the broad Yangtze, Nationalist China's last great defensive barrier, and swept government positions aside like puny earthworks in a raging tide. The Communists moved with impressive speed. In four days, they took Nanking, cut off Shanghai and captured half a dozen strategic Nationalist cities.'[35]

Communist soldiers crossed the Yangtze first in the relatively narrow, twisty section, dotted with islands, between Wuhu and Anqing.[36] They did so during the early evening of Wednesday 20 April, after what had been a warm day with little wind, few waves and little evidence of unusual activity. 'The trees on the opposite bank afforded some inviting shade, and there was absolutely no sign that a major military conflict was about to break out', according to a recent account.[37]

Then, at 5 p.m., communist artillery opened up, and an armada of tiny boats emerged from their hiding places. 'The troops embarked without lights, lying on the gunwales, their weapons resting on the edge of the boats', said an observer. 'Thousands of white and rust-red sails were hoisted to the wind. The boast pushed off with cheering cargoes.'[38] A communist radio broadcast embroidered this account, though not apparently by much: 'The river rang with silvery notes of bugles and martial music . . . Boats by the thousands shuttled between the northern and southern banks . . . As 1,000 guns belched fire and smoke, the Yangtze waters were lit up with a watery glare.'[39]

The first boat to cross safely landed troops near Wuhu. Other vessels were hit by machine-gun fire as they approached the river bank. There was some hand-to-hand fighting in the shallows. But the defence was shambolic. Tang Enbo rushed to the area to try to stop the rout but it was too late. The defence lines had collapsed, his forces (the Nationalists 20th, 88th and 55th armies) had retreated. By dawn on 21 April perhaps as many as 300,000 communist troops had crossed the river, where they were said to have established a salient that extended for some 75 miles with a depth of 12 miles.[40]

Later the same morning, Zhou Enlai dropped by the Six Nations Hotel in Beiping where the government peace delegates were staying, to inform them that the PLA had just crossed the river. The game was up. Even Zhu, the man many regarded as the most suave of communist leaders, was apparently not beyond a bit of swagger when the occasion warranted. He hoped that the news would be conveyed to an anxious Li Zongreng in Nanjing and encourage him to throw in the towel before it was too late.

A few hours later, the action switched to the stretch of river east of the capital, close to where it suddenly sweeps south and spreads wide to meet the sea. The man at the centre of things here was Sixto Mercado Tiongco, a Filipino-Chinese better known to the communist troops under his command as General Ye Fei. He was in charge of the 10th Group Army, spearhead of the Eastern Assault Group. Just shy of his thirty-fifth birthday, Ye's task was to get his 28th, 29th and 31st armies across the Yangtze opposite Jiangyin, the fortified strongpoint that guarded one of the few choke points along this section of the river.

This was challenge enough. But during the previous twenty-four hours a new one had emerged in the form of a British warship, HMS *Amethyst*, a 1,350-ton frigate, rapidly steaming upriver to relieve HMS *Consort* of guardship duties in Nanjing. Her presence was the cause of a curious interlude, a small one in the context of the struggle for China, but no less telling for that.

A naval vessel from Britain or another country had been stationed at Nanjing on a rotating basis for some time to deliver supplies and provide assurance to the anxious foreign community. Should the need arise, it would assist with evacuation. For reasons that were controversial at the time and never satisfactorily explained since, *Amethyst* was ordered to sail from Shanghai to Nanjing, a roughly 170-mile journey, on the morning 19 April to take over such duties. Royal Navy commanders seem to have believed that she would reach the capital on 20 April, and that *Consort* would be back close enough to the safety of Shanghai before expiry of the midnight deadline, after which the communists had said their armies would cross the Yangtze by force unless the government accepted their peace terms.

The '*Amethyst* Incident' has received much attention in China and elsewhere, and it is the repercussions rather than the details that are of interest here.[41] The bare 'facts' are that on the morning of 20 April, while steaming upriver towards Zhenjiang, close to where the Grand Canal joins the Yangtze, *Amethyst* came under fire from communist batteries on the north shore, to which she might have been much closer than was either prudent or admitted by the Royal Navy at the time and for long thereafter.[42] She was badly damaged, many of her crew killed and/or seriously injured. She ran aground at what naval charts then called Rose Island.

Subsequent attempts by *Consort* later the same day, and the cruiser *London* and frigate *Black Swan* on 21 April, both of which had sailed up from Shanghai, to rescue *Amethyst* failed. Several members of the crew of *Consort* and *London* were killed or died of their wounds during heavy exchanges with shore batteries. The communists said 252 Chinese lost their lives due to the naval bombardment. An RAF Sunderland flying boat, sent up from Hong Kong, managed to alight on the river and transfer a doctor and medical supplies to *Amethyst*, but it, too, came under fire and was forced to leave almost immediately.

Amethyst, capable of some movement but badly crippled, was thus alone and, in a matter of hours, beyond rescue. A ship of the Royal Navy, long used to patrolling and policing Yangtze waters, had been damaged, some its crew killed and the vessel itself now hostage to the revolutionary forces reshaping China. Protracted negotiations with the communists to secure its release floundered on the refusal of the *Amethyst*'s captain to admit that she opened fire first, apologize and provide compensation.

In his memoirs, Ye Fei recalled that his lieutenants advised him on 21 April (that is, the day after initial clashes) that there was a foreign naval vessel in the zone in which his forces were preparing to cross the river. 'Our orders from Party Central were that, in the event of conflict with the imperialists, we should not fire the first shot, but if the imperialists fired on us, we should definitely fire back', he wrote.[43] Yet these were tense times: 'I considered the situation – it was only half an hour before we were due to cross the river. I told my troops to hoist a signal and order the ship out of our military zone. But it did not move as instructed. Instead, sailors moved towards the stern and targeted their guns on our positions. This was no time for indecision, so I gave the order to open fire. Great plumes of water shot up as our shells hit the surface.'[44]

When Third Field Army HQ asked him whether the foreign warship or the communist batteries had fired first, he said it was the former. He then made a pact with a fellow officer to maintain this line (or lie), noting that the two of them 'laughed a good deal about it in later years'.[45] He went on to make a politically more substantive point: 'What we bombarded was an English warship. What we in fact hit was the nerve centre of the imperialists, at last making them put an end to their rash actions.'[46]

Forty-five British naval crew, plus at least three Chinese serving them, lost their lives in the '*Amethyst* Incident', the largest single group of foreign nationals to be killed in China's Civil War. Historian Robert Bickers described it as 'the last overt Western military action in Chinese territory'. It was followed by a full (and similarly final) military burial of the British fallen in Shanghai's Hongqiao cemetery.[47] 'Whatever may be the division of opinion in Britain, there can be no doubt that British opinion in China will support the view that the Navy was acting wisely and in accordance with the best traditions in going about its normal duties', said the British-owned *North China Daily News* in what is perhaps best described as a last imperial hurrah sounded from inside mainland China.[48]

Amethyst's 100-day ordeal would end on 31 July when she escaped down the Yangtze under cover of darkness to re-join the British Fleet at the mouth of the river. Thanks to Britain's gift for turning a humiliation into a triumph, her 'dash for freedom' became a symbol of national daring once the ship reached Devonport at the end of October and her crew were later feted in London. But before then, the incident provoked controversy and heart-searching about Britain's handling of relations with the revolutionary forces gaining control over the whole of China and forced a major reassessment of the dangers the communist armies posed to its position in Hong Kong.

As for Ye Fei, the presence of British warships in his combat zone was an unwelcome complication but far from the biggest problem he faced. The river was 1,500 yards wide at Jiangyin, known as the 'gate of the river defences'. Whoever controlled it possessed a vital 'jumping off' point for the south and the east of the Yangtze Valley. Earlier in April a senior Nationalist commander had visited the site with a US military delegation to discuss ways of strengthening it. As long as the Jiangyin fortress was in government hands, the communists could expect to have trouble crossing the river at this point. It was too wide to cross further east; while to do so to the west would be too close to Nanjing.

It was fortunate, then, that the communist underground had been at work among the garrison forces. Tang Junzhao, a key figure in the Party's Central China Bureau, had spread the message that the government's cause was lost via his relatives who were serving in the Nationalist armies and happened to hold important positions in the fortress. There was a Party cell on the inside. When the attack began, at 5.30 p.m. on 21 April, the defectors took Dai Rongguang, commander of the fort, prisoner and made sure that the fort's guns fired neither on the PLA troops as they stormed across nor the small harbours in the vicinity where they safely disembarked. 'We could have crossed the Yangtze without the rebellion at Jiangyin, but we probably would have sustained much heavier losses', Ye conceded.[49]

The defection of the Second Naval Flotilla, stationed close to Nanjing, also made life easier for the communists than it might have been. This, too, was at least partly attributed to the Party underground – though it could have occurred without much instigation given the government's poor treatment of its sailors, in common with its soldiers and airmen.

The key figure here was Lin Zun, forty-four, then in command of a fleet of some twenty-five vessels of various kinds. Nanjing had assigned the Second Flotilla to Yangtze defence duties at the end of 1948. The sailors were no happier about this than they were about the way in which the Civil War was going generally. Guo Shousheng, a senior GMD naval commander and classmate of Lin's, was an underground Party member. He urged Lin

Zun to defect, which he duly agreed to do. It was then just a question of timing and coordination.

Lin let the underground know, on the eve of the crossing, that he would not impede the passage of troops. Indeed, when the PLA launched its offensive, in the Wuhu region, he disobeyed orders from navy chief Gui Yongqing to interdict the armada. On 22 April, by which time the PLA had crossed at several points, Gui ordered the Second Flotilla and other naval units forces to withdraw to the safety of Shanghai. Again, Lin resisted. And when the officers discovered that Gui himself had fled Nanjing, and other senior officials had flown south to Guangzhou, there was anger in the officers' mess. 'The senior staff cursed their commanders that not a single one of them was ready to fight for the Nationalist cause', according to a Chinese account. On the morning of 24 April, the Second Flotilla mutinied or 'rebelled', as some sources prefer. Together with a further twenty-five vessels berthed at Zhenjiang, up river, its commanders declared for the communists, thus 'forming the basis of 'New China's navy'.[50]

In a matter of a few days, then, the PLA had crossed the Yangtze in large numbers, across huge distances, encountering desultory resistance at best from the Nationalist defenders. Mao's armies were now ready to sweep into the towns and cities along the southern bank that had constituted the government's heartland for much of the past two decades and extend the revolution deep into the remaining yet diminishing areas under its control. It seemed that there was little to stop them.

Notes

1   Liu Tong, *Juezhan: Huadong jiefang zhanzheng, 1945–1959* ('Decisive Battles: The War of Liberation in East China, 1945–1949') (Shanghai: Shanghai renmin chubanshe, 2017), p. 548.

2   The phrase is Frank Dikotter's in *Things Modern: Material Culture and Everyday Life in China* (London: Hurst & Co., 2007), p. 74.

3   Jeremy Brown and Paul G. Pickowicz (eds), *Dilemmas of Victory: The Early Years of the People's Republic of China* (Cambridge, MA: Harvard University Press, 2007), p. 24.

4   Dangdai zhongguo yanjiusuo bian (ed.), *Zhonghua Renmin Gongheguo shibiannian: 1949 nianjuan* ('Chronicle of the People's Republic of China – 1949') (Beijing: Dangdai zhongguo chubanshe, 2004), pp. 359–60.

5   Liu Tong, *Juezhan*, p. 548.

6   William W. Whitson, *The Chinese High Command: A History of Communist Military Politics, 1921–71* (New York: Praeger, 1973), p. 87.

7   Zhongyang yanjiuyuan jindaishi yanjiusuo, *Pan Zongwu xiansheng fangwen jilu* ('A Record of Interviews with Mr Pan Zongwu') (Taipei, 1992), p. 172.

8   Ibid., p. 173.

9   Liu Tong, *Juezhan*, p. 541.

10 Ibid.

11 Isabella Bird, *The Yangtze Valley and Beyond* (London: Virago Press, 1985), p. 60.

12 Li Tongfa, *1949 Da chetui* ('1949: The Great Withdrawal') (Taipei: Lianjing chuban shiye youxian gongsi, 2009), p. 45.

13 Junshi kexueyuan junshilishi yanjiubu (ed.), *Zhongguo renmin jiefangjun zhanshi: disanjuan, quanguo jiefang zhanzheng shiqi* ('History of the Wars fought by the Chinese People's Liberation Army. Vol. 3: The War of National Liberation') (Beijing: Junshi kexue chubanshe, 1987), p. 321.

14 John Leighton Stuart, *Fifty Years in China: The Memoirs of John Leighton Stuart, Missionary and Ambassador* (New York: Random House, 1954), p. 235.

15 Percy Finch, *Shanghai and Beyond* (New York: Charles Scribner's Sons, 1953), p. 340.

16 Liu Tong, *Juezhan*, p. 563.

17 Donggil Kim, 'Stalin and the Chinese Civil War', *Cold War History*, Vol. 10, No. 2 (May 2010), p. 195.

18 Ibid., p. 186.

19 Junshi kexueyuan junshilishi yanjiubu, *Zhongguo renmin jiefangjun zhanshi*, pp. 321, 325.

20 Dongil Kim, 'Stalin and the Chinese Civil War', p. 193.

21 Lyman P. Van Slyke, *Yangtze: Nature, History and the River* (Reading, MA: Addison-Wesley Publishing Company, 1988), p. 146.

22 Zhonggong Shanxi shengwei dangshi biangongshi (ed.), *1949 Shanxi ganbu nanxia shilu* ('1949 A True Record of the Shanxi South-bound Cadres'), Vol. I (Taiyuan: Shanxi renmin chubanshe, 2012), p. 1.

23 Ibid., p. 2.

24 Joseph W. Esherick, *Ancestral Leaves: A Family Journey through Chinese History* (Berkeley, CA: University of California Press, 2011), p. 218.

25 Huang Yongsheng (ed.), *Guangxi wenshi ziliao xuanji disanshiliu: Nanxia ganbu zai Guangxi* ('Guangxi Historical Materials, Vol. 36: South-bound cadres in Guangxi') (Nanning: Guangxi qu zhengxie wenshi ziliao bianjibu chu ban faxing, 1993), p. 2.

26 Zhonggong Shanxi shengwei dangshi biangongshi, *1949 Shanxi ganbu nanxia shilu*, p. 11.

27 The sources cited in this section are drawn from this literature.

28 Zhonggong Shanxi shengwei dangshi biangongshi, *1949 Shanxi ganbu nanxia shilu*, p. 15.

29 Ibid., p. 41.

30 Ibid., p. 90.

31 Junshi kexueyuan junshilishi yanjiubu, *Zhongguo renmin jiefangjun zhanshi*, p. 325.

32 Liu Tong, *Juezhan*, p. 548.

33 Ibid., p. 551.

34 Dangdai zhongguo yanjiusuo bian, *Zhonghua Renmin Gongheguo shibiannian 1949 nianjuan*, p. 372.

35 *Time*, 2 May 1949, p. 16.

36 The following account of the Yangtze crossing draws on Liu Tong, *Juezhan*, Chapters 38 and 39; William W. Whitson, *The Chinese High Command: A History of Communist Military Politics, 1921–71* (New York: Praeger, 1973), pp. 243–4, 332–3, 186–9; and Christopher R. Lew, *The Third Chinese Revolutionary Civil War, 1945–49: An Analysis of Communist Strategy and Leadership* (London: Routledge, 2009), pp. 129–44.

37 Liu Tong, *Juezhan*, p. 567.

38 Peter Townsend, *China Phoenix: The Revolution in China* (London: Jonathan Cape, 1955), p. 49.

39 *Time*, 2 May 1949, p. 16.

40 Liu Tong, *Juezhan*, p. 568.

41 Two recent summaries are, in English, Brian Izzard, *Yangtze Showdown: China and the Ordeal of HMS Amethyst* (Barnsley: Seaforth Publishing, 2015); and, in Chinese, Liu Tong, *Juezhan*, Chapter 39, pp. 577–86. The latter draws on a range of documentary sources to show that Mao and Zhou Enlai found the *Amethyst* Incident 'politically useful' for a while, but were not sorry when the vessel escaped, and may indeed have made it easier to do so than might otherwise have been the case, in order to avoid further friction with the imperial powers.

42 Izzard, *Yangtze Showdown*, p. 6.

43 Ye Fei, *Ye Fei Huiyilu* ('Reminiscences of Ye Fei') (Beijing: Jiefang chubanshe, 1988), p. 371.

44 Ibid.

45 Ibid., p. 372.

46 Ibid.

47 Robert Bickers, *Out of China: How the Chinese Ended the Era of Western Domination* (London: Allen Lane, 2017), p. 273.

48 *The Times*, 25 April 1949, p. 4.

49 Ye Fei, *Ye Fei Huiyilu*, p. 375.

50 Liu Tong, *Juezhan*, p. 570.

6

Taking the cities

'Overturning heaven and earth'

The Chinese Communist Party owed its survival, and by the late 1940s, its political ascendancy to the fact that it controlled large parts of the countryside. It was led by men who, of necessity, had been more successful in fomenting rural revolution than inspiring the country's relatively small number of industrial workers, scattered across government-controlled cities, to overturn the political order. The fact that by 1948 the CCP was in a position to topple Chiang's Nationalist government was due to its command of large peasant armies, which had only lately been equipped with modern weapons and organized along professional military lines. On the eve of its seizure of power, the CCP had not occupied and administered a single large city – with the exception of Harbin, hard up against the border with the Soviet Union, which it snatched from government hands in 1946 when Stalin's Red Army troops eventually withdrew from most of Manchuria.

During the course of 1949, the overwhelmingly rural character of China's revolution changed. Communist troops would capture all of China's major cities, most importantly those in the Yangtze Valley, source of the Nationalist government's political and economic power. The CCP was going to take these key citadels by force of arms if necessary; occupy them in the face of anticipated opposition from what it called the 'unarmed enemy',[1] run them more efficiently than the 'reactionary' forces they would soon replace; and turn them into showcases of Chinese communism, modern industry and international proletarianism. Mao recognized that the future of the revolution hinged on how the Party went about this work. In March 1949, a Central Committee directive warned: 'As soon we take over a city, we must focus on the restoration and development of the city's production . . . if we cannot improve the livelihood of workers first and then that of ordinary people, we shall certainly not be able to maintain our political power.'[2]

By April, the methods by which the CCP had gained control over China's cities varied. The PLA took the Manchurian cities of Changchun and Shenyang by long and bloody siege. It conquered Tianjin by storm. It subjected Beiping to a form of calibrated suffocation that finally persuaded its defenders to surrender and accept 'peaceful liberation'. And Nanjing, Chiang Kai-shek's capital for the past twenty-one years and symbol of what remained of his regime's power and prestige, it would take by vacant possession. Mao Zedong celebrated the event in a poem, referring to the 'heroic triumph' with which 'heaven and earth had been overturned'.[3] Symbolically, this was so; in practice, it was a subdued affair – as would prove the case, with the occasional exception, across much of the country.

Last hours in Nanjing

By mid-April, Acting President Li Zongren and those around him were painfully aware that the failure of the peace talks in Beiping meant they would soon have to abandon their capital. The speed with which they would have to do so, thanks to the scale and success of the communist crossing of the Yangtze, was more of a surprise. Divisions over how to defend south China had 'virtually opened our gates and invited the robber into our house' Li would later complain.[4] As the PLA crossed the Yangtze, he rejected blandishments from Beiping to stay in Nanjing, welcome the liberators and sign the peace accord in exchange for a position in the new dispensation.

Other senior civil and military officials had every intention of getting out, too. They scrambled to secure seats on the planes leaving for Guangzhou, which the government declared its new, 'temporary' capital, and for Taipei. A scene of pandemonium greeted Associated Press reporter Seymour Topping at the air strip closest to the city centre, where planes were being loaded 'in a frenzy for quick take-offs'. He watched a Nationalist general 'hoarsely shouting orders to soldiers to load his grand piano and other furniture aboard an air force plane', and saw legislators wearing pith helmets and carrying tennis rackets clamber aboard a plane bound for the south.[5] In Taipei, the British consul reported 'a veritable invasion of Government officials, Military Officers and members of the Legislative and Control Yuans, with some 50 planes arriving in one day'.[6]

The less fortunate Nationalist soldiers 'streamed out of the capital, weary and disorganised, along the dry brown roads leading through fields of green vegetables and yellow rape, southward and eastward towards the coastal cities of Shanghai and Hangzhou and the rugged mountains of Fujian and Jiangxi', *Time* reported.[7] Demolition teams destroyed such facilities as the attackers might easily put to use – the railway station, ammunition dumps, aircraft and aviation fuel, surplus vehicles and so on. The power plant and waterworks escaped destruction but would soon become targets for the Nationalist air force.

The issue of evacuation aside, there was the question of the overall Nationalist defence plan, now that communist troops had breached huge stretches of the Yangtze up and down river of Nanjing. On 20 April, in another late night conclave in Li's private residence, Bai Chongxi argued that both Nanjing and Shanghai be abandoned, his own forces withdraw from Wuhan south into Hunan, and a new defensive line be formed as a kind of screen to defend southwest China. Tang Enbo's forces should anchor the southeastern end of this line, along the Jiangxi–Zhejiang railway, while Bai's central China troops would prevent a communist advance into the 'rice basket' of Hunan, and the provinces to its south and west. Li agreed. But Chiang was still committed to holding Shanghai as long as possible so as to evacuate men and material to Taiwan.

These differences of opinion were papered over on 22 April when the severity of the situation brought Chiang out of 'retirement' in Xikou for a hastily arranged meeting with Li, Bai, He Yingqin and Zhang Qun in Hangzhou. It was the first time the former and the acting president had met since January. A brief encounter, it was held in the guest house of Air Force Academy where Li pressed Chiang once again to resume the presidency and take back control of the government and military. Li had assumed the acting presidency to conduct peace talks which had now failed. He said it was time for him to step down.

Chiang agreed it was time for a change of policy but was not (yet) ready to take up the reins. Instead, he pledged his full personal support for Li. He agreed that He Yingqin, as both defence minister and premier, should have full control over the military, and endorsed a statement to the effect that the government would fight the communists to the bitter end. Then came the sting in the tail: the GMD would set up an 'Extraordinary Committee', with Chiang as chair and Li as his deputy. It would have the power to approve all major decisions before they were passed to the government for implementation. Chiang had 'stepped up' but not in the manner Li hoped.

Li shunned attempts to persuade him to fly to the relative safety of Shanghai and instead returned to Nanjing with a reluctant He Yingqin. By the time he arrived back at his private residence on the evening of 22 April, the communists had penetrated the city suburbs and sporadic gunfire could be heard. 'The capital was a scene of desolation', Li recalled. 'Normally busy thoroughfares, such as Chungshan Road and Taiping Road, were deserted, stores were closed and the streets were empty of people.' He dressed for bed 'but could not sleep a wink'.[8]

At 4 a.m. the next morning, Saturday 23 April, He Yingqin telephoned Li and told him he must leave Nanjing immediately; he could not guarantee the acting president's safety beyond 6 a.m. Li 'put the receiver down in a daze', according to one of his aides.[9] He and his party of about thirty then set off for the airfield in the grounds of the former Ming Palace. The somewhat ramshackle vehicles in which they were travelling had to force their way through a constant stream of military traffic fleeing the capital. The sun was just coming up when they reached their destination, where He Yingqin was waiting for the party. He exchanged a few words with the acting president. Li then boarded his plane, the *Zhuiyun* ('Cloud chaser'), which circled the city, affording the passengers a last look at the capital, before it ascended into the clouds.[10] Li then instructed the pilot to head not for Guangzhou but to Guilin, his home town in Guangxi, where he would be able to rest and plan his next moves in a position of relative safety, surrounded by supporters.

Interlude

For Wu Yifang, principal of Jinling Girls' College and her staff, keeping the students together, ensuring their safety and maintaining the standard of teaching that had earned the Nanjing-based institution a high reputation had been a major challenge in the past few months. Of the 482 students who began the term, only about 100 remained when the communists entered the city. Some staff had left for Guangzhou, others for Taiwan.[11]

A communist underground cell had been active in the college in 1948. Perhaps it had a hand in persuading a handful of girls to cross the Yangtze (in the 'other direction') and join the 'political corps of the Liberation Army', as the Dean's Report put it, even before the victors arrived in the city.[12] Jinling girls had taken part in student demonstrations in April demanding that the government accept the communists' terms for ending the war. Many more would enthusiastically join the cause after the takeover because 'the attraction of youth to this big and victorious movement is so strong when once aroused that no one, not even parents, can divert interest into other channels'.[13]

In common with many others, the speed of the communist takeover surprised Eva Spicer, the perceptive Jinling history teacher. Partly this was because residents found it so hard to get their hands on genuine information. 'On Thursday [21 April] we were still hearing rumours of a possible month or so of resistance', she wrote. 'On Friday [22nd] things seemed pretty normal ... but there was heavy firing on Friday night.' Spicer cycled to campus on Saturday morning [23rd] only to be told by one of the Chinese faculty that she should 'not to go out, as the government was evacuating very rapidly, a good many [if not all] of the police had been withdrawn, and there was considerable disorder and looting on the street, and in fact, The Crisis Had Arrived'.[14]

It certainly was something of a crisis for Wu who learned from street posters that she had been appointed vice chair of a Public Safety Committee tasked with preserving order during the interval between the departure of the Nationalists and the arrival of the communists. The Nationalist garrison commander had made the appointment but then 'left in such a hurry that she [Wu] didn't get the letter [informing her] until later'.[15] A pacifist as well as a patriot, Wu had spent the past few months encouraging her students to concentrate on their studies rather than take part in protests. But she trod a careful path during the dying months of Nationalist rule, skilfully managing to 'dodge the personal invitations from Chiang Kai-shek and Song Mei-ling to go to Taiwan, and even refusing to accept the airplane ticket delivered to her by Chiang's aide in the last days before the Communist takeover', according to a recent history of the college.[16]

The Public Safety Committee soon had its work cut out: a brief but intense bout of looting occurred once the Nationalists left the scene, witnessed among many others, by Indian Ambassador K. M. Panikkar, who returned to Nanjing on what he described as the 'last Guomindang train' from Shanghai.[17] The capital presented what he described as a strange scene:

> Systematic looting of the houses of Guomindang leaders was underway, but it was done in a civilised and orderly manner, old women being helped by younger people to carry what they had collected! The mob did not destroy anything; they broke only such things as had to be broken, like doors, window frames etc which some people carried away quietly as if they were withdrawing a deposit from a bank.[18]

Li Zongren's residence, only recently vacated, was a prominent target. 'A mob swarmed up the long fir tree-lined drive to President Li's grey brick home', reported *Time*. 'A ragged boy shoved a porcelain sink through a smashed door panel to three of his friends outside. Li's housekeeper helped the looters take out the furniture, explaining: "The sooner they clean out the place the better. Then I will have peace." '[19]

After an interval, the Public Safety Committee, led by Ma Jingyuan, a retired Nationalist division commander, managed to impose some order and contacted communist troops just outside the city centre. As the main body of PLA soldiers marched in on 24 April, there was sporadic gunfire and a few explosions. Some fires were still burning, notably in the Ministry of Justice building. But there was little other commotion.

Troops quickly took control of key government buildings and no doubt took particular delight in lowering the Republic of China flag then still flying over the Presidential Palace, Chiang's former seat of power. However, the famous photograph by Zou Jiandong that depicts this scene was shot, not at the time in the manner of genuine news or war photography, but two days after the event in a carefully staged re-enactment. Claire Roberts, a historian of photography in China, described it as 'a fine example of an image constructed in order to evoke a particular historical moment'.[20]

In any event, the new arrivals in the Nationalist capital were confronted by the consequences of a hurried, ill-planned evacuation rather than organized resistance. 'Trucks laden with ammunition and medicine were left behind because the drivers fled', notes Chinese scholar Liu Tong. 'A small group of government troops were carrying so much silver coin that they could not flee fast enough. Reluctantly, they had to entrust some of it to other units because they valued their lives more than their money.'[21] Members of the Yangtze Detachment, the south-bound cadres, who arrived in the city some three weeks after the PLA vanguard, were billeted in the Ministry of

Communications building. 'The place was empty', some of them recalled. 'Apart from destroyed papers all over the floor, there was nothing there.'[22]

Nanjing's residents were keen to get their first sight of the 'enemy'. 'In the streets and squares of Nanjing, the Communists were orderly', reported *Time*. They sang or listened to harangues from their officers. They looked no different from their Nationalist brothers, except they were fresher, more soldierly. . . . people grouped around them and, with unaffected curiosity, stared at the invaders from the north.'[23] The sightseers displayed little enthusiasm but no hostility either, Ambassador Panikkar recorded after a tour of the city.[24]

Some foreign observers drew a comparison between the relatively enthusiastic reception the communists received from parts of the population when they took over Beiping and the apparent passivity of the public in Nanjing. They quizzed Wu Yifang about the matter. She pointed out that Beiping had been under siege for weeks and that many of the city's population had never much liked the 'southern' GMD regime which, among other things, had stripped their city of its status as the national capital. They were glad to see the back of it. Nanjing, by comparison, was built for and by the Nationalists; and many residents depended on the government for work. But Wu said another factor accounted for the cool response of some students: 'They had received many letters during the previous three months from friends in the north informing them that life under the new regime was not all they had hoped, that students there were getting very small food allowances [and] that there remain many restrictions on their freedom'[25]

The new order

The ease with which communist forces occupied the capital was matched by the competent way in which they took over the established organs of power and influence, rapidly 're-casting' them so they could fulfil the new regime's revolutionary purpose. This was the work of the Nanjing Military Control Committee, which, as its name implies, was dominated by the PLA. It was tasked, like its counterparts in other towns and cities under communist control, with suppressing resistance, maintaining order and generally running things until a new 'civil' administration, in which the 'south-bound cadres' would play an important role, could take on the job.

In addition to assuming the main functions of government, the Military Control Committee was quick to bring to heel the leading financial institutions, including the Central Bank of China, the Bank of China and the Bank of Communications, all of which were note-issuing banks. They became property of the communist authorities. The Nanjing police force, some of whose leaders fled with other senior Nationalists officials, was promptly reorganized, though many of those who had elected to remain behind were retained.

The importance to the communists of controlling the flow of information, one of the reasons for the movement's success up to this point, was apparent almost immediately as they took over Nanjing. Media organizations of what was described as the 'defunct Chiang Kai-shek party' – the Central News Agency, the Central Daily News (*Zhongyang Ribao*) and the National Salvation Daily (*Jiuguo Ribao*) among them – were simply closed down.[26] In the days that followed, all news organizations, Chinese and foreign-owned were required to register and adhere to an editorial policy designed to 'protect the people's liberties of speech and of the press; and also to deprive the reactionary elements of their liberties and of the press ...' In other words, they were obliged to tow the communist government's line.[27]

US news organizations came in for particularly sharp criticism; the new communist-controlled media urged the Chinese people to free themselves from 'news colonization'. Things had to change. 'As regards the reporting of foreign correspondents in China, it is impossible to let them enjoy the unlimited freedom they had during the KMT rule', said the *Nanjing Daily*. 'The Chinese people have the right to decide which news agencies or papers are hostile and must refrain from sending reporters to China.'[28] 'Reactionary' bookshops were also taken over, and new reading material shipped in from Beiping to fill shelves that were emptied of titles deemed unacceptable under the new dispensation. However, *Qianjin Bao*, the newspaper that reported this development, added: 'For research purposes, the [new] Xinhua Bookstore will keep three copies of each of the books taken over from the [reactionary] publishers and booksellers.'[29]

On 10 May, little more than two weeks after 'liberation', the Nanjing People's Government was formed under Liu Bocheng as mayor. Since Liu was also commander of the Second Field Army, the military was obviously still in charge, as was to be expected given Nanjing's symbolic importance, and the fact Nationalist planes had returned to bomb the city's power plant and the Nanjing to Shanghai railway line. However, the bombing was counterproductive. Eva Spicer scornfully noted: 'The Guomindang looks as though they might help to rally the people of Nanking behind the new regime ... their planes came back and bombed the city; they were manly aiming at more or less military objectives, but in trying to get the electric plant of the city ... they killed and wounded quite a number of civilians, children and adults'.[30]

One of the new municipal government's first moves was to introduce a curfew with a view, as the *Nanjing Daily* put it, 'to restore normal conditions and order, to maintain public peace and to avert destructive activities of the remnants of the reactionary KMT in the city'.[31] Lack of adequate coal supplies meant that Nanjing was deprived of electricity for some hours of the day, as had often been the case under the GMD.

Yet these problems aside, Knight Biggerstaff, a US scholar then based in the city, writing just less than a month after the occupants arrived, said the communists had done a remarkable job in the taking over of this city:

They have moved quickly and efficiently to deal with the essentials: police protection, electricity and water, food supplies, prices, public health, and transportation. There has been a lot of pious propaganda, but the necessary jobs have been done. The local people, who have seen a number of changes in government, seem unable to get over their astonishment at the efficiency of the administration, the evident goodwill and conscientiousness of individual officials, and the excellent behaviour of the soldiers.[32]

The 'ex-ambassadors'

Diplomats in Nanjing, accredited to a government that had abandoned its capital and moved to Guangzhou, adopted a wait-and-see attitude, in keeping with many ordinary residents. Most envoys, unlike their Soviet counterparts who for reasons already discussed had relocated south,[33] stayed put in the hope of establishing working relations of some kind with the new rulers, even though this was likely to fall far short of the full diplomatic ties that would be expected to arise from formal recognition of the new regime. For one thing, the communists had yet to set up a national government. For another, the United States, the key player, was distinctly unlikely to recognize such an entity when it was created – though an attempt would soon be made to start a dialogue of sorts in Nanjing.

For his part, Mao had set out the main lines of the Party's 'revolutionary diplomacy' in a Central Committee document issued on 19 January. They were later captured in pithy slogans typical of the CCP leader, referring to the need to 'make a fresh start'; 'clean the house before inviting in the guests'; and 'siding with the world socialist camp without reservation'.[34]

There could be no question of a communist-led Chinese government simply slotting itself into the network of diplomatic relations fashioned by its Nationalist predecessor: it was the work of a reactionary clique that had become a willing tool of the global imperialist camp led by the United States. China was in the process of liberation and transformation along socialist lines. It was moving from one 'camp' to another – namely, to the socialist camp led by Stalin and the Soviet Union.

Studied indifference, then, was the major feature of the CCP's policies towards the diplomatic establishment in Nanjing and its various offshoots elsewhere in the country. Yet as was the case when planning the Yangtze crossing, Mao (and Stalin even more so) was anxious not to provide the Western powers with grounds to intervene as communist forces extended their conquests and the Nationalist government collapsed. The communists' treatment of US Consul General Angus Ward in Shenyang, described earlier, was potentially a sensitive matter.[35] So was the handling of HMS Amethyst, the British warship damaged and still stranded on the Yangtze, much to the concern of politicians and public in the United Kingdom.[36]

There was an anxious moment when, early in the morning of 25 April, communist soldiers barged into US Ambassador Leighton Stuart's bedroom, woke him up, had a good look around the room and advised him that the items over which their eyes had just roamed 'would eventually go to people to whom they should belong anyway'.[37] Mao immediately gave orders that no such infringements occur again.[38]

In fact, 'diplomacy' as the Nanjing-based diplomats had known it practically became a thing of the past the moment the communists took over. Indian Ambassador Panikkar recalled:

> A day or two after the occupation we were politely but firmly informed that we would be given no diplomatic privileges and would be treated as only distinguished foreigners. We were alluded to as ex-ambassadors. There was no Foreign Office to deal with us but only a Foreign Personnel Bureau where our secretaries had to present themselves with an interpreter since all business was transacted in Chinese . . . We were not allowed the use of cypher or the privilege of using couriers. In fact, we had technically ceased to be diplomats.[39]

Leighton Stuart nevertheless sought dealings with the new authorities, if only on an informal basis. On 13 May he met Huang Hua, head of the new Alien Affairs office in Nanjing, who had set up shop in the compound of the former government's Ministry of Foreign Affairs. A short, trim thirty-nine-year-old, Huang was a graduate of Beiping's Yanjing University, of which the ambassador had been president. A degree of mutual respect and cordiality might be expected to grace the occasion of their meeting.

It was characterized more by a certain stiffness. Mao had advised Huang exactly what he could and could not say to the ambassador. The former would not amount to much unless the US agreed to cut all ties with the Nationalists. This was a non-starter: Washington might have (largely) given up on Chiang, but it was not ready formally to abandon his government, still less encourage a communist alternative. Thus, in June, when Leighton Stuart asked his seniors for permission to visit Beiping 'unofficially', at the invitation of his old university, but in fact to use the occasion to hold talks with Zhou Enlai, Washington declined. 'Diplomacy' as far as the ambassador was concerned was thus mainly a question of winding up his own mission and waiting for the communists to grant him permission to leave the former capital, which he was to do on 2 August.

These initiatives aside, there was little for most 'ex-diplomats' to do, other than monitor the situation in Nanjing and elsewhere as limited information flows allowed. With the apparent exception of British Ambassador Sir Ralph Stevenson, who did not feel he could leave his post until the fate of HMS

Amethyst was settled, most envoys became rather jittery with the passage of time. The unbearably hot summer in Nanjing that year did not help. And diplomats being diplomats, many of them wondered how they would ever get out of the city both from a practical point of view and with their dignity intact.

However, there was an upside to this diplomatic *ennui*. As the summer wore on, Eva Spicer and some her colleagues found that they could join the Embassy Club 'at very reasonable terms', where they could swim four days a week in the club pool, and enjoy 'Hamburgher [sic] sandwiches and coffee . . .'[40]

Defence of a 'dying cause': the taking of Taiyuan

Few people expected Chiang's armies to put up much of a fight for the capital: ultimately, the survival of the Nationalist regime did not depend on defending the symbolic seat of its power, even though its fall to the communists was a severe blow. By contrast, the battle over the fortress city of Taiyuan was a different story – one that illustrated the contrasting forces and patterns of conquest at work in China's Civil War. The provincial capital of Shanxi, one of the last Nationalist redoubts in north China, was finally captured by the PLA the day after they marched into central Nanjing.

Shanxi was the personal fiefdom of Yan Xishan, its Nationalist governor. Like the Guangxi leaders Li Zongren and Bai Chongxi, Yan acquired something of a national reputation in the 1930s by turning his domain into a 'model province'. Roads and railways were built, literacy and public health programmes championed, and reforestation encouraged. Also like the Guangxi leaders, Yan was often at odds with Chiang whose authority he accepted in name only while basking in the title 'Marshal' that the Nationalist leader bestowed upon him.

Each of these men, along with many other of the regional militarists who played an important role in Republican politics, would reject the accusation (for that is what it was) that they were 'warlords', a label applied at the time and since. They nevertheless owed much of their power and influence to the factors that made 'warlordism' common at the time: tight control of a distinct territory in which to raise revenues and troops, and the fostering of a distinct provincial or regional identity as a means of resisting encroachment by the central government or other 'outside' forces. Even in the heyday of his power, Chiang Kai-shek was forced to treat with rather than tame these regional satraps.

Yan had managed to retain something of his authority over Shanxi, despite Japan's occupation of Taiyuan during the war and the CCP's infiltration of much of the countryside thereafter. Shanxi, as noted earlier, was a recruiting ground for the south-bound Cadres sent out to take the revolution to cities and countryside south of the Yangtze. By the summer of 1948, the communists had confined Yan – now in his mid-sixties, a diabetic and giving every appearance of being exhausted – along with some 100,000 troops to his capital. This was situated on the flat loess soil that characterized much of the region and was practically surrounded by nearby hills and mountains. Fortunately for him, the city contained a steel works, several other large factories and a modern arsenal. It was also ringed with impressive defensive fortifications and nestled within 40-feet thick traditional city walls.

The battle for Taiyuan lasted six months, and not many of them had passed before land communications were cut and the central government had to supply the city with 200 tons of rice, flour and ammunition by air each day. This was a challenge for the pilots, many of them foreigners, who either dropped their cargoes as close to the target as possible or landed on a narrow airstrip, threw their loads out on the ground and took off again as soon as possible to avoid communist mortar fire from the nearby hills. 'We flew as many as twenty-eight airdrops a day', wrote Felix Smith, a Civil Air Transport pilot. 'Every time a C-46 flew over the besieged city, eight tons of supplies rained down.'[41]

PLA commanders besieging Taiyuan tried to persuade the defenders to give in. 'Captured prisoners were sent into the city with pledges that Yan's soldiers who surrendered would be treated well along with their dependants', according to an official account of the campaign.[42] Supplies of food were also proffered to the hungry troops. Some surrendered but the majority fought on, even when the communists launched their final campaign at the end of March. It began with an artillery bombardment by Lin Biao's Fourth Field Army, which sparked fires across the city, and ended in fierce street-to-street fighting during which the defenders were finally overcome.

A few weeks before the end came, Yen had told somewhat credulous visiting US reporters that he intended to commit suicide before giving up Taiyuan. In the event, he left for Nanjing in February and never returned, though he is said to have expressed the wish to do so, irrespective of the dangers. He had thoughtfully brought out with him the province's store of gold. Yan's key subordinates hung on to the bitter end. When it came, 'Yan's son-in-law and the chief of the gendarmerie were last seen trudging down the street at the end of a rope', said Smith. 'More than four hundred men, including Yan's nephew, swallowed cyanide capsules, and their bodies were cremated by their friends.'[43] Unlike central government troops, for whom flight to Guangzhou or Taiwan was an option, at least for a while, Yan's commanders in Taiyuan had nowhere to go. They had a single, non-transportable, stake in a local version of the old order and they were prepared to die for it. The taking of Taiyuan, which was completed on 24 April, was thus very different from that of Nanjing. As William W. Whitson put it: 'The defending army demonstrated surprising loyalty to a dying cause and to Yan Xishan, the last symbol of warlordism in Shansi Province.'[44]

The 'huge test': taking Shanghai

'Taking Shanghai is the final problem in the Chinese Revolution and a huge test for us', Chen Yi, commander of the Third Field Army, to whom Mao had allocated this task, told his senior officers on 10 May. 'How we handle the situation in Shanghai will be a matter of great concern throughout the entire country and to the world at large. If we do well, the democratic forces in the world will celebrate, cheer us on and rejoice. If we fail, they will lose hope in us.'[45]

Perhaps still not used to being on the winning side, Chen was concerned that the speed with which his forces forged the Yangtze and had by now forced the once seemingly formidable armies of Tang Enbo into a triangular pocket around the mighty metropolis of Shanghai had bred over confidence, perhaps even complacency, among his men. He was right to be worried. During their rapid advance into southeast China, some Third Field Army soldiers complained that they were spending all their time chasing rather than fighting the enemy. 'The enemy is a complete failure. We crossed the Great River without even firing a shot; all we do is pursue and attack; all the enemy can do is retreat', some of them said.[46] This was not what they had volunteered for. Neither was it what they had been told to expect as they stormed into the enemy's strategic heartland.

Perhaps Shanghai would prove the exception, the venue of a last stand, a decisive encounter of some kind? Not many residents, Chinese or foreign, seemed to think so. What was clear, as Chen Yi acknowledged, was that the stakes were huge. This was true for the communists who coveted the city; the Nationalists who at least pledged to defend it; the citizens of Shanghai, many of whom still worried over whether to stay or leave; and the people of China as a whole, who were watching proceedings with curiosity and concern.

It was hardly less significant for the outside world – especially for the 'West' and what was by now becoming known as the 'Soviet bloc'. For both these camps, the fate of China's most famous city figured large in the intensifying drama of the Cold War. The communist capture of Shanghai, assuming it transpired, would surely prove the single most important 'symbolic' episode to date in the rise of 'Red China'. It would mean a citadel of capitalist enterprise had fallen under the hammer and sickle, portending a major shift in global fortunes.

Getting ready

The communist high command planned the takeover of Shanghai with the kind of attention they had devoted to crossing the Yangtze. The 'shift in the Party's work from the countryside to the cities', the great theme of policies and pronouncements during the past few months, was put to no greater test than in running the most sophisticated commercial centre in China and one of the most famous cities in the world.

Not that the communists would be running it 'the same way' – at least not for long. Alongside the refrain of 'business as normal', which the Party championed to qualm Shanghai nerves, was that harsher critique of the city and much of what it stood for, drawing on the virulent mixture of Marxism and nationalism at the heart of the CCP's creed. According to this view, Shanghai was essentially a capitalist, parasitic even criminal city where consumption exceeded production, workers were exploited, vice flourished and gangs ruled. It served rich Chinese and foreigners, who until recently ran the place, rather than the ordinary people of China. It was a shameful symbol of all that was wrong with 'old' China – one that was about to be put right by the 'other' side of Shanghai, the birthplace of China's industrial working class, as well as many of the radical ideas and political movements that had challenged and changed China over the decades, the Communist Party among them. The Shanghai elite was going to be overturned, and city life reordered along very different ideological lines.

That was for the future. More immediately, Party leaders had three main issues on their minds as they prepared to move in and take over, as Chen Yi explained to his troops. First, Shanghai was where the interests of the foreign powers were more concentrated than anywhere else in the country. British and US warships were still berthed in the city or its vicinity. If PLA troops forcibly expelled the Nationalists, might it provoke armed intervention of some kind?

Second, if the Nationalists were to put up stiff resistance and war had to be fought in Shanghai itself, it would be like trying to 'beat a rat in a China shop'.[47] The destruction could be so great that it could have a serious effect on the economic reconstruction the communists planned for 'new' China.

Finally, and crucially, there was the question of competence. That is, the competence of the PLA, in league with the 'south-bound cadres' travelling in its wake, and the Shanghai Party underground, with whom it planned to link up, to take over the city and run it efficiently. If it failed to handle the takeover well, there could be strikes, power cuts and chaos, and Shanghai could be turned into a 'dead city', Chen Yi warned. Communist troops might then have to evacuate the place – a humiliating matter and one that could affect the outcome of the Civil War.

Close study of what made the city tick was essential for all military and civilian personnel, who hoped, in a matter of weeks, to run the place. To this end, the Party in early May organized a conference in Danyang, a county town some 150 miles northwest of Shanghai, to plan details of the takeover. Cadres from all over the country attended but the most important were the 'Shanghai experts', those working in the city, in some cases for years, who sneaked away to share their knowledge and advice with their would-be liberators. They included Liu Xiao, head of the Shanghai Party underground, Xia Yan, a left-wing playwright and cultural commentator, and Pan Hannian, recently returned from Hong Kong, where he carried out secret work for the Party, but would soon enter the public eye as a somewhat dapper, sophisticated deputy mayor of communist-ruled Shanghai.

Attendees at the Danyang Shanghai workshop are said to have examined some 200 separate books of materials concerning the city's political, economic, social and cultural situation compiled from documents obtained from the enemy or put together by the Party underground. Close attention was paid to handling what the Party called the 'national bourgeoisie' – owners of Chinese business enterprises that were neither controlled by, owned or depended on the Nationalist party or foreigners, and who were thus deemed to have a place in the new order, at least initially. This category included many, though by no means all, of China's famed 'Shanghai capitalists'. The proper treatment of foreigners and foreign enterprises was also discussed. So were plans to ensure adequate supplies of energy and food for the population. Study of police operations in Shanghai was an important aspect of the proceedings, as events during the takeover would soon prove. Frederic Wakeman Jr, a leading historian of the city, noted that a police training group was set up in Danyang ready to run specific precincts in the city.

The discussions at Danyang were to play an important part in the events that followed, as a recent Chinese account concedes: 'No matter whether big or small, all such matters had to be considered together and implemented in a comprehensive manner if [the takeover] was to succeed.'[48] Yet it was still the PLA that had to make the first move and bring Shanghai to heel. And its battle plan would depend to some extent on how the enemy planned to defend the city. This was the subject of a five-day military conference that began on 10 May in Suzhou, the scenic city about 50 miles west of Shanghai, at which Chen Yi and his commanders spelt out the options.

The first of them was to wage siege warfare against Shanghai of the kind already employed to deadly effect in Manchuria in 1948 and more recently in Taiyuan. This would reduce deaths and injuries among the communist troops but punish Shanghai's citizens. And since the Nationalists controlled access to the sea, via the Wusong Forts where the Huangpu river met the Yangtze, a siege would be hard to enforce: the enemy could both bring in supplies and easily escape should he wish to do so.

An alternative was to choose a weak spot in the enemy's defences – in this case, south of the Suzhou river (which meets the Huangpu at the city's well-known Suzhou Creek). The problem here would be that it would mean taking the fight right into the city centre, causing destruction in the process.

A better idea was to concentrate the attack first on Wusong, thus enveloping and avoiding the centre of the city. The enemy could expect to fight hard in this locality: it was his retreat path and he needed time to get troops, equipment and other assets out of Shanghai or to bring fresh supplies in. But it would at least spare the city and its people from the effects of fighting.

Nationalist end game

The Nationalists tried to keep the world, and especially the communists, guessing about their end game in Shanghai. Martial law was imposed on 23 April. Newspapers and radio stations were heavily censored. The great human exodus continued: Reuters reported 'heavy air arrivals [in] Hong Kong and Guangzhou of rich Shanghai merchants with service between Shanghai and Guangzhou said [to have] increased to 30 planes daily.'[49]

On 26 April, Chiang Kai-shek suddenly appeared on the scene, much to the surprise and fury of Li Zongren, it must be assumed. He and his retinue arrived on a naval frigate that they had boarded at the small harbour near Xikou; Chiang ordered it to head for the city rather than, as many expected, Taiwan. At the Hangzhou Conference, a few days earlier, he had rejected Li Zongren's request that he resume power, but it now seemed that he had come to take personal command of the defence of Shanghai. He promised another 'Stalingrad', telling military chiefs that they could expect a big change in the international scene that would result in the US coming to the aid of his government. Perhaps partly in response, marine insurance rates doubled for Shanghai vessels.[50]

But this was bluff and bluster. Chiang ordered Tang Enbo, who had some 200,000 troops under his control in the region, to hold Shanghai with the sole purpose of shipping as many men, and as much materiel and other assets as possible to Taiwan and to Zhoushan, south of Shanghai in the Gulf of Hangzhou, not far from Xikou. Chiang's strategy, apparently decided by him alone, thus resembled Dunkirk rather than Stalingrad: it was important for symbolic reasons to mount some sort of defence of the city, but more important still to evacuate as many resources as possible so that the Nationalists could fight another day on another shore. US Consul General John Cabot put things more bluntly: the Nationalists were 'carrying on a gigantic and sickening racket to strip the town clean before they hand it over'.[51] Chiang wanted to carry out the 'greatest possible removal of transportable equipment and other assets as well as personnel useful to the Communists'.[52]

Asset stripping aside, Nationalist soldiers also showed signs of 'digging in' – in both the city centre and the suburbs, where they erected a picket fence along the southwest and northern sides of Shanghai. The palisade attracted mockery and mirth, if of a rather grim variety. But it was a serious matter for the nearby villagers whose homes were destroyed to provide a field of fire: some 80,000 people were said to have been forced out into the countryside. 'Inside the shrinking Nationalist lines, sweating soldiers and coolies dug trenches, strung barbed-wire barricades, sowed "dragon's teeth" – thick rows of sharpened bamboo stakes pointed towards the approaching enemy', *Time* reported. 'If a stand were to be made at all, it would be made inside a belt of defense that extended 30 miles from the city's teeming center.'[53] Farmers were pressed into service, trees cut down and grave mounds levelled.

Consul General Cabot said the aim was to keep soldiers busy so they 'won't have time to think of running away'.[54] By the latter half of May, the Nationalists were said to had constructed some 4,000 pillboxes or blockhouses and 10,000 other military features designed to ward off attack.

In the city itself, the authorities ruled with what one reporter said was a 'trembling iron hand'.[55] He meant the government was losing grip. Yet it could still arrest and execute suspected communists. Peter Townsend was one of several people who witnessed a 'trial' outside police headquarters of three men accused of trying to overthrow the government. They were driven away in the back of a lorry to a major crossroads where 'the men were blindfolded. There was a burst of firing. One still struggled for life, and a nervous officer emptied his revolver into him.'[56] A furious Cabot declared: 'Even in Yugoslavia I never saw anything quite so crude and arbitrary as the recent wave of executions.'[57] The New China News Agency said 'at least 1,000 people had been executed by police and secret service agents during the month before the city's liberation'.[58]

The general rush for the remaining exits continued amid the somewhat eccentric displays of government determination to keep the communist armies out of the city. Townsend noted:

> Each street corner had its pillbox, yet at the airfield, taking furniture, dogs, household utensils, sometimes wearing three hats on their head, civil officials crowded the planes, and the ships up-anchoring were laden with passengers, buses, cars and grain, and the banks on the Bund, roped off in day time now, had empty vaults . . . suddenly you realised that this had been a rearguard action all along, keeping one channel open through which to drain off the wealth, the road to the port of Woosung.[59]

Shanghai seemed to be emptying. 'The city seemed sunk in a melancholy stupor', said Randall Gould, managing editor of the *Shanghai Evening Post and Mercury*.[60]

By this time, Chiang and his son Chiang Ching-kuo had sailed out of Shanghai, to the accompaniment of distant artillery fire. They landed in Zhoushan, where Tang Enbo was turning the island into a staging post for the evacuation of men and equipment to Taiwan. Chiang was concerned that the 'right sort of people' – that is, leading financiers, business leaders, senior civil servants and other prominent figures – were among those leaving the city. He feared, with some justice given what had happened in Beiping and Nanjing, that such people would be susceptible to communist overtures, coming either from the Party underground or other channels, to strike a deal, stay put and turn their enterprises, government departments and organizations over to the 'liberators'.

Liu Hongsheng, patriarch of the Liu family business who had decided against transferring all of his assets and activities to Taiwan a few months earlier, began to receive such messages as the communists encircled the city.[61] They were conveyed by one of his sons who, unbeknown to Liu, had joined the CCP during the war against Japan and worked undercover ever since. With the PLA on the outskirts, communist radio broadcasts urged the Lius to remain in Shanghai, promising they would be unharmed. Liu was not convinced. 'The Communists will never be our real friends', he told the family. He decided to move some of his business assets to Hong Kong and follow them there, despite government attempts to keep him on the mainland if he was not ready to go to Taiwan.[62] His arrival in the British colony meant he had shaken off the cold embrace of the Nationalists and, at least for the moment, avoided what the communists had promised would be a much warmer one. But it did not settle the matter of where he and his businesses should be based, either in his own mind or that of his large family – as would soon become apparent.[63]

Many foreigners in Shanghai also faced the dilemma of whether to leave or stay though, with certain important exceptions, they had less at stake than most Chinese. True, they might lose their livelihoods, in some cases considerable commercial assets, and abandon the pleasures of a certain lifestyle. But many of them had a homeland in which they could settle, even if, in the case of those born in Shanghai, they might never have visited it, nor much wanted to.

The exception were the stateless persons, notably White Russians who had fled Bolshevism and, at least initially, the roughly 20,000 Jews who had managed to escape Hitler's Europe for Shanghai in the late 1930s thanks to the city's lax immigration rules. Together, they constituted the largest group of foreigners in Shanghai. With the communist armies encroaching on their sanctuary, it was time to move on again. Fortune smiled on the city's Jewish community: the new state of Israel welcomed them, setting up an embassy in the old Russian Jewish Club to that end. 'About 10,000 Shanghailanders, including Russian and Sephardi Jews, found a home in Israel', according to one authority.[64] The International Refugee Organization came to the rescue of many others, either arranging for them to travel to Israel or to a holding camp in the Philippines, pending approval to emigrate to the United States, Canada, Europe or Australia.

Nationals of the foreign powers were aware that their governments could do little to protect them against whatever lay ahead. Towards the end of April, some twelve US naval ships moved down river, away from the city centre, to avoid becoming trapped in the narrow reaches of the Huangpu should the communists capture Wusong. The US government had urged its approximately 2,500 nationals in Shanghai to board the vessels and evacuate the city.

The Royal Navy also sailed out of Shanghai, keen 'to avoid the appearance of provocation' given that HMS *Amethyst* was still stranded on the Yangtze', reported *The Times*.[65] It said that 'a large measure of discretion is left to the people on the spot to determine what is best to be done in the interests of the British community', which was said to number some 4,000. 'The situation is anxious. There is little room for refugees in Hong Kong, so that evacuation means leaving China altogether and abandoning, probably for good, commercial interests of the greatest value to this [i.e. Britain] country.'[66] The next day it noted that 'a general evacuation of British subjects is not ... for the time being in prospect. Unless conditions become too hazardous, British businessmen will, it is believed, stay, with or without naval protection, and try to carry on trade under the new regime.'[67]

'Calculated among the liberated'

'We are not sure, but the guns may soon cease and we shall be calculated amongst the liberated', wrote Arthur Ludbrook, leader of the Salvation

FIGURE 6.1 *A train packed with refugees heads for Shanghai, which by early May PLA forces had cut off by land from the rest of China.*

FIGURE 6.2 *Communist troops enter Shanghai, China's most cosmopolitan city and its trade and financial centre.*

Army in China, on 21 May. He was writing from Embankment House, the Salvation Army headquarters in Shanghai, north of the Suzhou Creek, which would soon become a centre of military action. 'Nothing could be worse than life as lived in Shanghai these last months', he added. 'As I write streams of people are filling a couple of main streets, moving slowly, yet wedged in together to make progress almost impossible, going to – who knows!'[68]

CCP leaders were unwilling to order the PLA to move into Shanghai proper until they felt ready to administer the city efficiently. But they were not prepared to sit and watch while the Nationalists 'fleeced the city of the last remaining dollar', as US Consul General Cabot put it. Mao said as much to the commanders of the Third Field Army: the enemy was known to be moving men and materiel out via Wusong, and while this might be allowed to continue for a while, it must not do so for long. Shanghai should be

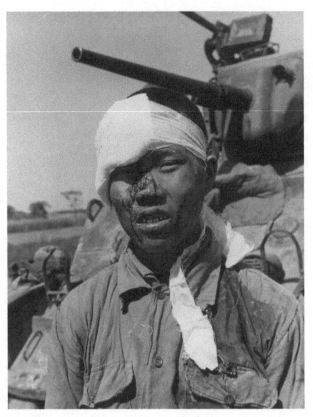

FIGURE 6.3 *The human face of war: A wounded Nationalist soldier near Shanghai during the retreat from advancing communist forces.*

attacked 'from the rear', as it were, its access to the sea cut off as soon as possible. The army could then enter the city and claim the prize. The attack on the Wusong area, where the Huangpu meets the Yangtze estuary, began on the night of 12–13 May. But the defenders put up more of a fight than expected and the PLA had to abandon a frontal assault in exchange for a slower approach that involved digging trenches in rice paddies to avoid withering fire from enemy pill boxes and fortified points.

The order went out on 21 May that the general advance on Shanghai would be launched on 23 May. Troops responsible for taking over the city centre were forbidden to deploy artillery or explosives so as not to damage buildings and so on. The PLA quickly overwhelmed the city's two main airports, in the western and southern suburbs, and Tang Enbo, realizing the end was close, left in a warship for the waters outside Wusong. The next day the PLA breached the city's unimpressive defensive perimeter.

Curiously, the Nationalists chose this moment to stage a 'victory rally'. On the morning of 24 May, on the orders of Tang, now nowhere to be seen, and to the bemusement of onlookers, troops and trucks took part in a parade against the background of store window posters proclaiming: 'We will fight to the last drop of blood! Shanghai will be the Communists' graveyard!'[69] They then hurried away. Other units were busy blowing up part of the Jiangnan shipyards, sinking oil tankers and destroying equipment in the international radio station.

Police chiefs were on the move, too. 'Trucks drew up in front of police stations, and squads of policemen with families and baggage climbed aboard for Wusong and the fleet of evacuation ships', according to Wakeman. 'As the Nationalists marched out, their flag was hanging from every home in accordance with an ordinance designating the day as a "victory celebration".'[70]

In the early hours of 25 May, communist soldiers in green fatigues penetrated to the city centre, filing down the very streets that less than twenty-four hours earlier witnessed the Nationalists' last hurrah. Their entry was largely uncontested. It was testimony to the Party's careful planning, the readiness of many, indeed most, of those in authority under the departing regime to hand over responsibility to the new, and the desire of the general public to see things return to 'normal' as soon as possible.

The smooth takeover of the police force was particularly striking: when the PLA advance guard turned up at the Central Police Station, officers came out to greet them and to surrender their station. The 'shadow police' teams in Danyang, where they had carefully planned for this moment, caught the train into the city, linked up with the Party underground in the precincts and took control of operations. Police officers who had served under the old order were encouraged to stay in post – on the understanding that they would now 'serve the people'.

The changeover at the top of the city administration also went smoothly. Wu Guozhen (KC Wu), Shanghai's long serving mayor, had resigned on 14 May citing illness. One of the first things his successor, Chen Liang, former Secretary of the Municipal Government, did was to urge residents to plant 'victory gardens' in anticipation of a long siege. But he soon decided that he was not prepared to serve 'the last shift on behalf of the Chiang dynasty' and turned his mind to finding a successor.[71] Understandably, there were few willing candidates.

Then Chen happened to listen to a communist radio broadcast in which a series of prominent Shanghai people, named by the Party, were urged to remain in post. Among them was Zhao Zukang, head of the Public Works department. 'Right', Zhao said to himself. 'The communists have chosen the next acting mayor for me – it's Zhao Zukang!'[72] A graduate of Cornell University where he had studied road and bridge construction, Zhao had already decided to stay put. A certain 'Miss Li' of the local underground had helped win him over: he supplied her comrades with maps of the suburbs that were doubtless helpful to the PLA as they planned their entry into the city. Zhao held the fort for a few days until Chen Yi, Commander of the Third Field Army, took over as Shanghai's first communist mayor.[73]

Troops who lacked maps could call upon help from the most knowledgeable people in Shanghai when it came to navigating the huge city. 'About 50 postmen in uniform arrived with their bicycles to act as guides to the troops in southern Shanghai', reported the New China News Agency. It was a 'classic example of the solidarity of workers . . . with the PLA'.[74]

The PLA encountered few pockets of resistance as they moved into the city. Only one of them amounted to much. It was in the area north of the Suzhou Creek, around the well-known Garden Bridge, where Nationalist forces commandeered the waterfront buildings, firing down from the rooftops at communist troops who attempted to cross the Creek.

It was a tense few hours for the PLA, some of whose men wanted to deploy artillery and end the resistance for good but were overruled by their officers; for the Nationalist troops, whose commanders realized that their cause was hopeless and that they were merely covering the evacuation of other units; and for the many foreigners holed up in Broadway Mansions, home among other organizations of the Foreign Correspondents' Club, the General Post Office and the Embankment Building, to which place of imagined safety the Salvation Army had moved its China headquarters. 'For two days the building [Embankment Building] was under fire with its thousand or more inhabitants crowded into the corridors for safety', Arthur Ludbrook said. But he was happy to advise his superiors in London that 'officers who live in the building are none the worse for the experience and headquarters functions as usual'.[75]

The stand-off at Suzhou Creek was brought to an end by the means communists employed on countless occasions to disarm their enemies: the 'turning' of Nationalist commanders by pointing out the futility of their cause; the need to avoid loss of life and damage to property; and powerful appeals to their patriotism. Chinese should not fight Chinese, was the message. On 27 May, Liu Changyi, Deputy Commander of the Shanghai-Wusong Garrison, surrendered his 40,000 men. All of the city was in communist hands, the evidence of the rout of government forces striking. Shi Youren, commander of the 8th Division of the Nationalists' 54th GMD Army, recalled the scene:

> On the afternoon of May 25th, the day Tang Enpo gave the order to evacuate the city, I set out in a jeep for Qiujiang Wharf. I hadn't been travelling very long when I ran into a traffic jam and it is was impossible to go any further. I got out of the vehicle and went ahead on foot to see what was going on. The road to the wharf was solidly blocked with vehicles of all kinds. It was then that I discovered that because the PLA had been shelling the wharf area, the drivers and their escorts had deserted their vehicles and rushed on board the ships in panic. When I got to the ships I saw that few of our troops had managed to get aboard . . . The

jetties were out of use and I personally had to be carried on board (by other soldiers presumably). The boat allocated to us was a 3,000 ton cargo vessel which had previously been used to transport 2,000 tons of flour. It could carry only 1,000 of our troops ... The situation was desperate and we had to throw overboard much of our ammunition. The crew wanted us to set off immediately, and although we were overloaded, we had no choice but to do so.[76]

Some 50,000 Nationalist troops are believed to have escaped Shanghai for Taiwan or Zhoushan. A much larger number was left behind. Most surrendered. Others scattered across the countryside, some of them to regroup and launch small-scale attacks on communist forces. Still others, if circumstances allowed, threw away their uniforms and made for home, in many cases hundreds of miles away.

Shanghai's new dawn

In common with the residents of other cities where the communists marched or fought their way in, the people of Shanghai were keen to get a glimpse of their liberators as soon as it was safe to do so. Randall Gould, among others, witnessed popular much enthusiasm for the regime 'as well as secret preparation for its arrival'.[77] This was the work of a numerically small but effective underground Party whose 'reached into police offices, government departments, railway yards, factories and schools', according to one observer.[78] There were certainly Party supporters at St John's, one of Shanghai's most famous universities. A pro-communist group would soon emerge there to lead the student body in transforming the institution.[79]

First impressions were a combination of admiration and disdain. The former arose when residents found that, during the first few days of their arrival, communist troops slept on the streets despite heavy rain, declined invitations to dry off in people's houses, rejected gifts of food and marched off to perform their ablutions in the Huangpu river rather than commandeer more convenient facilities for such purposes.

Nationalist soldiers had behaved very differently – as the young architect Chen Zhanxiang (known as 'Charlie Cheng' during his student days in Britain) saw first-hand as he watched them flee Shanghai, pilfering and looting as they did so. Despairing of China's future, Chen had already decided to move to Taiwan and had packed his belongings and bought an airline ticket accordingly. Then, gazing out of his apartment window, he saw the communist troops enter the city in a quiet, disciplined fashion. When, the next morning, they declined to accept the soup he and his wife had made for them, Chen took it back upstairs and broke down in tears. 'If a party can educate its army to behave in that way, why wouldn't I have faith in their ability to re-build the country?' he said. He promptly tore up his air ticket.[80]

The disdain was the product of an understandable but hardly flattering sense of Shanghainese superiority: residents knew their city was the most sophisticated in China and those now occupying it were country bumpkins. Writer Percy Finch spoke for many, Chinese and foreign alike, when he described the liberators as 'red-faced country boys ... hardened by long marches and campaigning but [who] retained all the gawkiness of their rural background; they gaped at skyscrapers, department stores, domed banks, towering office buildings, neon signs and monster signboards with the wide-opened eyes of villagers lost in a modern city'.[81] Such an army might be able to conquer the country, given the dire performance of Chiang's troops, but how could they be expected to run as complex and modern a city as Shanghai? Many worried that they could not, and that Shanghai would never recover. Others drew a more comforting conclusion: the city's new rulers would have to rely on established local talent and enterprise or see the city fare even worse than it had in the last months of Nationalist rule.

Many foreign businessmen, perhaps encouraged by the circulation of notices written in English to the effect that, provided they were engaged in 'normal vocations', they and their enterprises would be safe under the communists, were even more upbeat.[82] This perplexed US Consul General Cabot. The day after the takeover he attended a meeting of the US Chamber of Commerce where: 'The rejoicing couldn't have been greater if the city had been liberated by American forces. American and British businessmen were convinced – I can't think why – that they would do better under the Communists.'[83] There was a widespread feeling that, despite their anti-imperialist and pro-Soviet rhetoric, the communists would need to trade with the West to give their regime a fair chance of survival let alone achieve its hugely ambitious goals. Nowhere could such trade be conducted more conveniently than in Shanghai, whose future as an international city thus seemed assured. Disappointment lay in store for those who held such views.

Nevertheless, the speed with which normal life resumed surprised and pleased many. 'The changeover was like nothing that had been imagined', wrote Randall Gould. 'We had feared days or lawless disorder. Nothing of the sort occurred. One day the Nationalists, next day the Communists, while our erstwhile defenders rode down the Yangtze River and over to Formosa. It was as simple as that.'[84]

Traffic quickly took to the streets again. Shops and some banks reopened. Tuition resumed in some schools. Postal services, complete with new stamps, began again. Supplies of coal and grain arrived. On 1 June, the Yangtze was declared open to foreign trade, though not to foreign warships, and inland navigation to and from Shanghai resumed. The CCP's New China News Agency reported that half of Shanghai's privately owned factories were operating by 9 June and that all of them were expected to do so by the end of the month. Mayor Chen Yi held a series of meetings with senior business leaders, promising to assist them and reminding them of the difficulties they faced under Nationalist rule.[85]

Yet this was a 'new' normal, as a sharp-eyed UP reporter pointed out: 'Chen Yi's Field Army political department had opened an office at Bubbling Well Temple guarded by volunteer police. A poster at the entrance still proclaimed "death to all Communist traitors,"' said the despatch. 'Nearby, in the Burlington Hotel, 300 Government and Kuomintang officials were being guarded by five sentries.'[86]

It was never the CCP's plan simply to run 'old Shanghai' better than their predecessors. Rather, Party leaders were determined to reshape city society, and to do so at a time of continued insecurity and danger – much of it stemming from Nationalist air raids, a blockade of shipping and the threat that Chiang's armies might 'return' in force. The tense atmosphere tended to increase support for the new regime, as was the case elsewhere in the country. Almost daily reports about the arrest of Nationalist spies, the thwarting of attempts to assassinate Chen Yi, and plots to blow-up factories, banks and government buildings also made it easier to exert control over citizens' lives.

Under Mayor Chen Yi, the Shanghai Military Control Committee quickly took over public enterprises, including many schools and leading universities. It also adopted the Nationalists' system of household registration but brought it together with 'food ration cards and mass participation', to use Wakeman's phrase.[87] This meant that the police were in charge of issuing ration tickets. The creation of street and lane committees of residents, again welcomed by many as an expression of civic solidarity, made possible the social control and surveillance that the CCP deemed necessary to transform Shanghai society – and to identify and deal with those who resisted change.

Shanghai's diverse media was tamed to the same end. Two of the three leading newspapers, *Shen Bao* and *Xin Wan Bao*, were closed because of their previous anti-communist stance. Two others 'stopped publication voluntarily', as the rather pregnant phrase put it.[88] Two English-language papers lingered longer – considerably so in the case of the venerable *North China Daily News*: it survived until June 1950, when it made the mistake of reporting that the North Koreans had attacked first in the Korean War. Randall Gould's paper, *The Shanghai Mercury and Evening News*, stopped publishing in June 1949, a few weeks after the takeover, due to a wage dispute, which the paper was prevented from covering in its own pages. The upshot, according to Gould, was a handsome pay-off to the staff from New York (by the owners) and the sale of the printing machinery at a large net loss.

It would take another year at least before Shanghai's new identity as a socialist city completely eclipsed what was for many Chinese its disreputable past as a cosmopolitan, 'quasi-colonial entrepôt of trade, culture and intrigue', as one writer put it.[89] But within a few months of 'liberation', the break with the past was already profound. 'The liberation of Shanghai has broken the resistance of Chinese counterrevolutionaries whose forces had already been shattered into tiny fragments', proclaimed the New China

News Agency. 'Remnants in various parts of the country are unlikely to hold out much longer.'[90]

Notes

1   Tony Saich (ed.), *The Rise to Power of the Chinese Communist Party: Documents and Analysis* (New York: M. E. Sharpe, 1996), p. 1340.

2   Ibid., pp. 1340–1.

3   Mao Zedong, 'The People's Liberation Army Capture Nanking', April 1949. https://www.marxists.org/reference/archive/mao/selected-works/poems/poems19.htm (accessed 20 February, 2020).

4   T'ong Te-kang (with Li Tsung-jen). *The Reminiscences of Li Tsung-jen* (Boulder, CO: Westview Press, 1979), p. 513.

5   Seymour Topping, *Journey between Two Chinas* (New York: Harper & Row, 1972), p. 66.

6   TNA FO371/75801, 25 April 1949, p. 94.

7   *Time*, 2 May 1949, p. 16.

8   T'ong Te-kang, *The Reminiscences of Li Tsung-jen*, p. 516.

9   Liang Shengjun. *Jiang-Li douzheng neimu* ('The Inside Story of the Struggle between Jiang and Li') (Taipei: Xinxin wencongshu, 1992), p. 140, from which the scenes at the airport that follow are drawn.

10 Ibid.

11 SOAS archives, 'Papers of Eva Dykes Spicer', PP. MS92, 'Report from the Office of the Dean of Students', 11/48.

12 Ibid., p. 1.

13 Ibid.

14 Ibid., Private letter dated 30 April 1949 and marked not for quotation and only for private circulation, p. 1.

15 Ibid.

16 Jin Feng. *The Making of a Family Saga, Ginling College* (Albany, NY: State University of New York Press), 2009, p. 229.

17 K. M. Panikkar, *In Two Chinas: Memoirs of a Diplomat* (London: George Allen & Unwin, 1955), pp. 47–8.

18 Ibid., p. 49.

19 *Time*, 2 May 1949, p. 16.

20 Claire Roberts, *Photography and China* (London: Reaktion Books, 2013), p. 101.

21 Liu Tong, *Juezhan: Huadong jiefang zhanzheng, 1945–1959* ('Decisive Battles: The War of Liberation in East China, 1945–1949') (Shanghai: Shanghai renmin chubanshe, 2017), p. 570.

22 Zhonggong Shanxi shengwei dangshi biangongshi (ed.), *1949 Shanxi ganbu nanxia shilu* ('1949 A True Record of the Shanxi South-bound Cadres'), Vol. 1. (Taiyuan: Shanxi renmin chubanshe, 2012), p. 202.

23 Liu Tong, *Juezhan*, p. 570.

24 Panikkar, *In Two Chinas*, pp. 49–50.

25 Knight Biggerstaff, *Nanking Letters, 1949* (Cornell University: East Asia Papers Number 23, 1979) p. 44.

26 SOAS archives, 'Papers of Sir Lionel Lamb', PP. MS 380730, *Nanjing Diplomatic Press Service*, 11 May 1949, p. 8.

27 Ibid.

28 Ibid., p. 7.

29 Ibid., p. 8.

30 SOAS archives, 'Papers of Eva Dykes Spicer', PP. MS92, Private letter dated 30 April 1949 and marked not for quotation and only for private circulation, p. 4

31 SOAS archives, 'Papers of Sir Lionel Lamb', PP. MS 380730, *Nanjing Ribao*, 12 May, 1949, n.p.

32 Knight Biggerstaff, *Nanking Letters, 1949*, p. 54.

33 See Chapter 3, p. 89.

34 Dangdai zhongguo yanjiusuo bian (ed.), *Zhonghua Renmin Gongheguo shibiannian: 1949 nianjuan* ('Chronicle of the People's Republic of China 1949') (Beijing: Dangdai zhongguo chubanshe, 2004), p. 356.

35 See Chapter 2, p. 160.

36 See Chapter 5, p. 147.

37 Kenneth W. Rea and John Brewer (eds), *The Forgotten Ambassador: The Reports of John Leighton Stuart, 1946–1949* (Boulder, CO: Westview Replica Editions), 1981), p. 320; FRUS, *The Far East: China, Vol. VIII*, 25 April 1949. https://history.state.gov/historicaldocuments/frus1949v08/d857 (accessed 20 February 2020).

38 Liu Tong, *Juezhan*, p. 590.

39 Panikkar, *In Two Chinas*, pp. 52–3.

40 SOAS archives, 'Papers of Eva Dykes Spicer', PP. MS92. Letter to Family and Friends dated 29 August 1949.

41 Felix Smith, *China Pilot: Flying for Chennault during the Cold War* (Washington, DC: Smithsonian Institution Press, 1995), p. 115.

42 Junshi kexueyuan junshilishi yanjiubu (ed.), *Zhongguo renmin jiefangjun zhanshi:disanjuan, quanguo jiefang zhanzheng shiqi* ('History of the Wars fought by the Chinese People's Liberation Army. Vol. 3: The War of National Liberation') (Beijing: junshi kexue chubanshe, 1987), p. 362.

43 Smith, *China Pilot*, p. 117.

44 William W. Whitson, *The Chinese High Command: A History of Communist Military Politics, 1921–71* (New York: Praeger, 1973), p. 353.

45 Liu Tong, *Juezhan*, p. 601.

46 Ibid., p. 604.

47 Ibid., p. 601.

48 Ibid. pp. 600–1.

49 FRUS, *The Far East: China, Volume VIII*, 24 April 1949. https://history.state. gov/historicaldocuments/frus1949v08/d321 (accessed 20 February 2020).

50 *The Times*, 28 April 1949, p. 2.

51 FRUS, *The Far East: China, Volume VIII*, 11 May 1949. https://history.state. gov/historicaldocuments/frus1949v08/d361 (accessed 20 February 2020).

52 FRUS, *The Far East: China, Volume VIII*, 7 May 1949. https://history.state. gov/historicaldocuments/frus1949v08/d348 (accessed 20 February 2020).

53 *Time*, 16 May 1949, p. 19.

54 FRUS, *The Far East: China, Volume VIII*, 25 April 1949. https://history.state. gov/historicaldocuments/frus1949v08/d325 (accessed 20 February, 2020)

55 *Time*, 23 May 1949, p. 21.

56 Peter Townsend, *China Phoenix: The Revolution in China* (London: Jonathan Cape, 1955), p. 61.

57 FRUS, *The Far East: China, Volume VIII*, 11 May 1949. https://history.state. gov/historicaldocuments/frus1949v08/d361 (accessed 20 February 2020).

58 *SWB*, No. 9, 21 June 1949, p. 29.

59 Townsend, *China Phoenix*, p. 68.

60 Randall Gould, 'Shanghai during the Takeover, 1949', *The Annals of the American Academy of Political and Social Science*, Vol. 277, Report on China, September 1951, p. 183.

61 See Chapter 4, p. 114.

62 Sherman Cochran and Andrew Hsieh, *The Lius of Shanghai* (Cambridge, MA: Harvard University Press, 2013), p. 283.

63 See Chapter 8, p. 219.

64 Roman Malek (ed.), *Jews in China, From Kaifeng to Shanghai* (Sankt Augustin: Monumenta Serica Institute and the China-Zentrum, 2000), p. 413.

65 *The Times*, 29 April 1949, p. 4.

66 *The Times*, 25 April 1949, p. 4.

67 *The Times*, 26 April 1949, p. 4.

68 Salvation Army Heritage Centre. Letter from Arthur Ludbrooke, 21 May 1949, File No. CH1/1/3.

69 Percy Finch, *Shanghai and Beyond* (New York: Charles Scribner's Sons, 1953), p. 338.

70 Jeremy Brown and Paul G. Pickowicz (eds), *Dilemmas of Victory: The Early Years of the People's Republic of China* (Cambridge, MA: Harvard University Press, 2007), p. 32.

71 Chen Guanren, 'Gongwujuzhang Zhao Zukang ruhe dangshang guomindang zuihou yiren shanghai shizhang' ('How Public Works Chief Zhao Zuguang became the last GMD mayor of Shanghai'), CCP News, Party History Channel, pp. 1–2. http://dangshi.people.com.cn/n/2013/0707/c85037-22107403.html (accessed 20 February 2020).

72 Ibid.

73 Ibid.

74 *SWB*, No. 7, 7 June 1949, pp. 25–6.

75 Salvation Army Heritage Centre, Territorial Newsletter, Shanghai, 3 June 1949, File No., CH1/2/1.

76 Liu Tong, pp. 611–12.

77 Gould, 'Shanghai during the Takeover, 1949', p. 183.

78 Townsend, *China Phoenix*, p. 65.

79 Helen Zia, *Last Boat out of Shanghai: The Epic Story of the Chinese Who Fled Mao's Revolution* (New York: Ballantine Books, 2019), p. 269.

80 Wang Jun, *Cheng Ji* ('City Story') (Beijing: Joint Publishing Book Store, 2011), p. 78.

81 Finch, *Shanghai and Beyond*, p. 339.

82 *SWB*, No. 7, 7 June 1949, pp. 24–5.

83 Noel Barber, *The Fall of Shanghai: The Communist Take-Over in 1949* (Newton Abbot: Readers' Union, 1980), p. 164.

84 Gould, 'Shanghai during the Takeover, 1949', pp. 183–4.

85 *SWB*, No. 8, 14 June 1949, p. 21.

86 *SWB*, No. 6, 31 May, 1949, p. 22.

87 Jeremy Brown and Paul G. Pickowicz (eds), *Dilemmas of Victory: The Early Years of the People's Republic of China*, p. 43.

88 *SWB*, No. 6, 31 May 1949, p. 21.

89 Carolyn Wakeman and Ken Light (eds), *Assignment Shanghai: Photographs on the Eve of Revolution* (Berkeley, CA: University of California Press, 2003), p. viii.

90 *SWB*, No. 7, 7 June 1949, pp. 24–5.

7

Parallel worlds

Li licks his wounds

If Acting President Li Zongren regarded his flight from Nanjing in the early hours of 23 April as a low point in his political and personal fortunes, he would soon discover there was worse to come. His first problem was relatively inconsequential: once his plane had taken off, just hours before communist soldiers marched into the centre of the Nationalist capital, it ran into bad weather. He had surprised his pilot by instructing him to head for Guilin, capital of Guangxi province, rather than Guangzhou, the temporary seat of the central government, where many other senior officials had fled. But foggy conditions made landing in Guilin dangerous and he was forced to divert to Liuzhou, in central Guangxi, from where Li telephoned provincial governor Huang Xuchu to break the news that he was 'coming home' rather than joining the rest of the government, which would be left leaderless as a result.

Yet once Li and his party settled in Guilin, it quickly emerged that there was not enough money to fund the office of the acting vice-president. 'Three days after our arrival I was told that we had used up all the funds we had brought from Nanjing', a close aide complained. 'We didn't even have enough money to buy food! To tide us over, I had no choice but to borrow 3,000 silver dollars from the Guangxi Provincial Government and Guilin Bank.'[1] Though a tiny amount, this added to the burdens of a province already straining every resource to support hundreds of thousands of its own troops on the frontline to the north.

But what really marred Li's homecoming was the fact that the Nationalist cause, over which he had presided for the past three months, was in almost complete disarray. PLA troops had crossed the Yangtze in strength, virtually unopposed. The capital had fallen. A host of other cities that formed part of the government's political and economic heartland were about to do the same.

Among the lost territory was that of southern Anhui, the province in central China that straddled the Yangtze between Wuhan and Nanjing. This had been part of the Guangxi Clique's 'empire' since the start of the war against Japan, when Li Zongren was appointed regional commander. The PLA's crossing of the Yangtze brought Guangxi influence to a sudden end, forcing Governor Zhang Yichun (an Anhui man but a Guangxi appointee) and his entourage to flee. As elsewhere, Nationalist troops could not flee fast enough: the only limit to the PLA's advance was its capacity to administer the newly acquired territories and its over-extended supply lines.

The government still had many men in uniform, even though its armies now relied on a smaller population and diminished territory for material and moral support. But they varied in quality, the personal allegiances of their commanders, the amount and quality of equipment and supplies at their disposal, and, above all, in their willingness to fight. Tang Enbo's well-equipped troops were a case in point: they had withdrawn to Shanghai in the face of the PLA onslaught with a view to stripping the city of as many assets as possible before retreating to the Zhoushan Islands and Taiwan. Further north, Liu Anqi, another commander loyal to Chiang, was desperately trying to evacuate as many of his troops as possible from Qingdao, the remaining port north of the Yangtze still in Nationalist hands, from which the United States was also withdrawing its ships and marines in the face of a PLA assault that threatened to drive them into the sea.

In the interior, the most formidable, though not the best-equipped, troops were those of Bai's Central China Command. They stood directly in the path of the PLA's advance into south China, seat of the temporary capital, and were thus now the communists' primary target. Hu Zongnan, based in the former imperial capital of Xian in Shaanxi province, also commanded a large force. In principle, it constituted an obstacle to a communist advance into both southwest and northwest China, where local Moslem cavalrymen might also be expected to put up a fight. Further south, troops of the Guangzhou Pacification Command under Yu Hanmou, though smaller in number and poorly equipped, could if suitably led and organized surely be expected to mount a defence of the two 'Guang' provinces, Guangdong and Guangxi.

But little would be accomplished on the military front unless the Nationalists healed their political divisions. This would require Chiang, by now in control of the government's gold supplies, many of its troops and much of its US-supplied military equipment, Li, licking his wounds in Guilin, and the other Nationalist leaders, largely at a loss in Guangzhou, to bury their differences, conduct sweeping reforms and win the people of south China over to the fight against communism. It was a tall order. A. Doak Barnett, that acute observer of China on the eve of the communist conquest, had concluded, after travelling through the south, three months before the PLA crossed the Yangtze, that:

The government's rear is psychologically weak and vulnerable. If an evacuation southward is made, the government will find itself in a region where people have already lost faith in the fight. It will encounter distrust.

It may even encounter intense resentment and active opposition. With public morale at such a low ebb, the job of mobilizing support and reviving a spirit of resistance against the Communists will be colossal – if it is possible at all.[2]

By the time Li arrived in Guilin, the situation in the south had markedly deteriorated.

The mood in the communist-controlled north was upbeat by comparison. Mao and his military commanders were more confident of victory than ever in the immediate aftermath of the Yangtze crossing. With the Nationalist state collapsing before their eyes, they stepped up preparations to replace it. China thus consisted of parallel worlds in the spring and summer of 1949 – one of state-building, the other of state collapse; the end of one regime and the beginning of another.

'Chiang Kai-shek is our enemy': Guangxi's peace movement

Though Li and Bai Chongxi had long been prominent figures on the national stage, their power ultimately lay in their control over Guangxi and its chief resource – the province's fighting men. Gone were the days when they could run the place as a quasi-autonomous personal fiefdom and showcase of reform as they had during the 1930s: Chiang's government had made inroads during and after the war against Japan, weakening their once solid grip on their homeland. But the network of military and civilian officials that Li, Bai and Huang Xuchu, the third leader of the 'Guangxi Clique', had put together to administer the 14–15 million martial-minded yet war-weary, relatively poor people of the province still answered ultimately to them.

Moreover, troops from Guangxi constituted the core of Bai's Central China Command, which in the first two weeks of May was still clinging on to the central Yangtze city of Wuhan and was responsible for the defence of the whole of south China. Many of them had been on the front line of China's national and civil conflicts for the past thirteen years, often fighting far from home. And the defeat and/or retreat of the armies under Chiang's direct control during 1948 and early 1949 meant that it was Guangxi troops, and thus the Guangxi leaders, that now assumed critical importance in determining the future of the Nationalist cause. It is thus no surprise that Li's decision to recuperate in Guilin rather than join the government in Guangzhou worried many Nationalist leaders. Chiang was so concerned that he sent senior envoys to Guilin in a desperate attempt to persuade Li to move south, fearful that, exhausted by military setbacks and the failure of the national peace talks, he and Bai would treat with Mao.

*

Chiang's anxiety was well founded. When Li arrived in Guilin, a group of civilian leaders presented him with a document calling for a peace deal with the communists. Leading the charge was Li Renren, sixty-three, Chair of the Provincial Assembly. Highly respected as a former teacher as well as an administrator, Li Renren enjoyed close relations with both Li and Bai. He rallied other officials of a generally left or liberal persuasion to the cause. The Nationalist government was close to collapse, Li Renren explained. It was important to realize that Chiang Kai-shek, not the communists, was Guangxi's real enemy. Li and Bai still had 200,000 troops under their command, and thus possessed a bargaining chip with which to open talks. Some concessions would have to be made but a local deal could be struck – possibly via the good offices of Li Jishen, the prominent figure from Guangxi, who was now in Beiping in his capacity as head of the 'GMD Revolutionary Committee' (GMDRC), the breakaway Nationalist organization that had thrown in its lot with the communists. Another Guangxi peace advocate, provincial education chief Huang Puxin, said that on his part there could be no talk of fighting on unless he could move his family to Hong Kong, as Bai had done in the case of his own, numerous dependants. Bai was said to be incensed by the remark.

A stormy meeting of senior provincial officials followed at Li's Guilin's residence. As was the case when the Guangxi leaders met the previous month in Nanjing to discuss the peace plan that Huang Shaohong brought back from Beiping, Li responded mildly to the latest initiative. He respected the motives of those involved but said that the moment for peace talks had passed: they had been tried but failed due to the communist's lack of sincerity.

Bai, who had flown in from Wuhan, approached the matter with characteristic bluntness, attacking those who advocated surrender. Guangxi had to be ready to fight – only then might peace be possible, he insisted. To abandon the threat of force and then sue for peace was foolish. The reason he was determined to oppose the communists to the bitter end was 'not to protect his own position, but rather to defend the vital interests of the Chinese nation', according to one of those present. 'When the communists showed they were ready to tolerate different opinions and allow [political] space for opponents to operate, then would be the time to talk of peace.'[3]

The Guangxi peace initiative thus ended abruptly, at least for the time being. Bai ensured that those willing to surrender were removed from office – especially if they controlled the province's financial assets: they could be bargaining chips in talks with communists. Li Renren, by now a member of the GMDRC, would soon slip away from Guangxi to Beiping where he would take up a role in the new communist government. Huang Puxin left for Malaysia. Other Guangxi 'leftists' went to Hong Kong to wait and see how the Civil War ended before deciding their next move. The military faction of the 'Guangxi Clique', anti-communist to a man, had prevailed again. The province's civilian leaders were no match for the men in uniform – a hard truth of Republican-era Chinese politics.

Lin Biao vs Bai Chongxi: a duel resumed

The Guangxi generals did not fare so well in the battle against the communists along the middle reaches of the Yangtze. At first, Bai's headquarters in Wuhan, a centre of industry, major port and a key communications hub, seemed unperturbed by the stunning collapse of the Nationalist defence line in the face of the PLA's three-pronged crossing of the river to the east. The US Consul General in Hankou, which along with Hanyang (also on the north bank of the Yangtze) and Wuchang (on the south bank) constituted the 'tri-city' of Wuhan, found 'remarkable indifference [to the] disaster in east China' among Bai's commanders. Bai would not abandon the city until forced to do so because he needed the tax revenues to finance his troops, the consul asserted.[4] The location of a major iron and steel works, Wuhan also produced munitions, though output was much reduced by years of war and destruction.

Yet Lin Biao, whose Fourth Field Army was by now vastly superior in numbers and morale to the forces commanded by Bai, was bearing down hard on his old foe. His troops had marched the 800 miles from Beiping to the Yangtze in some forty days. Food stores, mobile hospitals and provision for animal shelter and fodder had been set up along the route, while 'at intervals of a few miles, signposts had given details of the next stage of the journey', the official New China News Agency reported. Information had even been given to the soldiers about the country through which they were travelling 'to discount rumours such as that the mosquitos in China were as "big as bees", and that people in the South "died like flies from tropical disease"'.[5] Even so, there were no grounds for complacency: the official history of the Fourth Field Army acknowledged that Bai was a formidable enemy and that its own troops were entering new terrain.[6]

Bai might have appreciated the compliment had survival of his forces not been at stake in the first few days of May. Lin's army had for some time pinned him down, as the PLA high command intended, while the Second and Third Field Armies crossed the Yangtze further east. But within a matter of days, the Second Field Army had not only swept into south China, it was surging west towards Nanchang, capital of Jiangxi province, from where it threatened to cut off Bai's planned retreat into Hunan. 'Bai Chongxi became like a finger jutting out into communist territory', Li Zongren observed.[7] The Central China Command needed to withdraw from Wuhan quickly or face amputation.

Many ordinary residents had already fled. 'Hankou has become a vacuum as people [have] left the city and fled south to Hengyang [in Hunan], Guilin and other places, or west to Guiyang [capital of Guizhou province]', *Minzhu Daily* reported. 'Believing that Bai Chongxi might demolish the city when the time comes for him to withdraw, the populace [that remains] is apprehensive. But though they are thinking of a local peace movement, nobody has the courage to start this openly ... [instead] they are secretly organising and preparing themselves to protect buildings in the city while waiting for the arrival of the liberation forces.'[8]

At first Bai's withdrawal was orderly. But panic set in when Zhang Gan, one of Bai's deputy commanders, surrendered to the communists along with 20,000 men. The Nationalist rear guard evacuated the city on 16 May and the PLA advance guard arrived a few hours later. The communists seemed 'unprepared to have Wuhan drop into their laps so suddenly', mused the US consul general. Nationalist demolition had seriously crippled the port, but small businesses were gradually opening and Wuhan was 'resuming normal appearance'.[9] Communist sources said workers had thwarted Nationalist plans to destroy transport equipment and facilities, in one case by covering 'locomotives in mud to mislead saboteurs, while hiding wheels and vital parts'.[10]

The situation was anything but normal in Nanchang, where Xu Qiming, another Guangxi general, was trying to blunt the threat that its capture would pose to Bai's new HQ in Changsha, capital of Hunan province, some 160 miles to the west. Xu, like Bai, was as committed to the anti-communist cause as he was proud of his identity as a Guangxi man. He complained that the defenders, led by Jiangxi's provincial governor and military chief, Fang Tian (a Chiang appointee), had no stomach for the fight. 'Fang was terrified and had no control over his forces. He wanted to desert Nanchang, but I told him that since he was the provincial governor he had to hang on for at least a few more days', he complained.[11] Xu travelled by train to Changsha to discuss the situation with Bai only to find on his return that Fang had fled. There was no option but to pull out of the city, which he did on 22 May. His forces then embarked on a long defensive battle in the Gan River valley, to the southeast of Nanchang, in an effort to slow the PLA advance and protect Bai's eastern flank.

News from other fronts was equally discouraging. On 20 May, the PLA had driven Hu Zongnan's forces out of Xian, opening the way for incursion deep into the northwest despite initial resistance on the part of Moslem cavalry under local leader Ma Bufang. That Ma's defence of his region only briefly impeded the advance of Peng Denghuai's Second Field Army was no surprise to Stalin. 'You exaggerate the forces of Ma Bufang', he cabled Mao in early June. 'In accordance with our information, he is not that strong.'[12] On 25 May, Shanghai had fallen. And Qingdao changed hands on 2 June when, in the words of the British consul general, 'General Liu sailed away about 9.45am leaving behind about 2,000 troops . . . and wholesale looting commenced at the wharf'.[13] Soldiers left ashore tried to commandeer a Norwegian vessel to take them to safety. It was a 'most marvellously quiet and peaceful takeover', the Consul observed. But he was perplexed: Judging from the 'weary, footsore and weather beaten' appearance of the communist troops who arrived, 'it was a mystery how they walked through the Nationalists'.[14] These military setbacks added to the political and economic woes unfolding in the rapidly diminishing territory under Nationalist control.

'Scraping the bottom of the barrel': the Nationalists in Guangzhou

Li Zongren, having quashed the Guangxi 'peace movement', refused to resume his duties as head of the government in Guangzhou until he received assurances from Chiang Kai-shek that he would be given a free hand in decision-making and access to the financial assets needed to prosecute the war. He also recommended that Chiang either resume the presidency or leave the country.

In a somewhat tortuous exchange of messages, Chiang insisted that the Ministry Defence had sole responsibility for military decisions. As for finances, it was true that he alone had taken the decision to transfer the government's gold and foreign exchanges reserves to Taiwan. But he had done so solely to prevent them from falling into the hands of the enemy. In future, budgetary allocations for military and other purposes would be made 'as normal'. As for Li's suggestion that he leave the country, Chiang replied: 'I have given more than 40 years of my life to the Revolution and the struggle to create an independent and free China. As long as some part of China is still free and there is a regime capable of preserving its independence, I am convinced there is hope.'[15] In the light of these assurances Li, more trusting than he had a right to be, left Guilin for Guangzhou on 8 May, to the relief of many in the Nationalist camp.

But it was more relief than belief, as Lewis Clark, senior US diplomat in Guangzhou, advised Washington: 'Li felt it necessary to come to Guangzhou, resume authority and ascertain whether Generalissimo will in fact behave. My best judgement is that he won't and that these maneuvers merely delay disintegration and that eventually Li will be led publicly to denounce Generalissimo and his machinations.'[16] This was a prescient observation, the only questions turning out to be those of timing and the precise events that would bring it to pass. Ten days after his arrival in Guangzhou, Li sent Gan Jiehou, a close aide who had been educated in the US, to Washington as his 'personal representative'. His mission was to persuade the administration to provide money and military equipment directly to Li and Bai for the defence of south China.

A tussle in early June over the formation of a new cabinet showed the fragile nature of the new accord between Chiang and Li. The latter insisted that Bai be appointed minister of defence, in which capacity it was imagined that he might be able to turn things around. This was far-fetched given the military setbacks of the previous few weeks; and in any event, Chiang would not hear of it. The post went instead to Yan Xishan, who succeeded He Yingqin as premier, and agreed to take on the defence portfolio as head of a 'war cabinet'. 'The choice of Yan Xishan, last surviving war lord, as premier, seems further evidence, if further evidence is needed, of complete bankruptcy GMD leadership', Lewis Clark wrote.[17] He drove the message home a few days later: 'New Premier Yan Xishan is an old man, old even for his 67 years. After long conversation, one would almost say he is in his dotage, and it is to this man free China is entrusting its destiny.'[18] A member of the Legislative Yuan, which Li persuaded to approve Yan's appointment, said: 'The Guomindang has scraped the bottom of the barrel.'[19]

The new government (and Chiang, often acting alone without Guangzhou's knowledge let alone its permission) sought to stabilize the situation on and off the battlefield. On 20 June, it imposed a sweeping naval blockade on every port from Manchuria in the north to Fujian in the southeast: foreign vessels were forbidden to steam into any communist-held harbour. When the British-owned SS *Anchises* approached Shanghai the next day, Nationalist aircraft bombed and strafed her with machine-gun fire.

The blockade, coupled with air raids on ports and other facilities, soon drained the commercial life out of Shanghai, Tianjin and lesser ports, all of whose trading communities were suffering from high taxes, unfavourable rates of exchange and limited communications with the wider world. It provoked strong opposition from both British and US governments, albeit to little avail. Washington and London were in any event not really at one on the issue. The former wanted to send ships into Shanghai to evacuate its nationals. London was under pressure from the British business community to keep it supplied with the goods and materials local firms needed to survive and hopefully prosper under communist rule.

The economy in Nationalist-held territory was in even worse shape. Finance Minister Xu Kan said in June that the cost of government and military operations totalled some 45 million silver dollars a month while monthly revenues, most of them from customs duties and the salt tax, came to 10 million dollars. The loss of customs revenues in Shanghai and Tianjin to the communists was an enormous blow, and Xu complained of having to go begging to Chiang in Taiwan for funds – only to be turned away empty-handed or with far short of what was required.[20]

Wary of printing money and fuelling even higher rates of inflation, the Guangzhou government on 3 July launched a new currency, the silver yuan. The Nationalists' hard currency reserves, now amassed in Taiwan, should have been enough to back the new issue, but Chiang, one step ahead of his rivals again, had earmarked the nation's gold to support the New Taiwan dollar, introduced on 15 June. Taiwan's economy soon began to stabilize; the urban economy in the mainland was close to collapse. 'The claim that the silver yuan was backed by reserves was fraudulent and the public hoodwinked', complained Li Zongren's aide.[21] The CCP's New China Agency described the episode as 'another large-scale robbery of the people by the Guomindang remnants before they are laid in their coffins'.[22]

Land reform: the Nationalists 'latch on'

The sense that the government was acting too little and often far too late was nowhere more apparent than in the case of its sudden enthusiasm for land reform. 'Land to the tiller' had been the rallying cry of Sun Yat-sen, founder of the GMD, to China's farmers. Considerable efforts were devoted to the study of and solution to China's land problem in the 1920s and 1930s, and in some parts of the country ambitious reforms attempted.[23]

But since Chiang turned on his party's erstwhile communist allies in 1927, land reform had remained more a matter of policy than practice: the central government lacked the will and the capacity to implement reform because, unlike the CCP, it failed to establish effective control over the countryside. This was one of the reasons why Mao was now on the brink of seizing national power and Chiang was rapidly losing it. In the closing stages of the Civil War the Nationalists decided they had to do more for the country's farmers. A Foreign Office official in London, hearing of this turn of events, commented: 'It is a pity action on these lines was not taken years ago . . .'[24]

Guangxi was one of the provinces in which such reforms were introduced, though an official responsible was to claim, after 1949, that the aim was to 'use "reactionary land reform" to counter "revolutionary land reform" of the kind championed by the communists'.[25] In the spring of 1949, provincial authorities conducted a survey to find out how much land was falling out of agricultural production. Landlords discovered to be in possession of such were required to sell their holdings to county-level governments before the spring planting. But few funds were available for this purpose and landlords were quick to resort to aliases in order to retain property within the family rather than sell it to would be owner-occupiers. Plans to ensure that a farmer (invariably a man) be allowed to own only 7 mu of land (1 mu = one-sixth of an acre) plus an extra 3 mu per son up to a maximum of 16 mu were 'not strictly enforced', noted one observer.[26]

In Guangxi, as in other areas, attempts at land reform lasted only as long as the Nationalist regime. More thorough and brutal methods would be employed once the communists gained control. They typically involved public meetings in which landlords were harangued by peasants who were encouraged to 'speak bitterness' about the exploitation they had suffered under the old order. Emotions ran high, as one might expect of occasions designed to 'settle accounts' in the rural class war. Landlords were dispossessed, usually physically mistreated and often killed, their land distributed to tenants or small owner-occupiers. The old order in the countryside of south China was uprooted in the early 1950s as violently as it had been in many parts of northeast and north China beforehand.

Chiang returns

On 1 July, Lester Knox Little, the inspector general of the China Maritime Customs Service, wrote in his diary: '1949 half over. Will I be in China on Dec 31? I doubt it but don't dare make any predictions.'[27] His uncertainty was understandable: unless dramatic changes occurred, there seemed every chance that the government he worked for might not exist by the end of the year.

On the same day that Little made these observations, Gan Jiehou, busily championing Li Zongren's cause in Washington, explained in a meeting with Secretary of State Dean Acheson how the acting president planned to ensure that large parts of mainland China were kept free of communism. Nationalist armies would hold two major defence lines for as long as possible in the hope that US aid would be forthcoming and/or the communist advance would either run out of steam or be halted by popular uprisings in areas already taken over.

The northern defence line ran from Xian in Shaanxi Province, west to Baoji and then south to Hanzhong. Its purpose was to keep the communists

FIGURE 7.1 *'Private Citizen Chiang': Chiang Kai-shek had given up the presidency in January but in July is shown here with his bodyguards in Taiwan, a few months before the communists completed their conquest of the mainland and 'his' government fled to the island.*

FIGURE 7.2 *Chiang Ching-kuo, Chiang Kai-shek's son, was both confidant and companion of his father during the year he lost power on the mainland.*

out of Sichuan, China's granary, to the south, and protect northwest China. Some 400,000 troops, including the formidable Moslem cavalrymen, were said to be available for this task. The southern defence line, a revised version of the one Bai Chongxi had drawn up immediately after the PLA crossed the Yangtze, ran from Changsha in Hunan, southeast to the coast along the border of Guangdong and Fujian provinces.[28] Bai's armies, which Gan by now overestimated at some 300,000, would hold this line, supported by local Guangdong forces. Guangzhou would be kept open to receive US aid or if necessary facilitate Nationalist retreat. Should the government have to give up Guangzhou, the small port of Guangzhouwan, to the southwest, could be held to serve the same function.

Acheson treated Gan courteously but was unimpressed. The lines supposedly being defended had in many areas already been breached. Gan failed to put forward realistic plans as to what equipment the Nationalists needed and how it would change the situation on the battlefield. Conversations about US aid for regional leaders and armies determined to resist communism continued and some funds were eventually dispersed. But though Washington sympathized with Li Zongren's position, it was no more willing to bankroll his wing of the Nationalist government than it was Chiang's. 'The US stood ready to assist China, but first China would have to give concrete evidence of its desire to help itself', Acheson told Gan.[29]

With Li and Chiang still at odds over how to avoid the complete collapse of their government such evidence was not forthcoming. While Li wanted to concentrate on defending the south and southwest, Chiang, at this juncture, felt the best place for any last stand was Taiwan and the southeastern province of Fujian, together with its offshore islands. Nationalist troops concentrations were split between southwest and southeast China accordingly, a situation the communists quickly exploited, once their armies were ready to resume their thrust south.

What brought home the fact that the split at the top of government was unbridgeable was Chiang's return to power in early July in everything but name.[30] In the space of just a few days, after weeks of secrecy surrounding his movements, he chaired a major meeting on military strategy in Taipei and gave an interview to US reporters in which he pledged to fight communism to the finish. He then embarked on a diplomatic visit to the Philippines, with whose President Elpido Rivera Quirino he signed an accord envisaged as the first step towards the creation of a regional anti-communist alliance known as the Pacific Pact.

Chiang feared that Washington had not only given up on him and his government but much of Asia as far as the threat of communism was concerned. As he put it to Lewis Clark, the senior US diplomat in Guangzhou: 'Since the US is not willing to take on the responsibility of leadership in the Far East, I have no option but to put together an alliance to that end myself.'[31] For Chiang, as for Mao, the struggle for China was part of a regional or indeed global battle for supremacy between the socialist and democratic camps. The US government, still keen to reduce rather than increase its commitments in Asia, was unimpressed. So was London. A Foreign Office official complained that, if Chiang's Pacific Pact materialized, it 'would be abortive and prejudice subsequent more sensible attempts to build up an anti-Communist front in S.E Asia'.[32]

On 14 July, Chiang arrived in Guangzhou, apparently without prior notice, to reorganize Nationalist party affairs and discuss defence plans with Li and other leaders. Once word leaked out that he had landed, Acting President Li and Premier Yan sped off to the airport to greet him but arrived too late.[33] Chiang's visit coincided with a pause in what had seemed the PLA's relentless southern advance due to flooding and supply problems; momentarily, a more optimistic mood prevailed in the temporary capital. Agreement was reached on the creation of the GMD's Extraordinary Committee, the party's new supreme decision-making organ, which was designed to coordinate and streamline decision-making at a time of national emergency. Chiang was chairman and Li one of the vice-chairs. Both men hoped the new body would prove an effective means of checking the power of the other. Only one of them would be disappointed at the outcome, and it was not Chiang Kai-shek. Li Zongren was marginalized – politically and soon personally. A CIA assessment described his effectiveness as 'little greater than that of a well-meaning warlord'.[34] He was also by now in poor health, a situation the left-leaning *Far Eastern Bulletin*, published in Hong Kong, was quick to turn to propaganda advantage: 'Li may be genuinely ill, but what ails him most is probably the shock of intense disappointment', it scoffed.[35]

Beiping: re-casting the country

By the summer of 1949 Mao and the other CCP leaders were settling down to life in more comfortable circumstances than many of them had known since embarking on their revolutionary careers. They faced plenty of challenges as the PLA extended control over ever larger chunks of the country, including its major cities. Restoring economic production, curbing inflation, maintaining public order and easing public anxieties over the Party's intentions were chief among them. It was not even clear, given Nationalist air raids and the naval blockade, that recent gains were irreversible. 'Just because we have won victory, we must never relax our vigilance against the frenzied plots for revenge by the imperialists and their running dogs', Mao warned. 'If they still hanker after adventures, they will send some of their troops to invade and harass China's frontiers.'[36]

Yet by mid-year, the Party had combined apparent military invincibility with a monopoly of hope regarding China's future. Mao and the men around him had fashioned a master narrative of national salvation, something the Nationalists failed to achieve throughout their long, bitter struggle against communism. The CCP promised the Chinese people 'liberation' – land for the peasants, an end to widespread injustices, of bullying at the hands of foreigners and of poverty and backwardness. There was to be a 'new China': a modern, industrialized country that the world would never look down on again. Such a powerful message overcame misgivings many might have about the Party's recourse to violence in the countryside and the new curbs on individual freedoms it imposed in the cities. China needed to change; that was undeniable. It was also widely accepted. Thanks to the Communist Party, it was at last going to happen.

Among those who thought so was Li Zhisui, thirty, a medical doctor from a wealthy family in Beiping who had left the country in December 1948 in pursuit of a brighter future in Hong Kong or Australia. In the event, he found neither prospect congenial, the first because he did not wish to be a 'disenfranchised subject of a foreign king', the second because of Australia's 'whites only' policy.[37] What shaped Li's future was the communists' capture of Beiping and their humbling of the Royal Naval frigate HMS *Amethyst* on the Yangtze a few months later. When his family wrote to him, urging him to return, Li was ready to comply. 'It seemed perfectly natural to me that China should be governed by the Communist party', he wrote. 'I worshipped the party. It was the hope of new China.'[38] Li and his wife Lillian Wu left Hong Kong for Beiping in mid-June 1949 even though they could earn more working abroad. 'If China under the Communist party could become rich again, I was willing to suffer hardship for my country', he declared.[39]

Li was at first struck by the shabby, drab appearance of Beiping and its residents who, men and women alike, 'dressed in communist blue or grey cotton washed so often as to be almost completely faded'. Yet 'the whole city seemed happy ... and the population welcomed the new communist government'. A bigger surprise was the fact he was assigned to duties not, as he hoped, in a city hospital or medical school but to the 'Labour University' in the Fragrant Hills outside Beiping. This was the closely guarded quarters in a former imperial park where Mao and the Party elite lived and worked. It took him some time to discover that he had been 'plunked unsuspecting into the very centre of the Chinese Communist Party', as he put it.[40] By a twist of fate, he would remain in this privileged position for the rest of his working life, thanks to his appointment a few years later as Mao's personal physician.

Mao's mastery of the country was not complete when the somewhat mystified Li Zhisui turned up at the CCP's headquarters, its seclusion, fresh air, flowers, lakes and the scent of pine trees a welcome alternative to the heat and dust of central Beijing. But he was certainly by now the most powerful man in China. The unrivalled leader of his party, he was hailed within its ranks as a master strategist and theoretician. To his authenticity as a peasant, and thus an ordinary son of the Chinese people, he added almost legendary status as a successful revolutionary leader, able to dissect China's national situation and place it in a global context. These attributes, together with his charismatic personality, had made him the object of a personality cult within the Party, and increasingly among the general public. His portrait, like his message, was becoming ubiquitous.

Yet if he was dominant, Mao was not (yet) domineering. Rather, his own triumphs and those of his Party were the fruit of collective leadership. The number two figure in the Party, Liu Shaoqi, and number three, Zhou Enlai, figured large in decision-making, along with Zhu De, the military commander, and the key generals in the field: Chen Yi in the southeast, Lin Biao (then a Mao favourite), in the south, Liu Bocheng, soon to head southwest, and Peng Dehuai, readying his forces to conquer the northwest. Mao was careful to allow his military commanders flexibility in achieving their objectives.

The military and political successes of the previous few years did much to account for this unity within the top ranks of the Party, which extended beyond the figures just mentioned. A common determination to transform China into a prosperous and powerful state had the same effect. Lack of either was the main cause of the divisions and diminishing authority of the Nationalist government in the south.

*

While it could draw on the rich experience of running large parts of China dating back to the late 1920s, the Party now faced the challenge of governing the entire country. Much of it was newly conquered. A large part of it was unfamiliar in the sense that the CCP had weak or almost no organizational presence in many areas, especially the south and southwest. Vested interests and even many ordinary people could be expected, at best, to be lukewarm about the idea of revolutionary change imposed by 'outsiders'. As Mao pointed out, many people, and foreigners in particular, felt the communists simply were not up to the job: 'They reckon that we will not be able to manage our economy, they are standing by and looking on, awaiting our failure.'[41]

Uncertainty over the Party's attitude towards the Soviet Union and its willingness to share power at home accompanied these doubts about its capacity to govern the country. Diplomats in particular continued to speculate about the extent to which the CCP was a genuinely Marxist party, Mao a potential 'Asian Tito', and whether it would be economic difficulties or the incompatibility between communist ideals and the supposedly individualistic nature of the Chinese people that would frustrate the country's new rulers. Mao did much to end such speculation with the publication, on 1 July, of *On the People's Democratic Dictatorship*, a key text of the times and one of the most important of his many writings.

In the space of a few pages, Mao summarized the development of human progress according to Marxism, reviewed the course of Chinese history since the Opium Wars, and explained the failure of efforts to reform China – until its advocates discovered Marxism, thanks to the Bolshevik Revolution of 1918.[42] History had shown there were limits to what China could learn from the reactionary imperialistic West. It had thus been necessary to abandon the pursuit of 'bourgeois democracy' for 'people's democracy' under the leadership of the working class. According to Mao, the Chinese 'people' consisted of the urban working class, the peasantry, the petty bourgeoisie (small businesses) and the national bourgeoisie (larger Chinese private firms). Since communist armies had overthrown the reactionary Guomindang, these groups or classes could now form a state of their own. Jointly, they would exercise dictatorship over 'feudal reactionaries' and 'the running dogs of imperialism', categories reserved for landlords, bureaucratic capitalists (those with close ties to the GMD) and Nationalist diehards of one sort or another. These were the class enemies whom it was necessary to suppress because, as Mao explained it, one should not show 'the slightest timidity before a wild beast'.

But in imposing this revolutionary new order at home China could not expect to stand alone. It must ally itself with the Soviet Union and the People's Democracies (of Eastern Europe). New China would 'lean to one side'. National interests would take priority whenever possible but within the context of an international united front with the socialist camp. Having seized power, the CCP now had to exercise it, which was a very different matter given the parlous state of the country. 'We shall soon put aside some of the things we know well and be compelled to do things we don't know well', Mao warned, referring to the challenges of economic construction that lie ahead. 'We must not pretend to know what we do not know. The Communist Party of the Soviet Union is our best teacher and we must learn from it.'

US Ambassador Leighton Stuart, isolated in his embassy in Nanjing and by now rather downcast at the defeat of his vision of a liberal future for China, began one of his last significant despatches to Washington with an ironical thank you to Mao for his 'unprecedentedly clear exposition of just where the top leadership of the CCP stands'. He said the principal tones of Mao's essay were those of:

> unswerving allegiance to the doctrine of world revolution by violence, of devotion to the USSR as the centre of revolutionary power, of destructive hatred of all opposing forces, of absolutism and irreconcilability of Communist creed with any other political or social theory. What are to us horrors of bloody struggle are to Mao and his associates only necessary, desirable surgery on (the) body politic of China.[43]

Stuart, in common with many other people, might have had a lot more to say had they known that, on Mao's orders, Liu Shaoqi was at this precise moment on a secret mission to Moscow in search of financial aid, technical assistance and what amounted to a guide on how to build a socialist state. Stalin was ready to comply on the first two points, reacting with humour and surprise when Mao cabled that China was willing to pay more than the 1 per cent annual interest originally attached to the loan. Liu and his comrades were told they were welcome to study and learn all they could from the workings of the Soviet state, though it would be best if they were to 'legalise their presence by declaring themselves to be a trade delegation from Manchuria'.[44] A team of Soviet experts accompanied Liu on his return train journey to Beiping. The CCP leadership's secretive – and successful – appeal to Stalin for aid was in sharp contrast with the earlier highly publicized, much criticized and unavailing efforts of Song Meiling to persuade President Truman to come to the rescue of her husband's ailing Nationalist government.[45]

However, by this time Washington had grown tired of China in more senses than one. The Truman administration's handling of the country had long been the subject of partisan contention, and Chiang's US supporters – the China Lobby – were searching among their fellow citizens for those they insisted had betrayed the Chinese leader. The guilty parties were said to be communists in the State Department, among others. The China Lobby was exercising more influence on US China policy than events in China itself.

It was in this context that, at Secretary State Dean Acheson's suggestion, the administration decided to produce a 'White Paper' to set out the record concerning US China policy as well as its consequences. Its aim was to explain, absolve and exonerate. The key message, accompanied by scores of historical documents, was that the United States was not responsible for the demise of Chiang's government. Acheson's Letter of Transmittal of 30 July 1949 said: 'The Nationalist armies did not have to be defeated; they disintegrated. History has proved again and again that a regime without faith in itself and an army without morale cannot survive the test of battle.'[46] China's Civil War 'was the product of internal Chinese forces, forces which this country tried to influence but could not. A decision was arrived at in China, if only a decision by default.'[47]

Another of the White Paper's assertions was that, due to the CCP's victory, China had once again succumbed to imperialism – this time that of the USSR. Acheson wrote: 'The Communist leaders have foresworn their Chinese heritage and have publicly announced their subservience to a foreign power, Russia, which during the last 50 years, under tzars and Communists alike, has been most assiduous in its efforts to extend its control in the Far East.'[48]

More than 1,000 pages in length, weighing three pounds and with a retail price of three dollars, the White Paper was published on 5 August.[49] The State Department was anxious that Ambassador Leighton Stuart leave China before it appeared. He did so on 2 August. Mao seized on both events to whip up anti-US sentiment and cut the ground from those Chinese, many of them liberal intellectuals, who were lukewarm about the triumph of communism and harboured friendly feelings towards the US. The White Paper was a welcome 'bucket of cold water for those who believe everything American is good and hope that China will model herself on the United States', he wrote.[50] 'Leighton Stuart has departed and the White Paper has arrived', he added a few days later. 'Very good. Very good. Both events are worth celebrating.'[51] A torrent of criticism of the White Paper engulfed communist newspapers and radio broadcasts for days. It included publication of a Chinese translation of Acheson's letter in the form of a textbook, accompanied by an editorial that refuted all its 'erroneous viewpoints'.[52]

Publication of the White Paper failed to stifle Truman's critics at home or free US China policy from entanglement in domestic politics. It did, however, dismay the Nationalist government in Guangzhou at a time when it was subject to a fresh round of military reverses. The most serious of these occurred on the Hunan front, where Bai Chongxi was engaged in a desperate attempt to prevent Lin Biao's forces sweeping south towards Guangzhou or advancing southwest into Guangxi.

Communist pressure and fear of defections among his own commanders had already forced Bai to shift his headquarters from Changsha, the Hunan capital, to Hengyang, about 80 miles to the south. But in early August disaster struck when Hunan Governor Cheng Qian announced that he had turned over his province to the communists, and a few days later his close associate Chen Mingren, commander of Bai's First Army, also deserted. In early September, Cheng Qian travelled by train to Beiping, where he was met by Mao, Zhou and other senior leaders. By that time the rest of South China was exposed to attack. Fear and then gloom settled over Guangzhou. Lester Knox Little wrote: 'These two events – defection in Hunan and White Paper in Washington – may be the one-two punch that finishes the Guomindang Government of China.'[53]

In fact, Bai managed to hold on to southern Hunan for a few more weeks. In mid-August, at the battle of Qingshuping, near Hengyang, he inflicted a heavy defeat on units of Lin Biao's army whose commanders thought the entire province was now theirs for the taking. It was the first significant reverse the PLA suffered for at least a year. But it was also Bai's last victory.

Gan Jiehou in Washington continued his increasingly desperate efforts to secure US aid for the defence of south China, but there was little else for the Nationalists to celebrate in August. Chiang Kai-shek, who had good reason to be offended by the US White Paper, largely kept his own counsel in public. Ching-kuo told his father of the contents of the White Paper and news of the Nationalist defections in Hunan just before he boarded a plane for the Republic of Korea and another round in his anti-communist diplomacy. 'Not only did this news not surprise him but he seemed very calm on receiving it', Ching-kuo noted in his diary.[54] Perhaps this was because Chiang Kai-shek had received assurances that at least the United States, unlike Britain, had no intention of recognizing the new state Mao would soon set up in Beiping.

Hong Kong: fortress or free port?

During the spring and summer of 1949, Britain was more concerned about the security threat to Hong Kong than the question of whether it should recognize China's anticipated new communist government. As discussed in Chapter 4, communist victories in the mainland, disruption to the China trade, an influx of refugees and increased activity on the part of both Nationalist and CCP elements in the territory alarmed the colonial authorities. Much of life seemed to go on as usual. But threat assessments were undertaken to determine Hong Kong's ability to cope with a united, communist China across the border, and internal security was tightened to deal with potential challenges to British rule. London was not complacent. But it decided there was no need yet to step up military defences: communist armies were still hundreds of miles away, and Nationalist defence lines, though stretched and weak, lay between them and the crown colony.

The shelling of HMS *Amethyst* and the PLA's crossing of the Yangtze on 20–21 April drastically altered this picture. Malcolm MacDonald, Britain's Commissioner for Southeast Asia, put the matter bluntly in an 30 April despatch to London:

Further [communist] victories in China in general and our naval reverse on the Yangtze in particular have gravely weakened our prestige . . . I fear that the effect of the *Amethyst* incident in particular is bad in Hong Kong . . . It is universally recognised by the Chinese as a sign of our impotence to resist Chinese Communists, and as an indication that we shall not have the strength to defend Hong Kong if Communists wish to press for rendition or capture of the colony.[55]

Hong Kong Governor Alexander Grantham concurred, noting uneasily that Qiao Mu, head of the communist New China News Agency in the colony, hosted a cocktail reception in the Hong Kong Hotel to celebrate the Yangtze crossing, and that 'an even larger celebration was held at one of the leading Chinese restaurants the next day'.[56]

The Attlee government responded by announcing in May that substantial reinforcements would be sent to Hong Kong, raising the number of troops to be deployed there over the next few months to 30,000–40,000. Air and naval support would be provided and a carrier group would arrive before long. The aim was to calm nerves in the colony and signal to the communists that Britain was determined to hang on to Hong Kong.

The first goal was achieved fairly easily, despite lingering memories in the community of the relative ease with which the Japanese had taken over in December 1941. A visit by Minister of Defence A. V. Alexander in June put some people's minds at rest. But the idea that reinforcing Hong Kong would send a signal to the communists was more problematic, in part because of uncertainty over communist intentions.

The CCP's opposition to imperialism was obvious: the communists were more nationalist than the Nationalists, who had themselves constantly clamoured for the return of Hong Kong. Moreover, during the summer, the Party and its allies stepped up criticism of the colonial government, especially over the Societies Ordinance which prohibited political organizations from operating in the colony if their aims and activities were unconnected to life in the territory. Hong Kong was the only place in China where personal liberties were secured and many in the colony wanted them to remain. But the government felt it had to keep the Civil War out of Hong Kong and used the new legislation to shut down the local branch of the Nationalist Party and prevent the CCP from forming one. GMDRC leader Li Jishen, who until he went north to join the communists had attacked Chiang's government from the shelter of Hong Kong, claimed the Societies Ordinance would turn the territory 'into a police state and deprive every Hong Kong resident of his democratic rights'. To deny local people 'organisational contact with the Mother country was tantamount to depriving them of the freedom of assembly organisation and residence'.[57]

Yet criticism of colonialism was one thing, determination to kick the British out of Hong Kong another. Complaints about alleged British mistreatment of Chinese in the territory (and, incidentally, in Southeast

Asia) were staples of Party propaganda. Explicit references to the need for an early end to foreign rule in Hong Kong were few and far between. London seemed exasperated yet strangely comforted. In mid-June the Foreign Office advised its Commonwealth partners that it had 'no reliable evidence of [communist] intentions and [that] it seems probable that the Communist leaders themselves have as yet reached no decision as to their own policy in regard to Hong Kong.'[58]

Perhaps this was just as well: policy towards Hong Kong had to be calibrated carefully given Britain's different, sometimes almost contradictory, goals as far as the colony was concerned. To start with, the essential weakness of London's position had to be considered: British forces, however large in number, could not expect to hold Hong Kong for long in the face of a determined military attack from the mainland. At best, their presence might raise the threshold of aggression. And while, for reasons of British prestige in Hong Kong and throughout Southeast Asia, it was essential to reinforce the colony, it was equally important not to do so in a way that provoked the communists. Fear that if this happened there would be repercussions for the British community in Shanghai prompted UK Ambassador Ralph Stevenson in Nanjing to urge London to tone down its language and even muzzle the UK media when it came to talk of defending Hong Kong.

For their part, British officials shied away from adopting a long-term policy on Hong Kong, and above all of talking about one. Nigel Brook of the Cabinet Office wrote on 12 May: 'It is not perhaps putting it much too high to say our only hope of hanging on to Hong Kong is to keep quiet about it.'[59] That was not so easy when the very existence of the colony seemed under threat. Harold Macmillan, a future Conservative prime minister, said in the House of Commons on 5 May that Hong Kong was the 'Gibraltar of the Far East. It must be held.'[60]

It was not the last time analogies of this kind were applied to Britain's toehold on the tip of China. The rapid advance of Chinese communism meant the colony would soon constitute a Cold War frontier. The question thus arose of whether efforts should be made to turn it into a 'fortress' or let it to continue to function mainly as free port, albeit one the British were determined to hang on to for strategic as well as commercial reasons. Officials in London and Hong Kong, along with the local business community, favoured the latter. 'Residents in the Colony would be the first to deplore it if the Island were turned into a fortress in reckless disregard of trade', said the *Far Eastern Economic Review*. 'Hong Kong would become merely a sterile camp.'[61]

This fate was avoided and compromise of a kind struck during the late summer of 1949, just a few months before communist forces arrived at the Hong Kong border. Britain would not (quite) turn the colony into an armed camp, but neither was it ready to give it up. On 19 August, Foreign Secretary Ernest Bevin wrote:

Just as we cannot foresee with certainty how the future of Berlin will develop but are convinced of the necessity of remaining there, so we are impelled to remain in Hong Kong without any clear indication of the extent or duration of the military commitment involved. In both cases the threat of Russian and Communist expansionism necessitates holding what we have and not withdrawing.[62]

Bevin also pledged that Britain would discuss the future of the territory only with a 'democratic' China. To do otherwise would 'hand the people of Hong Kong over to a Communist regime'.[63] This condition was soon dropped – a move that made it less embarrassing, just over thirty years later, when Britain opened negotiations with communist China on the handover of Hong Kong.

During September, as communist forces pressed on towards the beleaguered Nationalist capital of Guangzhou, some 80 miles to the north, British troops joined the growing influx of mainland refugees in Hong Kong. Whatever their presence did for local confidence, it created headaches for those tasked with accommodating them. Many soldiers were forced to billet under canvas in the New Territories. A commando brigade fared rather better, occupying the Jockey Club. In country areas, roads had to be built and bridges thrown up. Soldiers and sailors became 'a much more familiar street site than ever before', noted the *Far Eastern Economic Review*.[64]

More noticeable still were the refugees who continued to arrive in large numbers. Among them as the year came to a close was a twelve-year-old boy, Bai Xianyong, one of Bai Chongxi's seven children who, with their mother, had fled south for safety. Their new situation was something of a come down for this family of the Nationalist elite. Hong Kong presented a desolate scene; many of its habitable as well as its less habitable areas were overflowing with the casualties and victims of China's Civil War. 'There were lots of people living with us, including relatives who needed looking after and troops formerly under [father's] command', Bai recalled of his time in the Colony. 'People were forced to sleep outside of our building as well as in the stair wells and the corridors. The streets themselves were full of refugees.'[65]

On the move in south China

Bai Chongxi's family fared better than the millions of other people on the move in south China in an effort to stay ahead of the fighting or escape what they feared would be the unhappy consequences of communist rule. This was certainly true of Mei Jun, the young woman who at the start of the year left her village with Yingyang, her baby son, whom she entrusted to her mother-in-law in a Hunan hamlet, not far from Changsha where Bai had set up his new headquarters.[66] In March, Mei Jun had travelled on to Guangzhou where she hoped to re-join her husband, then in charge of a military unit responsible for security at Tianhe military airport, the main route in and out of the city for political and military leaders. There she saw something of the chaos unfolding in the city as officials and entire government departments, business leaders and diplomats arrived from Nanjing. Large numbers of soldiers and ordinary civilians followed. In the light of these scenes, and the seemingly unstoppable advance of the communist armies, she could no longer bear to be separated from her son. She would go north again and take him to a place of safety.

Yet by September, when Mei Jun eventually set out from Guangzhou, this was no easy matter. For one thing, she was 'going against the flow' of people, which was from north to south. For another, due to the fighting, the railway tracks had been lifted north of Hengyang station in Hunan. She and her escort had to walk some 25 miles along the track bed and country footpaths before they arrived at her husband's remote village. 'How far has the fighting got?' was the question that first greeted her.[67] As for Yingyang, he did not recognize his mother and clung stubbornly to his grandmother.

By the time Mei Jun decided to return south, railway services had resumed at Hengshan, north of Hengyang. But the train they hoped to catch was packed with refugees, many of whom clung to the outside of the carriages and squatted on every conceivable space along the carriage roofs. When it was about to leave, Mei Jun was in torment. It was impossible for her and Yingyang to get on board. 'Wouldn't it be best to leave the child with me rather than take him on the train?' asked her mother-in-law. Mei Jun seemed torn, 'alternately stretching out her hand to take the child and then withdrawing it', according to the account provided later by her daughter. Finally, she decided she must travel alone, telling her mother-in-law that she would soon be back. Her escort then thrust her through a carriage window 'as if she was a piece of freight or a parcel'. Mei Jun was south-bound again.

Also heading south around the same time was the Henan schoolboy Ya Xian who the previous November had left his middle school together with his classmates and teachers in the belief that, since the fighting had reached their hometown, it was better to be educated on the move than risk death or injury.[68] Some five months later, the Henan students met up with those from Hunan and they trekked south together in search of sanctuary. The group settled for a while in Yongzhou, a town on the Xiang river on the Hunan side of the Guangxi–Hunan border, where their teachers took over a local temple and taught as best they could and tried to keep up student morale by getting them to sing the national anthem.

The war had not yet reached Yongzhou. But there was little doubt that it soon would, raising the problem of where the students should head next. For many of them, it would be deep into Guangxi, ahead of Bai's fleeing armies. But not for Ya Xian and others among his group. While in Yongzhou, they recalled hearing for the first time about the 'wonders of Taiwan'. It was the 'Switzerland of the Orient', they were told. Taiwanese sugar cane was 'as thick as a rice bowl'. And fish were 'so numerous that nets were not necessary to catch them – they simply jumped out of the sea and the lakes into fishing boats'. It is not hard to believe such claims impressed naïve young people with little to rely on save their own resources and the desire to find a safe haven.

It was no surprise, then, that Ya Xian and others responded positively to a series of notices they saw pasted on the Yongzhou city walls. These called on young people of vigour, determination and a spirit of self-sacrifice to enlist in a new army then being raised in Taiwan. The recruitment campaign was part of efforts by Sun Liren, the US-trained general on whose skills both Chiang (at first) and Washington set their hopes for a Nationalist military revival. Recruits were told they could expect promotion to junior officer rank after three months training. Ya Xian was encouraged when reporting for duty to find that a fellow Henanese stepped forward and greeted him in his own dialect. He was even more pleased to be offered what amounted to a hearty meal: he and his classmates had not eaten meat for the past six months.

Despite objections from their teachers, the would-be soldiers left Yongzhou for Guangzhou, where Ya Xian remembered seeing his first movie, ironically a film about China's war against Japan. He left the mainland for Taiwan in August 1949, travelling on the deck of a ship full of soldiers. On arrival in the Taiwanese port of Gaoxiong, Ya Xian joined the Nationalist army's Communications Corps.

Mei Jun and Ya Xian's stories were those of loss and separation, an all-too-common experience for Chinese people during the Civil War. But occasionally there were happier outcomes. Douglas Sargent of the Church Missionary Society, who spent much of the late 1940s in the Anglican diocese of Hunan and Guangxi, relayed one such tale to his superiors about the effects of the war on people in his area. He began his 3 July letter from Guilin on a sad note: 'It is interesting, but infinitely saddening, to see all the old refugee problems turning up again; situations and conditions with which we were all too familiar during the war [i.e. China's war against Japan]. Each Sunday we find new members of our congregations – Christians from other places, fleeing from the Reds.'

But Sargent went on:

A week ago we had a very happy experience in this connection. A Christian, a bank clerk from Hankou [in Wuhan], had gone with his family to Liuchow [in central Guangxi]. And somehow on the way they lost a teen-aged son. The father was sent here [i.e. Guilin] for a little while on Bank business, and as he was on his way to early Communion here, whom should he see but his son walking down the road with a bundle on his shoulder. You can imagine the sense of relief and thanksgiving with which he attended the service.[69]

The vast majority of those crowding into trains, buses and ships in south China or who simply tramped along its highways and country lanes were less fortunate. Their travails would continue as China's Civil War forced them to forsake their homes, their families and their very roots in exchange for an uncertain future in unfamiliar, distant parts of the country. Yet though they were many, they were also a minority. The overwhelming majority of Chinese people were not directly affected by the fighting even if they were uneasy about the future. Most could not escape even they wanted to. And many of them regarded the by now obvious communist victory, an end to military conflict and the prospect of a new start for their country with some enthusiasm.

Notes

1   Liang Shengjun, *Jiang-Li douzheng neimu* ('The Inside Story of the Struggle between Jiang and Li') (Taipei: Xinxin wencongshu, 1992), p. 142.

2   Doak A. Barnett, *China on the Eve of Communist Takeover* (New York: Frederick A. Praeger, 1963), p. 99.

3   Liang Shengjun, *Jiang-Li douzheng neimu*, p. 145.

4   FRUS, *The Far East: China*, Vol. VIII, 26 April 1949. https://history.state.gov/historicaldocuments/frus1949v08/d327 (accessed 21 February 2020).

5   *SWB*, No. 5, 24 May 1949, p. 21.

6   Diseyezhanjun zhanshi bianxiezu, *Zhongguo renmin jiefangjun disiyezhanjun zhanshi* ('A History of the Battles Fought by the PLA's Fourth Field Army') (Beijing: jiefangjun chubanshe, 1998), p. 468.

7   T'ong Te-kang (with Li Tsung-jen), *The Reminiscences of Li Tsung-jen* (Boulder, CO: Westview Press, 1979), p. 522.

8   SOAS archives, 'Papers of Sir Lionel Lamb', pp. MS 380730.

9   FRUS, *The Far East: China*, Vol. VIII, 19 May 1949. https://history.state.gov/historicaldocuments/frus1949v08/d392 (accessed 21 February 2020).

10 *SWB*, No. 6, 31 May 1949, p. 22.

11 Zhongyang yanjiuyuan jindaishi yanjiusuo, *Xu Qiming xiansheng fangwenlu* ('A Record of Interviews with Mr Xu Qiming') (Taipei: Zhongyang yanjiuyuan jindaishi yanjiusuo, 1983), pp. 143–4.

12 Wilson Center Digital Archive. 'Stalin to Mao', 18 June 1949. https://digitalarchive.wilsoncenter.org/document/113379 (accessed 21 February 2020).

13 *Foreign Office Files for China: Part 1 Complete Files for 1949, A Listing and Guide to the Microfilm Collection* (London: Adam Matthews, 1999–2002), p. 9.

14 Ibid.

15 Zhang Liangren (ed.), *Chiang ching-kuo xiansheng quanji* ('The Complete Works of Mr Chiang Ching-kuo'), Vol. 1 (Taipei: Xingzhengyuan xinwenchu, 1991), diary entry, 3 May 1949, p. 431.

16 FRUS, *The Far East: China*, Vol. VIII, 9 May 1949. https://history.state.gov/historicaldocuments/frus1949v08/d352 (accessed 21 February 2020).

17 FRUS, *The Far East: China*, Vol. VIII, 5 June 1949. https://history.state.gov/historicaldocuments/frus1949v08/d435 (accessed 21 February 2020).

18 FRUS, *The Far East: China*, Vol. VIII, 16 June 1949. https://history.state.gov/historicaldocuments/frus1949v08/d461 (accessed 21 February 2020). Yan was in fact sixty-five in 1949.

19 *Time*, 13 June 1949, p. 23.

20 Cai Dengshan (ed.), *Huang Xuchu huiyilu – Li Zongren, Bai Chongxi yu Jiang Kieshi lihe* ('Reminiscences of Huang Xuchu – The Separation and Reunion of Li Zongren and Bai Chongxi with Chiang Kai-shek') (Taipei: Duli zuojia, 2016), p. 351.

21 Liang Shengjun, *Jiang-Li douzheng neimu*, p. 180.

22 *SWB*, No. 14, 26 July 1949, p. 31.

23 See Chapter 1, p. 41.

24 TNA FO371/13910, 10 September 1948.

25 Wang Ruilin (ed.), *Xinguixi jishi* ('A True Record of the New Guangxi Clique') (three volumes) (Nanning: Guangxi zhuangzu zizhiqu xinwen chubanju, 1990), Vol. 3, p. 221.

26 TNA FO 371/75841/ F12923, 'Economic Report for Guangzhou for the month of July 1949'.

27 Chang Chihyun (ed.), *The Chinese Journals of L. K. Little, 1943–54: An Eyewitness Account of War and Revolution. Vol 1* (London: Routledge online resource, 2017), Electronic Resource: 707.7/968.

28 See Chapter 6, p. 155.

29 FRUS, *The Far East: China*, Vol. VIII, 16 June 1949. https://history.state.gov/historicaldocuments/frus1949v09/d671 (accessed 6 January 2020).

30 Chiang was not yet ready to 'come out of retirement' and reclaim the title of president.

31 Zhang Liangren (ed.), *Chiang ching-kuo xiansheng quanji*, diary entry, 19 July 1949, p. 456.

32 TNA FO371/75802, 21 July 1949, p. 81.

33 *Time*, 25 July 1949, p. 19.

34 National Intelligence Council (NIC), *Tracking the Dragon: National Intelligence Estimates on China During the Era of Mao, 1948–1976*, 16 June 1949, ORE 45–49, CD-ROM, p. 14 or p. 51.

35 *Far Eastern Bulletin*, 20 May 1949, p. 2.

36 MZD *SW*, Vol. IV, 15 June 1949. https://www.marxists.org/reference/archive/mao/selected-works/volume-4/mswv4_64.htm (accessed 24 October 2019).

37 Li Zhisui (with the editorial assistance of Anne F. Thurston), *The Private Life of Li Zhisui* (New York: Random House, 1994), p. 38.

38 Ibid., p. 41.

39 Ibid., p. 39.

40 Ibid., p. 48.

41 Mao, *Selected Works*, Vol. IV. https://www.marxists.org/reference/archive/mao/selected-works/volume-4/mswv4_65.htm (accessed 25 October 2019).

42 Quotations in this and the following paragraph are taken from MZD *SW*, Vol. IV, 30 June 1949. https://www.marxists.org/reference/archive/mao/selected-works/volume-4/mswv4_65.htm (accessed 21 February 1949).

43 FRUS, *The Far East: China*, Vol. VIII, 6 July 1949. https://history.state.gov/historicaldocuments/frus1949v08/d478 (accessed 21 February 2020).

44 Wilson Center Digital Archive 'Memorandum of Conversation between Stalin and CCP Delegation', 27 Jun 1949, http://digitalarchive.wilsoncenter.org/document/113380 (accessed 25 October 2019).

45 See Introduction, p. 19.

46 *CWP*, Vol. I, p. xiv.

47 Ibid., p. xvi.

48 Ibid.

49 *Time*, 15 August 1949, p. 1.

50 MZD *SW*, Vol. IV, 14 August 1949. https://www.marxists.org/reference/archive/mao/selected-works/volume-4/mswv4_66.htm (accessed 25 October 2019).

51 MZD *SW*, Vol. IV, 18 August 1949. https://www.marxists.org/reference/archive/mao/selected-works/volume-4/mswv4_67.htm (accessed 28 October 2019).

52 *SWB*, No. 22, 6 September 1949, p. 27.

53 Chang Chihyun (ed.), *The Chinese Journals of L. K. Little, 1943–54*, Electronic Resource: 731.5/968.

54 Zhang Liangren (ed.), *Chiang ching-kuo xiansheng* quanji, diary entry, 6 August 1949, p. 460.

55 Brian Izzard, *Yangtze Showdown: China and the Ordeal of HMS Amethyst* (Barnsley: Seaforth Publishing, 2015), p. 101.

56 TNA FO 371/1607, 'Hong Kong Political Summary for April 1949', p. 30.

57 *SWB*, No. 8, 15 June 1949, p. 24.

58 British Library, India Office Records, 'Communism in China', IOR/L/WS/1/1231, Outward telegram from the Commonwealth Relations Office, 15 June 1949, p. 1.

59 S. R. Ashton, G. Bennett and K. A. Hamilton (eds), *Documents on British Policy Overseas, Series I, Volume VIII: Britain and China 1945–1950* (London: Routledge, 2002), p. 71.

60 *Hansard*, 5 May 1949, p. 1234. https://api.parliament.uk/historic-hansard/commons/1949/may/05/china-british-policy (accessed 21 February 2020).

61 *Far Eastern Economic Review*, 22 June 1949, p. 770.

62 Ashton et al. (eds), *Documents on British Policy Overseas,* p. 334.

63 Ibid., p. 336. The cabinet later agreed to remove the term 'a democratic' China for fear that its retention would 'preclude the UK from discussing Hong Kong at any time with a Communist government in China' (p. 338).

64 *Far Eastern Economic Review*, 7 July 1949, pp. 1–2.

65 Long Yingtai, *Da Jiang Da Hai 1949* ('Vast Rivers, Vast Seas 1949') (Hong Kong: Cosmos Books, 2015 edition), p. 151.

66 See Chapter 4, p. 116.

67 The quotations in this and the following paragraph are drawn from Long Yingtai, *Da Jiang Da Hai 1949*, pp. 68–9.

68 See Chapter 2, p. 58. The account of Ya Xian's journey that follows is drawn largely from Long Yingtai, *Da Jiang Da Hai 1949*, pp. 131–3.

69 Church Missionary Society Archives. Kwangsi-Hunan General Papers 1935–1951, G1 CH5/1 Reel 418. Letter from Sargent to Wittenbach, 3 July 1949.

8

Mao's new world

'The CCP is here to stay for some time'

On the afternoon of Saturday 1 October, Mao Zedong, dressed in a smart dark-brown version of the plain, high-collared tunic favoured by Chinese revolutionaries, ascended the Gate of Heavenly Peace, part of the Forbidden City in the centre of what was now to be known as Beijing, the new national capital.[1] On either side of him, overlooking Tiananmen Square, stood many of the generals who during the past eighteen months had defeated Chiang Kai-shek's best-equipped armies, and the senior Party figures who under his leadership had brought all but a handful of China's provinces under communist rule. A sprinkling of prominent non-Party members – including Song Qingling, widow of Sun Yat-sen and sister of Chiang's wife Song Meiling – joined the victors on this special day in China's history. The only foreigners granted such elevated status were members of a cultural and artistic delegation from the Soviet Union.

It was a moment many people, Chinese and non-Chinese, had been waiting for – in hope, fear or something in between. Twenty-eight years earlier, Mao had been one of the dozen or so delegates who attended the founding congress of the Chinese Communist Party in Shanghai. He spoke once on that occasion in July 1921, delivering a report on communist activities in Changsha, the nearest city to his home in the Hunan countryside. He was 'pale-faced', with a 'rather lovely temperament', noted one of those present. 'In his long gown of native cloth he looked like a Daoist priest out of some village.'[2]

He cut a different figure on that Saturday afternoon in 1949. Heavier set and reportedly not in the best of health, he had survived three decades of harsh revolutionary struggle to accomplish one of the great political triumphs of his and any era. It was symbolized by the neat ribbon that adorned his tunic bearing the two characters *zhuxi* – 'Chairman'. The 'village priest' had become leader of the world's most populous nation and, in the eyes of some, a revolutionary of global stature. Standing on the terrace of the ancient stone gate, the symbolic centre of Chinese political power, Mao was master of all he surveyed. Before him stretched a crowd of at least

200,000 people, many of them carrying banners and waving flags. They had thronged or been 'bussed' into Tiananmen Square to celebrate the long anticipated founding of the People's Republic of China and to acclaim Chairman Mao as their leader.

Among them was Li Zhisui, until now largely confined to the Party's semi-secret headquarters in the Fragrant Hills where he was one of the few Western-trained doctors trusted to look after the new elite. Li arrived early in the morning to find the square, specially cleared for the occasion, full of people, its flaky red surrounding walls neatly re-painted. Bright red banners proclaimed 'Long Live Chairman Mao Zedong!' and 'Long Live the People's Republic of China!' Li was overcome by the occasion. Mao 'had been my hero since my brother first told me he was China's messiah, and this was my first glimpse of my saviour',[3] he wrote.

The formal proceedings began with a rendition of the new national anthem, 'March of the Volunteers'. Mao then stood up to proclaim, in a single sentence, the founding of the People's Republic of China. When he pressed an electric button, the new national flag rose slowly up a giant flagpole erected for the purpose in the middle of the square. Its four small yellow stars, situated close to a much larger one in the top left-hand quarter and set against a blood-red background, depicted China's new political reality. The 'leading' star represented the CCP; the lesser ones, the four classes – workers, peasants, the petty and the national bourgeoisie – whom for Mao constituted the 'people' of the People's Republic of China. Heavy guns roared out in salute.

In his first speech before so large a crowd, Mao affirmed the people's victory over 'reactionary forces' before proceeding, somewhat anti-climactically, to read out a long list of names of those appointed to lead the various branches of the country's new government. He concluded by stating that the PRC was the sole legitimate government of China, and that it was willing to establish diplomatic relations with others around the world on the basis of equality, mutual benefit and respect for national sovereignty. By prior arrangement, the Soviet Union was the first to recognize the new regime, followed by several of its satellites in Eastern Europe.

A military parade followed during which a dozen or so planes of the small communist air force (including captured US-supplied Mustang P-51s) overflew the city. Taking the salute, PLA commander-in-chief Zhu De praised the troops for their heroic achievements but warned their work was not over. 'Enemy remnants are still colluding with foreign aggressors and carrying out counter-revolutionary activities', he said. 'We must devote all of our energies to achieving final victory in the people's war of liberation.'[4]

It was then the turn of the turn of the 'masses' to celebrate the new order, which many did with apparent, if choreographed, enthusiasm – a hallmark of large public events in China at the time and since. Two foreign scholars who found themselves among the crowd said their Chinese counterparts 'went wild with excitement' as they marched past the reviewing stand.

'Waving handkerchiefs they jumped in the air. Deafening shouts of "Long live the People's Republic of China!", "Long live Chairman Mao!" mixed with "There he is! He's waving to us!" . . . engulfed us like a mighty wave.'[5] Smaller scale celebrations took place in other cities under communist rule.

Events in Beijing cast a dark cloud over Guangzhou, more than 1,000 miles to the south, where Chiang Kai-shek was trying to rally a demoralized, divided Nationalist elite and decide where best to make his last stand. Li Zongren condemned the creation of the PRC as a 'distortion of the will of the Chinese people'. Moscow was 'pulling the strings in the treacherous acts performed by the Chinese communists'.[6] A few days earlier he had told the *Central Daily News* that time was on the government's side. Floods in the Yangtze valley and reliance on local people for supplies meant the communists were finding it hard to feed their troops. If the Nationalist army swapped passive for aggressive defence it would 'hasten the communists' collapse'. As long as it held on to the south and southwest, the US 'was certain to come to their assistance'.[7]

It is true that Congress was about to provide 75 million dollars for anti-communist activities in China, and that some of this money would find its way to south China. But time was running out. The administration's China policy had been set out in the recently published White Paper: there would be no new funding for Chiang's ailing regime. Shortly before Mao mounted the rostrum at Tiananmen, the counsellor in the by now understaffed and largely isolated US embassy in Nanjing wrote that, in view of China's recent history, it was wise to conclude that 'the CCP is here to stay for some time'.[8]

'"You are dictatorial": Dear Sirs, . . . that is exactly what we are'

In his *On the People's Democratic Dictatorship*, Mao Zedong made no secret of the kind of state he intended to found.[9] It reflected the circumstances in which it was born and the future its creators intended for their country: one of revolutionary transformation. But in the process, the conditions were created for tyranny – one that would lead to policy disasters on an epic scale, deprive millions of citizens of their human rights and shape the country's political behaviour for decades to come.

In 1949, however, it was widely agreed that China needed a strong state. The tasks ahead were daunting. Several Nationalist armies had yet to be defeated, their leaders captured or forced to quit. A large part of the population was exhausted by war, mired in poverty and/or plagued by deep insecurities. Millions of people had been displaced. Many would never return. The urban economy, still prey to the inflation that had destroyed the wealth of much of the middle class and now a victim of the Nationalist blockade, was barely functioning. Land reform had yet to begin in the huge territories the communists now controlled – Lin Biao warned that the urban population of Central China 'was still faced with a "feudalistic countryside"'.[10] Much of the outside world was hostile or otherwise ill-disposed to 'Red China', apart from the Soviet Union and its satellites.

Yet this generally bleak situation was also why the prospect of an end to the fighting, a new sense of national dignity, greater social justice and a stronger economy – all of which seemed to be promised by the foundation of the PRC – appealed to many Chinese. Mao's remarks, just prior to 1 October, that the Chinese people had 'stood up' and that their country would 'no longer be subject to insult and humiliation', resonated with many from tenant farmer to Western-educated professor.[11] The Nationalists had failed the country on nearly every count. For many, the 'New China' of Mao Zedong and the CCP seemed worthy of allegiance. It was also by now (almost) the only option: no other political force was in a position to run the country.

This did not mean that 'People's China' could count on the compliance of the people. The new regime had to strike a balance between securing consent and maintaining control. The enemy's armies might be on the brink of defeat, but their 'reactionary' ideas, ambitions, plots and schemes – enthusiastically supported by the United States – were deemed more dangerous than ever. 'Our revolutionary work is not completed', Mao warned on the eve of the PRC's founding. 'Under no circumstances must we relax our vigilance.'[12]

This explains why the PRC was founded as an executive rather than a deliberative state. It consisted of strong rather than 'independent' institutions. And it imposed few restraints on those in charge of them. The only formal rules governing its behaviour derived from the 'Common Programme' approved by Chinese People's Political Consultative Conference, the body the CCP had convened in September to legitimize its rule. Composed of representatives carefully selected for the purpose, the Consultative Conference was the closest thing the PRC had to a legislature. There was no constitution as such.

Nor was there felt to be much need for one – at least at first. After years of bitter struggle, Mao had seized control over more than half of the country and a much larger share of its population. This was no time to submit to 'checks and balances'. Chiang Kai-shek had often felt much the same: his government's fitful practice of constitutionalism during the previous two years had so weakened his personal authority that he had been forced to set up the GMD Extraordinary Committee to rule the diminishing territory under his jurisdiction.

The new government at first exercised a form of military rule. China was divided into six large administrative regions in which the army was responsible for keeping order and imposing a form of central control over the country that it had not experienced for decades while allowing for regional differences. This was often difficult because in many parts of the country the communists were both new arrivals and 'outsiders' serving far from home. Communist rule seemed somewhat distant to many people until officials and 'work teams' penetrated their villages.

No clear separation was made between Party and state in the new polity: Mao was chairman of both the Central People's Government and the Party, Liu Shaoqi was vice-chair of the government, while Zhou Enlai was premier and foreign minister. From the first, the Party was what mattered in the People's Republic. The government was a legal entity, necessary to administer and execute policy, and conduct relations with counterparts and international bodies around the world. But its leaders owed their authority to the CCP, which promptly set up branches in every ministry and department of the new administration.

The Central People's Government could claim to be fairly representative. It was a 'democratic coalition' in that it included members of those classes whom Mao said collectively constituted the 'people'. Many positions were filled by leaders of the 'democratic parties', as the small political organizations that had thrown in their lot with the CCP were known, or by so-called 'democratic personages'. Among them was Fu Zuoyi, the Nationalist general who surrendered Beiping (as it was then called), now made minister of water resources, and Li Jishen, one of six vice-chairmen of the Central People's Government. Few of these men can have had any illusions about where real power lay. But they, too, had nowhere else to go, short of leaving the country or throwing in their lot with the rapidly retreating Nationalists, which probably amounted to the same thing. On the other hand, their participation was important to the CCP: it helped win support for the regime, especially from intellectuals, without whom it would be difficult to run the country at all.

At province, municipality and country levels, so-called Representative Conferences were set up as a kind of transmission belt between the new politico-military authorities and ordinary citizens. Their role was to co-opt people of different background and opinions – though regulations stipulated that participation was restricted to those who 'opposed imperialism, feudalism, bureaucratic capitalism and supported the Common Programme'.[13] Party leaders complained that these organizations were not formed quickly enough, and that little was getting done on the policy front as a result. Where Representative Conferences were set up 'the collection of taxes, mopping up of bandits, reductions of rent and interest, settling of labour–capital disputes, carrying out of land reform and the development of production and cultural work proceeded more smoothly', claimed the New China News Agency.[14]

Rights and wrongs

China's new leaders abolished all of the Nationalists' legal codes and statutes, bringing the established justice system to a halt. A Chinese lawyer in Shanghai, summoned to a briefing on how the courts were to proceed, was surprised to be told that in future 'only the edicts of the Military Commission would be enforced, and that ... cases would be decided according to 'common sense'. Lawyers were not recognized because they were held to be the servants of capitalism ... Litigants must appear in court but lawyers cannot be heard.'[15] An observer of a trial involving a foreign missionary in Shanghai said he found it 'impossible to tell whether the magistrate was the judge or the public prosecutor; or even whether the missionary had been summoned as witness or defendant!'[16]

In the new 'people's courts', informal settlement was favoured over legal adjudication and mediation commissions were set up. They frequently instructed disputants to 'pair off and thrash out their differences', according to one observer.[17] Another novelty was the 'mass trial' in which serious cases, usually involving political crimes, were conducted before a large crowd, partly as 'a device to educate the onlookers'.[18] These occasions often ended with the execution of those accused or found guilty, which usually amounted to the same thing. From the beginning, law was an instrument of policy in the PRC; thirty years would pass before China acquired a criminal code worth the name.

The Common Programme, whose fifty-eight articles constituted an odd mix of policy intentions, quasi-constitutional definitions of the new order and a pledge that violence would be used against those who opposed it, set out the government's aims. In addition to land reform, they included equal rights for women and the promise of universal franchise.[19] It also contained guarantees of individual freedom worthy of the most liberal of democracies – except they did not extend to such arbitrary categories as landlords, bureaucratic capitalists and 'reactionaries'. Such ('non-') people were to be suppressed, which was why Mao insisted that the army, the people's police and the people's courts must be strengthened. 'To the hostile classes the state apparatus is the instrument of oppression', he explained. 'It is violent, not benevolent.'[20]

All foreign privileges were to be rescinded and treaties signed by Chiang's government reviewed to determine whether they harmed China's national interests. If so, they would be abrogated. Foreign countries whose territories included Chinese people were warned that the new government would 'do its utmost to protect their proper rights and interests'.[21] British officials took particular note of this, mindful of the implications for their administration of Hong Kong and Malaya.

Restoring economic order

Rehabilitation of economy was a top priority. This, too, was a tall order. The communists inherited little in the way of gold and foreign currency reserves; Chiang had shifted most of them to Taiwan. With war continuing in the south, southwest and northwest, expenditure far outstripped revenues, as had been the case under the Nationalists. Ivan Kovalev, Stalin's man on China, told his chief in December 1949: 'State finances and monetary circulation are in a completely unsatisfactory state.' He estimated the budget deficit (as a percentage of income) to be 29.2 per cent for central China and 43.2 per cent for northwest China.[22] Finance Minister Bo Yibo said that even in 1950 'military and administrative expenditure would absorb 60 per cent of the Budget since there would be 9 million people, including the armed forces, government and educational personnel, who would be paid by the state'.[23]

The PLA was ordered to 'take part in the work of production and construction from the spring of 1950 in order to improve its own livelihood and reduce public expenditure'.[24] In the countryside, the programme to reduce rent and interest, a prelude to land reform in the newly liberated areas, was expected to boost the harvest, along with the fact that millions more farmers now already owned their own land. Figures for industrial and agricultural output in 1949 were something of a disaster, amounting to 49.9 per cent and 80 per cent respectively of China's record, set in 1936, just before the start of the Sino-Japanese War.[25]

For many citizens and as well as businesses, 'liberation' meant a tightening of belts. 'People should help balance the budget by reducing consumption and buying Victory Bonds', state media said.[26] The plan was to issue 200 million such bonds in 1950, redeemable at value determined by the commodity index to protect investors. Sales would be aimed at 'industrialists, merchants, rich families, retired government officials and retired army officers'.[27] Such groups soon came under strong psychological and political pressure to purchase the bonds and show their loyalty to the regime.

Imaginative methods of fund-raising were sometimes adopted at the local level. In September, shortly after the communists set up a new provincial government in Changsha, capital of Hunan, three foreign oil companies with offices in the city were told that they had to contribute 25 per cent of a 600 million renminbi 'loan' to support military operations. They at first refused and received letters in which the 'bullying and threatening tone was remarkable', according to the local British consul.[28] They decided to pay up, despite instructions to the contrary from their head offices, in the interest of future operations and the 'safety of all employees'.[29]

The almost worthless gold yuan introduced by Chiang's government quickly went out of circulation. But rapid deprecation of the renminbi, the new currency that replaced it, meant that the old silver dollar staged a comeback: by May it was worth more than a US dollar. By the autumn inflation was again a serious issue in the cities. The regime declined to solve the problem by printing money. Instead, it tied wages to the price of essential commodities and conducted bank transactions on the same basis. A statement from the Head Office of the Bank of China, now under 'new management', read:

The Parity Savings Deposit is introduced with a view to encouraging thrift savings, developing sinking funds for production and insuring living standards. Depositors of current deposits and fixed deposits for periods of ½ or 1 month shall be restricted to organised labour, office clerks, teachers and students . . . The maximum amount of deposit per month shall not exceed the depositor's monthly wage, or in the case of a student, his monthly cost of board.[30]

Prices gradually began to stabilize, a welcome novelty for city dwellers.

Another success, certainly relative to the Nationalists' record, was the rapid centralization of financial decision-making and creation of a national financial bureaucracy. Trade was the first economic activity to fall under its remit. The national budget was not far behind. By the end of 1949, key decisions on trade, finance and other economic matters were being made in Beijing. Provincial and local governments were forbidden to spend the taxes they raised; the days of regional autonomy would soon be over.

Labour and capital

The Common Programme promised to protect private property and encourage private business. Socialism was not an avowed goal – at least not yet. Liu Shaoqi insisted it should not be proclaimed as such 'since it would easily create confusion as to the practical steps which had to be taken today'.[31] However, there were few grounds for believing that Mao had jettisoned such aims now that he was at last in a position to implement them. In any event, the emphasis was at first on rapid industrialization – for both welfare and security reasons. 'Only if we develop our industry and do not let our economy become reliant on foreign countries can we provide a basis for the independence and sovereignty of our nation and guarantee a prosperous life for our people', said PLA commander Zhu De.[32]

His remarks were an early indication that New China would favour industry over trade, and concentrate on building up the domestic economy rather than expanding commercial links with the wider or at least the Western world. Politics, ideology and the Nationalist blockade all tended towards this end though they did not make it inevitable: it would take the outbreak of the Korean War in June 1950, followed by China's participation in the conflict the following November, to do that. Nevertheless, the communist conquest meant that 'maritime China' was almost bound to became a Cold War frontier rather than the largely porous zone across which flowed capital, people and ideas, as had been the case for much of the previous century. Taiwan, Hong Kong and nearby countries host to large numbers of overseas Chinese lay on one side of this frontier; 'continental China' or the PRC on the other.

Economically, Shanghai suffered particularly badly once relief that the changeover had occurred with relatively little violence and destruction passed off. China's global city rapidly lost its raison d'etre. 'Between the upper and nether millstones of the blockade and the Communist controls and taxation, merchants and industrialists of all nationalities have been ground', complained the China Association, the lobby group for British business in China.[33] The Party was unsympathetic. A few months after 'liberation', it announced plans to relocate two million residents to the interior so that they could 'take up useful occupations or engage in the agricultural production', as the *Far Eastern Economic Review* put it. 'Those earmarked for removal included unemployed shop employees and their families, 650,000 urban poor, 170,000 loafers and 100,000 refugee landlords.' The aim was to 'offset the effects of the blockade and build up a new Shanghai'.[34]

Despite these developments, Mao insisted that the national bourgeoisie had an important role to play in New China. 'Our present policy is to restrict capitalism and not to eliminate it', he said.[35] In a visit to Tianjin in the spring of 1949, Liu Shaoqi upbraided local Party leaders for their heavy-handed treatment of commercial activity in the city. His remarks, which were well publicized, eased some of the anxieties of business leaders across the country. On the other hand, they did not offer much comfort to the country's proletariat in whose name the CCP had seized power.

Many workers evidently took seriously the idea that they were now 'masters of the country' and demanded an immediate improvement in their conditions. As early as April, the Central Committee complained that due to spontaneous strikes in cities already liberated, 'the struggle between capital and labour was such as to result in a state of anarchy'.[36] Labour strife was particularly severe in Shanghai thanks to capital flight, factory closures and the departure (usually to Hong Kong or Taiwan) of the owners. Between June and December 1949, there were 3,324 strikes or labour disturbances in the city. The previous highest figure was 280 incidents, in 1946, according to historian Elizabeth J. Perry.[37]

The Party urged owners and workers across the country to end labour unrest under the slogan, specially coined for the purpose, that 'private and public interests, labour and capital must both benefit'.[38] Li Lisan, deputy chairman of the new All China Labour Federation, said: 'Workers should not let themselves be mistaken by the parallels with land reform; there could be no doubt that the (re)distribution of factory installations would spell ruin for the workers.' The time 'had not yet arrived' for the 'complete abolition of capitalist exploitation'; both private and state capital were needed to boost industry.[39]

It may have been statements of this kind that persuaded Liu Hongsheng, the Shanghai business leader who had fled to Hong Kong in April and transferred some of his business there, to return.[40] Family pressure also played a part.

During his six months in the colony, Liu's second son constantly urged him to go home. 'The new government is lenient, reasonable, dead honest, hardworking, practical, patriotic, humble and they certainly mean well', he told his father.[41] Liu's wife tried a different tack: 'It's sad that you and I have been separated so long even in our old age. The nights are long and are filled with too many dreams.'[42] Liu's mistress, a Christian, couched her appeal in religious terms: 'Under God, I know that our heavenly Father will look after you, and I hope that God will let us see each other again soon.'[43]

In the event, it was emissaries sent to the colony by Zhou Enlai that did the trick. They explained that Liu had nothing to fear should he return to Shanghai and that business opportunities there were more promising than those in Hong Kong. He at last made up his mind. 'I am an old man already over sixty', he told the family. 'All of my enterprises are in China, so I'll go back and not stay abroad as a white Chinese.'[44]

Arrangements were made for his clandestine departure to prevent interference by Nationalist agents. On 2 November, he boarded a steamer bound for Tianjin. On arrival, Zhou invited him to talks in Beijing, during which the premier urged him to persuade other capitalists to follow his lead and help build up the country. Once back in Shanghai, Liu became a vocal supporter of the new government, at least in public.

'"Liberation" is intensely political'

The creation of a 'people's' government with its own flag, currency, national anthem and capital city constituted the mere trappings of victory as far as Mao was concerned in 1949. Even the new government's political and economic programme could be seen as but one aspect of the revolution he intended to carry out now that the CCP controlled most of the country. He was determined to create a new nation not just a new state, and to transform the entire lives of the Chinese people not merely their politics and economy. It was a project of huge scale and great vision – and one Mao would before long implement with great brutality.[45] If there was no immediate recourse to terror during the takeover in 1949, there was no doubt that conditions were being put in place to exercise it.

The Party was determined to shake people out of their often narrow frames of reference and force them to transfer their loyalties to new, national and revolutionary causes. To this end, citizens in every walk of life were furnished with what in effect were new identities. These centred around class and an individual's status as either an urban or rural resident – the great social divide in China at the time and for long thereafter. 'Classifying the population was a great bureaucratic challenge for the state', writes Felix Wemheuer of the early years of the PRC.[46] It rose to the challenge, penetrating society to an extent China had not seen before.

The registration of every household in Beijing was an example. It was undertaken by the municipal police whose ranks were reorganized for the purpose and renamed the Public Security Bureau. By mid-November all 439,000 families (total population 1.95 million) were issued with a household registration certificate. Before long, every urban citizen acquired a personal dossier on entering the workforce that would stay with them for the rest of their lives. Class soon became the most critical factor in determining individual fortunes. At one (positive) end of the spectrum were the categories of 'revolutionary cadre' and 'industrial worker'. At the other were the new regime's undesirables – the 'capitalist', the 'rightist' or, still worse, the 'counterrevolutionary'. Access to land, higher education, the military, Party membership and much else in Chinese life would soon depend on where one was located on this politically loaded spectrum.

Social engineering on the scale Mao envisaged required tight control over all sources of information and particularly the media, which the Party had been careful to make its mouthpiece wherever it had imposed its rule. One of the first things the communists did when they occupied the cities in 1949 was to close or censor newspapers and radio stations that had been loyal to the Nationalists or were of independent hue.[47] New organizations were set up in their place. But there was still something of a battle over content. 'Recently, media organisations have published news items without seeking prior approval from the relevant authorities', the Party complained in November. 'They have then been forced to put out corrections . . . causing practical and political mistakes.'[48] It later criticized what it called 'anarchy and lack of discipline' on the news front.[49]

Most media were eventually tamed, their output consisting of what one observer defined as 'information', chiefly in the form of government announcements; 'education', consisting largely of 'study' materials; and 'propaganda', either relaying the wicked actions of reactionaries and imperialists or the heroic achievements of those who boosted production or spread the values underlying the new order.[50] Dull uniformity prevailed in a once lively press. The Party had already ordered local radio stations across the country to relay Beijing's version of domestic and international news, giving birth, in June 1949, to China's first genuinely *national* but often fairly uninteresting newscast.[51]

Most foreign news organizations fared no better. Only journalists from countries that recognized the new government were allowed to file despatches. This 'automatically clamps the lid on all United States and other Western power news services and newspapers', complained *The New York Times*.[52] It was also something of a turning point: a good deal of what the Western world learned about New China would in future have to rely heavily on the observations of those based in Hong Kong and elsewhere outside of the country. News organizations from Russia, her satellites and Yugoslavia, all of which recognized the regime, were spared the ban. Given the 'colour' of their governments, Beijing expected them to report 'favourably' on socialist China.

Tight control of the media was just one aspect of the mobilization of society in support of the Party's aims and ideals. Another was the creation of 'mass organizations' in which people came together to pursue common interests according to their professional status or personal preoccupations. In the first week of March, not long after it occupied Beiping, some 20,000 young people were brought together to celebrate the creation of the National Federation of Students. In April, the first congress of the New Democracy Youth Federation was convened. Amid great fanfare, the All-China Literacy Workers Association met for the first time in June–July. The following month, the All-China Federation of Trade Unions was formed.

Senior leaders such as Zhou Enlai and Liu Shaoqi frequently addressed the most significant of these conclaves, and their remarks were then given extensive, uncritical coverage in the media. The substance of what they had to say was remarkably consistent, despite the different interests and specialist nature of many of the audiences they addressed. The main theme – a veritable anthem resounding throughout society in print and spoken word, in slogan, image and almost every art form – was that of the allegedly epoch-defining difference between the 'old' China and the 'new'; between the horrors of life under Chiang's feudal reactionary government and the bright prospects in store thanks to 'liberation'. Problems were not ignored, the evil schemes of the enemy never downplayed. But extravagant praise for the new dispensation and its leaders was the order of the day, irrespective of context or occasion.

For most ordinary citizens, the biggest change in their lives following liberation was the virtually obligatory attendance at meeting after meeting. 'From July onwards, Shanghai was turned into a huge adult education centre', noted the perceptive French reporter Robert Guillain. 'Everywhere, in government office, factory, banking-house, workshop, store, school and university, an orgy of meetings and lectures is going on; the people are being "re-educated" on a grand scale.'[53] A UPI report from Shanghai said: 'Instruction was provided in Communist philosophy with special reference to the democratic principles as expounded in Mao Zedong's writing and speeches. The courses include "debates and free discussions".'[54] A foreign professor at Tianjin's Nankai University wrote: 'Everyone is expected to spend at least two hours every day in political study. The . . . movement has . . . become extraordinarily widespread. There is hardly a corner of Chinese social life into which it has not penetrated.'[55]

The purpose of these gatherings was to spread the Party's message and help people re-mould their outlook and very personality through the study of Marx, Lenin and Mao (and often Stalin). Party leaders wanted to convince and convert, to empower and enlighten but above all to *change* those they ruled. They were also keen to know on whom they could rely, and to single out, ostracize and punish those thought likely to resist the new order.

Self-criticism was an important part of these proceedings. It enabled those who found it hard to come to terms with the new ways of thinking to get things off their chest, and provided opportunities for the more loquacious and perhaps less sincere to say their piece. Esther Cheo Ying, seventeen, inspired by Mao's revolution and keen to see her father again, had made her way to China from England, where she had spent the past eleven years. Attached to a unit of Lin Biao's Fourth Field Army based near Beiping, she was soon caught up in the meetings routine. 'The afternoons and after our four o'clock meal we spent in innumerable meetings and self-examinations, always searching for motives and reasons in everything we did or thought', she wrote. 'Our meetings were mainly ... discussing and analysing our faults and listening to what others thought of our behaviour and attitude.'[56] The pressures to conform were immense, the penalty for non-compliance the charge that one was unpatriotic or worse 'reactionary'.

Public participation in politics, a patchy affair at best under the Nationalists, was thus almost obligatory once the communists took over. 'Millions of China's citizens live and breathe politics, all the more eagerly because it is for the first time', wrote Alun Falconer, a sympathetic observer of the new order in Shanghai. '"Liberation" is intensely political.'[57] Public space in China was being filled, as the Party intended, with politics and propaganda. Private space, where personal thoughts and activities, as well as those of closely knit communities such as family members or friendships are shared, was rapidly diminishing.

Language and discourse were early casualties. 'The classification of the people in terms of class status gave rise to a new language of good and evil', notes Felix Wemheuer. 'Abstract class categories took on vivid and concrete form in personal stories delivered through propaganda, literature and films.'[58] The revolutionary lexicon, with its rich store of 'positive' terms such as 'comrade', 'liberation', 'worker', 'peasant', 'democratic personage', 'Chairman Mao', and so on, and its negative archetypes of 'reactionary', 'Chiang's bandit gang', 'imperialist', 'landlord', and so on, soon became part of everyday speech. This made it easier for the Party to incite public hatred of enemies, real or imagined. In newspaper articles or informal conversation, in leaders' speeches or the casual remarks of prominent citizens, the condemnation of class enemies was prized over conventional civilities.

The Chinese 'calendar' also changed in 1949 – and not just because from 1 October China's new rulers jettisoned the Nationalists' method of counting the years from the creation of the Republic of China in 1912 and adopted the Gregorian calendar. Public life acquired a new rhythm built around a different set of public holidays, invariably accompanied by parades and processions.

Maria Yen, a student at Beijing University, described the new holidays as a 'nerve stimulant' injected by the authorities 'into what would have been an inadequate emotional life without them'. She wrote:

Red May Day started off the big procession of official festivals during the summer and fall of the Communist year. July 1st came next, the anniversary of the founding of the Chinese Communist Party in 1921. Then we celebrated August 1st, the birthday of the People's Liberation Army. October 1st is the new National Festival, celebrating the official founding of the People's Republic in 1949. Stalin's seventieth birthday, on December 21, 1949, which our papers told us was being hailed as a historic milestone all over the world, was greeted in Beijing by two days of city-wide celebrations . . .[59]

The 'armour of the regime'

The capacity of the CCP to mobilize large numbers of people in many parts of the country that had only just come under its control was extraordinary, even though it could draw on years of experience doing so on a smaller scale. Genuine public enthusiasm for change, grounded in deep dissatisfaction with Nationalist rule, must have accounted for much of this since, as the Party often admitted, it suffered from a serious shortage of trained personnel in 1949. Journalist Robert Guillain put the number of those who constituted what he called the 'armour of the regime' at less than ten million. 'Out of that number 3 million are, according to recently published figures, members of the Party', he wrote. 'If we picture the situation with these few million ardent enthusiasts superimposed on a mass of 450,000,000 people, we have the essential clue to the whole situation in the New China.'[60]

Party membership had expanded dramatically during the Civil War but this was a mixed blessing. In 1947, Mao warned that 'landlords, rich peasants and riff-raff' had sneaked into its 2.7 million-strong ranks.[61] By October 1948, the total had reached three million but again it had proved necessary to correct 'Left mistakes' that affected rich peasants, damaged private business and overstepped the mark in 'suppressing counterrevolutionaries'.[62] The People's Daily said the majority of Party members in north China (as elsewhere) came from the peasantry whose 'very low level of culture and understanding of Marxism and Leninism' often caused deviations in the prosecution of Party policies.[63]

Liberation made joining the Party more attractive: there were 5.8 million members by 1950, some 1.1 per cent of the population. But it also tended to create a two-tier Party consisting of those who had joined before 1949 and thus often risked their lives for the Revolution, and those who jumped on the bandwagon. Once in power, CCP leaders saw no need to deprive themselves of privileges and perquisites when it came to living conditions, job allocation, access to information and so on. By their reckoning, the CCP was a 'vanguard' party: it had led the Revolution.[64] The victors surely deserved some spoils.

*

Since it lacked enough qualified people of its own to run the country, the new government was keen to retain as many existing personnel as possible, especially if they were highly skilled. Many civil servants, bankers, professors and journalists simply carried on their duties as before – as long as they were not senior members of the GMD and underwent the required study and thought reform. But some were sacked, apparently without good reason. In October the Central Committee upbraided the authorities in Hunan for dismissing all but forty of the 330 staff of the Salt Bureau, a move it said 'violated instructions and caused people to lose hope'.[65] Work was found for those who had lost their jobs.

Where considered desirable, members of the local Party underground were appointed to certain roles in government. But the backbone of the new regime consisted of the young *cadres* or bureaucrats (by no means all of them Party members) whom the CCP had recruited in their hundreds of thousands to serve at various levels once the enemy armies had fled or surrendered. The 'south-bound cadres' who followed the PLA across the Yangtze were a case in a point.[66]

Cadres were the archetypes of New China, their appearance and behaviour almost bywords for much of what observers regarded as good and bad about Mao's regime. Eva Spicer, the Jinling College history teacher who was by now coming to terms with life in Nanjing under communist rule, took tea with one of her former students who had joined the cause and been assigned to work for the New China News Agency. 'She was dressed in the blue uniform, which is one better than the rather yellow khaki, but is not well cut, and looks far from smart', she said of her guest.

> She is provided with two of those a year, one padded garment, and a coat (if she had not had one). She is fed (three meals a day), and if she takes her children back to Beiping with her (at the moment they are with her husband in Shanghai, she has been travelling for almost two years) they will be fed and educated, and I presume clothed. They are given what is now the equivalent of about one silver dollar a day to buy, as she said, 'toilet paper, soap and peanuts'. I think it would be enough for the first two items. I haven't priced soap lately, but I don't think you would get very fat on the number of peanuts you could buy.[67]

Esther Cheo Ying, in the suburbs of Beijing, was similarly turned out and provided for. 'We were given our food, our winter and summer uniforms and two pairs of cloth shoes', she recalled. 'Each month we had a little pocket money which just about covered our basic needs, such as a piece of soap, and for the girls, a very coarse woody paper for use as sanitary towels.'[68]

In their blue or khaki uniform, topped by a cloth cap which they often wore in the office, the cadres made 'strange conquerors', wrote Robert Guillain.[69] A source told a reporter from *The Times* that the communists wanted everyone to live like a cadre, whom he described as someone who:

feeds at a communal mess, eating one of the three grades of food – or 'three pots' as the Chinese call it – depending on his rank in the hierarchy. The regime houses him, clothes him, educates his children, and sends him to hospital when he is sick. His salary is microscopic, lower than a houseboy's, really little more than pocket money. He cannot accept invitations from non-party friends except, with special permission, from relatives. He is expected to be completely incorrupt – and is.[70]

This particular correspondent seemed unaware that women featured prominently in the ranks of Guillain's 'strange conquerors'.

Cadres set sartorial as well as political standards. 'The most obvious change after the Liberation was the steady increase in gray uniforms on the campus', wrote Maria Yen of her university.[71] Western-style suits and bright dresses were forsaken for dull, cotton-padded (in winter) 'Lenin suits' to show that those who wore them had forsaken the past. Powder and rouge became rare. Pigtails were lopped off, leaving a bob hairstyle just long enough to cover the ears. Such obvious evidence that people had embraced the 'new life' was a good way of avoiding attention and criticism, she noted.[72]

Cornered and constrained: the 'West' gets ready to bow out

As it consolidated its hold over the country, Mao's government presented a unique challenge to the merchants, missionaries, diplomats, teachers, scholars and others who made up the foreign, mainly Western community in China. They owed their presence in the country to an earlier, now discredited dispensation. They faced something they had never encountered before: an apparently strong, centralizing state capable, as historian Daniel H. Bays put it, of 'demanding their compliance if not their allegiance'.[73]

'New China' was founded on a highly negative set of ideas about the impact on the country of foreigners in general and Westerners in particular. With few exceptions, they were cast as the beneficiaries, if not the agents of the imperialism that had done such harm to China for so long. Moreover, they tended to be haughty and superior – a view until now too easily tolerated by Chinese who had obviously lost their sense of national dignity. Such sentiments, apparently sanctioned by the 'scientific' ideology of Marxism championed by China's new rulers, conformed with the deeper strains of anti-foreignism to which some Chinese were prone.

In light of this, the new government's handling of the foreign community in 1949 had a kind of logic to it – even though (and perhaps even because) it caused frustration and despair among those on the receiving end. The communists ignored most foreigners when they took over the cities, though they did restrict their movements.[74] This at first was of most concern to members of the Western diplomatic community who were keen to establish a working relationship with the new authorities, if only to learn more about their intentions, and to maintain their own dignity as envoys. But that was not forthcoming. Henceforth, dignity depended on diplomatic recognition of the new regime, and this required the severance of official ties with the Nationalists. No Western country was ready to do that until the dust had settled, which it did not until the very end of 1949.

In the meantime, indignities prevailed. Throughout the year and in some cases beyond, staff in Western embassies and consulates were treated as ordinary foreigners. They were deemed to have no right to speak on behalf of their governments or to engage on official business with any branch of the new Chinese administration. Their letters and phone calls went unanswered, their privileges and interests were for the most part denied.

Some, mostly US, diplomats received rougher treatment. Angus Ward, US consul in Shenyang, spent most of 1949 under house arrest or in prison on charges of assaulting a Chinese member of his staff during an argument over pay, and engaging in espionage.[75] He was only released in December.

In July, police in Shanghai detained, beat and then denied medical treatment to William Olive, US vice-consul, after he had for some reason driven his car into a public parade. Olive acted as he had 'because he thought he was a vice-consul of the United States', the New China News Agency said.[76] His attitude towards Shanghai's new rulers was that 'of a master which an American vice-consul used to adopt in dealing with the Guomindang reactionaries', chimed in the *Liberation Daily*.[77] Olive was released after signing a letter of apology. He left China shortly afterwards.

In October, Paul Paddock and Culver Gleysteen, respectively consul and vice-consul in Dalian (then known in the West as Dairen), on the southern tip of Manchuria, were finally allowed to leave their post. They and their local staff had endured more than a year of harassment at the hands of both the Soviet and Chinese authorities who jointly administered the city.[78] Beijing even created difficulties over granting permission to the remaining US diplomats in Nanjing to leave the country, despite the fact that Mao had 'celebrated' the departure of Ambassador John Leighton Stuart in August.[79] By the end of the year, the US had shuttered all of its diplomatic missions in China apart from the consulates in Beijing and Shanghai, both of which closed early in 1950.

It was not all bad news for foreigners in 1949 – though in this particular case it was due to the actions of the Nationalist rather than the communist government. In June, Lester Knox Little, inspector general of the Maritime Customs Service, finally managed to persuade his superiors in Chiang's administration to pay the pension benefits due to foreign members of the service who had retired. 'I signed checks for 220,00 pounds and US$85,000 today being 70% of pension benefits to the 65 or so foreigners who are being voluntarily retired today', Little wrote in his diary on 30 June. 'I have never signed cheques with more pleasure, and when I can pay out the 30% balance, I shall be very happy. In spite of all difficulties, the Chinese government will have fulfilled its obligations at least to its retired Customs staff . . .'[80] Chinese members of the service, many of whom also had cause for concern about their future, complained that Little put up less of a fight when it came to securing their future.

Many in the missionary community were similarly troubled as 1949 came to a close. Whatever their affiliation, missionaries were often close to the ground and could see at first hand something of the public dissatisfaction with the Nationalists as well as the hopes stirred by the promise of a new start under the communists. Pledges by the new government to protect freedom of religion, which was included in the Common Programme, were welcome. As Daniel H. Bays pointed out, some Protestants, missionaries and Chinese alike 'were hopeful that some kind of Sino-foreign Protestant community could continue to exist, and make a Christian contribution to the "new China"'.[81] The US Presbyterian Church was among them. In December 1949 it expressed its 'earnest desire' to continue missionary activity in communist China. 'As evidence of this continuing policy, missionaries are remaining at their posts of service in China and new missionaries have already gone or are preparing to go', the denomination's Board of Foreign Missions declared.[82]

Yet others felt that this was a tall order given the history, character and policies of the men now running the country. Arthur Ludbrook, head of the Salvation Army in China, spoke for many when he said: 'The new Government objects to foreigners working in Missions and is not happy that it is necessary for Missions to receive foreign money . . . The People's Government in future hopes to do all Emergency Relief Work themselves – certainly they do not wish for the help of Foreigners or Foreign Organisations.' He informed his headquarters in London: 'With regret we have to report that Prison Work has been stopped by the New Government. At the end of the year all our activities, except contact with one or two foreign prisoners, had ceased. Often we sense the end of our International Army in China is near . . .'[83]

He was right. By and large, missionaries were able to continue their work during the changeover and beyond, albeit under closer scrutiny and tighter regulation as the communists imposed their rule. Medical doctors and teachers at mission-funded or foreign-managed schools and universities, such as Eva Spicer in Nanjing, were required to register and account for their presence in China. They were not immediately told to leave. But the course had been set and it was just a matter of time: the coming of communism meant China's missionary community was headed for the exit.

The foreign merchant community was at first of a different mind.[84] This was largely because its members were driven by more earthly pursuits and had significant assets to protect. Yet by the end of July, a combination of high prices, heavy taxation, unfavourable exchange rates and, perhaps above all, the Nationalist blockade drove some of its British members to despair. The China Association took up their case with the government in London. If Britain was unable do anything to lift the blockade, 'the Association could only advise members to cut their losses as soon as they felt they must', it warned.[85]

Britain could not do anything. And many firms did leave Shanghai for Hong Kong or elsewhere. The effectiveness of the Nationalist blockade eventually weakened. But before long so did the hopes of the Western business community that life would continue along 'normal lines' under communism. Instead, new hardships lay in store: foreign firms were forced to stay open for the next year or so, even though there was often little business to conduct. They then had no alternative but to write off or sell at 'fire-sale' prices their assets in exchange for permission to cease trading and allow their principals to leave the country.[86]

To some, there was an element of predictability about this. In a minute written in November 1949, A. A. E. Franklin, a Foreign Office official, complained about the 'over-righteous indignation of the Shanghai "taipans" [business bosses] that somebody's else's war is being allowed to interfere with their business'. The taipans were misreading the times, he contended. 'Some appreciation of the traditional Chinese conception of international affairs is absolutely essential to an understanding of what is going on now.' He continued:

> Mao Zedong, as a patriot, doubtless shares many of the prejudices of the late-lamented Empress Dowager [the notably anti-foreign figure who dominated affairs in the last dynasty], the grey coolie uniform notwithstanding. In this respect they [the communists] are in the classical Chinese tradition. At best the foreigner is a necessary evil. To show him that he is not allowed to boss anybody about, you concentrate on humiliating him and making him lose face. The charm of the process is that by so doing you yourself gain face and the common man of China will undoubtedly think the more of you for it if you succeed in pulling it off.[87]

New China's new friends

If there was an element of truth to Franklin's description of the new government's attitude towards foreigners, there was also a strong element of caricature. China's leaders *were* ill-disposed towards much of what the foreign community in Shanghai and elsewhere stood for because its roots lay in their country's national humiliation. Yet they were also what today would be regarded as 'globalists'. It was simply that their cosmopolitan sympathies were directed towards the socialist world led by the Soviet Union rather than the West. They were 'leaning to one side', as Mao had phrased it. By first shunning and later expelling the West from China, they had, in yet another respect, reconfigured the international system. As historian Robert Bickers puts it, they had embarked on a 'change of partners, and a new phase in the attempted development of China in collaboration with foreign allies and foreign experts. It was out with the old and in with the new . . .'[88]

China's communists were as active in this new international space as circumstances allowed. They were not complete novices when it came to global diplomacy: Dong Biwu, a member of the Party's Central Committee, was a member of the Chinese government delegation that in June 1945 attended the founding congress of the United Nations in San Francisco. To a limited extent, the CCP could claim to have played a part in creating the post-Second World War order.

But by 1948 the Cold War had cast a pall over this order, and China's communists participated enthusiastically on the Soviet side in the struggle for global supremacy. An example was the 'attendance' of Guo Moruo, a leading literary figure who had thrown in his lot with the Party, at a meeting of the Soviet-sponsored World Peace Council in Paris in April 1949. The French authorities declined to let many delegates, Guo included, into their country, so he took part in a separate conclave in Prague linked to the Paris event. On returning to China, he declared that the CCP's victory in the Civil War

> had changed the balance of power between the forces of peace – led by the Soviet Union – and those of aggression – led by American imperialists . . . In the past, China had constituted 'the biggest foreign market' for imperialist countries which had generally treated the Far East as their colonies and 'life-line'. The liberation of China would encourage the process of colonial revolution; in this sense it was a guarantee of peace in the Far East and throughout the world.[89]

Another senior Party official returned from taking part in the Ninth Congress of the Czechoslovak Communist Party and the Second Congress of Polish Trade Unions as well as the World Peace Council with even more encouraging news. 'Well-known revolutionary leaders in every country had agreed that the victorious revolution in China constituted the third great victory of mankind since the October Revolution and victory in the anti-fascist Second World War', he enthused.[90] Such remarks emphasized the global significance of China's year of revolution: it had changed the world.

China's communists were also keen to host Soviet-led or 'Soviet-friendly' international events themselves. It was a useful means of boosting the legitimacy of their regime as well as displaying its achievement before a friendly audience. The first of these was the Trade Union Conference of

Asian and Australasian Countries, which met in Beijing in November. It was 'more like an international conference of communist parties than a trade union gathering', a fact that is said to have irritated Stalin.[91] But it was an expression of the international outlook of China's new leaders: they wanted their country to contribute to the global struggle for liberation of the kind they had so recently won at home.

They also had to deal with more practical and indeed critical matters on the foreign policy front. The Soviet camp aside, most countries, and especially those that 'mattered', still recognized what was left of the Nationalist administration as the legitimate government of China. Worse, the Nationalists continued to occupy China's seat in the UN and, as one of the organization's founders, enjoyed permanent membership of its powerful Security Council. The Nationalist delegation to the UN spent much of the autumn trying to persuade the world body to support a resolution condemning Soviet imperialism in China. Shortly after the founding of the PRC, Zhou Enlai informed UN Secretary General Trygve Lie that 'the so-called delegation of the Guomindang government had no right whatsoever to represent the Chinese people, and demanded that the United Nations immediately abolish all the rights of the "delegation" to participate in the United Nations'.[92] There was no question of the PRC taking China's seat at the 'top table' until the United States embarked on the normalization of its own relations with the communist state. Twenty-two years would pass before this came about.

In the meantime, New China was in need of economic, technical and military support to rebuild the country, meet the demands of its people and defend the revolution against its enemies at home and abroad. Given the circumstances, there was only one place from which such support could come.

On 5 October, four days after the founding of the People's Republic, the Soviet–Chinese Friendship Association was inaugurated amid much fanfare in Beijing. Song Qingling, New China's most prominent woman, gave the opening address. In what *The New York Times* described as a 'futile gesture', the Nationalist government in Guangzhou ordered her arrest along with that of eighty-three communists and their collaborators.[93] Liu Shaoqi, the CCP's point man on Soviet affairs following his secret talks with Stalin in July, disclosed to the meeting that there were some 200 Soviet technical experts already at work in China, most of them in Manchuria. They were paid the same as Chinese engineers of the same grade – unlike their American and British counterparts who had always demanded very high wages, he said. By this time, the Soviet Union had detonated its first atomic weapon, placing the socialist camp, at least symbolically, on the same footing as the US, leader of the capitalist or 'free' world.

Alexander Fadeyev, leader of the Soviet Cultural Delegation whose members had been on the rostrum at Tiananmen when Mao founded the People's Republic, had a message for the wider world arising from the friendship between the USSR and China. 'Let the bourgeois idiots of the imperialist camp in America and Western Europe pipe their old tune that China is backward', he was reported as saying. 'From now on the Chinese nation is one of the most progressive and highly civilised nations, pointing out the path for all mankind.'[94]

Soviet influence on public life in New China was soon visible. The appearance of posters showing images of Stalin and Lenin was a case in point. Eyebrows were raised when these first appeared in Shanghai, until recently the archetype of Chinese capitalism. Liliane Willens, who had been born in the city to White Russian parents, 'wondered how the People's Republic could justify its friendship with this "big brother" that had not yet relinquished control of the Chinese port of Dairen [Dalian]'. On seeing posters of Stalin, Lenin and Marx alongside Chinese leaders, she 'was amused that the Chinese would show respect to these new "devils"'.[95]

Public respect for the Soviet experts who arrived in China was in short supply, according to some sources. 'Information reaching Consulate General from many quarters shows rapidly swelling tide [of] Chinese charges and bitterness re greedy Soviet greedy encroachments', wrote the US consul in Shanghai.[96] Among many complaints, he reported Chinese anger 'that North China had shipped many trains of its food to Russia when China's food needs [are] great', and spoke of the threat of 'violent Chinese reaction' to the fact that a recent Soviet cultural delegation had been 'avid in buying up metals etc while in Shanghai'.[97] The *New York Times* said that other foreigners in China had 'become adept at spotting the new arrivals from their clothes and general demeanour. The newcomers are reported to be usually poorly dressed and many of them visit Beijing tailors soon after their arrival for new suits and new fur coats.'[98]

There were relatively few Soviet experts in China in 1949, which is probably why they made a big impression. But the encounter between Soviet and Chinese communists would soon blossom into a fully-fledged fraternal relationship that reached into almost every area of life. In the 1950s, Soviet expertise, funds, personnel, complete industrial plant, machinery and weapons flowed into China on a grand scale. The PRC's forms of government, legal procedures, arts, architecture, cityscapes and even its sciences were all shaped by the experience. And in a 'reverse flow', thousands of Chinese studied in the Soviet Union and its satellites. Among them were two men – Jiang Zemin and Li Peng – who as Party leader and premier respectively would dominate Chinese politics in the 1990s.

Such developments could not easily take place in the absence of a formal treaty of friendship and alliance between the Soviet Union and the PRC. No such pact existed at the close of 1949. Moscow had long helped bankroll, arm and advise China's communists, often causing misgivings and setbacks for both parties. Now that the CCP had conquered China and created a new state, the principals – Joseph Stalin and Mao Zedong – would have to meet face to face. The communist world had suddenly acquired a huge, populous and important new member. It was up to the established and the new titan of the communist world to work out how they might best pursue their joint and individual national interests.

To this end, amid great secrecy and in apparently apprehensive mood, Mao on 6 December boarded an armoured train in Beijing bound for Moscow and his first journey outside China. A small group of experts and support staff accompanied him, along with a wagon full of gifts for Stalin – rhubarb, radishes and onions from Shandong, fine quilts from Hunan, tea from Zhejiang, *maotai*, the fiery spirit, from Guizhou, and premium brand cigarettes from Shanghai.[99] Unhappy over this display of largesse, Mao is said to have had the wagon decoupled.[100] He was about to end what had been an extraordinary year at home with what he hoped would be a triumphant stride onto the world stage.

Notes

1   See Introduction, note 2. p. 24.

2   Alexander Pantsov (with Steven I. Levine), *Mao: The Real Story* (New York: Simon & Schuster, Kindle edition, 2013), pp. 101-2.

3   Li Zhisui. *The Private Life of Chairman Mao* (New York: Random House, 1994), p. 51; Frank Dikotter, *The Tragedy of Liberation: A History of the Chinese Revolution, 1945–57* (London: Bloomsbury, 2013), p. 41.

4   Dangdai zhongguo yanjiusuo bian (ed.), *Zhonghua Renmin Gongheguo shibiannian: 1949 nianjuan* ('Chronicle of the People's Republic of China 1949') (Beijing: Dangdai zhongguo chubanshe, 2004), p. 569.

5   Allyn Rickett and Adele Rickett, *Prisoners of Liberation* (San Francisco, CA: China Books, 1981), pp. 22–3.

6   *SWB*, No. 25, 11 October 1949, p. 33.

7   *SWB*, No. 24, 4 October 1949, p. 44.

8   FRUS, *The Far East: China*, Vol. VIII, 3 September 1949. https://history.state.gov/historicaldocuments/frus1949v08/d593 (accessed 22 February 2020).

9   See Chapter 7, p. 197.

10 *SWB*, No. 14, 26 July 1949, pp. 29–30.

11 MZD *SW*, Vol. 5, 21 September 1949. https://www.marxists.org/reference/archive/mao/selected-works/volume-5/mswv5_01.htm (accessed 21 February 2020).

12 MZD *SW*, Vol. 5, 21 September 1949. https://www.marxists.org/reference/archive/mao/selected-works/volume-5/mswv5_01.htm (accessed 21 February 2020).

13 New China News Agency, Beijing, 4 December 1949.

14 *SWB*, No. 34, 13 December 1949, p. 34.

15 TNA FO371/75836, 6 July 1949, 'Copy of a Memorandum from Mr John Gadsby re Meeting of the Bar Council of Shanghai'.

16 Otto Van Der Sprenkel (ed.), *New China: Three Views* (London: Turnstile Press, 1950), p. 106.

17 *The New York Times*, 11 December 1949, p. 42.

18 Ibid.

19 Felix Wemheuer, *A Social History of Maoist China* (Cambridge: Cambridge University Press, 2019), p. 58.

20 Tony Saich (ed.), *The Rise to Power of the Chinese Communist Party: Documents and Analysis* (New York: M. E. Sharpe, 1996), p. 1370.

21 The Common Program of the Chinese People's Political Consultative Conference, 1949, Article 58. https://sourcebooks.fordham.edu/mod/1949-ccp-program.asp (accessed 20 November 2019).

22 Wilson Center Digital Archive, 'Report, Kovalev to Stalin', 24 December 1949, p. 3 http://digitalarchive.wilsoncenter.org/document/113441 (accessed 2 February 2020).

23 *SWB*, No. 34, 13 December 1949, p. 30.

24 Ibid., p. 33.

25 Dangdai zhongguo yanjiusuo bian (ed.), *Zhonghua Renmin Gongheguo shibiannian: 1949 nianjuan*, p. 838.

26 *SWB*, No. 34, 13 December 1949, p. 19.

27 *SWB*, No. 38, 10 January 1950, p. 343.

28 TNA FO371/83357/F111/1, 'Hankow Despatch', 27 October 1949.

29 Ibid.

30 TNA FO371/83272/C10121/1, China Association Annual Report, 1949–1950, p. 7.

31 *SWB*, No. 23, 27 September 1949, p. 23.

32 Dangdai zhongguo yanjiusuo bian (ed.), *Zhonghua Renmin Gongheguo shibiannian: 1949 nianjuan*, p. 425.

33 TNA FO371/83272/C10121/1, China Association Annual Report, 1949–1950, p. 2

34 *Far Eastern Economic Review*, 1 September 1949, p. 278.

35 Tony Saich (ed.), *The Rise to Power of the Chinese Communist Party*, p. 1373.

36 Dangdai zhongguo yanjiusuo bian (ed.), *Zhonghua Renmin Gongheguo shibiannian: 1949 nianjuan*, p. 388.

37 Jeremy Brown and Paul G. Pickowicz (eds), *Dilemmas of Victory: The Early Years of the People's Republic of China* (Cambridge, MA: Harvard University Press, 2007), p. 60.

38 Dangdai zhongguo yanjiusuo bian (ed.), *Zhonghua Renmin Gongheguo shibiannian: 1949 nianjuan*, p. 409.

39 *SWB*, No. 5, 24 May 1949, p. 27.

40 See Chapter 7, p. 165.

41 Sherman Cochran and Andrew Hsieh, *The Lius of Shanghai* (Cambridge, MA: Harvard University Press, 2013), p. 285.

42 Ibid., p. 287.

43 Ibid.

44 Ibid., p. 288.

45 For a recent account see Dikotter, *The Tragedy of Liberation*; and for an earlier one, Richard L. Walker, *China Under Communism: The First Five Years* (New Haven, CT: Yale University Press, 1955).

46 Felix Wemheuer, *A Social History of Maoist China*, p. 39.

47 See Chapter 6, p. 159.

48 Dangdai zhongguo yanjiusuo bian (ed.), *Zhonghua Renmin Gongheguo shibiannian: 1949 nianjuan*, p. 682

49 Ibid., p. 713.

50 Otto Van Der Sprenkel (ed.), *New China: Three Views*, pp. 13–14.

51 Dangdai zhongguo yanjiusuo bian (ed.), *Zhonghua Renmin Gongheguo shibiannian: 1949 nianjuan*. p. 411.

52 *The New York Times*, 7 October 1949, p. 10.

53 Van der Sprenkel (ed.), *New China*, p. 91.

54 *SWB*, No. 9, 21 June 1949, p. 27.

55 Van der Sprenkel (ed.), *New China*, pp. 14–15.

56 Esther Cheo Ying, *Black Country to Red China* (London: Vintage 2009), p. 38.

57 Alun Falconer, *New China: Friend or Foe?* (London: The Naldrett Press, 1950), p. 66.

58 Felix Wemheuer, *A Social History of Maoist China*, p. 63.

59 Maria Yen, *The Umbrella Garden: A Picture of Life in Red China* (New York: Macmillan, 1954), pp. 101–2.

60 Van der Sprenkel (ed.), *New China*, p. 85.

61 Saich, *The Rise to Power of the Chinese Communist Party*, p. 1199.

62 Ibid., pp. 1318–19.

63 FRUS, *The Far East: China*, Vol. VIII, 9 July 1949. https://history.state.gov/historicaldocuments/frus1949v08/d488 (accessed 21 February 2020).

64 Wemheuer, *A Social History of Maoist China*, p. 19.

65 Dangdai zhongguo yanjiusuo bian (ed.), *Zhonghua Renmin Gongheguo shibiannian: 1949 nianjuan*, p. 664.

66 See Chapter 5, p. 140 et seq.

67 SOAS archives, 'Papers of Eva Dykes Spicer', PP MS92, Letter dated 23 June 1949.

68 Esther Cheo Ying, *Black Country to Red China*, p. 34.

69 Van der Sprenkel (ed.), *New China*, p. 85.

70 *The Times*, 10 August 1949, p. 4.

71 Yen, *The Umbrella Garden* pp. 72–3.

72 Ibid., p. 73.

73 Daniel H. Bays, *A New History of Christianity in China* (Chichester: John Wiley & Sons, 2012), p. 159.

74 See Chapter 6, p. 160.

75   See Chapter 2, p. 71.

76   *SWB*, No. 13, 19 July 1949, p. 26.

77   Ibid.

78   FRUS, *The Far East: China*, Vol VIII, 26 October 1949. https://history.state.gov/historicaldocuments/frus1949v08/d1138 (accessed 10 December 2019).

79   See Chapter 7, p. 199.

80   Chang Chihyun (ed.), *The Chinese Journals of L. K. Little, 1943–54: An Eyewitness Account of War and Revolution. Vol 1* (London: Routledge online resource, 2017), Electronic Resource: 707.7/968.

81   Daniel H . Bays, *A New History of Christianity in China*, p. 149.

82   *The New York Times*, 11 December 1949, p. 46.

83   Salvation Army Heritage Centre *North China Territory Report 1949*, p. 7, File no. CH1/2/1, 'Social Operations', section p. 1.

84   See Chapter 2, p. 66 and Chapter 6, p. 176.

85   DBPO, p. 326.

86   See Robert Bickers, *Out of China: How the Chinese Ended the Era of Western Domination* (London: Allen Lane, 2017), especially Chapter 8.

87   DBPO, pp. 406, 407.

88   Bickers, *Out of China*, p. 251.

89   *SWB*, No. 6, 31 May 1949, p. 28

90   *SWB*, No 12, 12 July 1949, p. 28.

91   Jung Chang and Jon Halliday, *Mao: The Unknown Story* (London: Jonathan Cape, 2005), p. 358.

92   Home News Library of the Xinhua News Agency (compilers), *China's Foreign Relations: A Chronology of Events*, 1949–1988 (Peking: Foreign Language Press, 1989), p. 3.

93   *The New York Times*, 9 October 1949, p. 1.

94   *SWB*, No. 25, 11 October 1949, p. 27.

95   Liliane Williams, *Stateless in Shanghai* (Hong Kong: China Economic Review Publishing [Hong Kong] for Earnshaw Books, 2010), p. 223.

96   FRUS, *The Far East: China*, Vol. VIII, 16 December 1949. https://history.state.gov/historicaldocuments/frus1949v08/d729 (accessed 13 December 2019).

97   Ibid.

98   *The New York Times*, 19 November 1949, p. 6.

99   Dangdai zhongguo yanjiusuo bian (ed.), *Zhonghua Renmin Gongheguo shibiannian: 1949 nianjuan*, pp. 763–4.

100 Dikotter, *The Tragedy of Liberation*, p. 122.

9

End games

By the time Mao arrived in Moscow in mid-December to begin his first foray in international diplomacy, his arch-rival Chiang Kai-shek had also reached his final destination in this tumultuous year in the lives of the two men. There, however, the similarity stops. Though Mao was uneasy about the prospect of meeting Stalin and securing the kind of alliance 'New China' badly needed, he was the undisputed victor in China's Civil War. Chiang, on the other hand, had been forced from the mainland to Taipei, his government, along with his own career, apparently in ruins.

Yet though of huge significance, the difference between success and failure, victory and defeat in the struggle for control over China was not absolute. This owed much to the Nationalist 'endgame' on the mainland and the ways in which the rest of the world was forced to adjust, not only to a 'New China' after 1949, but to a country with a dual identity, prey to bitter mutual hostility and locked in fierce competition for the loyalty of the Chinese people and the rest of the world. The endgame began with the PLA's advance on Guangzhou, the Nationalist's temporary capital, in the run-up to the proclamation of the PRC on 1 October.

'Our position is critical'

In mid-September, the US consulate general in Guangzhou reported that Li Zongren, apparently despairing of Gan Jiehou's efforts in Washington to secure US aid for the defence of south China against communism, requested that the following message be passed to Vice-Admiral Oscar Badger, Commander of the US Seventh Fleet:

Chinese Government Guangzhou is in extremely critical position. Within next week or 10 days decisive battle expected Hunan which will decide fate of Guangzhou. General Bai Chongxi will face combined armies Lin Biao and Liu Bocheng. Generalissimo's [i.e. Chiang Kai-shek] actions indicate we can expect no support from Air Force and funds for Guangzhou Government from Taiwan be completely stopped near future with no hope future Taiwan financial aid. Without funds our Government will collapse. If US intends any military, financial or moral backing, regardless amount, the time is now. Our position is critical.[1]

Summoned to meet Li and Bai, the US assistant naval attaché found the two Guangxi leaders in better spirits than their message suggested. 'Li appeared fresh, alert, kindly as ever, although he and Bai had been in conference all during day and evening', the attaché reported. 'Bai appeared tired, thoughtful but with usual dry humour.' They 'obviously consider immediate financial or military aid, in whatever amount, the only hope of saving present government against Communists and freeing it of the Generalissimo'.[2]

Time was running out for both objectives. Nor would US aid make much difference even if it were available: State Department officials complained that the war plan Li had shared with them a few days earlier was 'obviously hastily put together' . . . and a 'further demonstration of the unrealistic thinking which has always prevailed in Nationalist circles'.[3]

More to the point, the communists had acquired seemingly unstoppable momentum. PLA troops had penetrated deep into northwest China and were now scarcely more than 150 miles north of Guangzhou, from which city many nervous Nationalist officials and residents were fleeing by plane, ship, train, car, bus or on foot south to Hong Kong and beyond. Elsewhere in the areas still under Nationalist control, generals and their troops, provincial governors and politicians, civic leaders and many ordinary people readied themselves in various ways for the collapse of the regime and the arrival of the communist armies.

Yet it was not entirely clear that the fight had finally gone out of all the political and military factions in the Nationalist government. Chiang's government was feeble and discredited but it was not yet dead. The longer it survived, the bigger the challenge it presented to the legitimacy of Mao's new state.

For precisely these reasons, regime survival was Chiang's priority as his world crumbled in the final weeks of 1949. His aim was to be the 'last man standing' in any rump Nationalist government and emerge as the sole recipient of any outside aid. He was convinced that it was up to him to rescue and rejuvenate China, despite what many regarded as evidence to the contrary. Lester Knox Little, by now the outgoing head of the China Maritime Customs Service, was surprised to find Chiang looking 'well, perfectly calm and entirely free from any sign of nervousness or worry', when he called on him at his residence in Taipei in late October. 'He obviously has a great reserve of strength – spiritual, perhaps – or a complete lack of sensibility . . . I could not help admiring him, even though he must be held principally responsible for the tragedy through which China is passing.'[4]

It was not even clear where the last stand was to be made. There were several options, in addition to the fairly obvious one of Taiwan, to which Chiang had transferred as many resources as possible during the course of

1949. Yet scholar Lin Hsiao-ting has shown that Chiang often regarded the island as more of an insurance policy than the inevitable site for a last stand.[5] His personal authority there was not as secure as it seemed. And in the minds of many Taiwanese and some foreign governments (though not most Chinese), doubts persisted over Taiwan's precise legal status, pending the signing of a peace treaty with Japan. For all these reasons and more, Chiang was reluctant to withdraw his government entirely from the mainland unless there was no alternative.

Guangzhou conquered

Li Zongren's warning in mid-September that a decisive battle was about to take place in Hunan that would determine the fate of south China and thus the government of his Guangzhou proved correct. The PLA's Heng-Bao campaign (named after the two Hunan cities – Hengyang and Baoqing [modern Shaoyang] – over which it principally was fought) inflicted a serious blow on Bai Chongxi, who lost some 47,000 men in the space of a few weeks. Lin Biao and his Fourth Field Army were undoubted victors in this latest encounter with their arch-foe: Bai was forced to withdraw west into Guangxi, his morale-boosting victory over Lin's armies at Qingshuping in early September a thing of the past.[6]

A few days later, Soviet journalist Konstantin Simonov, attached to Lin's armies, drove through Hengyang, the recently abandoned location of Bai's Central China Command. 'It was a town of nearly 200,000 but when the GMD pulled out so did much of the population – to the surrounding villages – out of fear that there would be hand-to-hand fighting in the streets', he wrote. Wreckage was evident in the city alongside the abandoned defensive works such as pill boxes. Together with the shuttered shops and the dilapidated houses this 'made a rather dismal impression'.[7]

Some of Bai's forces escaped intact but their move west opened the way for the PLA drive south to Guangzhou, which Mao and the high command had prioritized. It was important to crush the Nationalist government or at least deprive it of the access to the outside world afforded by Guangzhou's port, major rivers and abundant maritime connections. Bai Chongxi's army, now largely isolated and bottled up in Guangxi, could be dealt with later.

The taking of Guangzhou was made easier than it might have been by continuing divisions between Chiang Kai-shek and Li Zongren over where to stand and fight. Li and Bai had spent much of the summer planning the defence of the two 'guang' provinces – namely Guangdong, location of Guangzhou, and their own Guangxi – which they believed they could hold for some time, especially if supplied by sea. Leading Cantonese generals Yu Hanmou, Zhang Fakui and Xue Yue, all backed the idea.

Chiang also pledged to defend Guangdong to the last, but it was not the only option as far as he was concerned. He certainly did not want all of the

Nationalists' military assets in south China put at risk in defence of the temporary capital. And he was concerned that, should the government manage to hold Guangzhou, he would face the prospect of at least one rival as leader of the Nationalist cause. That would threaten him personally and, in his view, place his country in even greater jeopardy.

Associates of Li Zongren complained bitterly that Chiang deliberately sabotaged the defence of south China. He had starved Bai of the necessary funds, air cover and equipment to hold Hunan, ordered the withdrawal of troops from both of his flanks, and criticized the Cantonese generals for supporting Li's plans for a 'last ditch stand'.[8] Thanks to Chiang's 'meddling', Guangzhou was rendered virtually defenceless.[9] Bai was said to have been so full of 'disgust and resentment' over the fact that his troops had not been paid that he would in future 'fight only for Guangxi with whatever means he can muster from his native province'.[10]

Chiang seemed unperturbed. He had for some time planned to shift the government to Chongqing, the capital during the war against Japan, or perhaps to another city in the southwest, should the military and political situation in Guangzhou deteriorate. Preparations to that end had been under way as early as the end of May – less than a month after the Nationalists moved to Guangzhou following the fall of Nanjing. This was because 'circumstances [generally] did not favour the central government at that time so the cabinet made plans to move to yet another location', writes Lin Tongfa in his study of the Nationalist's 'Great Withdrawal'. But 'the issue was handled in a low-key way so as not to have a negative effect on the military situation: it was therefore deemed best to send individual departments to different places'.[11] However, most of the places selected were in or around Chongqing.

Civil servants and politicians were understandably reluctant to make yet another move as long as Guangzhou was not under immediate threat. But by mid-August it was, and the government said that 12,000 persons, comprising 8,500 dependants and 3,500 inessential personnel, were scheduled to depart the city. Two thousand top officials would stay behind ready to go to the airport '"briefcase in hand" to follow Acting President Li Zongren . . . to Chongqing, where they will set up offices close enough to airport to be able to get out to Formosa when Sichuan is lost', a US diplomat reported.[12] A correspondent for *The Times* wrote: 'It is impossible not to feel sorry for some of these officials. After spending the war years in Chongqing, followed by sojourns of varying length in Nanjing, Shanghai and Guangzhou, they again find themselves back in the war-time capital. Nor are any of them confident that Chongqing can hold out for long.'[13]

Indeed, many of them decided to cut out the Chongqing leg of the search for safety altogether. 'Although the Chinese Nationalist Government have decided to move from Guangzhou to Chongqing we understand that most Government departments will be partially transferred to Formosa which will become the main policy-making centre', wrote the British consul in

Taipei in mid-September.[14] He noted that the Ministry of Foreign Affairs had established an office in Taipei, which would house the archives; that Lester Knox Little, inspector general of Maritime Customs, had moved his staff to Formosa; and that each of the five main branches of government had set up offices in the island. 'Over one hundred legislative Yuan members, several hundred government officials and a number of Guomindang Executive Committee and Party members have taken refuge in Formosa from Guangzhou', he advised London in October.[15]

The fall of Hengyang on 8 October sealed Guangzhou's fate. Large Nationalist formations still guarded the northern approaches to the city. But both they and their commanders lacked the will to stop troops of Lin Biao's Fourth Field Army and the Second Field Army under Liu Bocheng from swooping south. Local guerrilla units, long active in the more remote areas of Guangdong, joined forces with the regulars. By the time of the 'double ten' anniversary (the tenth day of the tenth month – the day in 1911 when republicans overthrew the Manchu monarchy), gunfire could be heard in Guangzhou. It must have lent poignancy to the anniversary greetings President Truman sent to Li Zongren to mark Republican China's national holiday. The president's message was a matter of diplomatic routine, *The New York Times* advised its readers – though it conceded some 'viewed it as an affirmation of continued United States support of the Nationalists in their fight with the Communists'.[16]

Two days later the government announced that it would transfer operations to Chongqing with effect from 15 October. 'The large scale evacuation of Government personnel from Guangzhou to Chongqing had been going on for several days and was nearly completed', government radio said.[17] Six aircraft had been put at the disposal of the diplomatic community to allow them to transfer personnel to the new temporary capital. Most diplomats preferred to go to Hong Kong. Even as the mass exodus got under way, and three columns of communist troops closed in on the northern and eastern suburbs, the Nationalists promised to put up a fight – as they had pledged to for other cities shortly before they fell. On 9 October, Generals Yu Hanmou and Xue Yue swore to 'defend Guangzhou to the death' and to 'live or die in the city'.[18] Two days later Lester Knox Little wrote:

> It looks as if the government is evacuating Guangzhou as quickly as possible, and I shall be surprised if any responsible official is to be found there a week from today . . . We are seeing plenty of history being made again around and about the Guangzhou Delta, and I confess that I find it stimulating and exciting to be in the thick of one part of it.[19]

The next day, 12 October, Li Zongren and other senior leaders left the city. Revealingly, they headed in different directions. Li flew to Guilin, the by now nervous Guangxi capital, 'for a rest' before travelling on to Chongqing. Premier Yan Xishan went to Taipei for discussions with Chiang Kai-shek.

The Cantonese generals headed for Hainan, where they hoped to muster as many of their troops as possible ahead of whatever came next.

Before leaving, Nationalists soldiers blew up a major bridge over the Pearl River whose cantilever structure *The New York Times* described as 'the finest in China'.[20] They also destroyed facilities at the city's two main airports and set fire to munitions stores. 'The last Nationalist officials have left Guangzhou, which only awaits the arrival of the Reds', Little observed. 'After all the talk and boasts, not a shot was fired by the 'defenders' of the city, who skedaddled as fast as they could – after needlessly blowing up the great Pearl River Bridge. Like a spoiled child who destroys a child's sand castle just to be nasty.'[21]

There were scenes of panic as residents rushed to buy up supplies. Nationalist soldiers forced their way on to planes or ships to take them to Hainan or Guangzhouwan, the last remaining serviceable ocean port in south China. Others headed up the West River into neighbouring Guangxi. Properties in the city's wealthier districts were looted, their owners having fled to Hong Kong. However, a section of the municipal police remained on duty, 'having been warned by underground cells to continue their services', according to *The New York Times*.[22]

Later on 14 October, quiet fell over Guangzhou as it awaited its 'liberators'. They arrived about 7 p.m. and promptly took over the major buildings in the city centre that had served as the Presidential Office, the seat of the Cabinet, the Guangdong Provincial Government and the Municipal Police Station. This and the arrival of other forces from the eastern suburbs meant that 'Guangzhou had been liberated', the Fourth Field Army's official history declares.[23] With its international audience in mind, *Time* adopted a breezier tone: 'With scarcely more than a quiet sigh, Guangzhou last week passed under Communist rule. There was no resistance in the city that had given refuge to China's dying Nationalist government . . . A million Chinese carried on impassively while the Red underground among them emerged for jubilant street parades . . .'[24]

Hong Kong: tightrope walking

The communist conquest of Guangzhou meant that it was only a matter of time before PLA soldiers came into contact with British security forces along the border of Hong Kong. Officials in both London and the colony were fairly certain that the communist advance would stop at the border – as trains on the Kowloon to Guangzhou Railway line now did. 'Through trains', in common with direct air and shipping links, had suddenly become a thing of the past even though for the next few weeks the 'frontier' itself would remain as porous as it had been before the arrival of the PLA. There were no signs that the new regime was bent on reclaiming the colony: it had too many other things to do. But London had sent in reinforcements to

FIGURE 9.1 *Where two worlds met: A British police inspector and a PLA irregular in October stand either side of the boundary marker between Hong Kong and China.*

maintain internal security and signal to the communist leaders that it had no intention of abandoning its outpost on the edge of what was now 'Red China'.[25] The arrival along the border in mid-October, first of communist irregulars and then of formal PLA units, put that theory to the test.

At Shataukok, the village divided by the border between Hong Kong and China, '35 uniformed regular Communist troops arrived and formally took over responsibility for the administration from the elders of the village chamber of commerce', *The Times* reported on 19 October.[26] 'At Shenzhen, further west, there is a now a small garrison of regular Communist troops.' A British police officer made contact with communist guerrillas who told him they were under strict instructions 'to avoid any kind of incident with British forces' and 'move into new positions along the frontier only after the Nationalists had moved out'. The government's annual report happily recorded at the end of the year that 'there were no incidents, and relations between the British and Chinese authorities on the frontier have been formal and correct'.[27] Indeed, the situation was said to be so peaceful on the day communist troops appeared that 'only two miles from the border British residents played golf', noted the *Daily Telegraph*.[28]

FIGURE 9.2 *Communist volunteers (of various ages) in late October shout out their support for Mao Zedong in Shenzhen, close to the Hong Kong border.*

Percy Chen, son of a former Chinese foreign minister and at the time a left-leaning lawyer in Hong Kong, was one of a small group of people who went north to greet the PLA. They crossed the bridge at Shenzhen where they were surprised to be met by

> boys not more than thirteen or fourteen years old. They were dressed in gray uniforms with puttees on their legs and straw sandals on their feet, had Mauser revolvers hanging by leather straps over their right soldiers, and wore gray caps with a red star on their front. These were the famed Red Devils, who acted as orderlies and messengers, and performed duties other than combatant ones.[29]

The proximity of the PLA was a symbol of the changed situation facing Hong Kong following the communist conquest of south China. The colony had, as it were, acquired a new neighbour – one that was strong, well disciplined, tightly organized and politically opposed to much of what Hong Kong stood for, including the very concept of continued foreign rule. Britain was about to find that governing the territory would prove a more complex, sensitive and risky matter than it had been when the Nationalists were in charge.

Coping with the continuing influx of refugees was an example. Chinese flocked into the colony at the rate of over 10,000 a week at the time of the fall of Shanghai in May and again in October when the conquest of Guangzhou was imminent, according to the government.[30] For much of this time, Guangzhou was the last major city still under Nationalist control and one of the last places in the country where the government was issuing passports. Hong Kong and thus the wider world were within reach. Those with the means, the motive and the courage flocked south as quickly as they could. 'Hong Kong saw another influx of evacuated Guangzhou residents into the already overpopulated Colony', observed *The New York Times* on 14 October.[31] 'Sixty planes landed at Kai Tak airport and about 6,000 persons arrived by train.' The government said passenger traffic on the Guangzhou–Kowloon railway in 1949 reached 4.7 million, an 80 per cent increase over the past two years.[32]

Hu Yaohen, a teenager from Hubei who made his way to the territory with his father, recalled walking across the bridge that separated China from Hong Kong.

> They [officials on the Hong Kong side] would just say 'Where do you live?', in Cantonese. I remember my father just handed them some gold. And they let us by. The Hong Kong government didn't know how to deal with all the refugees. We ended up living on the side of the mountain . . . There were about 300 people living there when we arrived. It got up to about three thousand after a few weeks.[33]

Officials were relieved that no large formations of Nationalist soldiers crossed into the colony. Instead, they fled southwest to Hainan or east to Taiwan. But Governor Alexander Grantham was worried about a future wave of refugees, which he feared would come from north or central China, probably by way of Taiwan. 'Hong Kong cannot stand any more influx on significant scale', he advised London. '. . . and Taiwan has a very large number of refugees from the mainland who will probably want to move on soon at all costs.'[34] He announced that, effective from 11 November, all foreign nationals would require a visa to enter the colony save those coming from the mainland, which meant in effect those entering overland via Guangdong. It proved impossible to implement such a scheme.

The government made more progress with plans to register the Hong Kong population, another necessity given its growing size and fears of subversion. Under the Registration of Persons Ordinance, people were to be issued with identity cards that, if necessary, would entitle them to food and other essential supplies. 'Before the end of the year well over 120,000 persons had been registered in the Colony', according to the government's annual report.[35]

Hong Kong's desire to remain neutral in China's unfinished Civil War – another necessity if the colony was to survive and prosper given the new circumstances – required skilful tightrope walking. Controversy over the ownership of most of the assets of the two government-owned Chinese airlines made this apparent. Prior to losing much of the mainland, the Nationalist government ordered eighty-three planes belonging to China National Aviation Corporation (CNAC) and Central Aviation Transport Corporation (CATC) to fly to Hong Kong to avoid confiscation by the communists. However, in November, pilots and crew flew thirteen of the aircraft to Beijing, where they were feted as national heroes. At a dinner to celebrate their defection, Zhou Enlai said the action of the airlines' staff 'marked the starting point of the Chinese people's civil aviation which had boundless prospects'.[36] More planes were on the point of flying north when the Hong Kong government intervened and grounded them.

The Nationalists restructured ownership of the airlines in favour of the United States in the hope that the rest of the fleet could be kept out the clutches of Beijing. However, the matter was then placed before the Hong Kong courts, by which time Britain had recognized the PRC, implying that it was bound to hand the aircraft over to China. Washington, anxious that if they got hold of them the communists could use the planes against the Nationalists in Taiwan, threatened London with sanctions. The upshot was that, while the Hong Kong courts ruled in favour of Beijing, they instructed Grantham to hold the aircraft until legal process had been exhausted. This finally happened in 1952, when a ruling of the Privy Council in London declared in favour of the 'US owners' of the airlines. Governor Grantham expressed himself unhappy over what he described as 'a sorry business'.[37]

More humdrum but hardly less sensitive were the government's moves to curb CCP (and Nationalist) activities in the colony. Beijing frequently took the Hong Kong authorities to task for, in effect, outlawing the Communist Party and 'persecuting' local left-wing or 'progressive' individuals.[38] The colonial government did not yield; indeed, it took special measures to break up what it regarded as 'Red Schools' where it feared the communists were fostering insurrection among the young. 'These had to be closed down and, in the most flagrant cases, the teachers deported', Grantham insisted.[39] More leniency was shown when it came to flying the new PRC national flag. Lester Knox Little wrote in his diary for 10 October: 'I saw a great many Communist flags flying in Hong Kong today . . . Communist flags have been banned in Singapore but not in Hong Kong. A sign of the times.'[40]

Communist influence in Hong Kong's trade union movement was another potent issue now that the CCP was in control over the border. The communists in effect controlled the 25,000–30,000 members of the Hong Kong and Kowloon Federation of Trades Unions which enrolled an estimated 12 per cent of the colony's workforce. It had a strong presence in the utilities as well as the port. The influx of capital and skills from Shanghai meant more factories in Hong Kong – and thus potentially more power for the unions. In its annual review of the labour situation, the government expressed concern over the 'rather darker' outlook towards the end of 1949.[41] Police action was necessary to end the occupation by workers of the Hong Kong Match Factory; and a strike on the tram ways, encouraged by the new rulers in Guangzhou, turned into a confrontation with the government in 1950 that the latter eventually won. It showed the 'government was master in its own house', Grantham recalled.[42]

Hong Kong thus ended 1949 on a different note and in a different mood than it had begun. There was relief that the Chinese Civil War seemed to be over, at least in its most brutal phase. And there was no immediate external challenge to British rule, as many had feared would be the case at the height of HMS *Amethyst* incident. But strength and subtlety were required on the part of the authorities if the colony was to flourish and its inhabitants enjoy peace, stability and liberties of the kind unavailable elsewhere in China. With the former in mind, the Hong Kong government in December 1949 granted itself emergency powers, which Grantham (and his successors) reserved the right to evoke on a piecemeal basis irrespective of whether a formal state of emergency was declared.

Guangxi graveyard

Shortly after he had forced Bai Chongxi's armies west into Guangxi, opening the way for the conquest of Guangzhou, Lin Biao offered an assessment of his great Nationalist rival. 'I consider Bai Chongxi the most capable of the Guomindang Generals – not that that is saying much', he told Soviet

MAP 9.1 *Guangxi graveyard: Where Lin Biao's Fourth Field Army crushed the Nationalist government's last significant military resistance, led by Bai Chongxi.*

journalist Konstantin Simonov during an interview at his Hengyang headquarters. But he had 'years of fighting experience and is a better commander than the rest . . .' As for his troops, 'there are a great many old campaigners among them, and their fighting capacity is above [the] average of Chiang Kai-shek's army.'[43]

In other words, Bai was not beaten yet, and it fell to the commander of the PLA's Fourth Field Army to make sure he was. 'Now we are faced with our last objective: to liberate Guangxi, surrounding and annihilating the whole of the Guomindang force that is holding it – the largest fighting force the Guomindang still has', Lin said.[44] Bai had rejected CCP peace overtures on several occasions, most recently in August, when at a press conference in Hong Kong, Huang Shaohong, a member of the government peace delegation, formally broke with the Guomindang and tried to persuade his fellow Guangxi men to follow suit. A few did so, but not the provincial military chiefs. They, like Bai himself, would have to be broken on the battlefield. The best place to so this was in Guangxi itself. It would shatter Bai's reputation on his own turf and show the independent-minded people of Guangxi that the communists were now in charge.

The plan, attributed to Mao and the high command rather than Lin, was to envelope Bai's armies in a huge 'horse-shoe' formation whose tips or prongs would eventually meet, preventing his escape. It was important to put direct pressure on Bai but not so much that he and his armies could escape before they could be surrounded. The Fourth Field Army would deploy a total of some half a million men to the Guangxi campaign, calling on Second Field Army troops for support in the southeast of the province. That was close to twice the size of Bai's army which was also poorly equipped by comparison. In an attempt to ensure that Bai could at least pay his troops, CIA operatives oversaw the delivery of 'formidable piles of cash [in HK dollars] that filled two large wicker baskets' to his headquarters in Guilin, according to a recent account.[45] It was not clear to what use, if any, the money was put.

Divisions hampered plans for the defence of Guangxi, as they had at almost every stage during this year of catastrophe on the battlefield. But on this occasion, they appeared to perplex the man usually acclaimed for quick decision-making: Bai himself. General Xu Qiming, commander of Bai's 10th corps, recalled a tense meeting in Guilin in which 'Chiang [who was not present] wanted [Bai] to retreat into Yunnan, Li had his mind set on withdrawal to Hainan and I favoured a move into French Indochina. Bai was confronted with the most difficult decision of his life.'[46]

Military leaders had considered the option of fleeing across the border into French Indochina for some time. At the local level, Guangxi Governor Huang Xuchu held several rounds of informal talks with Vietnamese nationalist leaders to this end. Chinese officials even raised the matter with US diplomats in Guangzhou. The latter expressed themselves 'amazed' when asked to 'persuade [the] French Government to agree to entry of Bai's forces into Indochina and remain there apparently indefinitely'.[47] It was up to the Chinese government to approach Paris, not the Americans, came the brusque reply.

Xu conceded that it might be necessary to fight the French if they tried to stop Chinese troops entering their territory but 'they had so few forces on the ground, that they would find it impossible to stop an army as large as ours from crossing into their territory'.[48] And if the border intrusion provoked an international incident, so much the better: it might wake the Americans up.[49] At least flight into Indochina was a strategy for survival; the alternatives pointed to utter defeat.

Zhou Enlai, aware of the Nationalists' plan, issued stern warnings to the French authorities in Indochina not to intervene in China's Civil War. He did so even as he and Mao were themselves seeking Stalin's permission to send PLA forces across the border in support of Ho Chi Minh, the Vietnamese revolutionary leader. Stalin declined, advising a colleague privately that he 'was not pleased with the way the CCP planned to handle the Vietnam issue', according to historian Odd Arne Westad.[50]

Bai decided he would make a stand in Guangxi for as long as possible and withdraw south to Hainan, hopefully via the Leizhou Peninsula, when it was not. The Guangxi soldiers were expected to put up a stiff fight now that their backs were against the wall. The province would practise 'total war'. The provincial government, which had shifted from Guilin to Nanning, further south and west, would 'strengthen the defence works and clear the fields', as an aide described it.[51] Along the railway and roads leading into northwest Guangxi 'everything that might be useful to the communists was gathered up and placed out of reach. This included livestock and food; not a needle and thread was to remain.'[52] A policy of 'every ten households has a gun and produces a soldier' was introduced in an effort to turn the civilian population into a popular militia.[53]

With the war about to enter Guangxi, it was important to ensure that the province's civilian officials remained loyal. They were required to take 'an anti-communist oath' which, according to the government news agency, forbade them to 'cooperate with the Communists by passing on information, providing food, guiding Communist forces or leaving behind – in case of evacuation – cooking utensils for the use of the PLA. They also promised to report any discovery of Communist spies or agents to the military authorities immediately.'[54]

Rivalry for control of what remained of the central government cast a shadow over the imminent military showdown in Guangxi. On leaving Guangzhou, Li Zongren flew first to Guilin and then on to Chongqing, the new temporary capital. He received a warm welcome from the public but was alarmed that the local commanders were loyal to Chiang rather than himself. 'Everything I said and did was known to Chiang's people; I could have been arrested at any moment', he recalled.[55] Moreover, local newspapers had begun referring to Chiang as 'president' rather than 'director' of the

GMD. Li believed Chiang might force him to relinquish the acting presidency when, as expected, he arrived in the city in the next few days. He therefore left for Kunming, capital of Yunnan, to discuss anti-communist resistance with provincial governor Lu Han. Chiang and Li would never meet, nor trust each other, again.

The rift was sealed by Li's sudden decision to leave China for the United States. His few days in Kunming had convinced him that Lu Han would not long hold out in Yunnan. Indeed there was a risk that he would try and reach a deal with the communists by kidnapping Chiang or even Li himself. On 13 November, Li flew to Guilin, which by now was 'jittery and scared' at the approach of the communist armies.[56] During a tense conference Li, Bai and other military commanders reviewed the options. Bai again seemed 'unfocussed and at a loss', observed an aide. He was 'facing the biggest defeat in his life'.[57]

The only way to avoid disaster seemed to be withdrawal to Hainan. On 16 November, Li flew to the island to assess the situation. It was not encouraging. A *New York Times* reporter, visiting the main town of Haikou around the same time, wrote:

> Within the past six weeks more than 100,000 [Nationalist troops] have arrived in this city of 250,000. They arrive by ancient steamer, landing craft, junks and sampans. Ragged and weary, they wade ashore through the shallow surf, each carrying a bundle of the pitifully few things he could save ... Many have lain ill on the sidewalks for days. Malaria is common and there is a danger of typhus and cholera. Unpaid for months, the soldiers try to sell their few belongings for food.[58]

In despondent mood, Li flew back to Nanning, where he fell seriously ill from a suspected duodenal ulcer. Rather than risk his life, he decided it would be better to seek medical treatment in the United States and return to China as soon as possible, perhaps with a pledge of US support. He summoned Bai, Governor Huang Xuchu and a few other senior figures to his bedside to break the news. It was the last time the three main leaders of Guangxi Clique met. 'For more than thirty years, Huang, Bai and I had worked closely together. Now we had parted ways', Li observed.[59]

On 19 November, Li advised Premier Yan Xishan by telegram of his decision to leave the country. He also asked Bai to fly to Chongqing and share the news with Chiang, who was trying to rally support for a last stand in Sichuan. Chiang gave Bai a pep talk. History showed the country always made progress when the two men worked together, Chiang told him. 'However grave the current situation, there is a way forward as long as we cooperate.'[60] It was reconciliation of a kind after a year of disastrous divisions between the two men, rooted in two decades of distrust. But it was only skin deep. And soon it would hardly matter as far as Chiang was concerned.

On 20 November, Li left for Hong Kong where he entered the colony's Taiho hospital. Chiang sent emissaries to the patient in an unsuccessful attempt to persuade him to return. Chiang 'wants someone else to continue "holding the bag" for him and to take public responsibility for loss of mainland', US diplomats observed sourly.[61] But Li's days of 'holding the bag' were over. Denied diplomatic passports by his own government, he and his entourage flew out of Hong Kong on 5 December on personal travel documents.

When Li left China he believed Bai might still have a chance of keeping the communists out of part of southern China. 'Before he left, Li gave me a letter to deliver to Bai in Hainan', a close aide recalled. 'It requested that he concentrate his forces there and wait for Li's return from surgery in the United States. The two men could then plan their next steps.'[62] In fact, the battle for Guangxi was nearly over. The ruthless efficiency with which Lin Biao crushed Bai's armies confirmed his reputation as the superior strategist of the two and the most talented commander in the Civil War.

Lin's central thrust forced Bai to abandon Guilin and northwest Guangxi for the imagined safety of the south. An eyewitness described a tragic scene: 'Abandoned military vehicles were left alongside the road, and soldiers and civilians marched in a steady stream south.' Such trains as were running 'were crowded with soldiers, refugees and their dependants'.[63] The communist New China News Agency provided a different take: Bai's troops 'left a trail of destruction as they fled . . .; railway bridges were in ruins, scuttle boats blocked the river crossings, cooking utensils in civilian homes had been smashed and the inhabitants driven into the mountains'.[64]

Guilin fell on 22 November, Liuzhou in central Guangxi on 25 November and Wuzhou, the main commercial central on the West river in the southeast, on the same day. Instead of putting up stiff resistance, Bai's men proved a 'spent force', as one provincial official put it.[65] Many Guangxi soldiers, weary of fighting for so long, 'simply deserted and made their way home', said another.[66] Guerrillas of the Guangdong–Guangxi and Guangxi–Yunnan–Guizhou Border Columns assisted the PLA regulars, most of whom were northerners and unfamiliar with local conditions. The Guangxi irregulars were not as numerous as those that had linked up with the PLA in the conquest of Guangzhou. But they were a force that, in the words of a political commissar of the Second Field Army, will 'help us take the battle into Guangxi and then to administer the province. Their role should not be underestimated.'[67]

During the last week in November and the first few days of December, Bai sought to get a grip on the situation from a beleaguered Nanning. It was by now far too late to defend Guangxi, as he told Republican Senator William Knowland, who flew in from Hong Kong to meet him on 2 December. Knowland was a fierce critic of Truman's opposition to further aid for the Nationalists; Lester Knox Little described him as 'the last straw at which the GMD is grasping'.[68] Bai asked Knowland to ensure that any aid in future be directed to Hainan, where he and his armies would soon be based. Since PLA forces were by now just a few miles outside Nanning, he urged the senator to leave as soon as possible, which he did on 3 December. The following day, Bai himself, together with provincial governor Huang Xuchu and other senior leaders, left Hainan. None of them would return to the mainland.

The fiercest fighting for control over Guangxi occurred in the south and east of the province, along the border with Guangdong. In and around Bobai and Baihe, two otherwise fairly undistinguished country towns, Bai's main armies were decimated. Their commanders were caught out by the speed of the PLA advance. Their plans to hold a corridor along which men and equipment could retreat south to Hainan lay in ruins.

General Xu Qiming provided a first-hand account of the chaos and catastrophe that engulfed Nationalist forces further west, along the 'escape road' from Nanning to the then small port of Qinzhou, from which it was hoped troops could also cross to Hainan. Xu insisted that escape to the island was impossible: there were not enough boats and no suitable harbours either in Qinzhou or Hainan. Troops fleeing south would 'have the ocean ahead of them and enemy at the rear. With no boats to get us across, the most likely outcome is extermination of our forces.'[69]

So it proved. En route to Qinzhou Xu ran into what remained of troops led by Huang Jie, who had decided to head for French Indochina with as many of his men as possible. An air-force plane carrying orders from Bai said it was too late to reach Hainan: Xu would have to follow Huang Jie into the mountains of southern Guangxi and thence into French territory. 'It was the last order Bai would ever issue to his troops', a close associate noted.[70]

Since communist regulars were pursuing Huang, it was also dangerous to follow the Nationalist retreat. Indeed, Xu was soon forced to fight on two fronts. His army was destroyed as a fighting unit and he himself narrowly avoided capture. Together with his personal security detail he spent the following few weeks hiding in the mountain villages of southern Guangxi and the outskirts of Qinzhou. He eventually made his way to Guangzhou and thence to Hong Kong where his wife, who had already settled in the colony, was astonished to see her husband again given that he had been listed as missing. 'When Bai heard of my escape he ordered Lin Pixian [another Guangxi general then in Hong Kong] to give me 20,000 dollars', Xu recalled. He promptly abandoned the military life for the study of Chinese medicine.[71]

Another (temporary) disappearance caused by communist conquest of Guangdong and Guangxi was that of a non-combatant, one Ye Yuanzhang, commissioner of customs in the former treaty port of Pakhoi (Beihai). Ye reported ultimately to Lester Knox Little, the inspector general who, as noted, had by now left the mainland. Ye's last telegram to his superiors, dated 6 December 1949, read:

URGENT. Communist forces reported 30 li (about 10 miles) from *Hoppo* [Customs office] and expected to arrive Pakhoi tomorrow. Mass evacuation Nationalist troops now in progress. Self and staff will remain at post as instructed. If no further report from me, Goodbye.[72]

The fall of Guangxi brought Bai Chongxi's career as a military commander and key political player during the events of 1949 to an abrupt end. On arriving in Hainan, he spent most of his time in a warship patrolling the waters off Qinzhou in the hope that some of his soldiers might yet escape. Few managed to do so. An official account of the battle said the PLA had put out of action 172,990 Nationalist troops along with 90 senior ranking officers. Some 20,000 soldiers had managed to escape into French Indochina. 'The PLA had wiped out the last and the largest remaining Nationalist fighting force on the mainland.'[73]

Whether or not these curiously precise figures were accurate, it was clear that Bai's armies had been cut to pieces. The French promptly disarmed those of his soldiers that had managed to flee across the border and confined them to camps. Bai was a general without troops; a military leader whose political influence had evaporated; a national figure for whom there was no longer role in his country's life. The headquarters of his Central China Command, which at the start of the year were located in the industrial city of Hankou and exercised control over the entire middle Yangtze, now operated out of a Catholic church in Haikou, the largest town on an undeveloped island of which the Nationalists controlled only the coastal fringe. Communist guerrillas had held sway in the interior for years.

Liang Shengjun, a close aide who did not see his boss during the height of the recent fighting but joined him afterwards in Hainan, was astonished by Bai's changed appearance. A few weeks earlier, he had appeared composed and in a bright mood even though the communists were bearing down on his province. Now he looked 'thin and pallid, his eyes dull, his spirits low, his voice barely more than a murmur'.[74]

There was now only one course open to Bai – a move (or retreat as he must have regarded it) to Taiwan, where he could expect to exercise little influence and be monitored by Chiang's agents. Li Zongren's departure and Bai's military defeat meant Chiang need no longer fear the Guangxi faction. But he saw no need to forgive his erstwhile rivals, especially Bai who in the telegram he sent almost exactly a year ago had urged him to retire.[75] Bai left Hainan for Taipei on 30 December – and a largely unhappy later life, full of regret over the loss of the mainland and (vain) hope that it might be recovered.

By comparison, Lin Biao ended the year on a triumphant note. On 19 December he left Guangxi for Changsha from where he issued a statement commending the Fourth Field Army on its actions. The annihilation of Bai's forces would 'prove to be of vital significance for shortening the war', he declared.[76] Lin was right. He had one more major act to perform in the Civil War: the 'liberation' of Hainan for which planning soon began.

Filling out the frontiers

Remarkably, the communist conquest of south China coincided with that of the vast expanses of the northwest. This required the PLA to negotiate even more difficult terrain and longer distances than that south of the Yangtze. Victory was no less sudden or complete.

Chiang's government had never been able to bring Gansu, Qinghai, Ningxia and the even more remote Xinjiang province to heel. Its authority throughout this relatively under-populated region rested on limited subventions from the central government in exchange for public expressions of loyalty on the part of regional leaders who largely went their own way. China's new rulers were determined to impose their will throughout the country, gain access to the northwest's rich resources and ensure there was no room for 'reactionaries' or 'imperialists' in even the most distant parts of 'People's' China.

The military obstacle to this goal consisted of the armies of the Ma clan of Moslem warlords who had ruled much of Gansu, Qinghai and Ningxia throughout the Republican period, and central government troops under Hu Zongnan. Neither were in a strong position to defend the status quo, even though by means of a surprise attack in early June they managed to check the westward march of Peng Dehuai's First Field Army. Partly as a result of this victory, Chiang appointed Ma Bufang, the leading Ma, as political and military chief of the northwest to replace Zhang Zhizhong, who in April had switched roles from government peace delegate to supporter of the CCP.[77] Ma Honggui, governor of Ningxia, was made his deputy.

But Chiang's failure to supply the Ma armies with weapons and ammunition drove their leaders to despair. 'We called on General Ma [Honggui] again on August 15 and found [the] General interested in talking about only one thing—bullets', US officials reported from Guangzhou. 'He stated that he had asked Central Government officials [in] Guangzhou and Generalissimo in Formosa for bullets, but answer was invariably no. He said he even proposed borrowing bullets with a promise to return them when fighting was over, but answer was same.'[78]

Lack of the means to fight, and the failure of Hu Zongnan to coordinate (critics said even to cooperate) with Ma's armies, enabled the First Field Army to resume its drive west with little opposition. Lanzhou, capital of Gansu, fell in August; Qinghai and Ningxia did so the following month. Ma Bufang made his way to Hong Kong and thence to Mecca; Ma Honggui moved to Taiwan.

That left Xinjiang, only some 6 per cent of whose population were ethnic Chinese compared with an estimated 77 per cent Uighur and other Turkish-speaking peoples, as the remaining part of northwest China largely untouched by the Civil War.[79] Tao Zhiyue, the local military commander, could see which way the wind was blowing. He decided to spare the province from fighting by announcing a break with the Nationalists on 25 September and surrendering to the First Field Army commanders a few days later. A period of uncertainty followed in a region long riven with factional as well as ethnic differences. At the end of the year Peng Dehuai was able to report to Mao that, thanks to the re-education of Tao's troops and reorganization of the provincial government 'on national democratic principles', the overall situation in Xinjiang had begun to stabilize. But if no longer so rebellious, the region faced financial crisis. 'I consider it necessary for great assistance to be given from the Soviet Union', Peng said.[80] It was not long in coming.

As 1949 drew to a close, Tibet alone seemed unaffected by the struggle for control of China proper. Its religious rulers regarded their vast homeland, sandwiched between India and China, as an independent country. In July, they expelled the small resident Nationalist Chinese mission in Lhasa on the grounds that its members might defect to the CCP. The communist and the Nationalist governments both protested though neither could do anything about it.

That, too, would soon change. In early November, the Tibetan government wrote to Mao requesting talks. 'Tibet has been an independent country since ancient times, having never been ruled by foreign powers', the letter said. 'We hope you will guarantee that the PLA will not cross into Tibetan territory.'[81] Three weeks later, the Tibetans asked the British government for assistance should Mao fail to comply.[82] Neither stratagem succeeded: in October 1950, the PLA entered Tibet, crushing resistance to Chinese rule – at least for the time being. Britain was unable to do anything, even if it had wanted to. In 1951, the Dalai Lama, Tibet's spiritual leader, signed an agreement with Mao that essentially preserved the social and economic status quo in his homeland in exchange for accepting Chinese sovereignty. It was the kind of local peace deal that, albeit in different circumstances, some Guangxi leaders had hoped to reach with the communists in 1949 – until Bai Chongxi overruled them.

Undignified exit: Chiang's last days in the mainland

In December 1949, the remaining bastions of Nationalist rule in southwest China fell amid scenes similar to those that had accompanied the government's retreat from most other major cities during the course of the year. From mid-November Chiang spent much of his time in Chongqing, the new temporary capital, where he tried to stiffen the resolve of the regional militarists and hang on in the mainland as long as possible. High-level meetings took place. Stern pledges to fight to the finish were made. Ever more optimistic defence plans were announced. But there was a pronounced air of unreality to the proceedings: commanders and their armies lacked the will as well as the capacity to resist.

Yunnan Governor Lu Han, whose fiefdom appeared to offer a basis for longer-term resistance based on its geographical position and tradition of semi-independence, played a pivotal role in this mini-drama. In some ways, he was lucky to have kept his job thus far: in the summer, Li Zongren and Bai Chongxi, aware that he was in secret discussions with the communists, had proposed removing Lu and replacing him with their own man. 'Bai realised that an order alone would not achieve this and military action was required', recalled Guangxi Governor Huang Xuchu. 'Detailed plans for a military strike were drawn up.'[83]

Chiang intervened, preferring to handle matters in his own way. He held a 'pep talk' with Lu, who at first complied with Chiang's request to curb left-wing activities in Kunming, the provincial capital. At the same time, Lu may have been behind an offer to the United States that Yunnan 'break with Central Government, accept American protectorate and American troops, and to follow orders of American military, political and economic advisers' in the struggle against communism.[84] The advance of the PLA towards Yunnan made this plan impractical even had Washington agreed with it. On 11 December, Lu sued for peace with the communists. The takeover took time to complete and Nationalist forces under General Li Mi retreated into Burma, from where they continued to launch cross border raids into Yunnan during the early 1950s, often with CIA support. This was a nuisance as far as the government in Yunnan was concerned but not much more.

Few expected Chongqing to hold out for long. On 21 November, the government announced that it would move northwest to Chengdu, which Chiang imagined might be easier to defend. Pandemonium ensued. The roads were chock-a-block with trucks carrying people and equipment, cars and pedestrians trying to get away. Government buildings were empty save for a few people left behind to burn documents and files.[85]

By 25–26 November, the PLA had almost managed to surround Chongqing. On 29 November, gunfire could be heard from the house in which Chiang was staying. Ching-kuo urged his father to leave for the airport immediately. But it was difficult to get there because the road was blocked by vehicles heading in the same direction. Ching-kuo noted in his diary: 'Three times we had to stop because of chaotic traffic and on one occasion we had to get out of our vehicle walk for a bit before we managed to complete our journey in a jeep.' When they reached the airfield, Chiang and his party 'spent the night in an aeroplane'.[86] They took off (in a different plane) for Chengdu in the early morning of 30 November.

Pilot Liu Hongfei recalled:

I was piloting one of the last two B-25s to take off from Baishiyi airport in Sichuan with old President Chiang to Chengdu. There were still many dependants waiting to take off, and . . . one of the president's guards was forced to lie and tell them there were still five more planes coming to pick them up. We were forced to bomb the runway after we took off, so the CCP would not be able to use it. The soldiers left behind realized the situation and started to fire at us . . .[87]

The PLA's Second Field Army entered Chongqing on the afternoon of the same day.

Chiang spent ten days in Chengdu, from which the sound of gunfire could soon be heard. There was now only one choice as far as his next move was concerned: Taipei, capital of Taiwan. The decision to relocate the capital a fourth time in nine months was made public on 8 December. But keen to maintain at least symbolic ties with the mainland, he announced the creation of a supreme military headquarters in Xichang, southwest of Chengdu, in what was then the province of Xikang. Future military resistance to the communists would be coordinated from there, though the defection on 11 December of Xikang Governor Liu Wenhui meant it did not last long.

Seventeen aircraft ferried officials from a nervous Chengdu to the relative safety of Taipei. More might have been available had it not been for the defection of thirteen planes belonging to the national airline to Beijing a few days earlier. On the morning of 10 December, while Mao Zedong was undertaking his leisurely train journey across central Asia to meet Stalin in Moscow, Chiang and his party hurriedly left for Chengdu airport, where they boarded a DC3 for the long flight over communist-controlled territory to Taipei. 'Chiang's face bore a sorrowful expression as he boarded the plane', said a fellow passenger of the Nationalist leader's last few moments on the mainland. 'He did not utter a single word.'[88]

Taiwan: living on borrowed time

The Nationalist government's flight from the mainland to Taipei not only bore the hallmarks of a final act for Chiang, it pointed to the end of any vision of a non-communist China. The island looked anything but secure, even though it was situated some 100 miles offshore. In August, the PLA's Third Field Army had driven the Nationalists out of Fuzhou, capital of Fujian province, opposite Taiwan. In October they did the same in Xiamen (Amoy), potentially controlling both southern and northern ends of the Taiwan Straits. Formosa's closest links with continental China were cut; the two closest harbours from which an invasion could be launched were in communist hands.

In fact, there had been something of a reprieve on the military front. When on 24 October the PLA mounted an assault on the island of Jinmen

(Quemoy), barely a mile or two away from Xiamen, it was rebuffed by a heavily reinforced Nationalist garrison. Fierce fighting took place over the next three days. Artillery and, on the government side, tanks and fighter bombers were deployed. Nearly 10,000 communist troops were killed or captured in what an official history of the PLA described as 'a major setback in our war of Liberation'. It attributed the disaster to 'a slackening of the guard and blind optimism on the part of senior commanders', and referred to 'insufficient understanding of how to wage amphibious warfare'.[89] Chiang Ching-kuo visited the island for a few hours the day after fighting broke out. He described in his diary travelling in a jeep to General Tang Enbo's HQ and seeing corpses, wounded and captured soldiers along the route. 'I was enormously moved by the heroic fight the defenders had put up . . . It was our first victory of the year and a starting point for our recovery of the mainland.'[90]

Yet victory in the battle of Guningtou (named after the village in Jinmen where the bloodiest fighting took place) was small compensation for the disastrous defeats of the past two years that had driven the government into exile in Taiwan. At most it provided a little breathing space and boosted the flagging morale of a largely disorganized Nationalist elite struggling to consolidate its hold over the island. This daunting task fell, in the first instance, to Wu Guozhen (KC Wu), former mayor of Shanghai, who on 16 December succeeded Cheng as Taiwan governor. As an earnest of his dedication, he is said to have 'kept cyanide capsules with him'.[91] A British official observed: 'New civilian government has been designed to win American approval and resumption of aid by institution of drastic reforms.'[92]

Taiwan had been under martial law since May, partly in an attempt to curb suspected communist infiltration and control the behaviour of the huge numbers of soldiers, refugees and others who had arrived in search of safety. The British consul in Taipei provided a glimpse of what the authorities were up against:

> Conditions in Jilong [the island's main harbour, close to Taipei] are chaotic, the harbour is crammed with military shipping and no merchant shipping . . . can get in. Although the troops were originally destined for South China and ordered not to land, the officers have taken matters into their own hands claiming that the troops are starving, and have threatened to shoot the harbour authorities if hindered in landing.[93]

Anger among local Taiwanese over the bad behaviour of mainland soldiers, and the new arrivals generally, was another potential source of unrest.

Taiwan was also preparing for a communist attack. General Sun Liren, whom Chiang had earlier charged with raising a new army, had been appointed commander of the island's defence headquarters. A curfew was in effect in coastal areas. The government said conscription would be introduced in 1950. Now that the mainland had been lost, Taiwan had to shoulder responsibility for funding and directing the fight against the communists, placing a potentially huge burden on its economy and citizens.

In fact, Taiwan's economy proved a more promising part of an otherwise unhappy picture during the second half of 1949. The introduction of a new currency in June helped insulate it from inflation; locals and exiles alike handled money they could believe in. Taiwan was also quick to change trade partners following its isolation from the mainland. The British consul noted approvingly in November: 'Trade with Japan and Hong Kong has developed rapidly of late. More chemical fertiliser has been purchased and the target for the rice harvest of 1.2 million tons may well be achieved.'

More remarkable still was the government's progress with land reform – a key factor that helped the communists win control of the Chinese countryside and thus triumph in the Civil War but which the Nationalists failed to tackle seriously before it was too late.[94] Prior to the reforms, an estimated 70 per cent of Taiwan's 3.8 million farmers were tenants who paid rent ranging from 46 to 62.5 per cent of their total yield. The government imposed a limit of 37.5 per cent. It also compensated landlords rather than confiscating their property and killing them in the manner of the mainland. Farmers soon benefited. 'The income of the tenant farmers was estimated to have registered an average gain of 30 per cent, ranging from 0.9 per cent to as high as 70 per cent in comparison with the pre-reform period', claimed one observer shortly after the measures were introduced.[95] In these reforms as in others, the government benefited from the fact that Taiwanese people were relatively well-educated compared with their mainland counterparts. The literacy rate in the island was said to be 'more than 70 per cent', a legacy of Japanese rule.[96]

Yet for many observers at the close of 1949 a more pressing matter overshadowed these positive developments. It was whether the Nationalist government could survive for very long in its new home. There were slender grounds to think so. Guningtou might have demonstrated the PLA's lack of preparedness when it came to amphibious warfare but there could be no doubt about the CCP leadership's resolve to remove Chiang and reunite the island with the mainland. The Third Field Army, under General Chen Yi, was soon at work planning how to bring this about.

The threat of financial collapse also stalked the authorities, despite the positive trends in the economy. The provincial budget was said to be in balance at the close of 1949. But this overlooked the fact that the central government met only one quarter of the expenses of the large number of armed forces on the island, leaving the local government responsible for a sum equivalent to its entire annual budget. Gold and foreign exchange reserves could help balance the books for a while but not for long. 'The summer of 1950 would therefore appear to be the most dangerous period for Formosa if no positive measures such as economic and military aid are taken to help keep the island outside the Communist orbit', warned the British consul.[97]

Inept leadership and poor administration also persuaded many observers that Taiwan must fall to the communists before long. A CIA assessment said: 'Not only do the armed forces suffer from inept leadership, but all the worst aspects of the Nationalist Government are apparent in its maladministration of the island. These factors invite and facilitate Communist infiltration, which is already in progress.'[98] London was of similar mind. M. E. Dening, assistant secretary of state at the Foreign Office, wrote: 'I would not like to estimate how long Chiang Kai-shek can retain possession of Formosa, but I think we must accept the possibility that sooner or later it will turn communist. If anyone has any intelligent suggestions as to how this can be averted, we should be very glad to receive them.'[99]

In the case of the United States such analysis soon became policy, much to Chiang's concern. National Security Council document 48/2, which President Truman approved on 30 December 1949, stipulated that Washington would continue to maintain diplomatic relations with the Nationalist government 'until the situation is clarified'. There was no question of recognizing Mao's regime. It also pledged to deny Taiwan to the Chinese communists through diplomatic and economic means, including a ban on the export of strategic materials to what had by now become known as the 'communist bloc'. But it added: 'the strategic importance of Formosa does not justify overt military action ... so long as the present disparity between our military strength and our global obligations exist.'[100]

The message was unmistakable: unless conditions changed, there were clear limits to what the United States was willing to do to prevent the PLA completing its conquest of China. Chiang and his government were largely on their own. At the precise moment that Soviet leader Joseph Stalin was embracing Mao Zedong as a new partner in the socialist world and pledging to defend the PRC, President Truman formally loosened the ties that once bound his country to Nationalist China. It was a striking testimony to the upheavals that had taken place during the course of 1949 – the year China changed and much of the world along with it.

Notes

1   FRUS, *The Far East: China*, Vol. IX, 16 September 1949. https://history.state.gov/historicaldocuments/frus1949v09/pg_549 (accessed 6 January 2020).

2   Ibid.

3   Ibid. 6 September 2020. https://history.state.gov/historicaldocuments/frus1949v09/pg_547.

4   Chang Chihyun (ed.), *The Chinese Journals of L. K. Little, 1943–54: An Eyewitness Account of War and Revolution. Vol 1* (London: Routledge online resource, 2017), Electronic Resource: 810.7.

5   Lin Tongfa, *Da chetui* ('The Great Withdrawal') (Taipei: Lianjing chuban shiye youxian gongsi, 2009), p. 72 et seq.

6   See Chapter 7, p. 200.

7   Thomas W. Robinson, *A Politico-Military Biography of Lin Piao, Part 1, 1907–1949* (Santa Monica, CA: Rand, 1971), p. 192.

8   Liang Shengjun, *Jiang-Li douzheng neimu* ('The Inside Story of the Struggle between Jiang and Li') (Taipei: Xinxin wencongshu, 1992), pp. 189–91 for an example of the Guangxi 'critique' of Chiang at this stage.

9   The description is that of a US diplomat following a meeting with one of Li Zongren's advisers. See FRUS, *The Far East: China*, Vol. VIII, 24 October 1949. https://history.state.gov/historicaldocuments/frus1949v08/d640 (accessed 9 January 2020).

10 *The New York Times*, 9 October 1949, pp. 1, 6.

11 Lin Tongfa, *Da chetui*, p. 179.

12 FRUS, *The Far East: China*, 12 August 1949. https://history.state.gov/historicaldocuments/frus1949v08/pg_484 (accessed 8 January 2020).

13 *The Times*, 25 August 1949, p. 23.

14 TNA FO 371/75804/F12354, 28 August 1949, p. 41.

15 TNA FO 371/75804/F15933, 19 October 1949, p. 38.

16 *The New York Times*, 11 October 1949, p. 10.

17 *SWB*, No. 26, 18 October 1949, p. 23.

18 Diseyezhanjun zhanshi bianxiezu (ed.), *Zhongguo renmin jiefangjun disiyezhanjun zhanshi* ('A History of the Battles Fought by the PLA's Fourth Field Army') (Beijing: jiefangjun chubanshe, 1998), p. 546.

19 Chang Chihyun (ed.), *The Chinese Journals of L. K. Little, 1943–54*, Electronic Resource: 789.6.

20 *The New York Times*, 15 October 1949, p. 1.

21 Chang Chihyun (ed.), *The Chinese Journals of L. K. Little, 1943–54*, Electronic Resource: 794.9.

22 *The New York Times*, 14 October 1949, p. 1.

23 Diseyezhanjun zhanshi bianxiezu (ed.), *Zhongguo renmin jiefangjun disiyezhanjun zhanshi*, p. 550.

24 *Time*, 24 October 1949, p. 22.

25 See Chapter 7, p. 201.

26 *The Times*, 19 October 1949, p. 3.

27 Colonial Reports, *Hong Kong 1949* (London: His Majesty's Stationery Office), p. 1.

28 *Daily Telegraph*, 17 October 1949, p. 1.

29 Percy Chen, *China Called Me: My Life Inside the Chinese Revolution* (Boston: Little, Brown and Company, 1979), p. 389.

30 Colonial Reports, *Hong Kong 1949*, p. 2.

31 *The New York Times,* 14 October 1949, p. 1.

32　Colonial Reports, *Hong Kong 1949*, p. 11.

33　Mahlon Meyer, *Remembering China from Taiwan: Divided Families and Bittersweet Reunions after the Chinese Civil War* (Hong Kong: Hong Kong University Press, 2012), p. 41.

34　TNA FO371/75944/F17601, 24 November 1949, p. 56.

35　Colonial Reports, *Hong Kong 1949*, p. 7.

36　*SWB*, No. 31, 22 November 1949, p. 36.

37　Alexander Grantham, *Via Ports: From Hong Kong to Hong Kong* (Hong Kong: Hong Kong University Press, 2012 edition), p. 163.

38　See Chapter 7, p. 201.

39　Grantham, *Via Ports*, p. 115.

40　Chang Chihyun (ed.), *The Chinese Journals of L. K. Little, 1943–54*, Electronic Resource: 789.6.

41　Colonial Reports, *Hong Kong 1949*, pp. 18–21.

42　Grantham, *Via Ports*, p. 148.

43　Robinson, *A Politico-Military Biography of Lin Piao*, pp. 194–5.

44　Ibid., p. 199

45　Kevin Peraino, *A Force So Swift: Mao, Truman, and the Birth of Modern China, 1949* (New York: Crown, 2017), pp. 219–20.

46　Zhongyang yanjiuyuan jindaishi yanjiusuo (ed.), *Xu Qiming xiansheng fangwenlu* ('A Record of Interviews with Mr Xu Qiming') (Taipei: Zhongyang yanjiuyuan jindaishi yanjiusuo, 1983), p. 148.

47　FRUS, *The Far East: China*, Vol. VIII, 23 October 1949. https://history.state. gov/historicaldocuments/frus1949v08/d638 (accessed 13 January 2020).

48　Zhongyang yanjiuyuan jindaishi yanjiusuo, *Xu Qiming*, p. 148.

49　Ibid., p. 147.

50　Odd Arne Westad, *Decisive Encounters: The Chinese Civil War, 1946–1950* (Stanford, CA: Stanford University Press, 2003), p. 317.

51　Liang Shengjun, *Chise gongbuxiade Guangxi* ('Guangxi under the Red Terror') (Hong Kong: Ziyou chubanshe, 1951), pp. 3–4.

52　Ibid., p. 4.

53　Wang Ruilin (ed.), *Xinguixi jishi* ('A True Record of the New Guangxi Clique') (Nanning: Guangxi zhuangzu zizhiqu xinwen chubanju, 1990), Vol. 3, pp. 278–9.

54　*SWB*, No. 25, 11 October 1949, p. 34.

55　T'ong Te-kang (with Li Tsung-jen), *The Reminiscences of Li Tsung-jen* (Boulder, CO: Westview Press, 1979), p. 544.

56　Tang Degang (with Li Zongren), *Li Zongren Huiyilu* ('The Reminiscences of Li Zongren') (Hong Kong: Nanyue chubanshe, 1987), p. 665.

57　Liang Shengjun, *Chise gongbuxiade Guangxi*, p. 212.

58　*The New York Times*, 14 November 1949, p. 8.

59　T'ong Te-kang, *The Reminiscences of Li Tsung-jen*, p. 545.

60 Bai Xianyong, *Fuqin yu minguo* ('Father and the Republic') (Hong Kong: Tiandi tushu youxian gongsi, 2012), Vol. 1, p. 322.

61 FRUS, *The Far East: China*, 25 November 1949. https://history.state.gov/historicaldocuments/frus1949v08/d693 (accessed 14 January 2020).

62 Cheng Siyuan, *Bai Chongxi zhuan* ('A Biography of Bai Chongxi') (Hong Kong: Nanyuechubanshe, 1989), p. 320.

63 Liang Shengjun, *Chise gongbuxiade Guangxi*, p. 5.

64 *SWB*, No. 33, 6 December 1949, p. 34.

65 Zhang Renmin, 'Qianguibian dadao Yang Biao kanggong xunguo ji' ('A Record of the Anti-Communist Martyr Yang Biao of the Guizhou–Guangxi Border Area'), *Qun Qiu* (HK), No. 118 (1962), pp. 28–9.

66 Liang Shengjun, *Chise gongbuxiade Guangxi*, pp. 219–20.

67 Jin Lixin, *Zhongnan jiefang zhanzheng jishi* ('A True Record of the Liberation War in Southern China') (Beijing: Renmin chubanshe, 2004), p. 438.

68 Chang Chihyun (ed.), *The Chinese Journals of L. K. Little, 1943–54*, Electronic Resource: 837.1.

69 Zhongyang yanjiuyuan jindaishi yanjiusuo, *Xu Qiming*, p. 150

70 Cheng Siyuan, *Bai Chongxi zhuan*, p. 319.

71 Zhongyang yanjiuyuan jindaishi yanjiusuo, *Xu Qiming* p. 157.

72 Chang Chihyun (ed.), *The Chinese Journals of L. K. Little, 1943–54*, Electronic Resource: 29.5/931). There was no further report – at least to the Republican-era customs service. Ye remained in service under communist rule but was subject to intensive re-indoctrination, because, as he put it, 'of his rank and because he occupied a 30-acre house with servants provided by the Service'. He went to Taiwan in 1956 (ibid. 36.0/931).

73 Guangxi tongzhiguan (ed.), *Guangxi Jiefang shiji* ('A True Record of the Liberation of Guangxi') (Nanning: Guangxi renmin chubanshe, 1990), p. 10.

74 Liang Shengjun, *Jiang-Li douzheng neimu*, pp. 218–19.

75 See Introduction, p. 22.

76 *SWB*, No. 37, 3 January 1950, p. 32.

77 See Chapter 3, p. 101.

78 FRUS, *The Far East: China*, Vol. VIII, 15 August 1949. https://history.state.gov/historicaldocuments/frus1949v08/d561 (accessed 16 January 2020).

79 *The Times*, 22 September 1948, p. 5.

80 Wilson Center Digital Archive, 29 December 1949. https://digitalarchive.wilsoncenter.org/document/176327 (accessed 17 January 2020).

81 Dangdai zhongguo yanjiusuo bian (ed.), *Zhonghua Renmin Gongheguo shibiannian: 1949 nianjuan* ('Chronicle of the People's Republic of China 1949') (Beijing: Dangdai zhongguo chubanshe, 2004), p. 665.

82 Ibid.

83 Huang Xuchu, 'Guofu you yue qian yude kunchunzhiju' ('The Situation in Kunming at the Time of the Move of the Capital from Guangzhou to Chongqing'), *Qun Qiu*, No. 145, pp. 9–10.

84 FRUS, *The Far East: China*, 15 November 1949. https://history.state.gov/historicaldocuments/frus1949v08/d675 (accessed 20 January 2020); Lin Hsiao-ting, 'The Civil War and Modern China's Ethnic and Frontier Politics, 1947–53', *Asian Profile*, Vol. 37, No. 2 (April 2009), p. 109 et seq.

85 Lin Tongfa, *1949 Da chetui*, p. 290.

86 Zhang Liangren (ed.), Chiang Ching-kuo, diary entry for 29 November 1949, p. 490.

87 Joshua Fan, *China's Homeless Generation: Voices from the Veterans of the Chinese Civil War, 1940s–1990s* (London: Routledge, 2009), pp. 36–7.

88 Zhou Hongtao, *Jianggong yu Wo* ('The Revered Jiang and I') (Taipei: Tianxia wenhua chubanshe, 2003), p. 161.

89 Junshi kexueyuan junshilishi yanjiubu (ed.), *Zhongguo renmin jiefangjun zhanshi: disanjuan, quanguo jiefang zhanzheng shiqi* ('History of the Wars fought by the Chinese People's Liberation Army. Vol. 3: The War of National Liberation') (Beijing: junshi kexue chubanshe, 1987), pp. 340–1.

90 Zhang Liangren (ed.), Chiang Ching-kuo diary entry for 26 October 1949. p. 412.

91 Steve Tsang, 'Transforming a Party State into a Democracy', in Steve Tsang and Hung-mao Tien (eds), *Democratization in Taiwan: Implications for China* (Basingstoke: Macmillan, 1999), p. 2.

92 TNA. FO371/75805/F18919, 18 December 1949, p. 81.

93 TNA FO371/75805/F8556, 11 June 1949, p. 24.

94 See Chapter 1, p. 42 and Chapter 7, p. 191.

95 Wang Gung-hsing, 'Nationalist Government Policies, 1949–1951', *The Annals of the American Academy of Political and Social Science*, Vol. 277, Report on China (September 1951), pp. 218–19.

96 Ibid., p. 220.

97 TNA FO371/75805/F19647, 14 December 1949, p. 117.

98 National Intelligence Council (NIC), 'Survival of Non-Communist regimes, October 1949 Taiwan', p. 09/8.

99 DBPO, p. 397.

100 FRUS, *The Far East: China*, Vol. VII, Part 2, 30 December 1949. https://history.state.gov/historicaldocuments/frus1949v07p2/d387 (accessed 22 January 2020).

10

Afterwards

1949's long shadow

On 31 December 1949, a year to the day that Chiang Kai-shek informed his colleagues during that New Year's Eve soiree in Nanjing that he would step down so they could open peace talks with the communists, the CCP Central Committee issued a communiqué to all ranks within the PLA and the entire Chinese nation:

> In 1949, thanks to the selfless efforts of the People's Liberation Army and the support of the Chinese people all over the country, all of the mainland has been liberated save for Tibet, and some 2.6 million enemy troops have been put out of action. Due to this magnificent victory, imperialism and the rule of the reactionary GMD have been overthrown once and for all, and the People's Republic of China has been founded. The glorious tasks that lie ahead for the PLA and the Chinese people in 1950 are to liberate Taiwan, Hainan and Tibet, wipe out the remnants of the Chiang Kai-shek clique, complete the unification of China and prevent imperialist forces from establishing any sort of foothold in China. With the completion of this victory, the Chinese people can and must devote their energies to peaceful construction.[1]

The triumphalist tone was perhaps excusable in the victors but would have grated with the losers of China's Civil War. They included thousands of Nationalist troops now marooned in the mainland, bottled up in Hainan or fleeing across the border into French Indo-China; Chiang's rump Nationalist government, forced to seek sanctuary in an uneasy Taiwan; and the millions of people whose lives were disrupted or ruined by the conflict, many of them now refugees in unfamiliar places with little more to their name than the clothes they stood up in.

The communists' military victory was sudden, traumatic and seemingly irreversible. The entire Chinese mainland had been 'liberated' or 'lost', depending on which side one stood in the conflict. China had 'switched camps', exchanging its ambiguous identity as a partner of the West for the supposedly comradely embrace of the Soviet Union: at the close of the year, news of the outcome of Mao's visit to Moscow was anxiously awaited in Washington and London as well as in Beijing and Taipei.

But if there was much that was decisive about the events of 1949, there was also a major item of unfinished business: China's unification. Would there soon be one country that called itself by that name or two – i.e. the Republic of China and the People's Republic of China? What *kind* of China, or indeed 'Chinas' would the Chinese people and the rest of the world have to live with as a result of 1949? And what would the answers to these questions mean for diplomacy and statecraft, defence and security, peace and prosperity in the region and beyond?

The world would not have to wait long to find out. Neither would it find it easy to put the matter to rest. More than seventy years later, the Chinese people, their governments in Beijing and Taipei, the United States and Japan – to mention just a few of the interested parties – are still confronted with the consequences of China's unfinished Civil War. The prospects for peace in the Asia Pacific region, home of the largest share of the world's population and the main source of global economic growth, to a large extent depend on the way in which this critical issue in the story of China's national rejuvenation is resolved.

At the start of 1950, when the PLA had all but completed its conquest of the mainland, the Western powers broadly agreed that China's future was a matter for the Chinese people and that they should be left to get on with it. The US was reluctantly drawn to this conclusion, despite the vigorous efforts of the China Lobby of pro-Chiang supporters in Washington, and the fact that it was likely to mean all of China became communist. This was an uncomfortable moment in the career of Chiang Kai-shek, ensconced in his 'Nationalist Party Director's Office' in Yangmingshan, the mountain retreat north of Taipei. He had just lost the mainland. Now his international friends and partners were lining up to desert him.

In a White House statement on 5 January, President Truman said the US would 'not provide military aid or advice to Chinese forces in Formosa' or do anything that might 'lead to involvement in the civil conflict in China'.[2] The following day Britain recognized the PRC in the hope that it would protect British investments in Shanghai and make it easier to hang on to Hong Kong.[3] On 12 January, US Secretary of State Dean Acheson attributed the Nationalists' defeat to 'the grossest incompetence ever experienced by any military command', and stipulated that both Taiwan and South Korea lay outside what the US considered to be its line of defence in the Pacific.[4]

As 'victor', Mao Zedong enjoyed a more encouraging start to the year, the first month of which he spent in one of Joseph Stalin's dachas in the outskirts of Moscow. But, left to his own devices and largely ignored by the Soviet leaders, he too grew frustrated with the behaviour of his international partner.

Mao's allegiance to Stalin and the Soviet Union was not in doubt. A US diplomat in Moscow said the purpose of his visit was 'personally to report to the throne the acquisition of vast new territories and hundreds of millions of people for Stalin's empire'. It was a 'stupendous birthday gift for Stalin'.[5]

Yet Stalin was still suspicious of Mao on doctrinal grounds and may also have been concerned about the strategic implications of his victory. China was many hundreds of miles from the centre of power in the Soviet Union. Mao's revolution was made at home rather than in Moscow. Stalin would probably have to treat the PRC as an ally rather than another 'satellite' of the kind his country had helped set up in Eastern Europe. Perhaps with this in mind, Soviet negotiators drove a hard bargain in the negotiations that concluded with the signing on 14 February 1950 of the Sino-Soviet Treaty of Friendship, Alliance and Mutual Assistance.

At least Mao left Moscow with what he came for: a defence pact with the Soviet Union, financial aid (if a modest US$300 million dollars) and much-needed technical advice. He could now concentrate on planning the assault on Hainan and Taiwan (where success would mean the destruction of Chiang's government), and implementing the revolution. If there was in Taipei a feeling that things were coming to an end, there was a sense in Beijing that they were just beginning.

But it was only a beginning. At the start of 1950, the CCP had yet to establish firm political control over large parts of the country, especially south of the Yangtze and the Northwest. The communists controlled the towns and cities in the newly liberated areas but not the countryside, an ironic reversal of the revolutionary process prior to 1949. And in the cities, it was often the 'national bourgeoisie' – businessmen, liberal intellectuals, professionals, students, the urban young in general – who were the most enthusiastic supporters of the new regime. Workers tended to be less keen due to the Party's insistence that, even in 'New China', profits and production had to take priority, while the peasants, finding the heavier taxes they had to pay offset reductions in rent and interest rates, were sometimes driven to taking up arms against the new order.

Chastened but undeterred by these problems, Mao and the Party pressed on with their domestic agenda. Land reform, rapid industrialization, social reforms designed to end gender discrimination and a general re-moulding of the minds of the Chinese people were among the priorities. So was furthering the 'revolutionary' foreign policy on which Beijing had embarked in order to cement its position as an important member of the socialist bloc. China's leaders hoped that their experience of revolution, encapsulated in Mao's teachings, would resonate in what would soon become known as the 'Third

World'. Within weeks of the founding of their new state, they began providing military aid and advice to Ho Chi Minh in his attempt to evict the French from Indochina.

In March 1950, Lin Biao launched the long-awaited assault on Hainan Island. Chiang had already taken the difficult decision to withdraw (as he had from the Zhoushan archipelago, south of Shanghai) in order to reduce his defence lines. It was a sensitive issue because it weakened the credibility of his pledge to recover the mainland. It also made it harder to impose an effective blockade of the Chinese coast. But Taiwan's survival had to come first.

Familiar scenes of panic, chaos and tragedy unfolded at the dockside as troops and civilians struggled to escape. Among the evacuees was Mei Jun, the young woman who had left her son in Hunan the previous summer, spent several weeks in Guangzhou and then made her way to Hainan.[6] She had recently given birth to a daughter, Yinda, whom she carried on her back as she embarked on one of the evacuation ships. Many of the larger vessels earmarked for this purpose were too big to dock; smaller ones had to ply between them and the harbour. 'People pulled themselves up ladders to get over the ship's rails and into the boats like so many spiders', she recalled. 'Many could not make it and fell into the water . . . Cries of help went up . . . but no one paid any attention. Cotton shoes bobbed up and down in the harbour . . . Wounded soldiers who had protected the retreat lay on the dockside crying in pain . . . Those on board the ships could only look back helplessly, abandoning them to their fate.'[7]

Mei Jun's ship took her to Gaoxiong, the major port in southern Taiwan. It was the last leg in a perilous journey that had begun in January 1949, some fifteen months earlier. During the course of it she had left her son behind but, with new-born daughter, was about to start life as a permanent exile.

Chiang Kai-shek had long believed that his own and therefore China's fate would be decided by a wider war between the world's communist and democratic countries. He hoped this would happen before he lost the mainland. By the spring of 1950, it looked as though it would not do so before he was driven off Taiwan: CIA reports indicated that the Third Field Army had assembled a force of close to half a million men and an armada of junks for an assault on the island.

Chiang's luck then suddenly changed. North Korean leader Kim Il-sung secured Stalin's permission to order his troops across the border, destroy the South Korean state led by Syngman Rhee and unify the Korean peninsula. Stalin told Mao that if he disagreed, Kim would have to delay the attack. Mao did not and on 15 June North Korean troops crossed the 38th parallel.

Twelve days later President Truman announced that, given events in Korea, the US would regard the occupation of Taiwan by communist forces as 'a threat to the security of the Pacific area and to United States forces performing their lawful and necessary functions in that area'.[8] Accordingly, he ordered the US 7th Fleet to prevent any attack on the island. There was a condition: Chiang was to cease all military operations against the mainland. Though unwelcome, this was a price worth paying for a US security guarantee that Chiang and other Nationalist leaders believed had been far too long in coming. Suddenly, the survival of their regime was no longer the most immediate issue. Reform and reorganization could begin – in the interests of Taiwan and China as a whole.

The Korean conflict was also a turning point for Mao's China. By October 1950, US-led forces operating under the auspices of the UN had beaten Kim's

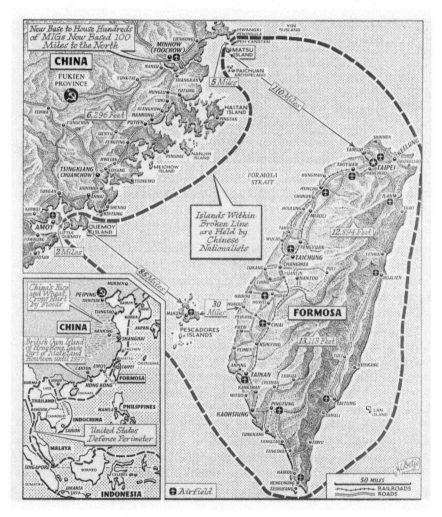

FIGURE 10.1 *Fortress Formosa: From December 8, Chiang shifted the seat of his Nationalist government to Taipei, capital of Taiwan. (The small map depicts the US defence perimeter as defined in mid-1950.)*

FIGURE 10.2 *'Two Chinas'. A Nationalist soldier in early 1950 gazes at 'Red China' (or the PRC) from the fortified island of Jinmen – then, as still the case today, part of the Republic of China or Taiwan.*

armies back north of the 38th parallel. They seemed to be closing in on the Chinese border. Stalin advised Mao that Kim's regime was on the brink of collapse. He responded by committing thousands of PLA troops, 'badged' for the purpose as 'Chinese People's Volunteers', to the conflict. After weeks of bitter combat, they fought the mainly US forces to a standstill around the 38th parallel, a source of pride to many Chinese at the time and since.

As far as Mao was concerned, the immediate price of involvement in the Korean War was a lost chance to liberate Taiwan. It also resulted in Western sanctions that deprived his country of many of the materials needed for economic reconstruction. But the conflict had larger consequences few could foresee at the time, chief among them the West's determination, in partnership with Asian countries where possible, to 'contain' revolutionary China. Here lies the origin, among other things, of the Southeast Asian Treaty Organization, US military involvement in Vietnam and the series of bilateral US security alliances (with Japan and South Korea, for example) that to this day seek to 'hem China in', much to Beijing's irritation.

From its beginnings, containment created a heightened sense of tension at home that Mao used to accelerate the transformation of his country and implement his revolutionary fantasies, often irrespective of the costs.

The CCP would have conducted land reform in the newly liberated areas, extended public ownership of the economy and suppressed criticism of its rule irrespective of China's participation in the Korean War. Socialism, even though Party leaders downplayed the term in the early years of the PRC, was always the goal. But these and other measures that imposed unprecedented control over people's lives would not have been introduced with such speed or accompanied by such brutality had China not believed itself to be at the mercy of reactionary forces at home and imperialists abroad.

It was against this background that Mao launched repeated campaigns during the 1950s to eliminate 'counterrevolutionaries', suppress critical thinking and generally root out all forms of opposition, real and imagined. The decade also witnessed happier outcomes. China's rapid industrialization, funded for the most part by the agricultural surplus made possible by land reform, was among them. Dramatic improvements in life expectancy and literacy rates and increases in living standards accompanied the appearance of factories, roads, railways and bridges across the country. Most of these developments, both positive and negative, were made possible by the CCP's creation of a strong, centralized state with unprecedented power over the lives of its citizens. Infused with revolutionary purpose and the will to impose it on its citizens, Mao's People's Republic made China a 'nation' in a sense that had not been the case under the Nationalists.

But a breakdown in relations with the Soviet Union, beginning in the late 1950s, paved the way for even more ambitious – and disastrous – schemes to revolutionize China and, hopefully, inspire revolutionaries elsewhere in the world. A chief consequence of the Great Leap Forward (1958–60), an attempt to establish communism overnight, was the death through famine of some 30 million people. That of the Cultural Revolution (1966–76), one of the chairman's last acts, was to wipe out many of the physical traces of China's past and destroy the country's intellectual life. By the late 1970s, it was widely accepted in China that the revolution that began in 1949 had gone badly wrong but that it is was far too dangerous to say so. The economy was close to breakdown, the Chinese people psychologically shattered. The PRC was not so much contained as isolated.

Thanks to the events of 1949 and shortly thereafter, the people of Taiwan and Hong Kong were spared these unhappy experiences. Indeed, the two territories had embarked on very different kinds of journeys.

Shortly after Chiang moved his capital to Taipei, he set about reforming the Nationalist Party whose failings he said were responsible for his defeat. He complained that his regime had 'crumbled like soil collapsing and a tile being shattered'.[9] In many respects Chiang had the advantage of a clean slate despite the legacy of defeat and loss of the mainland. In March he resumed the presidency of the Republic of China; Li Zongren, in the United States, though a vocal critic of Chiang, was by now a spent force. The political and military factions (such as the Guangxi clique) that once bedevilled Nationalist politics were powerless, most of the leading families that used to dominate the party forced into retirement. A system of political officers was inserted in the military. A KGB-style security apparatus was created. Every member of the Nationalist party was required to re-register.

These moves strengthened the once decrepit Nationalist party-state. But unlike the situation facing Mao, there were limits on how far Chiang and his fellow leaders would and could go. Mao was ruthless enough to become a genuine dictator; Chiang was dictatorial in manner and temperament, a rather different matter. Moreover, these aspects of Chiang's personality were tempered by the fact that he was Confucian in outlook and a defender of traditional Chinese values rather than a disciple of Marx and Lenin. He also sought to reconcile his impulse to dominate political life with the constraints set out in the constitution of 1946, even though he continued to use the national emergency created by 'communist rebellion' to justify the suspension of some of its provisions.

There is no question that Chiang's government dealt harshly with its opponents. Martial law was maintained in the interests of internal security as well as fear of external attack. The regime hunted down alleged communists in the diaspora and persecuted local Taiwanese who advocated independence. But the Nationalist leader had to be careful to retain US backing and win support from the Taiwanese people, many of whom were bewildered and unhappy over what was happening to their island under his rule.

One thing that the sometimes contradictory political forces at work in Taiwan during the early 1950s did deliver was political stability and social order. This created a favourable environment for economic growth. Perhaps surprisingly, policy did the same: the Nationalist government was less predatory in Taiwan than it had been on the mainland. It protected industry but also privatized many public concerns. It provided cheap credit and encouraged import substitution, particularly in the chemical, textile and fertilizer industries. It had the advantage of a sound currency (backed by gold and foreign exchange reserves shipped from the mainland) and US economic aid. And in the estimated 1.2 million mainlanders who made their way to the island, it had an influx of talent as well a source of additional labour.

What most of these exiles had in common was that they knew very little about Taiwan but believed it did not matter because they would not be there long. Nationalist leaders continually proclaimed the temporary nature of their presence. Chiang's armies were going to recover the mainland. The exiles would return to their homes and families. It was a question of 'one year to prepare, a second to counterattack, a third to "mop up" and complete success in five years', as the slogan put it.[10] It took some time for many of them to realize that Taiwan was home.

The mainland diaspora created enormous problems for Taiwanese society, many of them still apparent decades later, as explained elsewhere in this book.[11] The sudden 'insertion' of a large group of people from different parts of the mainland changed the composition of a population previously divided between a small number of indigenous Taiwanese and the much more numerous ethnic Chinese who had arrived over the centuries from Fujian. Generally speaking, the new arrivals spoke a variety of Mandarin or Shanghainese and mixed more easily with each other than they did with their hosts. Many of them, perhaps especially politicians, civil servants and professionals, also brought with them a sense of entitlement undiminished by the fact they were now exiles. This hardly went down well with 'genuine' locals.

Yet there was another side to the story. A significant proportion of the upper ranks of mainland Nationalist society fled to Taiwan between 1948 and 1952, the largest influx occurring in 1949. In absolute terms, the number was small but for Taiwan it 'was a source of fresh blood', as Lin Tongfa puts it.[12] This was because scholars arrived in Taiwan as well as soldiers, business leaders as well as landlords, artists, architects and filmmakers as well as unemployed civil servants. So did large amounts of capital, machinery and equipment and 'know-how'. A significant share of the mainland's 'stock' of innovation, entrepreneurial flair and general talent decamped to the frontier of the Chinese world, making an important contribution to Taiwan's economic take-off.

Hong Kong was the other major beneficiary of mainland capital, labour and expertise during and after the communist victory in 1949. Here, too, the influx of what were regarded at the time as refugees was thought to be temporary. Chinese people had always flowed in and out of Hong Kong. They did so in large numbers during times of emergency. Once the fighting was over most of the new arrivals would surely return. That they did not created one of the defining features of 'modern' Hong Kong: a predominantly settled rather than a floating population.

Another, related, feature was the imposition of a hard border between the crown colony and the PRC. Chinese security forces took the lead in restricting freedom of movement from China to Hong Kong; the British authorities, alarmed at the large number of refugees already in the colony, stepped up controls on their side a few months later. By mid-1950, the border between Hong Kong and China had something of the characteristics of a Cold War frontier. Chinese could travel from Hong Kong to China relatively easily but there was no guarantee they would be allowed to return. The British were especially reluctant to let in those who did not speak Cantonese, and were thus deemed to have no strong connections with Hong Kong society.

The colony's rapid industrialization was also a result of events across the border in 1949. A UN embargo on the sale to China of strategic goods imposed as a result of its participation in the Korean War and a US embargo on trade with the PRC of any kind made life difficult. But they were also midwives to Hong Kong's commercial 're-birth'. The territory shifted its focus from China trade to export manufacturing. Looking back after nearly two decades of 10 per cent GDP growth per annum, a Hong Kong government report said that, thanks to the injection of Shanghai experience and capital, the colony had been granted a 'ten to fifteen year start in industrialization over many other Asian countries'.[13]

Another striking legacy of 1949 in Hong Kong was the relationship that took shape between the colonial and the communist authorities concerning the status and government of the territory. Beijing was in doubt about the former: Hong Kong was Chinese territory, snatched from it in war, and destined to return when conditions were ripe. As for governance, the British insisted it was their responsibility alone but that they would exercise it in such a way as not to offend the powerful neighbour across the border, a policy that reflected what Governor Alexander Grantham and his successors would refer to as 'realism'. It boiled down to ruling out the possibility that Hong Kong might become independent; pledging not to 'politicize' the colony by conducting radical constitutional reform; clamping down on Nationalist organizations; and limiting the activities of third countries and other 'interested parties' in the territory.

Spats and tensions between Britain and China over Hong Kong were frequent during the 1950s and 1960s. Occasionally they were serious. But due to restraint on both sides, the colony retained its separate identity under British rule, embraced capitalism wholeheartedly and continued to enjoy the individual liberties guaranteed by the rule of law. Indeed, it was so successful that these attributes were at the heart of the 'One country, two systems' formula attributed to Chinese leader Deng Xiaoping under which Hong Kong would return to Chinese sovereignty on 1 July 1997. The former colony would constitute a Special Administrative Region of China in which Hong Kong people would run their own affairs, and the capitalist way of life, personal freedoms and rule of (common) law remain unchanged.

Rather surprisingly, this arrangement survived intact until the second decade of the twenty-first century. It was brought to an end by the determination of Xi Jinping, the CCP's assertive, authoritarian leader, to increase Beijing's influence in the territory. Such moves sparked public unease and, before long, protracted, violent protests, exacerbated by poor handling and political incompetence on the part of Carrie Lam, Hong Kong's chief executive. In July 2020, twenty-three years to the day that China recovered sovereignty over Hong Kong, Beijing bypassed the local legislature and imposed a 'National Security Law' of its own making on Hong Kong. The measure severely curbed individual freedoms, compromised the territory's judicial independence and authorized central government organs of state security to operate openly in the territory. A major aspect of the 'difference' between Hong Kong and the rest of China, so strikingly apparent since 1949, was brought to an end almost overnight.

*

While mainland China and Taiwan, or the People's Republic and the Republic of China, embarked on different trajectories in 1949 they retained one thing in common: deep-seated mutual hostility based on their long history of bloody conflict and rival claims to constitute the sole legitimate government of China. Chiang and the Nationalists spoke continually about 'recovering the mainland' by force, Mao and his fellow CCP leaders of their determination to 'liberate' Taiwan by the same means. The propaganda, on both sides, was relentless and vituperative.

They soon tested each other's military mettle along with the willingness of their backers, the US and the USSR, to get involved in China's Civil War. In 1954, shortly before Chiang's government was due to sign a mutual defence treaty with Washington, the PLA subjected the Nationalist-held island of Jinmen to heavy artillery bombardment. In response to this first Straits Crisis, the US Congress passed a resolution allowing American troops to defend parts of ROC territory outside of Taiwan island and the Pescadores (Penghu). Washington did not want to get dragged into war with China over these territories but neither did it want Chiang to lose them since they were considered vital for the defence of Taiwan.

In 1958, Mao decided to test the United States' commitment to Chiang with another artillery assault on Jinmen, this time reinforced by naval and air blockade. As Nationalist and communist planes fought for supremacy, ships of the US Seventh Fleet kept the island's garrison supplied by transporting men and equipment to within three miles of Jinmen and then transferring their cargoes to Nationalist vessels for the last leg of the journey. Mao, surprised by the determination of the Nationalists to retain Jinmen and angered by the reluctance of the Soviet Union to back his cause, lifted the blockade and reduced the shelling to alternate days. The status quo in the Taiwan Straits survived the stand-off in Fujian province.

It continued to do so until the early 1970s when US rapprochement with the PRC, exemplified first by the visit to Beijing in 1971 of Henry Kissinger, President Richard Nixon's national security advisor, and then of the president himself a year later, altered the terms of engagement between all the parties. Washington had by this time abandoned its twenty-year campaign to prevent the PRC from taking China's seat in the United Nations; in October 1971 the international body voted in favour of Beijing and expelled Taiwan.

The price of Nixon's reconciliation with the PRC was abrogation of both the defence treaty and formal diplomatic relations with the ROC. He considered it worth paying to secure Beijing's (cautious) support in the wider struggle against the Soviet Union and begin the withdrawal of US troops from Vietnam. The Taiwan Relations Act, passed by Congress in March 1979, obliged the US to regard Chinese attempts to unify the island by military means as a matter of 'grave concern' and pledged to supply its government with weapons so it can 'maintain a sufficient self-defense capability'.[14] This astutely crafted piece of US domestic legislation has formed the foundation of Taiwan's security to this very day. But the decision to recognize the PRC ended the pretence that Taiwan was 'China' and hastened the ROC's retreat from the international stage.

Radical changes in the PRC during the 1980s had a similar effect. Deng Xiaoping's economic reforms cast communist China in a new light. Not only was Mao dead (he died in 1976, one year after his rival Chiang), the same seemed to be true of much of what he stood for. After decades of seclusion and self-sufficiency, China had decided to 'join the rest of the world'. It was an inspiring story made more so by the fact that it pointed to lucrative commercial opportunities for the rest of the world. Chinese business leaders in Hong Kong, Taiwan and elsewhere were quick to seize upon them. Indeed, CCP leaders had these communities in mind when they launched China's Open Door policy: it was in part an attempt to lure back some of the money and talent that left the mainland in 1949.

Deng also offered new terms to Taiwan: the island could retain almost every aspect of its way of life – save for its name, flag and foreign policy – if it would agree to become part of the PRC. The CCP leaders hoped that their counterparts in Taipei, chastened by their relative diplomatic isolation, would be amenable to such an offer. However, Deng warned Taiwan's leaders that Beijing refused to rule out the use of force to bring the island back into the fold.

Chiang Ching-kuo, who had succeeded his father as head of the Nationalist party, rejected the offer. In 1986 he embarked on reforms of his own, lifting martial law, legalizing opposition parties and removing restrictions on the media. The Nationalists had always claimed to represent 'Free China'; they could soon claim to preside over the creation of the first genuinely democratic Chinese society. In 1991, the 'temporary provisions' to the constitution that Chiang had imposed in 1948 to grant him greater power in the struggle against communist rebellion, were finally abolished. Yet there was an irony at work here: genuine democracy in Taiwan made (voluntary) unification with China contingent upon the acceptance of the Taiwanese electorate rather than the preference of its leaders.

During the 1990s, trade and tourism across the Taiwan Straits blossomed. Among those making the journey were thousands of old Nationalist soldiers anxious to see their former homes again after a long absence and before it was too late. Yet this was often a dispiriting exercise, as the present author noted some time ago:

> Many of the travellers discovered that the mainland was not home at all. The first returnees were often horrified by the poverty they saw in some parts of the country and saddened by the grasping attitude of many of their compatriots, relatives included. There had been dark days in Taiwan, but the Nationalists had neither broken the spirit of those they ruled, nor destroyed China's traditional culture, customs and manners as the communists evidently had.[15]

Disillusion among the dwindling members of the 1949 generation who visited the mainland was soon overshadowed by the commercial opportunities that China's rapidly expanding economy presented. In 1949, China was a very poor, predominantly rural country. Sixty years later, it was a reasonably prosperous, primarily urban one. Three decades of reform and engagement with the wider world had transformed China economically. It was by then the fastest growing major economy in the world and the second largest in dollar terms. Millions of people were lifted out of poverty.

These achievements owed a great deal to Deng's reforms and those that followed. But Mao's contribution to the creation of contemporary China, though marred by bloodshed and tragedy on an epic scale, cannot for that reason easily be dismissed. It is a fine point. How to appraise the period from 1949 to 1979 in the making of today's China is a matter of judgement that scholars and others, Chinese as well as non-Chinese, will wrestle with for decades. Even then, they may fail to reach any firm conclusions.

In any event, Taiwanese firms invested billions of dollars in China during the first decade of this century. Hundreds of thousands of Taiwanese entrepreneurs settled in the Yangtze valley and elsewhere: the flow of talent and capital from continental to maritime China that began in the late 1940s was at last being reversed. As a result, Taiwan's economy became tied to the mainland more closely than it had ever been. CCP leaders believed that economic dependency combined with their common cultural heritage was bound to make Taiwanese people more amenable to the idea of reunification.

This was not the case. In fact, fear that it might – as well as concern over China's increasing threats to use military force against Taiwan – persuaded voters in the Taiwan elections of 2000 to reject the Nationalists and back the opposition Democratic Progressive Party (DPP). Newly elected President Chen Shui-bian was careful to tone down the pro-independence rhetoric of his party so as not to antagonize Beijing or cause anxiety in Washington. But relations with Beijing entered the deep freeze even though cross-Straits ties as a whole continued to grow.

The return to power of the Nationalists under Ma Ying-jeou in 2008 eased some of the tensions between the two former adversaries. And in 2015, towards the end of his second term, Ma and Xi Jinping, Chinese president as well as chairman of the CCP, held talks in Singapore: the two governments declined to recognize each other but their ruling parties did so. Not since August 1945, when Mao and Chiang held talks in Chongqing, had the leaders of the two political parties that shaped modern China met face to face. However, the second meeting proved as unproductive as the first.

In the meantime, China's military spending during the previous twenty years ensured that the PLA enjoyed close to full-spectrum superiority over Taiwan's much smaller forces. There were concerns that the Chinese military might soon be able to prevent the US from coming to the rescue of the island in the event of attack. The threshold to an assault seemed to be getting lower. Beijing heightened anxieties by staging provocative military exercises which it accompanied with stern warnings about the fate of those who hoped to keep China divided.

Yet again this approach failed to deliver. In 2016, and then again in 2020 though by a larger margin, Taiwan's voters returned the DPP to power, this time under Tsai Ying-wen, the island's first woman president. Her victory was in part a result of anxiety among Taiwan's voters over what was happening in Hong Kong, where the 'one country, two systems' formula for reunification (which Beijing had offered to Taiwan as early as 1981) was under obvious strain. But it was also an act of defiance in the face of China's intimidation of Taiwan, which took the form of a ban on individual tourist travel by Chinese citizens designed to punish the island economically, pressure on the few countries that still recognized Taiwan to switch ties to Beijing, and the funnelling of money into the Taiwanese media to influence the election.

Xi Jinping warned that the issue of Taiwan's reunification cannot be passed 'from generation to generation'. The decision to lift term limits on his period in office, along with his tightening of control over society as whole, suggested that he wished to go down in history as the man who reunified China. To achieve this in 2021, the centenary of the founding of the Chinese Communist Party, would be especially gratifying – both for Xi and the Party leadership in Beijing. A large part of Xi's 'China Dream', his great scheme for national rejuvenation, would thus be realized.

But as of this writing, the chances that reunification will be accomplished by peaceful means seem negligible at best. It is more likely that, more than seventy years after 1949, China's Civil War will remain unfinished and that it may even resume.

Notes

1   Dangdai zhongguo yanjiusuo bian (ed.), *Zhonghua Renmin Gongheguo shibiannian: 1949 nianjuan* ('Chronicle of the People's Republic of China 1949') (Beijing: Dangdai zhongguo chubanshe, 2004), p. 833.

2   Harry S. Truman, 'Statement on Formosa', 5 January 1950. https://china.usc.edu/harry-s-truman-'statement-formosa'-january-5-1950 (accessed 31 January 2020).

3   See Chapter 2, p. 72.

4   Dean Acheson, 'Speech on the Far East', 12 January 1950. https://www.cia.gov/library/readingroom/docs/1950-01-12.pdf (accessed 31 January 2020).

5   FRUS, *The Far East: China*, Vol. VIII, 18 December 1949. https://history.state.gov/historicaldocuments/frus1949v08/d731 (accessed 30 January 2020).

6   See Chapter 7, p. 203.

7   Long Yingtai, *Da Jiang Da Hai 1949* ('Vast Rivers, Vast Seas 1949') (Hong Kong: Cosmos Books, 2015 edition), pp. 38–41.

8   Wilson Center Digital Archive, 'Statement by the President, Truman on Korea', 27 June 1950. https://digitalarchive.wilsoncenter.org/document/116192.pdf?v= cd0b66b71d6a0412d275a5088a18db5d (accessed 31 January 2020).

9   Steve Tsang, 'Transforming a Party State into a Democracy', in Steve Tsang and Hung-mao Tien (eds), *Democratization in Taiwan: Implications for China* (Hong Kong: Hong Kong University Press, 1999), p. 1.

10 Lin Hsiao-ting, 'The Civil War and Modern China's Ethnic and Frontier Politics, 1947–53', *Asian Profile*, Vol. 37, No. 2 (April 2009), p. 402.

11 See Chapter 4, p. 109.

12 Lin Hsiao-ting, 'The Civil War', p. 6.

13 Wong Siu-lun, *Emigrant Entrepreneurs: Shanghai Industrialists in Hong Kong* (Hong Kong: Oxford University Press, 1988), p. 8.

14 The Taiwan Relations Act, 1 January 1979, p. 2. https://photos.state.gov/ libraries/ait-taiwan/171414/ait-pages/tra_e.pdf (accessed 10 February 2020).

15 Graham Hutchings, *Modern China: A Companion to a Rising Power* (London: Penguin Books, 2001 edition), p. 410.

PRINCIPAL CHARACTERS AFTER 1949

Bai Chongxi Moved to Taiwan where he held a series of honorary positions and was monitored by agents of an unforgiving Chiang Kai-shek; died in 1966 still dreaming of recovering the mainland.

Bai Xianyong Moved from Hong Kong to Taiwan aged fifteen; became a prominent writer and later the biographer of his father.

Chen Cheng Served as premier (head of government) of the ROC in Taiwan, championed reforms and economic development of the island; died in 1965.

Chiang Ching-kuo Became premier and then president of the ROC in Taiwan; set Taiwan on the road to democracy in 1986–7 by lifting martial law, ending a ban on opposition parties and relaxing media censorship; died in 1988.

Chiang Kai-shek Resumed the presidency of the ROC in Taiwan in March 1950; ruled the island oppressively while presiding over its rapid economic development; retained US recognition as head of the government of 'China'; died in 1975.

Fu Zuoyi Served the PRC as minister of water resources until 1972; despite his role in 1949, was unable to protect his family during Mao's Cultural Revolution; died in 1974.

He Yingqin Moved to Taiwan and played no further role in government; died 1987.

Hu Shi Spent the last part of his life in Taiwan; died 1962.

Huang Shaohong Remained in Beijing; criticized as a 'Rightist' in the 1950s and attacked again in Mao's Cultural Revolution during which, in 1966, he committed suicide.

Li Zhisui Appointed Mao's personal physician; survived the Cultural Revolution; left China for the US in 1988; author of *The Private Life of Mao Zedong*; died 1995.

Li Zongren Resided in the US until 1965, when he returned to China in what was a publicity coup for the PRC; died in Beijing in 1969.

Lin Biao   As leader of the PLA in the 1960s helped launch the Cultural Revolution and then used the military to 'hold the ring' during the chaos that ensued; said to have planned to assassinate Mao and, when it failed, to have died in a plane crash en route to the Soviet Union in 1971.

Lester Knox Little   Retired as Inspector General of the Chinese Maritime Customs Service in early 1950; died 1981.

Liu Hongsheng   Feted by CCP leaders as 'national capitalist', he was at first spared various crackdowns on corrupt business practices but not the sweeping nationalization of private enterprise in the mid-1950s when his firms were taken from him; died 1956.

Liu Shaoqi   Identified as successor to Mao until the early 1960s when the two fell out over economic and ideological issues; toppled during the Cultural Revolution; died in prison in 1969.

Mao Zedong   Transformed his country in many positive ways, but also plunged its people into mass movements and campaigns that, in the case of the Great Leap Forward (1958–60) and the Cultural Revolution (1966–76), cost millions of lives; died in 1976; still revered by CCP – and many Chinese – as founder of 'New China'.

Mei Jun   March 1950, arrived at Gaoxiong, southern Taiwan, where she rented a vegetable stall to earn a living; Long Yingtai, Mei Jun's next child, born in 1952, chronicled her mother's odyssey.

Eva Spicer   Left China in November 1950; died in 1974.

Ya Xian   Left the mainland for Taiwan via Guangzhou; became well-known writer and poet in Taiwan.

Yan Xishan   Fled to Taiwan in December 1949; retired in 1950; died 1960.

Zhang Zhizhong   Served the PRC government in various capacities; helped secure CCP control over the northwest; died 1969.

Zhou Enlai   Premier and foreign minister of 'New China', popular with many Chinese people even though he failed to curb and was sometimes complicit in Mao's revolutionary excesses; died 1976.

SELECT BIBLIOGRAPHY

Archives consulted

Church Missionary Society, Oxford
King's College London
Salvation Army Heritage Centre, London
School of Oriental and African Studies, London
Sheffield University

Books and periodicals

Armitage, David. *Civil Wars: A History in Ideas*. New Haven, CT: Yale University Press, 2017.

Asbrink, Elisabeth. *1947: When Now Begins*. London: Scribe Publications, 2017 (Kindle edition).

Ashdown, Paddy. *A Fortunate Life: The Autobiography of Paddy Ashdown*. London: Aurum Press, 2009.

Ashton, S. R., Bennett, G. and Hamilton, K. A. (eds). *Documents on British Policy Overseas, Series I, Volume VIII: Britain and China 1945–1950*. London: Routledge, 2002.

Association for Diplomatic Studies and Training Foreign Affairs Oral History Project. 'Elden B. Erickson', Interviewed by Charles Stuart Kennedy. Initial interview date: 25 June 1992.

Bai Xianyong. *Fuqin yu minguo* ('Father and the Republic'). 2 volumes. Hong Kong: Tiandi tushu youxian gongsi, 2012.

Barber, Noel. *The Fall of Shanghai: The Communist Take-Over in 1949*. Newton Abbot: Readers' Union, 1980.

Barnett, Doak A. *China on the Eve of Communist Takeover*. New York: Frederick A. Praeger, 1963.

Bays, Daniel H. *A New History of Christianity in China*. Chichester: Wiley-Blackwell, 2012.

Bellis, David. *Old Hong Kong Photos and the Stories They Tell*. Volume 1. Hong Kong: Gwulo, 2017.

Bennett, Gill. *Six Moments of Crisis inside British Foreign Policy*. Oxford: Oxford University Press, 2014 edition.

Bernstein, Richard. *China 1945: Mao's Revolution and America's Fateful Choice*. New York: Alfred A Knopf, 2014 (Kindle edition).

Bickers, Robert. *Britain in China: Community, Culture and Colonialism, 1900–1949*. Manchester: Manchester University Press, 1999.

Bickers, Robert. *Out of China: How the Chinese Ended the Era of Western Domination*. London: Allen Lane, 2017.

Biggerstaff, Knight. *Nanking Letters, 1949*. Cornell University: East Asia Papers Number 23, 1979.

Bird, Isabella. *The Yangtze Valley and Beyond*. London: Virago Press, 1985.

Bradie, Anne-Marie and Brown, Douglas (eds). *Foreigners and Foreign Institutions in Republican China*. London: Routledge, 2013.

Brown, Jeremy and Pickowicz, Paul G. (eds). *Dilemmas of Victory: The Early Years of the People's Republic of China*. Cambridge, MA: Harvard University Press, 2007.

Buck, John Lossing. *Land Utilisation in China: a Study of 16,786 Farms in 168 Localities, and 38,256 Farms in Twenty-Two Provinces in China, 1929–1933*. Three vols. Nanjing: Nanjing University Press, 1937.

Buruma, Ian. *Year Zero: A History of 1945*. London: Atlantic Books, 2013.

Byron, John and Pack, Robert. *The Claws of the Dragon: Kang Sheng – the Evil Genius Behind Mao – and His Legacy of Terror in People's China*. London: Simon & Schuster, 1992.

Cai Dengshan (ed.). *Huang Xuchu huiyilu – Li Zongren, Bai Chongxi yu Jiang Jieshi lihe* ('Reminiscences of Huang Xuchu – The Separation and Reunion of Li Zongren and Bai Chongxi with Chiang Kai-shek'). Taipei: Duli zuojia, 2016.

Chang, Carsun. *The Third Force in China*. New York: Bookman Associates, 1952.

Chang Chihyun (ed.). *The Chinese Journals of L. K. Little, 1943–54: An Eyewitness Account of War and Revolution. Vol 1*. London: Routledge online resource, 2017.

Chang, Jung. *Mao: The Unknown Story*. London: Jonathan Cape, 2005.

Chang, Sidney H. and Myers, Ramon H. *The Storm Clouds Clear over China: The Memoir of Ch'en Li-fu, 1900–1993*. Stanford, CA: Hoover Institution Press, 1994.

Chassin, Lionel Max. *The Communist Conquest of China: A History of the Civil War, 1945–1949*. London: Weidenfeld & Nicolson, 1966.

Chen, Percy. *China Called Me: My Life inside the Chinese Revolution*. Boston: Little, Brown and Company, 1979.

Cheng Siyuan. *Li Zongren xiansheng wannian* ('The Later Life of Mr Li Zongren'). Beijing: Wenshi ziliao chubanshe, 1985.

Cheng Siyuan. *Zhenghai mixin* ('A Political Life behind the Scenes'). Hong Kong: Nanyue chubanshe, 1988.

Cheng Siyuan, *Bai Chongxi zhuan* ('A Biography of Bai Chongxi'). Hong Kong: Nanyue chubanshe, 1989.

Cheo Ying, Esther. *Black Country to Red China*. London: Vintage, 2009.

Chiang Kai-shek (with an Introduction by Lin Yutang). *China's Destiny*. New York: The Macmillan Company, 1947.

Chiang Kai-shek (with Notes and Commentary by Philip Jaffe). *China's Destiny & Chinese Economic Theory*. New York: Roy Publishers, 1947.

Chiang Monlin. *Tides from the West*. Taipei: China Culture Publishing Foundation, 1957.

Ch'ien Tuan-sheng. *The Government and Politics of China, 1912–1949*. Stanford, CA: Stanford University Press, 1950.

Chin, Tsai. *Daughter of Shanghai*. London: Chatto & Windus, 1988.

China Handbook Editorial Board for the Nationalist Government. *The China Handbook 1950*. New York: Rockport Press, 1950.

Cochran, Sherman and Hsieh, Andrew. *The Lius of Shanghai*. Cambridge, MA: Harvard University Press, 2013.

Colonial Reports, *Hong Kong 1948, 1949, 1950*. London: His Majesty's Stationery Office.

Cowley, Robert (ed.). *What If? Military Historians Imagine What Might Have Been*. London: Pan Books, 2001.

Cradock, Percy. *Know Your Enemy: How the Joint Intelligence Committee Saw the World*. London: John Murray, 2002.

Craft, Stephen G. *V.K. Wellington Koo and the Emergence of Modern China*. Lexington, KY: The University Press of Kentucky, 2004.

Dangdai zhongguo yanjiusuo bian (ed.). *Zhonghua Renmin Gongheguo shibiannian: 1949 nianjuan* ('Chronicle of the People's Republic of China 1949'). Beijing: Dangdai zhongguo chubanshe, 2004.

De Bary, Wm Theodore. *Sources of Chinese Tradition*, Volume II. New York: Columbia University Press, 1960.

Dikotter, Frank. *Things Modern: Material Culture and Everyday Life in China*. London: Hurst & Co, 2007.

Dikotter, Frank. *The Age of Openness: China before Mao*. Hong Kong: Hong Kong University Press, 2008.

Dikotter, Frank. *The Tragedy of Liberation: A History of the Chinese Revolution, 1945–57*. London: Bloomsbury, 2013.

Ding Yonglong and Sun Zhaiwei. *The Collapse of the Nanjing Government*. Henan: Henan People's Publishing House, 1992 edition.

Diseyezhanjun zhanshi bianxiezu (ed.). *Zhonguo renmin jiefangjun disiyezhanjun zhanshi* ('A History of the Battles Fought by the PLA's Fourth Field Army'). Beijing: jiefangjun chubanshe, 1998.

Dittmer, Lowell. *Liu Shaoqi and the Chinese Cultural Revolution*. New York: M. E. Sharpe, 1998.

Dong Shigui, Zhang Yanzhi. *Beiping hetan jishi* ('A True Record of the Beiping Peace Talks'). Beijing: Wenhua yishu chubanshe, 1991.

Dong Xianguang. *Jiang zongtong zhuan Vol 3* ('A Biography of President Jiang'). Taipei: Zhonghua wenhua chuban shiye weiyuanhui, 1954.

Dower, John W. *Embracing Defeat: Japan in the Wake of World War II*. New York: Norton Paperback, 2000.

Eastman, Lloyd E. *Seeds of Destruction: Nationalist China in War and Revolution, 1937–1949*. Stanford, CA: Stanford University Press, 1984.

Eastman, Lloyd E. *Family Field and Ancestors: Constancy and Change in China's Social and Economic History, 1550–1949*. Oxford: Oxford University Press, 1988.

Eastman, Lloyd E, Ch'en, Jerome, Pepper, Suzanne, van Slyke and Lyman, P. (eds). *The Nationalist Era in China, 1927–1949*. Cambridge University Press, 1991.

Elegant, Robert S. *China's Red Masters: Political Biographies of the Chinese Communist Leaders*. New York: Twayne, 1951.

Esherick, Joseph W. (ed.). *Remaking the Chinese City: Modernity and National Identity, 1900–1950*. Honolulu: University of Hawai'i Press, 2000.

Esherick, Joseph W. *Ancestral Leaves: A Family Journey through Chinese History*. Berkeley, CA: University of California Press, 2011.

Fan, Joshua. *China's Homeless Generation: Voices from the veterans of the Chinese Civil War, 1940s–1990s*. London: Routledge, 2009.

Falconer, Alun. *New China: Friend or Foe?* London: The Naldrett Press, 1950.

Feis, Herbert. *The China Tangle: The American Effort in China from Pearl Harbour to the Marshall Mission*. New York: Atheneum, 1966.

Fenby, Jonathan. *Generalissimo: Chiang Kai-shek and the China He Lost*. London: Simon & Schuster, 2003.

Fenby, Jonathan. *Crucible: Thirteen Months That Forged Our World*. London: Simon & Schuster, 2018.

Fernandes, Moises Silva. 'How to Relate with a Colonial Power on its Shore: Macau in the Chinese Foreign Policy, 1949–1965.' *Bulletin of Portuguese/Japanese Studies*, Vol. 17 (December 2008), pp. 225–50.

Finch, Percy. *Shanghai and Beyond*. New York: Charles Scribner's Sons, 1953.

Foreign Office Files for China: Part 1. *Complete Files for 1949: A Listing and Guide to the Microfilm Collection*. London: Adam Matthews, 1999–2002. http://www.archivesdirect.amdigital.co.uk/FO_China

Foreign Relations of the United States, *The Far East: China 1948 Vols VII–VIII; 1949 Vols VIII–IX*. https://history.state.gov/historicaldocuments/truman

Gould, Randall. 'Shanghai during the Takeover, 1949.' *The Annals of the American Academy of Political and Social Science*. Vol. 277. Report on China, September 1951.

Goncharov, Sergei, N., Lewis, John W. and Xue Litai. *Uncertain Partners: Stalin, Mao and the Korean War*. Stanford, CA: Stanford University Press, 1993.

Grantham, Alexander. *Via Ports: From Hong Kong to Hong Kong*. Hong Kong: Hong Kong University Press, 2012 edition.

Guangxi tongzhiguan (ed.). *Guangxi Jiefang shiji* ('A True Record of the Liberation of Guangxi'). Nanning: Guangxi renmin chubanshe, 1990.

Hamilton, William Stenhouse. *Notes from Old Nanking, 1947–1949: The Great Transition*. Canberra: Pandanus Books, 2004

He Fangzhou. 'Zailun taonan' ('More on Running Away'). *Lun Yu*, 16 March 1949.

Ho, Daphon D. 'Night Thoughts of a Hungry Ghostwriter: Chen Bulei and the Life of Service in Republican China.' *Modern Chinese Literature and Culture*, Vol. 19, No. 1 (Spring 2007), pp. 1–59.

Home News Library of the Xinhua News Agency (compilers). *China's Foreign Relations: A Chronology of Events, 1949–1988*. Peking: Foreign Language Press, 1989.

Hood, George. *Neither Bang nor Whimper: The End of a Missionary Era in China*. Singapore: The Presbyterian Church in Singapore, 1991.

Hooper, Beverley. *China Stands Up: Ending the Western Presence*. London: Allen & Unwin, 1986.

Huai Xiang. *Li Zongren yu zhong-mei fandongpai* ('Li Zongren and the Sino-American reactionary clique'). Hong Kong: youzhou shuwu, 1948.

Huang Xuchu, 'Guofu you yue qian yude kunchunzhiju' ('The Situation in Kunming at the time of the move of the capital from Canton to Chongqing'). *Qun Qiu*, No. 145.

Huang Yongsheng (ed.). Guangxi wenshi ziliao xuanji disanshiliu: Nanxia ganbu zai Guangxi ('Guangxi Historical Materials, Vol 36: South-bound Cadres in Guangxi'). Nanning: Guangxi qu zhengxie wenshi ziliao bianjibu chu ban faxing, 1993.

Hung, Chang-tai. *Mao's New World: Political Culture in the Early People's Republic*. Ithaca, NY: Cornell University Press, 2011.

Hutchings, Graham. 'A Province at War: Guangxi during the Sino-Japanese Conflict, 1937–45.' *The China Quarterly*, No. 108 (December 1986), pp. 652–79.

Hutchings, Graham. *Modern China: A Companion to a Rising Power*. London: Penguin Books, 2001 edition.

Ingrams, Harold. *Hong Kong*. London: Her Majesty's Stationery Office, 1952.

Izzard, Brian. *Yangtze Showdown: China and the Ordeal of HMS Amethyst*. Barnsley: Seaforth Publishing, 2015.

Jacobs-Larkcom, Dorothy. *As China Fell*. Ilfracombe: Arthur H. Stockwell, 1976.

Jarman, Robert L (ed.). *China: Political Reports 1911–1960*, Vols 8 & 9. Cambridge: Archive Editions Limited, 2001.

Jin Chongji. *Zhuanzhe niandai: Zhonguode1947* ('The Turning Point: China in 1947'). Beijing: Sanlianshudian, 2002.

Jin Feng. *The Making of a Family Saga, Ginling College*. Albany, NY: State University of New York Press, 2009.

Jin Lixin. *Zhongnan jiefang zhanzheng jishi* ('A True Record of the Liberation War in Southern China'). Beijing: Renmin chubanshe, 2004.

Jowett, Philip. *Images of War: Chiang Kai-shek versus Mao Tse-Tung. The Battle for China 1946–1949. Rare Photographs from Wartime Archives*. Barnsley: Pen & Sword Military, 2018.

Judt, Tony. *Reappraisals: Reflections on the Forgotten Twentieth Century*. London: William Heinemann, 2008.

Junshi kexueyuan junshilishi yanjiubu (ed.). *Zhongguo renmin jiefangjun zhanshi:disanjuan, quanguo jiefang zhanzheng shiqi* ('History of the Wars fought by the Chinese People's Liberation Army. Vol. 3: The War of National Liberation'). Beijing: junshi kexue chubanshe, 1987.

Kau, Michael Y. M. and Leung John, K. *The Writings of Mao Zedong, 1949–1956*: Vol. 1, September 1949–December 1955. New York: M. E. Sharpe, 1986.

Kidd, David. *Peking Story: The Last Days of Old China*. London: Aurum Press, 1988.

Kim, Donggil. 'Stalin and the Chinese Civil War.' *Cold War History*, Vol. 10. No. 2 (May 2010), pp. 185–202.

Kubek, Anthony. *How the Far East Was Lost: American Policy and the Creation of Communist China, 1941–1949*. Chicago: Heny Regnery Company, 1963.

Kwarteng, Kwasi. *Ghosts of Empire: Britain's Legacies in the Modern World*. London: Bloomsbury, 2011.

Lai Tse-han, Myers, Ramon H. and Wei Wou. *A Tragic Beginning. The Taiwan Uprising of February 28, 1947*. Stanford, CA: Stanford University Press, 1991.

Lapwood, Ralph and Lapwood, Nancy. *Through the Chinese Revolution*. People's Books Cooperative Society, 1954.

Lary, Diana. *China's Republic*. Cambridge: Cambridge University Press, 2007.

Lary, Diana. *The Chinese People at War: Human Suffering and Social Transformation, 1937–1945*. Cambridge: Cambridge University Press, 2010.

Lary, Diana. *China's Civil War: A Social History, 1945–1949*. Cambridge: Cambridge University Press, 2015.

Leighton Stuart, John. *Fifty Years in China. The Memoirs of John Leighton Stuart. Missionary and Ambassador*. New York: Random House, 1954.

Lew, Christopher R. *The Third Chinese Revolutionary Civil War, 1945–49: An Analysis of Communist strategy and leadership*. London, Routledge, 2009.

Li Ao, *Li Ao Huiyilu* ('The Reminiscences of Li Ao'). Taipei: Li Ao chubanshe, 1999.

Li Zhisui. *The Private Life of Chairman Mao*. New York: Random House, 1994.

Liang Shengjun. *Chise gongbuxiade Guangxi* ('Guangxi under the Red Terror'). Hong Kong: Ziyou chubanshe, 1951.

Liang Shengjun. *Jiang-Li douzheng neimu* ('The Inside Story of the Struggle between Jiang and Li'). Taipei: Xinxin wencongshu, 1992.

Lieberthal, Kenneth G. *Revolution and Tradition in Tientsin, 1949–1952*. Stanford, CA: Stanford University Press, 1980.

Lin Hsiao-ting. 'The Civil War and Modern China's Ethnic and Frontier Politics, 1947–53.' *Asian Profile*, Vol. 37, No. 2 (April 2009), pp. 105–17.

Lin Hsiao-ting. *Accidental State: Chiang Kai-shek, the United States and the Making of Taiwan*. Cambridge, MA: Harvard University Press, 2016.

Lin Tongfa. *Zhanhou Zhongguode bianju: yi Guomindang wei zhongxinde tantao* ('Post-war Changes in China: An Exploration Focusing on the Guomindang'). Taipei: Taiwan shangwu yinshuguan youxian gongsi, 2003.

Lin Tongfa. *1949 Da chetui* ('1949: The Great Withdrawal'). Taipei: Lianjing chuban shiye youxian gongsi, 2009.

Ling, Oi Ki. 'Demise of the Missionary Enterprise.' In R. G. Tiedemann (ed.), *Handbook of Christianity in China, Volume Two: 1800 to the Present*. Leiden: Brill, 2012.

Liu Chengang and Wang Yuping. *Liu Fei jiangjun zhuan* ('A Biography of General Liu Fei'). Beijing: tuanjie chubanshe, 1998.

Liu, F. F. *A Military History of Modern China, 1924–1949*. Princeton, NJ: Princeton University Press, 1956.

Liu Shaotang (ed.). *Minguo dashi rishi* ('Chronology of the Republic of China'), Vol 3. Taipei: Fuji wenxue zazhishe, 1979.

Liu Tong. *Zhongguode 1948 nian: Liangzhong mingyunde juezhan* ('China in 1948: A battle that decided between two destinies'). Beijing: Sanlian shudian, 2006.

Liu Tong, *Juezhan: Huadong jiefang zhanzheng, 1945–1959* ('Decisive Battles: The War of Liberation in East China, 1945–1949'). Shanghai: Shanghai renmin chubanshe, 2017.

Loh, Christine. *Underground Front: The Chinese Communist Party in Hong Kong*. Hong Kong: Hong Kong University Press, 2010.

Long Yingtai. *Da Jiang Da Hai 1949* ('Vast Rivers, Vast Seas 1949'). Hong Kong: Cosmos Books, 2015 edition.

Lynch, Michael. The Chinese Civil War, *1945–1949*. Oxford: Osprey Publishing, 2010 (Kindle edition).

Mackinnon, Stephen R., Lary, Diana and Vogel, Ezra (eds). *China at War: Regions of China, 1937–1945*. Stanford, CA: Stanford University Press, 2007.

Maddison, Angus. *Chinese Economic Performance in the Long Run*. Paris: OECD, 1998.

Maddison, Angus. *The World Economy: A Millennial Perspective*. Paris: OECD, 2001.

Malek, Roman (ed.). *Jews in China, From Kaifeng to Shanghai*. Sankt Augustin: Monumenta Serica Institute and the China-Zentrum, 2000.

Mao Zedong. *Selected Works Vols IV & Vol V*. Peking: Foreign Languages Press, 1969 & 1977). http://www.marx2mao.com/Mao/Index.html

McGregor, Richard. *Asia's Reckoning: The Struggle for Global Dominance*. London: Allen Lane, 2017.

Melby John F. *The Mandate of Heaven: Record of a Civil War, China 1945–49*. London: Chatto & Windus, 1969.

Meisner, Maurice. 'The Significance of the Chinese Revolution in World History.' Asia Research Centre Working Paper 1. London School of Economics and Political Science, 1999. http://eprints.lse.ac.uk/21309/

Merkel-Hess, Kate. *The Rural Modern. Reconstructing the Self and State in Republican China*. Chicago: University of Chicago Press, 2016.

Meyer, Mahlon. *Remembering China from Taiwan: Divided families and bittersweet reunions after the Chinese Civil War*. Hong Kong: Hong Kong University Press, 2012.

Mitter, Rana. *A Bitter Revolution: China's Struggle with the Modern World*. Oxford: Oxford University Press, 2004.

Mitter, Rana. *China's War with Japan, 1937–1945: The Struggle for Survival*. London: Penguin, 2013.

Monitoring Service of the British Broadcasting Corporation, *Summary of World Broadcasts, Part V: The Far East*. Caversham Park, Reading: 1949–50

National Intelligence Council (NIC). *Tracking the Dragon: National Intelligence Estimates on China During the Era of Mao, 1948–1976*. Pittsburgh: Government Printing Office, 2004.

Naval Intelligence Division. China Proper, Vol III: Economic Geography, Ports and *Communications*. London: Geographical Handbook Series, 1945.

O'Neill, Mark. *The Miraculous History of China's Two Palace Museums*. Hong Kong: Joint Publishing (HK) Ltd, 2015.

Pan Ling. *Old Shanghai. Gangsters in Paradise*. Singapore: Heinemann Asia, 1993 edition.

Pang Dunzhi. *Qingsuan Guixi* ('Settling Accounts with the Guangxi Clique'). Guangzhou: Nanqing chubanshe, 1950.

Panikkar, K. M. *In Two Chinas: Memoirs of a Diplomat*. London: George Allen & Unwin, 1955.

Pantsov, Alexander (with Steven I. Levine). *Mao: The Real Story*. New York: Simon & Schuster, Kindle edition, 2013.

Pepper, Suzanne. *Civil War in China: The Political Struggle, 1945–1949*. Berkeley, CA: University of California Press, 1978.

Pepper, Suzanne. *Keeping Democracy at Bay: Hong Kong and the Challenge of Chinese Political Reform*. Lanham, MD: Rowman & Littlefield, 2008.

Peraino, Kevin. *A Force So Swift: Mao, Truman, and the Birth of Modern China, 1949*. New York: Crown, 2017.

Radchenko, Sergey and Wolff, David. 'To the Summit via Proxy-Summits: New Evidence from Soviet and Chinese Archives on Mao's Long March to Moscow, 1949.' *Cold War International History Project Bulletin*, Issue 16 (Fall 2007/ Winter 2008), pp. 105–82.

Rea, Kenneth W. and Brewer, John C. (eds). *The Forgotten Ambassador: The Reports of John Leighton Stuart, 1946–1949*. Boulder, CO: Westview Replica Editions, 1981.

Renmin chubanshe bianjibu (ed.). *Disanci guonei geming zhanzheng da shibiao* ('A Chronology of the Third Revolutionary Civil War'). Beijing: renmin chubanshe, 1983.

Rice, Condoleezza. *No Higher Honour: A Memoir of My Years in Washington*. New York: Crown Publishers, 2011.

Rickett, Allyn and Rickett, Adele. *Prisoners of Liberation*. San Francisco, CA: China Books, 1981.

Roberts, Claire. *Photography and China*. London: Reaktion Books, 2013.

Robinson, Thomas W. *A Politico-Military Biography of Lin Piao, Part 1, 1907–1949*. Santa Monica, CA: Rand, 1971.

Ronning, Chester. *A Memoir of China in Revolution*. New York: Pantheon Books, 1974.

Rowan, Roy. *Chasing the Dragon: A Veteran Journalist's Firsthand Account of the Chinese Revolution, 1946–49*. Guilford, CT: The Lyons Press, 2004.

Saich, Tony (ed.). *The Rise to Power of the Chinese Communist Party: Documents and Analysis*. New York: M. E. Sharpe, 1996.

Schell, Orville and Delury, John. *Wealth and Power: China's Long March to the Twenty-first Century*. London: Little, Brown Book Group, 2013 (Kindle edition).

Schram, Stuart. *Mao Tse-Tung*. Harmondsworth: Penguin Books, 1966.

Schram, Stuart. *The Political Thought of Mao Tse-tung*. Cambridge: Cambridge University Press, 1989.

Sebestyen, Victor. *1946: The Making of the Modern World*. London: Pan Books, 2015 (Kindle edition).

Shai, Aron. *The Fate of British and French Firms in China, 1949–54*. Basingstoke: Macmillan Press, 1996.

Shakya, Tsering. *The Dragon in the Land of Snows: A History of Modern Tibet since 1947*. London: Pimlico, 1999.

Short, Philip. *Mao: The Man Who Made China*. London: I. B. Tauris, 2017.

Smith, Felix. *China Pilot: Flying for Chennault during the Cold War*. Washington, DC: Smithsonian Institution Press, 1995.

Snow Philip. *The Fall of Hong Kong: Britain, China and the Japanese Occupation*. New Haven, CT: Yale University Press, 2003.

Tang Degang (with Li Zongren). *Li Zongren Huiyilu ('The Reminiscences of Li Zongren')* (Chinese language edition). Hong Kong: Nanyue chubanshe, 1987.

Tang, James Tuck-Hong. *Britain's Encounter with Revolutionary China, 1949–54*. New York: St. Martin's Press, 1992.

Tang, James Tuck-Hong. 'From Empire Defence to Imperial Retreat: Britain's Post-war China Policy and the Decolonization of Hong Kong'. *Modern Asian Studies*, Vol. 28, No. 2 (May 1994), pp. 317–19.

Tanner, Harold M. *The Battle for Manchuria and the Fate of China: Siping 1946*. Indianapolis, IN: Indiana University Press, 2013.

Taylor, Jay. *The Generalissimo's Son: Chiang Ching-kuo and the Revolutions in China and Taiwan*. Cambridge, MA: Harvard University Press, 2000.

Taylor, Jay. *The Generalissimo: Chiang Kai-shek and the Struggle for Modern China*. Cambridge, MA: Harvard University Press, 2009.

T'ong Te-kang (with Li Tsung-jen). *The Reminiscences of Li Tsung-jen*. Boulder, CO: Westview Press, 1979.

Topping, Seymour. *Journey between Two Chinas*. New York: Harper & Row, 1972.

Townsend, Peter. *China Phoenix: The Revolution in China*. London: Jonathan Cape, 1955.

Tsang, Steve (ed.). *A Documentary History of Hong Kong: Government and Politics*. Hong Kong: Hong Kong University Press, 1995.

Tsang, Steve. *The Cold War's Odd Couple: The Unintended Partnership between the Republic of China and the UK, 1950–1958*. London: I. B. Taurus, 2005.

Tsang, Steve and Tien Hung-mao. *Democratization in Taiwan: Implications for China*. Hong Kong: Hong Kong University Press, 1999.

Tsou, Tang. *America's Failure in China, 1941–1950*. Three volumes. Chicago: University of Chicago Press, 1963.

Tucker, Nancy Bernkopf (ed.). *China Confidential: American Diplomats and Sino-American Relations, 1945–1996*. New York: Colombia University Press, 2001.

US Department of State. *The China White Paper August 1949*, two vols. Stanford, CA: Stanford University Press, 1967.

van der Sprenkel, Otto (ed.). *New China: Three Views*. London: Turnstile Press, 1950.

van de Ven, Hans. *Breaking with the Past: The Maritime Customs Service and the Global Origins of Modernity in China*. New York: Columbia University Press, 2014.

van de Ven, Hans. *China at War: Triumph and Tragedy in the Emergence of the New China, 1937–1952*. London: Profile Books, 2017.

Van Slyke, Lyman P. *Yangtze: Nature, History and the River*. Reading, MA: Addison-Wesley Publishing Company, 1988.

Wakeman Carolyn and Light Ken (eds). *Assignment Shanghai: Photographs on the Eve of Revolution*. Berkeley, CA: University of California Press, 2003.

Wales, Nym. *Red Dust: Autobiographies of Chinese Communists*. Stanford, CA: Stanford University Press, 1952.

Walker, Richard L. *China Under Communism: The First Five Years*. New Haven, CT: Yale University Press, 1955.

Wang Chaoguang. *1945–1949: Guogong zhengzheng yu zhongguo mingyun* ('1945–1949: The Political Struggle between the Nationalists and the Communists and China's Destiny'). Beijing: shehui kexue wenxian chubanshe, 2010.

Wang, Chi. *A Compelling Journey from Peking to Washington. Building a New Life in America*. Lanham, MD: Hamilton Books, 2011.

Wang Gung-hsing, 'Nationalist Government Policies, 1949–1951.' *The Annals of the American Academy of Political and Social Science*, Vol. 277, Report on China (September 1951), pp. 213–23.

Wang Jun, *Cheng Ji* ('City Story'). Beijing: Joint Publishing Book Store, 2011.

Wang Meizhi and Zhang Huoshi, *Jinling tanmeng: Li Zongren in 1949* ('Nanjing Illusions: Li Zongren in 1949'). Beijing: Tuanjie chubanshe, 2007.

Wang Ruilin (ed.). *Xinguixi jishi* ('A True Record of the New Guangxi Clique'), three vols. Nanning: Guangxi zhuangzu zizhiqu xinwen chubanju, 1990.

Wang Weili (ed.), *Jiangjieshide wenchen wujiang* ('Jiang Jieshi's Civilian and Military Officials'). Taipei: Balilulun chubanshe, 1992.

Wang Xiaojue, *Modernity with a Cold War Face: Reimagining the Nation in Chinese Literature across the 1949 Divide*. Cambridge, MA: Harvard University Press, 2013.

Wang Yuping. *Liu Fei jiangjun zhuanlue* ('A Short Biography of General Liu Fei'). Beijing: Tuanjie chubanshe, 1998.

Wemheuer, Felix. *A Social History of Maoist China*. Cambridge: Cambridge University Press, 2019.

Westad, Odd Arne. *Decisive Encounters: The Chinese Civil War, 1946–1950*. Stanford, CA: Stanford University Press, 2003.

Westad, Odd Arne. *Restless Empire: China and the World since 1750*. New York: Basic Books, 2012.

Whitson, William W. *The Chinese High Command: A History of Communist Military Politics, 1921–71*. New York: Praeger, 1973.

Wilson Center Digital Archive. International History Declassified: https://digitalarchive.wilsoncenter.org/

Winfield, Gerald F. *China: The Land and the People*. New York: William Sloane Associates, 1948.

Winnington, Alan. *Breakfast with Mao: Memoirs of a Foreign Correspondent*. London: Lawrence & Wishart, 1986.

Wong Siu-lun. *Emigrant Entrepreneurs: Shanghai Industrialists in Hong Kong*. Hong Kong: Oxford University Press, 1988.

Wong, Young-tsu. 'The Fate of Liberalism in Revolutionary China: Chu Anping and His Circle, 1946–1950.' *Modern China*, Vol. 19, No. 4 (October 1993), pp. 457–90.

Worthing, Peter. *General He Yingqin: The Rise and Fall of Nationalist China*. Cambridge: Cambridge University Press, 2016.

Wu Xingyong, *Huangjin midang: yijiusijiunian dalu huangjin yuntai shimo* ('The Chinese Secret Archives of Gold: How the Mainland's Gold Was Moved to Taiwan'). Nanjing: Jiangsu renmin chubanshe, 2009.

Wu Yuexing (ed.). *Zhongguo xiandaishi dituji, 1919–1949* ('Atlas of Modern Chinese History, 1919–1949'). Beijing: Zhongguo ditu chubanshe, 1997.

Xiang, Lanxin. *Recasting the Imperial Far East: Britain and America in China, 1945–1950*. New York: M. E. Sharpe, 1995.

Xiao Zhihua and Shang Ruobing. *Xiao zhuge: Bai Chongxi wai juan* ('An Unofficial Biography of Bai Chongxi'). Henan: Henan renmin chubanshe, 1991.

Yang Kuisong, *Guomindange de 'liangong' yu 'fangong'* ('The Guomindang's "Unity with the Communists" and "Anti-Communism"'). Beijing: shehuikexuewenxian chubanshe, 2008.

Ye Fei. *Ye Fei Huiyilu* ('Reminiscences of Ye Fei'). Beijing: jiefang chubanshe, 1988.

Yen, Maria. *The Umbrella Garden: A Picture of Life in Red China*. New York: Macmillan, 1954.

Yick, Joseph K. S. *Making Urban Revolution in China: The CCP–GMD Struggle for Beiping-Tianjin, 1945–1949*. New York: M. E. Sharpe, 1995.

Yin Shi. *Li–Jiang guanxi yu Zhongguo* ('The Li–Jiang relationship and China'). Hong Kong: Ziyou chubanshe, 1950.

Zhang Liangren (ed.). *Chiang ching-kuo xiansheng quanji* ('The Complete Works of Mr Chiang Ching-kuo'). Vol 1. Taipei: Xingzhengyuan xinwenchu, 1991.

Zhang Renmin. 'Qianguibian dadao Yang Biao kanggong xunguo ji' ('A Record of the Anti-Communist Martyr Yang Biao of the Guizhou–Guangxi border area'). *Qun Qiu* (HK), No. 118, 1962.

Zhang Renyi, *1949 Zhongguo Shehui* ('1949: Chinese Society'). Beijing: Shehui kexue wenxian chubanshe, 2005.

Zhang Zhizhong. *Zhang Zhizhong huiyilu* ('The Reminiscences of Zhang Zhizhong'). Beijing: Wenshiziliao chubanshe, 1985.

Zhengxie Nanyangshi (ed.). *Nanyang jiaoyu qunqiu* ('The Spring and Autumn of Nanyang Education'). Nanyang wenshi ziliao, No. 9, 1993.

Zhonggong Shanxi shengwei dangshi biangongshi (ed.). *1949 Shanxi ganbu nanxia shilu* ('1949 A True Record of the Shanxi South-bound Cadres'), 2 vols. Taiyuan: Shanxi renmin chubanshe, 2012.

Zhonggong zhongyang dangshi yanjiushi (ed.). *Zhonggongdang shi dashi nianbiao* ('A Chronology of Major Events in the CCP's History'). Beijing: Renmin chubanshe, 1987.

Zhongguo renmin zhengxie shanghuiyi guangxi zhuangzu zizhiqu weiyuanhui (ed.). *Guangxi wenshi ziliao xuanji* ('Selected Materials on Guangxi history'), Vol. 9, Nanning: Wenshi ziliao yanjiu weiyuanhui, 1991.

Zhongyang yanjiuyuan jindaishi yanjiusuo (ed.). *Xu Qiming xiansheng fangwenlu* ('A Record of Interviews with Mr Xu Qiming'). Taipei: Zhongyang yanjiuyuan jindaishi yanjiusuo, 1983.

Zhongyang yanjiuyuan jindaishi yanjiusuo (ed.). *Bai Chongxi xiansheng fangwen jilu* ('A Record of Interviews with Mr Bai Chongxi'), 2 vols. Taipei: Zhongyang yanjiuyuan jindaishi yanjiusuo, 1984.

Zhongyang yanjiuyuan jindaishi yanjiusuo (ed.). *Pan Zongwu xiansheng fangwen jilu* ('A Record of Interviews with Mr Pan Zongwu'). Taipei: Zhongyang yanjiuyuan jindaishi yanjiusuo, 1992.

Zhou Hongtao. *Jianggong yu Wo* ('The Revered Jiang and I'). Taipei: Tianxia wenhua chubanshe, 2003.

Zhou Quan. *Guixi jiepou* ('An Anatomy of the Guangxi Clique'). Hong Kong: Qixing shuwu, 1949.

Zia, Helen *Last Boat out of Shanghai: The Epic Story of the Chinese Who Fled Mao's Revolution.* New York: Ballantine Books, 2019.

INDEX

Note: Page numbers in *italics* indicate figures and maps. Page numbers followed by an "n" refer to end-of-chapter notes. Page numbers in **bold** provide descriptions of principal characters.